E. Saccente

INTERNATIONAL ECO

C000147153

Written and published with the support of the
Australian Institute of International Affairs

INTERNATIONAL ECONOMIC PLURALISM
Economic Policy In East Asia And The Pacific

Peter Drysdale

ALLEN & UNWIN Sydney Wellington London Boston
In association with
The Australia–Japan Research Centre, Australian National University.

© Peter Drysdale 1988
This book is copyright under the Berne Convention. No
reproduction without permission. All rights reserved.

First published in 1988
Allen & Unwin Australia Pty Ltd
8 Napier Street, North Sydney, NSW 2059 Australia

Allen & Unwin New Zealand Limited
60 Cambridge Terrace, Wellington, New Zealand

Unwin Hyman Limited
15-17 Broadwick Street, London W1V 1FP England

Allen & Unwin Inc.
8 Winchester Place, Winchester, Mass 01890 USA

National Library of Australia
Cataloguing-in-Publication entry:
 Drysdale, Peter.
      International economic pluralism: economic policy in
      East Asia and the Pacific.

      Bibliography.
      Includes index.
      ISBN 0 04 335062 3.
           0 04 350075 7 pbk.

      1. East Asia — Economic integration. 2. Pacific Area —
      Economic integration. 3. East Asia — Economic policy.
      4. Pacific Area — Economic policy. I. Title.

337.1

Library of Congress Catalog Card Number: 88-71346

Set in 10.5/11.5pt Plantin by Sabagraphics Ltd, New Zealand

Printed by Kim Hup Lee Printing Co Pte Ltd Singapore

Contents

Tables

Figures

8

Preface

This book had its origins in a project that was conceived just over 18 years ago. At that time I was privileged to receive a grant through the Australian Institute of International Affairs to undertake a study tentatively entitled 'Japan and Australia in a Pacific Economic Community'.

I had already completed some work on this subject, to which my interest had been drawn in the course of preparing my doctoral thesis on Australia–Japan economic relations and the analysis of international trade flows. While at Hitotsubashi University in Tokyo on dissertation fieldwork from the Australian National University, I was associated with Kiyoshi Kojima and engaged in the cut and thrust of debate about the emergence of 'a Pacific economic community' to counterbalance what was then taking root in Europe. My first written piece on this subject was published in a journal produced by my student friends at Hitotsubashi as part of a program of international activities in which they were involved.

Later, in 1967, I took part in the preparations that led to the First Pacific Trade and Development Conference, held at the Japan Economic Research Center, Tokyo, in January 1968. This meeting was inspired by the interest in Kojima's work on the idea of a Pacific free trade area. The focus of the meeting was on existing and possible future trading arrangements, and specifically on the feasibility of a Pacific free trade area, among the economically advanced market-oriented nations of the Pacific. I was invited to prepare a paper analysing the impact of the free trade area proposal on Australia's trade and economic interests. This conference crystallised my commitment to the study of the East Asian and Pacific economy and of Australia's place within it. To participants in the conference, the need for analysis of Pacific economic policy problems, and for communication among researchers around the region, appeared far greater than had been initially perceived. A Pacific free trade area seemed very much a second-best solution, but it was thought extremely worthwhile to consider other possible economic policies and institutional arrangements for greater regional economic cooperation. Most of us felt it important to address explicitly the needs and interests of the developing countries of Asia and the Pacific in any discussion of regional cooperation. Thus began what has already been almost half a lifetime's research and other work on Australia's economic interest in the East Asian and Pacific economy.

The grant from the Australian Institute of International Affairs was instrumental in launching my own and other Australian efforts in this field. It required an initial period of study in the United States, an associated visit to Europe, a period of fieldwork in Japan in 1968–69, and follow-up research immediately after my return to Australia. I proceeded from the Second Pacific Trade and Development Conference to a sojourn at Harvard University where I was associated with Henry Rosovsky. The period at Harvard was one of exciting discovery. Rosovsky was then chairman of the Committee on Black and African Studies and in the middle of the storm that raged around the revolution on that issue. My first lunch with him and Albert Hirschman at the Harvard Faculty Club was consumed with the passion of that debate. This may seem remote from the Pacific economy, but it is not. For in this milieu I learned about pluralism — not the word, for I do not recall its having been mentioned at all in those days, but the real meaning of the notion and its centrality to the American polity and its survival.

From Harvard I was introduced into policy and research circles in Washington and elsewhere, and I enjoyed greatly my first experience with the concerns and perspectives of North America. A brief period at Oxford University, whence I had my first encounter with Europe, allowed the space to refine for publication a paper on 'Japan, Australia and New Zealand: the Prospect for Western Pacific Economic Integration', and then I returned to Japan and Hitotsubashi, the university of my graduate student days. In the northern summer of 1969 I completed a detailed study of the Japanese minerals and energy consuming industries and the resource goods trade with Australia, a study which was to establish another major stream in my research over the following decade.

After my return from Japan, I was engaged by the Asian Development Bank to work on its famous study, *Southeast Asia's Economy in the 1970s*, where I joined with Saburō Ōkita and Kiyoshi Kojima in contributing the analysis of foreign economic relations. This study, and the opportunity it afforded for developing research associations in Southeast Asia, was a happy complement to the work on which I had already embarked in Japan and North America. It provided the initial funding for the development of what subsequently became the Australia–Japan Research Centre and the Australian–ASEAN Research Project trade and economic data bank (now the International Economic Data Bank), and it made possible a whole new range of quantitative analyses of developments in the Pacific economy.

A number of papers followed in rapid succession from this activity, some of which were commissioned and published by the Australian Institute of International Affairs, and at the end of 1972 the original project was virtually complete. Or so it seemed. What happened, in fact, was that the work on Australia, Japan and the Asian–Pacific region had developed a life of its own — by a process in which I was now totally enmeshed, and which consumed my energies in many directions. The theme of the research had begun to attract the attention, if not always the enthusiasm, of policymakers. In April 1972 the first steps were taken to set up a joint program of research involving

Australian and Japanese economists to complete a report to the governments of Japan and Australia on *Australia, Japan, and Western Pacific economic relations*, under the direction of Sir John Crawford and Saburō Ōkita. I was heavily committed to coordinating this huge collaborative research effort and drafting the report.

There was a more fundamental intellectual challenge. I had by this time become aware that my work on the idea of some form of Pacific regional organisation or association (not regionalism in the form of a discriminatory free trade area, but regionalism involving collective agreements on modes of economic cooperation and the development of mechanisms to make them possible) did not fit comfortably into the conceptual framework conventionally applied to the study of international economic exchange.

In my doctoral thesis on Australia and Japan I had concluded that

> . . . [to] ignore the effect of imperfect knowledge and limited horizons (associated with the importance of political, cultural, and historical factors) on the attainment of economic goals is surely to ignore one of the most significant facts of economic life. If this is true of economic life within nation-states, how much more true is it of that area of economic affairs which involves contact between the peoples of separate nation-states! The unfamiliarity that breeds at least caution and reticence, at worst fear and hatred built on fear, no less limits the realisation of greater, if not optimal, national and international welfare . . . simply to increase the familiarity and reduce the uncertainties in commerce between nations, or between any two nations, can also provide a major and positive contribution to human economic welfare — as, indeed, it has for Japan and Australia.

This was the wellspring of my conception of the value to be derived from building new regional associations and organisations. But the analytic constructs of the theory of international trade did not give much guidance on the value or effect of such international organisational structures. Most of the colleagues with whom I taught were probably sceptical of the connection between their professional interests in the theory of international economics found in contemporary textbooks, and my research in this area. I had to elaborate my intuitions and convince them in the way of professional communication, rather than rely upon tolerant curiosity. This was also critical to pursuing the policy interest.

Going down this intellectual path would take me well beyond the conception of the original project for the Institute of International Affairs. Hedley Bull, who was then managing the Institute's research activities, was extremely sympathetic and patient. Eventually John Legge, who had taken over Hedley Bull's responsibilities, commanded the extension I sought to introduce new research and lay out 'some philosophical issues' — the ideas contained in chapter 2.

The genesis of the present book was thus both exhausting and exhilarating. Its final shape and structure owe much to support and encouragement from other sources. A watershed in my research and thinking over the past ten years or so was the preparation in 1979 of a paper with Hugh Patrick, then at Yale University, for Senator John Glenn's United States Congressional Committee on Foreign Relations with Asia and the Pacific, 'Evaluation of a Proposed Pacific Regional Economic Organisation'. This paper, and the study completed in Japan soon afterwards under the government of Prime Minister Ōhira by a study group led by Ōkita, saw a substantial elevation in political, as well as research, interest in the themes of this book.

The book itself is a product of Pacific cooperation and exchange. The labour of its writing was completed largely at the Australian National University, Yale University and Osaka, Kobe and Kyoto Universities in Japan. The periods of study at Yale were made possible by the award of a Fulbright Grant, which allowed me to spend six months as scholar-in-residence at the Economic Growth Center, and supported my work with Hugh Patrick on the Congressional Research Service paper. There I made the intellectual advance of integrating interests in the theory of public choice and the theory of international exchange with the purpose of my enquiry into the rationale for economic regionalism. This may have been a simple advance, but I think it was a necessary and useful one. It certainly provides some comfort to me in the communion I have with scholars and policymakers alike. The periods in Japanese universities were made possible by grants from the Japan Society for Promotion of Science, funded by the Japanese Ministry of Education. The congenial environment provided by Iwao Nakatani (my friend from student days) and his students at Osaka and colleagues at Kobe and Kyoto encouraged progress with writing. Essential to the completion of the book was the support of the Australia–Japan Research Centre, in the Research School of Pacific Studies at the Australian National University, through facilities such as the International Economic Data Bank and associated research programs.

To these people and institutions I am most grateful. The particular support of successive directors of the Australian Institute of International Affairs, particularly Alan Watt, Tom Millar and Ralph Harry and their research committees, is deeply appreciated. Although they could not have foreseen or understood the by-ways and by-products of the work that they set in motion, they retained their faith in its value and its completion, and of such faith real miracles are made.

Nothing in the somewhat autobiographical nature of these prefatory remarks more than faintly hints at the extent and nature of my personal obligation to the many colleagues and students who encouraged the development of my thinking on the subject of this book, or the institutions that have provided succour over the years. A list of those who have influenced the work would encompass virtually all my many friends and acquaintances in Northeast and Southeast Asia, North America, the Southwest Pacific and elsewhere. Under these circumstances, I can but limit my personal acknowledgments to a few of the most significant influences.

Sir John Crawford was, until his recent death, a constant source of encouragement and a critical reference point in all my work on the Pacific economy. My personal debt to him is beyond measure. It derives from the good fortune of working closely with him on these and other matters over the last 25 years of his life and, through this, reaping the harvest of his powerful intellect and immense experience. I discovered only relatively recently how, as a young man 50 years earlier, he had struggled, more masterfully than I, with some of the same ideas with which I struggle in this book, about the framework of agreements and understandings necessary for gainful international economic exchange. His contribution to the debate is the brilliant piece on the turmoil of Australia's relations with the region before the war, 'Australia as a Pacific power', published in 1938.

Kiyoshi Kojima sparked my intellectual energy towards trying to come to grips with all the dimensions of the idea of a Pacific economic community. Friend and protagonist, he was instrumental in my focusing on the idea of a Pacific economic community at an early stage, and in causing me to strive to get my ideas straight over all the years since I was a graduate student in his tough but loving care. Saburō Ōkita contributed in a very different way. His remarkable capacity to absorb wisdom from all sides and to deal with men and women in many countries on many levels has always symbolised for me the value and potential of the Pacific idea, well beyond any mere economic advantage it may bring to the peoples of the region.

I also acknowledge warmly Hugh Patrick's labours with me on this and related works. The productivity and warmth of our association are the fruit of his incisive mind and generous friendship. I also owe a special debt to Larry Krause for going over the manuscript before its publication.

I am especially fortunate in my friends and colleagues Ross Garnaut, Ben Smith, Iwao Nakatani and Nancy Viviani, who have in various ways teased this book out of me. They have acted as creative sounding boards, contributed ideas here and words there, carried the burden of its creation, but most of all shared a sense of what I was trying to do. James Jordan's lively assault on the manuscript in its penultimate form helped me to clarify the argument. These people, and many others, shaped my ideas and helped me to look at Pacific economic cooperation from more than one point of view.

The argument in chapters 8 and 9 draws heavily on material published elsewhere, and I record my thanks to the editors of the *Economic Record* and *Asian Survey* for permission to make use of them in this volume.

I must also acknowledge the assistance of the staff of the Australia–Japan Research Centre, especially Peta English, Kim-Lan Ngo, Corinne Boyles, Janet Healey and Frank Foley, for their work and care in editing and processing the manuscript, and Prue Phillips, Jeremy Whitham and Jong-Soon Kang for data and research assistance.

My final acknowledgements to my parents, wife and son are of a rather different character. They have contributed to this book in very crucial ways. Scribes of years gone by were commonly confined to monasteries, and the completion of an enterprise such as this makes one appreciate why the practice might have been felt generally necessary. Liz and Ben bore the costs of my wrestling with the writing, as well as one or two advantages, as their excursions to Nara, Kyoto and elsewhere created the solitude and incentive to be done with it. Their support and care sustained my efforts. My parents are responsible for encouraging, by processes subtle, generous and profound, my appreciation of the values and concerns that led me to this work on Australia's relations with its neighbours in Asia and the Pacific and on the economics of international pluralism. To them I offer this inadequate expression of my thanks.

Peter Drysdale
Canberra

1 Perspectives

The Pacific is the fastest-growing region in the world economy, and is rapidly becoming a major centre of world trade and economic activity. The growth performance of the Northeast and Southeast Asian economies over the past twenty-five years in particular has been quite remarkable. East Asia's share of world gross national product (excluding Eastern Europe) increased from 9 per cent in 1962 to 18 per cent in 1985 (Table 1.1). Moreover, its share is projected to rise to 22 per cent by the turn of the century.[1]

Table 1.1 Shares of Pacific and other regions in world GNP and trade, 1962 and 1985 (per cent)

	Share in GNP		Share in world exports		Share in world imports	
	1962	*1985[b]*	*1962*	*1985[b]*	*1962*	*1985[b]*
Australia	1.3	1.3	1.9	1.2	1.7	1.3
Japan	4.5	12.4	3.9	10.0	4.5	7.0
China	3.3	2.5	0.6	1.5	0.5	1.5
Other Northeast Asia	0.5	1.1	0.7	4.4	1.5	4.1
ASEAN	1.0	1.8	3.3	3.9	3.3	3.0
East Asia, total	**9.3**	**17.8**	**8.5**	**19.8**	**9.8**	**15.6**
North America	45.8	39.8	21.7	16.5	17.3	23.9
New Zealand and other Pacific	0.4	0.3	0.7	0.4	0.6	0.4
Pacific, total	**56.8**	**59.2**	**32.8**	**37.9**	**29.4**	**41.2**
Western Europe	30.9	26.7	45.8	41.4	50.7	40.7
Middle East	1.4	2.5	2.9	3.6	2.5	4.2
Rest of world	10.9[a]	11.6[a]	18.5	17.1	17.4	13.9
World, total	**100.0**	**100.0**	**100.0**	**100.0**	**100.0**	**100.0**

Notes: a Centrally planned economies not included.
　　　　　b 1985 data include estimates.
Sources: International Economic Data Bank, Australian National University; *Statistical Yearbook of the Republic of China* 1985; *United Nations Yearbook of International Trade Statistics* 1965

During the 1970s East Asia's growth performance remained strong while other industrial economies slowed down. As a result, per capita incomes in East Asia are now much closer to the average for industrial countries than they were twenty-five years ago. In 1962, per capita income in Japan was only 54 per cent of the average for industrial countries; by 1984 it was 93 per cent. For Hong Kong, Korea and Taiwan over the same period, per capita incomes rose from around 10 per cent to 22 per cent of the average

15

for advanced industrial countries, while for the ASEAN countries they rose from 5 per cent to 7 per cent. This is true not only of the market economies in East Asia and the Pacific but also of China, a country which is emerging as a major force on the regional and world economic stages.

The economic growth of East Asia has been closely associated with, and facilitated by, outward-looking trade and industrial development policies. East Asia's share of world export trade has more than doubled since 1962, and now represents almost one-fifth of all international trade (see Table 1.1). Much of that trade growth has been concentrated in the Pacific region. This bias towards intra-regional trade means that a large share of the benefits of East Asia's trade growth is accruing within the Pacific region.

Particular Pacific countries have benefited from this expanding East Asian trade. In the early 1950s nearly 65 per cent of Australia's trade was with the United Kingdom and other European countries, and only 30 per cent with Pacific countries. Today those shares are exactly reversed. The United Kingdom was replaced by Japan in the late 1960s as Australia's major trading partner, and since then Korea, Taiwan and China have increased their shares of Australia's trade. East Asia now accounts for about 45 per cent of Australia's export trade, more than three times its share of three decades ago.[2]

Some of the growth and redirection of Pacific countries' trade is due to the changing relative importance of the region in world trade, while the rest is attributable to strengthening complementarities and special connections in trade among these countries. In the course of rapid industrialisation, the densely populated, natural-resource-poor East Asian economies have been highly complementary to economies rich in natural resources such as Australia, North America, and some of the Southeast Asian economies. This, together with geographic proximity, ensures that the importance of East Asia to other Pacific countries has grown more rapidly than might be expected from East Asia's increased contribution to world trade. The significance of regional trade as a proportion of the total trade of Pacific economies rose steadily from the mid-1960s to the early 1980s (Table 1.2).

Table 1.2   Regional trade as a share of total for Pacific economies, 1964–66 and 1979–81
(per cent)

	Share of exports going to other Pacific economies		Share of imports coming from other Pacific economies	
	1964–66	1979–81	1964–66	1979–81
Australia	49.9	61.8	44.8	60.1
Japan	57.2	56.1	53.7	50.6
China	56.5	68.3	46.3	69.1
ASEAN NICs	44.8	62.3	61.7	66.2
Other ASEAN	62.4	77.6	62.8	66.8
North America	41.8	47.7	51.0	51.0
Pacific, total	**46.1**	**55.0**	**52.5**	**55.0**

Source: International Economic Data Bank, Research School of Pacific Studies, Australian National University

Projections of future trade highlight the growing importance of the Pacific in the world economy and in world trade. Pacific trade growth depends on the maintenance of trading opportunities for East Asia in the rest of the world, and hence on an open international trade regime. These facts have significant implications for shaping a sensible approach to international commercial diplomacy in an era of great change in the structure of world trade and the world economy.

This book will explore the question of commercial diplomacy and will seek to establish the relationship between the regional and global economic interests of countries in East Asia and the Pacific, in particular the countries of the Western Pacific. It will also review the nature and progress of interest in Pacific economic cooperation arrangements.

To answer questions about the interest of East Asian and Pacific countries in international commercial diplomacy and the idea of closer regional economic cooperation, it is necessary to lay out some simple, but important, analytic starting points. Indeed, an important theme developed in this essay is that the relationship between global and regional trading interests has often been confused, both in the literature and in the discussion of policy, because the framework within which the efficiency of regional trade and economic cooperation initiatives is commonly analysed addresses largely the wrong questions. This book suggests another approach. It seeks, in chapter 2, to clarify the nature of the policy issues confronting the dynamic and trade-oriented Pacific economies through welding the elements of the theory of international economic exchange together with elements of the theory of public choice.

Hence the importance of the *trade regime as an object of policy* needs to be underlined as the first analytic starting point.

Regional and international trade and other economic exchanges cannot develop and flourish without a confident framework of commitments to cooperative economic policy behaviour. The international trade regime provides a more or less confident framework within which trade and other economic exchanges may take place in the international market place. The origins of the framework for cooperative international economic exchange are many and varied — they sometimes have a political or even a moral basis, as did the emergence of the GATT and the other international economic institutions in the postwar period; they may derive from political alliance or strategic association (the European Economic Community, Comecon, ASEAN); or they may be a product of common economic and political interests which are encouraged by proximity.

A second starting point is to emphasise that regional action which aims at strengthening the framework for confident international economic exchanges does not need to involve *discriminatory policy* rules, European style. Indeed, a major conclusion of this book is that an important requirement for Pacific economic cooperation is to ensure consistency between global goals and regional or bilateral collective action to foster closer economic cooperation, so important is the strength of the world trading and economic system to the countries of East Asia and the Pacific. A corollary is that regional action can at times be by far the most effective route to further and faster pursuit of global objectives. In this sense, the Pacific economy and the economic policy response of Pacific countries are increasingly central to the health of the world economy.

Around 55 per cent of the trade of Pacific countries is intra-regional with other Pacific countries, although the region has only a 38 per cent share in all world export trade (see Tables 1.1 and 1.2).[3] A detailed study of regional trade data and analyses of complementarity, bias and intensity in Pacific trade flows reveals that, despite close economic relations among Pacific countries, to a great extent the *potential* for Pacific economic integration and complementarity is as yet unrealised. The detailed evidence of this potential is assembled and analysed in chapter 4.

One widely recognised characteristic of the Pacific economic community is the heterogeneity of Pacific countries (in political, cultural, social, institutional and economic terms), and this heterogeneity is frequently contrasted with the homogeneity of the Atlantic community. How should this influence the approach to international economic policy within the Pacific region? What problems are associated with the conduct of international economic diplomacy among heterogeneous nation states, and what instruments of international economic policy are crucial in overcoming these problems, given certain common goals and interests?

The literature on the theory of international trade does not address these questions, because it has been constructed upon the assumption of a homogeneous, not a pluralist, international community. A core element in the argument of this book seeks to redress this omission, since any realistic appraisal of international economic policy strategy for the Pacific community has to accommodate the fact of heterogeneity and the divergent, even conflicting, interests that are a consequence of heterogeneity. This empirical imperative encourages general insights into characteristics and effects of international economic policy which have not hitherto been sufficiently taken into account.

Despite their heterogeneity, the countries of the Western Pacific have two overriding *common interests*. The first is in strong economic growth and development — and these *development ambitions* cannot be achieved without an outward-looking or trade-oriented approach to strategies for economic development. This is the lesson of East Asian industrialisation experience over the past several decades — in the case of Japan, in the case of the East Asian newly industrialising countries and in the case of the third-generation Japans in Southeast Asia. The second common interest is the political and diplomatic interest in *neighbourly cooperation*. Even the remnants of ideological confrontation within the Pacific theatre (in Indo-China and the Korean peninsula) are qualified by the power of the interest in neighbourly cooperation.

These common interests provide the simple but substantial focus for economic policies directed towards closer Pacific economic cooperation and the building of a Pacific community over the decades ahead.

At a minimum, the very idea of a Pacific community is an effective means of promoting vigorous interest in the trade, investment and growth potential of the region as a whole, and for counterbalancing the declining relative economic importance of the older industrial countries in Europe — it is a useful rallying call for private and national energies, given the potential for regional development.

But are there more tangible international economic policy interests among the countries within the Pacific community? What are the real policy choices for Pacific countries in promoting their trade and development ambitions in the next decade or two? Trade policy issues are where some of the most serious challenges to East Asian and Pacific development ambitions have emerged in the past decade and a half.

The trade policy priorities and strategies of Pacific countries (especially Japan) need to be reassessed in the context of a dynamic and rapidly changing regional economy and the major shifts in the balance of world economic power that have been associated with this and other developments in the world economy. In both the regional and in the broader international context, the Pacific countries cannot operate on the assumption that other countries' trade protection systems are data in formulating their own approaches to trade policy. A corollary is that there is a certain urgency in international trade diplomacy about the task of defining the bases for initiatives aimed first, at securing the growth of new markets for both traditional and newly expanding exports from Pacific countries; and second, at ensuring continued access to markets with growth potential in the face of pressures towards increased protection. These pressures have derived, in the global arena, from stagnant production and trade growth, and are inevitable, in the course of regional trade and economic transformation, as the comparative advantage of industrialising countries declines in agriculture, in manufacturing involving heavy use of resources and energy, and eventually in labour-intensive manufacturing activity.

There are two areas of strategic interest for Pacific trade policies and commercial diplomacy if the potential benefits of Pacific growth are to be fully realised — the first is the issue of the pattern of protective policies within regional economies; the second is the global trade policy regime.

PROTECTIVE POLICIES WITHIN REGIONAL ECONOMIES

The evolution of the pattern of protective policies within the regional economy has been closely related to changing patterns of comparative advantage and disadvantage in the process of growth and industrialisation. Comparative advantage and competitiveness in trade specialisation reveal themselves in a dynamic context and can be stifled or nurtured by the extent and structure of trade regulation and trade protection. In the course of dynamic industrialisation and trade growth, such as has occurred in the Western Pacific region, certain industries in some countries prosper and expand while others become inefficient and should be allowed to contract. Often, as inefficient industries face increasing trade competition from neighbouring countries, they are inclined to demand — and they frequently secure — protection in one form or another. In the course of industrialisation, the agricultural sector has become less competitive in resource-poor countries and more heavily protected in this way. The same trend is evident in the way in which labour-intensive manufacturing activities receive protection at a later stage in the process of industrialisation. Such protection has distorted the structure of trade growth in agricultural and manufactured goods.

Changes in approach and emphasis in commercial policy during the process of economic growth and industrialisation can be anticipated, to a significant extent, and hence are susceptible to influence. Since protection damages trade interests and limits the scope for growth, there is room for sensible cooperation on a regional basis to limit the extension of protectionism in the course of further industrialisation. A critical interest in trade policy strategy is thus the anticipation of growth markets and changing comparative advantage, so that market access can be preserved through negotiated arrangements before protection becomes significant and entrenched. Such arrangements may involve comprehensive government-to-government agreements, but could equally well involve government initiative and support for securing commodity agreements or arrangements at the industry level. In the past, trade policy machinery in the Pacific countries has not been geared to take advantage of these possibilities, nor to integrate trade interests at this level with broad interests in commercial diplomacy, in global forums. The rationale for such initiatives in Pacific economic policy is developed in this book.

This first strategic interest for Pacific trade policy and commercial diplomacy is reflected in the established pattern of commercial policies and their effect on regional trading opportunities. Trade complementarity within the region is constrained, despite marked differences in comparative advantage, because most countries have already erected substantial barriers to imports of the various products in which they have a strong comparative disadvantage.[4] One example is barriers to imports of labour-intensive manufactures, the largest suppliers of which are the newly industrialising countries of Northeast Asia. Another example is the extremely high barriers to imports of food other than feedgrains into Northeast Asian markets. These barriers restrict trade between Australia and the region, while the United States, the world's largest supplier of feedgrains, benefits. An important example is the escalation of protection for primary resource processing in Asia. About 90 per cent of the value of Japanese and South Korean imports of fuels, minerals and metals (excluding petroleum) is made up of ores and concentrates, and virtually all the remainder is lightly rather than highly processed because of this feature of commercial policy and practice.[5] These barriers to trade limit the potential complementarity within the region; their modification would greatly strengthen regional trade and growth links.

Japan's call for a new round of multilateral trade negotiations and Australia's initiative in organising consultations among the officials of some Western Pacific countries on multilateral trade policy interests in the mid-1980s provided a starting point for a new commercial diplomacy, including the staging of multilateral negotiations relevant to East Asia and the Pacific region. Should comprehensive trade negotiations involving Europe and other countries beyond the Pacific within the GATT not prove feasible in the late 1980s, Pacific countries will still be able to proceed independently with multilateral negotiations and mutual reduction of trade barriers. While there has been talk from time to time by United States officials of pressing ahead with discriminatory freeing of trade within the region, this approach would not be in the interests of the countries of East Asia and the Western Pacific. The benefits of mutual reduction of trade barriers among Pacific countries on a *most-favoured-nation* basis would accrue significantly to countries within the region. It is thus in the interest of Western Pacific countries to press for multilateral and non-discriminatory trade liberalisation among Pacific countries, whether Europe comes to the party or not. This interest is elaborated in chapters 8 and 9.

THE GLOBAL TRADE POLICY REGIME

There are two important issues at stake here. The first relates to Japan's position at the leading edge of Western Pacific growth in the global economy, and to the continuing interest of Western Pacific countries in an open international trade regime. A much bigger and stronger Japanese economy now has to manage trade relations with the major economic powers on a more or less equal footing — and this includes difficulties with access to new markets for exports of highly sophisticated manufactured goods.

The second issue relates to the positions of the newly industrialising countries of East Asia, including China, and to their interest in the preservation and extension of a non-discriminatory trading regime in which access to established international markets is kept open. A characteristic of the trade expansion of the newly industrialising countries of East Asia is the process of their taking over market share (first in textiles and other labour-intensive manufactured goods trade) from Japan, and then, gradually, from one another. Arrangements that discriminate against their trade growth in favour of established traders would adversely affect their trade and development ambitions and regional trade interests. As well as this indirect stake, Western Pacific countries have a direct interest in the principle of non-discrimination in trading arrangements, since the highly controlled markets for agricultural commodities and labour-intensive or other manufactured goods are susceptible to the type of manipulation that corrodes the market shares of particular suppliers — usually the new and the relatively weak.

In the earlier postwar period, East Asian and Western Pacific countries (even including Japan) might have been able to operate on the assumptions that the international trade regime was firmly in place, and that the protection systems of other countries were data in the formulation of their own approaches to international economic policy. This was a luxury of the period in which the United States was large and rich enough, relative to every other country and also to the Pacific region, to be able to maintain the trade rules and system. Neither Japan nor the Western Pacific countries collectively can enjoy that luxury any more.

The Western Pacific countries have a particularly big stake in the existence of a confident trade regime. Japan is coming to have an important responsibility in sustaining and extending the GATT trade regime, and Australia for example is supportive of Japan in that role. Trade policy leadership responsibilities obviously represent a political as well as an economic burden for which there is only indirect recompense. This involves the effort of addressing the tough political problems (associated in Japan with agricultural protection, in the United States with steel, automobiles, electronics and textiles, in Australia with protection for much of the manufacturing sector), and of building an international partnership in the Pacific that will make it manageable. This will be easier if there is some sort of Pacific economic coalition in these matters. Only benefit can result from a purposive effort towards the development of a strong and constructive Pacific voice in international commercial diplomacy.

Perhaps in no other part of the world are there such strong trade and development ambitions as among the Pacific economies. Frustration of these ambitions is likely to create considerable political tension within the region. A central issue for Pacific countries is to devise the approach to foreign economic policy that will most effectively support these trade and development endeavours as well as providing a sufficient measure of trade and economic security in the face of less favourable developments elsewhere in the world economy. Closely related issues include the encouragement and direction of foreign investment, technology, and information flows towards the purposes of regional development. There are five broad interests that might be identified in East Asian and Pacific economic diplomacy. They can be stated quite simply as a prelude to the argument of this book; their explanations are its theme.

Foremost is the preservation of a *framework for economic security*. An important element in this is commitment to rules and principles upon which can be based a liberal international economic order promoting a relatively free, multilateral flow of goods, services and capital. Such a regime for international economic exchange underlies, for example, an industrialising nation's confidence in being able to trade its manufactures and obtain supplies of raw materials; a resource-poor nation's confidence in reliance on specialisation in the steady supply of raw materials as a route to economic security; and a resource-rich nation's confidence in international markets as a foundation for economic prosperity. It has evolved under the aegis of the great postwar global trading and monetary institutions. But for many East Asian and Pacific economies the protection provided by the global trading system has only been indirect, and these countries have had little influence in areas such as resource trade arrangements and trade access for developing countries.

A more substantial element in the economic security of the Pacific community in the postwar period has been the patronage and hegemony of the United States. The emerging shifts in relative economic power and the new alignment of international economic interests in the Western Pacific mean that the position of the United States can no longer be taken as given. Are there arrangements in the Pacific, supportive of global institutions and consistent with their main objectives, that could buttress the framework for Pacific and world economic security?

Second, there is the interest of Pacific countries in commitments to *expansive and competitive international economic relations*. Open trade, investment, and technology competition among the larger economies in East Asia and the Pacific form one interest that can be perceived as mutual by the small economies of the region. Another is a readiness by the advanced economies in the Pacific to find constructive and beneficial solutions to the problems of competition in specific sectors inherent in the evolving structure of Pacific economic growth. What policies are necessary to make these commitments feasible?

Third, *fair dealings with foreign companies and investors* are at the very foundations of an efficient and open international economy. They have to be built more strongly into the diverse political and institutional environments that constitute the Pacific economic community.

Fourth, there is a related interest in the *economic and strategic position of the Pacific countries* as the communist states of Asia, particularly China, open up their relations with the rest of the world. Asia and the Pacific are far more important than pawns in the ongoing bilateral relationships between the two superpowers. Furthering their economic and political interests in accommodation with the communist states of Asia, including the Soviet Union, will require in the future more consultation and cooperation among Pacific countries if complementary economic and political objectives are to be achieved.

Finally, the United States and Japan, on whom other Pacific countries are so dependent in their external economic relations, are at the centre of regional economic interests. As Japan expands its economic influence in the Pacific, it is important for all — the United States, Japan, and the other Western Pacific countries — that these two great industrial powers do not fall out of step. Unilateral economic actions by either the United States or Japan, or bilateral actions by both, are rapidly transmitted to the smaller nations of the region, with great impact upon their economies. There is an interest in *broadening the framework of the bilateral economic relationship between the United States and Japan* to incorporate the interests of other Pacific countries more fully and automatically.

These are the large and complex themes with which this book seeks to deal. Chapter 2 elaborates some principles whereby alternative economic policy regimes in the Pacific might be assessed. Chapter 3 reviews the development of the Pacific economy and common interests in economic policy in East Asia and the Pacific. Chapter 4 details the development of Pacific· trade interdependence and the substantial regional and global interest in further Pacific economic integration. Chapter 5 examines the important characteristics of the critical resource and agricultural trade relationships in the Pacific. Chapter 6 looks more closely at the nature and implications of the outward-looking development strategies of the newly industrialising countries in the Pacific, and chapter 7 at the sources of financing for regional economic development. The concluding chapters seek solutions to the policy interests and problems raised in these chapters.

NOTES

Chapter 1

1   See S.B. Linder *The Pacific Century: Economic and Political Consequences of Asian-Pacific Dynamism* Stanford: Stanford University Press, 1986, Table 4, p.12. Recent projections made by the Australia–Japan Research Centre, Australian National University, suggest a higher share, around 25 per cent.

2   Economic Planning Advisory Council (EPAC) 'International Trade Policy' *Council Paper* No. 18, 1986, p.9.

3   Japan Member Committee, Pacific Basin Economic Council *Pacific Economic Community Statistics* Tokyo: PBEC Japan Member Committee 1986, p.43. Based on trade matrix for 1984.

4   The term 'trade complementarity' is defined in a precise way in chapter 3. The concept can be understood broadly to mean the extent to which one country's specialisation in commodity exports matches another country's specialisation in commodity imports. Empirically this will be influenced by the effect of trade policies on the structure of each country's trade.

5   Kym Anderson et al. 'Pacific Economic Growth and the Prospects for Australian Trade' *Pacific Economic Papers* No. 122, Australia-Japan Research Centre, Australian National University, May 1985, p.35.

2 Nature of the policy issues

The economic behaviour and policy decisions of one country in an interdependent world have important effects on the economic opportunities and policy approaches of other countries.[1] It is necessary, therefore, to establish institutions and procedures which reduce uncertainties and anxieties in each country about the behaviour and foreign economic policy of other countries if the potential advantage of economic interchange is to be fully realised. Increasing economic integration among countries, and the presence of opportunities for further integration within a stable institutional framework, heighten the value of, and the need for, such institutions. The countries of the Pacific now form such a group of countries, with considerable potential for further mutually beneficial integration and with a substantial role to play in the global arena.

The Pacific economy is heterogeneous in terms of the economic size of its members, their standards of living, their cultures, their ethnic composition, their ideologies, and their social institutions. The variance in per capita income among Pacific countries contrasts sharply with the variance in per capita income among Atlantic community countries: the coefficient of variation is 0.98 for the Pacific, more than double that of the Atlantic community, which is only 0.39.[2] Yet, as detailed in chapter 3, the scale of economic interaction among Pacific countries ranks alongside that within the Atlantic. At first glance, the case for developing regional institutions would seem as strong for the Pacific as it was in years past for the Atlantic community, where an elaborate set of mechanisms for consultation and exchange of economic information and various other institutional arrangements has been in place for many years.[3] Reducing the uncertainties and anxieties associated with their heterogeneity through building up a stronger framework for regional economic relations offers large potential gains to countries in the Pacific. It also requires measures that will ensure proper recognition of the diverse objectives of very different countries and of the interests of the smaller and weaker economic partners in the Pacific.[4] These conclusions depend upon a line of argument that begins with the explanation of some quite fundamental propositions about the nature of economic cooperation and its benefits.

The initial step in the argument is to consider some abstract set of countries, each with a degree of market power. The theory of games suggests that, in the absence of some framework for making and communicating commitments to pursue mutually beneficial exchange strategies, restrictive and exchange-reducing strategies will be pursued. Within sovereign states, trust in contracts and commercial agreements may be built upon reputation and familiarity, but it also derives from enforceability through the authority of the state. Binding contracts, in this sense, are not available in the conduct of international exchange. Hence there is value in creating mechanisms or arrangements which allow states to communicate their perceptions of what are dominant strategies, and, in the dimensions in which they agree, to commit themselves to pursuing those strategies, with the retaliatory consequences of breaking promises also made clear. Where there is a lack of enforceability, the development of compatible incentives is a key issue. It is not only possible, but extremely likely, that subsets of the 'world' set of countries may agree in many more dimensions of action than does the 'world' group. Hence an essential step in the argument is the conclusion that there is a gain to be had from developing regional as well as 'world' forums to facilitate international exchange. There are good reasons to believe that the Pacific now constitutes such a subset of countries, and the bases upon which such a judgment may be made, such as the intensity of their trading relationships, are canvassed. The rest of the argument in this chapter explores alternative forms of regional cooperation (favouring regional arrangements which are non-discriminatory), and examines the character of social choice in a pluralist society and the important requirements for international economic pluralism.

NATIONAL INTEREST AND THE INTERNATIONAL COMMUNITY

An appropriate framework for economic cooperation is usually taken for granted in literature which analyses the mutual gains from specialisation and voluntary economic exchange.[5] Self-interested economic units (individual traders or nation states) are shown to gain through the exchange of commodities and services. These gains from trade recommend economic cooperation and exchange. Although there is the possibility of conflict over the sharing of the net surplus from trade — a conflict which is prominent in a two-trader model and reflects the presence of some monopoly power[6] — when there are many traders the element of conflict is reduced, so that in the limit, each trader in a competitive market is a pure price-taker. An elementary but critical fact is that this 'economically efficient' solution, including its most complex variants, requires a framework for cooperative exchange in the form of laws, institutions or understandings which will establish well-defined property rights and make trade contracts binding or somehow reliable. In the case of trade between nation states, the nature of understandings or agreements and the degree of confidence thereby provided between trading partners are crucial to realising the potential gains from trade.[7]

The importance of these observations needs to be demonstrated from first principles, since it is commonly understated in the theory of international economic policy. The problem can be most simply explained by appeal to the theory of games. The theory of games covers many potential exchange situations, but the branch most relevant to the economic problems considered here is the theory of games in which the exchange outcomes reflect the possibility of mixed interests, where partners have common interests in some situations but conflicting interests in others.[8] Mixed-interest games can be compared with identical-interest games, in which each partner's interests are exactly the same, and opposite-interest games, where interests are exactly the opposite, such as in the two-partner zero-sum game. Mixed-interest games capture the real nature of international trade and other economic exchange, through which there are mutual gains to be had but in which there is also the potential for conflict, in the form of restricting trade, withdrawing from trade, and even coveting the resource endowments upon which trade is based.[9] This game contrasts with the identical-interest (positive-sum) game assumed in the basic competitive models of an exchange economy, where the restriction or freeing of trade hurts or benefits each partner in the same direction.

Figure 2.1   Two-trader exchange game

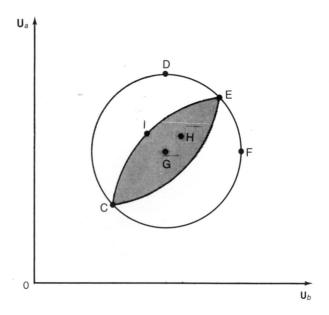

Figure 2.1 can be used to depict two mixed-interest exchange situations between a pair of trading partners, country *A* and country *B*. Economic welfare levels (*U*) are measured along each axis in the diagram, country *A*'s on the vertical axis and country *B*'s on the horizontal. The analysis starts from the assumption that each country is an ordered and sovereign entity which aims to maximise its national economic interests through the attainment of high

welfare levels. The initial assumption, therefore, is that each country has the ability to maximise some social welfare function of the Bergson–Samuelson form. In technical terms, Figure 2.1 represents a two-trader exchange game in which the pay-off vectors do not lie on a monotonically increasing line (as they would in an identical interest game) but are instead dispersed over a two-dimensional area.[10] Points in this area represent the various possible combinations of economic gain which could result from the adoption of different strategies by the two partners in the exchange.

In the first case, the possible pay-off vectors are described by the circular area enclosed by *CDEF*. Suppose *G* represents a point of relatively low trade involvement. Both partners have a common interest in moving away from *G* to the upper righthand boundary, *DEF*. Both will benefit, for example, if they move from *G* to a point like *E* which lies to the right of and above *G*. But the partners clearly have different interests in choosing among the various points between *D* and *F*, country *A* preferring *D* over *E* and country *B* preferring *F* over *E* and, of course, *F* over *D*. *E* represents a cooperative strategy for both countries (they impose no trade penalties on each other) and yields the maximum combined gain. But *D* yields more gain to country *A* where it adopts a non-cooperative strategy (imposes trade penalties) while country *B* maintains a cooperative strategy (does not impose trade penalties), whereas *F* yields more gain to country *B* when it adopts a non-cooperative strategy and country *A* does not. So there will be an incentive for each partner to adopt generally non-cooperative strategies on the basis of rational self-interest, as these strategies have the promise of yielding gains such as at *H*, where both countries are both better off than they would be if they were the lone partner holding to a cooperative strategy! There are many such circumstances in which the partner adopting a noncooperative strategy can either gain more than the partner adopting a cooperative strategy or has the potential to lose less than might otherwise have been the case, and this capacity is illustrated in the figure within the space under the arc *DEF*. Without deliberate cooperative action, non-cooperative approaches can dominate strategic choice in these circumstances.

This analysis incorporates the essence of the well-known *prisoners' dilemma game*. In the trade/restrict-trade context, the *prisoners' dilemma* game can be stated in terms of the following pay-off matrix.

			Partner B	
			Trade	*Restrict trade*
			β_1	β_2
	Trade	α_1	10,10	6,11
Partner A				
	Restrict trade	α_2	11,6	7,7

In this two-partner (non-zero-sum) game, partner *A*'s strategy, α_1, and partner *B*'s strategy, β_1, are *cooperative strategies* in which no tariffs are imposed by either country. Partner A's, α_2, and partner B's, β_2 are *non-cooperative strategies* in which trade restrictions or tariffs are imposed.

Each partner helps the other's interests when choosing cooperative strategies and harms the other's interest when choosing non-cooperative strategies. A *cooperative solution* is achieved with the choice of strategies α_1, β_2; a *non-cooperative solution* obtains when α_2, β_2 are chosen. Again, unless *binding* and *enforceable* agreements are possible between the two partners the pay-off structure rewards the partner who uses a noncooperative strategy over a cooperative strategy. However, where agreements are possible it is perfectly rational and feasible for partners to choose 'strongly dominated' cooperative strategies and improve their joint benefits from trade.[11]

In the second case, the possible pay-off vectors are delineated by the shaded lenticular area *CIE*. In this exchange there is an unambiguous common interest in moving from a point such as G to a point such as E, but there are conflicting interests in the combination of less than optimal outcomes within the shaded lenticular pay-off space. This case can perhaps be thought of as a representation of the exchange possibilities between two partners in a many-partner exchange. In these circumstances the restriction of trade prevents both countries from reaching the most preferred position and the largest gains from trade, and hence cooperative trade strategies appear extremely attractive, since the imposition of trade restrictions reduces the welfare of each trader from its free trade strategy maximum. However, non-cooperative strategies may still come to dominate. Point E represents only one solution through exchange, and there is no inevitability in its attainment without the interposition of an appropriate framework for cooperative exchange. Within the shaded pay-off space, arguments analogous to those introduced in the first case apply with equal force.

This conclusion might seem to sit paradoxically alongside the conventional wisdom in international trade theory, which suggests that it is an advantage to cooperate through pursuing a free trade strategy even when partners adopt policies that retreat from trade specialisation.[12] But the fact is that only in the rarest circumstances can it be imagined that each partner will have identical interests in the retreat from trade specialisation, so that commonly the interest in noncooperative strategies is strong unless agreements to secure trade cooperation are possible. The structure of trade gains, and losses, from a retreat from trade may take many shapes, depending on the relative sizes of the trading partners involved and the features of the particular commodity markets that are relevant. This will be true even in a purely economic context; and where national welfare is affected by non-economic arguments it will assuredly be true. The point is that there is no a priori reason for supposing that the partners will have identical interests, nor, to put it another way, that all possible pay-off vectors will lie on a line, such as OE, passing through the origin of Figure 2.1. As Hawtrey has observed:

> So long as welfare is the end, different communities may cooperate happily together. Jealousy there may be, and disputes as to how the national means of welfare should be shared. But there is no inherent divergence of aim

in the pursuit of welfare. Power, on the other hand, is relative. The gain of one country is necessarily loss to others . . . conflict is of the essence of the pursuit of power.[13]

The threat of arbitrary and 'negative' restrictions by trading partners — the potential product of any one of a wide and powerful collection of political, security–strategic and economic factors — holds back commitment to further involvement in trade.[14] This is a persuasive inhibition to exchange, and the inhibition is more persuasive still where levels of ignorance and uncertainty are high.[15]

Here it is important to note that the choices facing country A and country B are not merely to trade or not to trade, but could involve strategies which redistribute the gains from trade between partners or have the level of trade hinge upon conditional strategies. In the simplest exchange model there is also the option to steal. There is no strict analogy in the context of international exchange, which requires a more complex model for analysis, but the imperialistic option might be thought of as roughly analogous.[16] To observe that there are constraints on such 'unsocial' or 'internationally unacceptable' behaviour, albeit constraints which sometimes involve costs of enforcement, does not deny its relevance. Indeed, it merely serves to underline the fact that where mixed interests are commonplace *the partners to economic exchange become better off only by formally or tacitly agreeing to pursue cooperative trading strategies*. Such agreements are worthwhile so long as their enforcement is less costly to achieve than the joint gains that derive from them. Thus, although traders with selfish (or rational interest) motives benefit from exchange, and this can be depicted as the beneficial outcome of purely 'individualistic' activity, it can be seen that in actuality 'the invisible hand' theorem presumes a system of collective choice comparable in sophistication and complexity to the market system it governs.[17]

It is strongly evident in the first case described above that when these understandings or agreements are absent, non-cooperative strategies are likely to dominate. In Figure 2.1 the arcs DE and EF surround space which, once the process of retreat from cooperation begins, provides an incentive to rational traders to restrict exchange, as the pay-off structure rewards the non-cooperative over the cooperative partner. One variant on this behaviour pattern arises in the optimum tariff/export-tax case discussed in international trade theory, where the incentive to restrict trade derives from an ability to shift the terms of trade in one's own favour through the use of commercial policy instruments.[18] But there are many other pervasive variants which do not necessarily require that monopoly power in exchange be the sole motivation for inflicting damage (or exercising power) in the more general sense that is encompassed in these models. The exchange between Iran and the United States in recent times merely represents an extreme example. The activation by the United States of trade embargoes against the Soviet Union after the Afghanistan crisis is another. There are many normal circumstances in which partners retreat from trade to each other's cost in order tacitly to counter the potential threat of non-cooperative trading strategies.[19] This insecurity in trade takes many forms, and is nurtured and exploited by vested protectionist interests.[20] It lies at the base of attitudes, behaviour and policies in many countries that distort and restrict beneficial specialisation in international trade.

It may be argued that such game theory problems are less endemic a feature of international exchange than is suggested here, because the conditions required to make them so are not always satisfied or are readily overcome. The possibilities seem to abound for traders to communicate in order to make irrevocable commitments or agreements governing trade and to share information about strategy, and the game of international trade is repetitive. Certainly, if the apposite conditions do not hold, the prisoners' dilemma outcome will be hard to sustain. Yet to argue in this way underlines the crucial point that the explanation of such possibilities (and the understanding of the limits to such possibilities) assumes a critical interest in international trade and economic policy. The metaphor of the simple mixed-interest game is therefore critical to understanding why these conditions to sustain cooperative economic behaviour are an important policy interest. This point distinguishes the treatment here from that in the standard literature on international economic policy.[21] It is a key to understanding policy priorities in Asia and the Pacific and, it might be added, in an international economy undergoing considerable systemic change.

This argument illuminates the basis for concern and alarm among advocates of liberal trade at the appearance of monopoly or cartel behaviour in international trade, however rationally based in terms of producer or consumer self-interest.[22] The propensity for non-cooperative strategies to dominate, as exhibited in the structure of behaviour analysed here, is very real. From this perspective, cooperative trade strategies depend on a framework for exchange which must be nurtured and then carefully protected once established. If this framework is not strong and confident, the pursuit of cooperative strategies is unlikely and the mutual gains from trade commensurably limited.

The pursuit of rational self-interest through a system of voluntary international economic exchange requires the collective act of establishing such a framework. Such problems of collective choice are synchronous with the existence of recognisable international groups or communities.[23] Hence the aspects of policy which affect the choice of an appropriate framework for trading within the international community assume a special significance. The trade regime itself emerges as a most important object of policy.

DOMAINS FOR INTERNATIONAL COLLECTIVE ACTION

International agreements and understandings thus emerge as important pillars on which gainful economic interdependence is built. Growing world economic interdependence over the past several decades is certainly in part the result of both technological developments in industrial countries favouring specialisation within larger and larger international markets and the lowering of transportation and communications costs. But, importantly, it is also a consequence of the various institutional and policy commitments that followed the Second World War and built a stronger framework for international exchange and financial settlements.[24]

The process of international economic integration is far from complete, nor has its progress been in any sense uniform throughout the world economy.[25] The levels of integration within the international economy reflect, among other factors, the framework of tacit or explicit arrangements and understandings within which cooperative economic exchange has occurred. Trade among industrial countries generally grew much more rapidly than among other countries in the earlier postwar period. Integration also proceeded much more rapidly among these countries. The Atlantic community and the European community have taken economic integration further than most groups of countries, the latter within the framework of a customs union arrangement and measures encouraging broader economic and political union.

A central question is what criteria can be elicited to determine appropriate domains in which to further collective action aimed at strengthening the arrangements for cooperative international economic exchange and the gains from closer economic integration.

Closer economic integration has many possible roots. It can originate through commitments — multilateral, regional, or bilateral — which are based simply upon a recognition of the gains to be had from closer international economic cooperation and interaction. The great postwar multilateral institutions, such as the General Agreement on Tariffs and Trade (GATT), were based on such commitments.[26] It can germinate within a system of common cultures and social institutions; historically the close commercial ties among the British Empire countries had such origins. It may spring from ideological alignments, as among the Comecon countries and, more broadly, among the countries of the Western bloc. It may be encouraged by the advantages that contiguity presents in economic exchange. Or it may grow out of other non-economic interaction among nation states, such as membership of a common political alliance. Both relative contiguity and membership of a common political alliance provided starting points for closer Pacific economic integration. In Europe a commonly felt threat to external security prompted the formation of the EEC.[27] Any of these factors, separately or in some combination, can provide the impetus and rationale for collective action which effectively promotes closer economic integration within the international community of nations.

A wide range of studies of international political and economic systems reveals a great diversity of approaches over time and in different circumstances towards developing institutional frameworks aimed at fostering economic integration. The classic literature on the shaping of the Atlantic community stresses the relationship between the preconditions for integration and the feasibility of alternative approaches to integration.[28] The relative homogeneity among European nations and their common security interests, for example, were critical factors in encouraging the elaboration of a comprehensive framework for economic and, later, political union. Heterogeneity limits the scope for comprehensive union among many countries. However, a heterogeneous group of highly complementary economies can develop an intensive pattern of economic transactions fostered by propinquity, common political associations and a strong coalition of interests, which both encourages and requires closer policy coordination and economic association. Just such an intensive pattern of economic exchange has developed among the diverse countries of the Pacific.

Complete integration among a group of nations might be thought to require not just 'common' commodity markets or 'common' factor markets but also a tendency towards the equalisation of commodity prices and of the prices of the factors of production within them.[29] Common cultural and institutional factors offer one avenue to encouraging international market integration in this sense, and to creating the increased sensitivity of one nation's markets to developments in the markets of other countries which is one of the important consequences of integration. Another avenue is presented by the low resistances to bilateral or regional trade which arise from geographic proximity.[30] This proximity is a particularly important factor, inducing geographic concentration in trade for whole classes of commodities, such as minerals and raw materials, which are bulky in relation to their value and costly to transport.[31]

The systematic study of international trade resistances is, surprisingly, a new branch of economic enquiry, but it yields some useful general observations.[32] The cost of overcoming resistances to international trade varies across bilateral trading relationships, and as a result the price at which commodities are offered for international sale or purchase also varies according to the bilateral trading relationship within which the transaction is made. The effect of resistances on relative commodity prices provides incentives for the development of close trading ties among particular groups of trading nations. Low resistances are commonly associated with proximity. But other factors are also influential in determining the structure of trade resistances. In addition to objective trade resistances, which are the product of distance and transport costs or government policies that discriminate between trading partners, traders face various subjective resistances to trade, including imperfect knowledge of trading opportunities and the absence of confident and established business relationships.

Low transport and communications resistances interact with low institutional, political and other resistances to generate high intensities in trade and other economic relations, such as have developed among the economies of the Pacific.[33] Low resistances to trade on some trading routes encourage the processes of market and institutional integration more strongly among some groups of countries than among others. These discontinuities and fragmentations in otherwise more or less interconnected world markets are important in the management of foreign economic relations within the relevant policy horizons.[34] Indeed, their contours define important domains for collective action to secure agreements among groups of countries about a framework for economic exchange, as well as agreement on the policy coordination required, in one form or another, to manage the development of closer economic integration. The trade relations among Pacific countries will be analysed in detail in chapter 4 in order to explore the extent to which they provide such a domain for international collective action.

The distinction between institutional and market integration throws further light on what determines an appropriate domain for international action on the trade regime.[35] Institutional integration refers to the legal agreements and institutional arrangements which facilitate economic exchange among a community of nations. Market integration refers to the intensity of transactions in the markets for goods and factors of production within the community. If a circumstance exists where there are no governmental or direct institutional barriers to intracommunity transactions, but markets are in fact not linked because of either high transportation costs or the ignorance of trading opportunities, then institutional integration exists but market integration is underdeveloped. If, however, there are institutional and legal barriers to trade and capital movements but market ties survive, market integration is frustrated by the lack of institutional integration. This distinction is useful, not so much to draw attention to these different processes in integration as to underline the interaction between them. Institutional and market integration involve an important two-way interaction, in which close economic ties and common economic problems set the requirements for institutional arrangements, and institutional arrangements influence the degree of economic and political cohesion. Institution-building can usually neither wholly precede nor wholly follow the integration of economic markets.[36]

The distinction between institutional and market integration also highlights the scope for advancing integration arrangements on several fronts and at different levels. The literature in international economic theory might seem to take another position: that international economic policy should generally be multilateral in focus to be efficient and constructive. An argument which stresses the importance of the institutional framework within which international economic exchange is to take place prescribes no such automatic policy guideline. From this perspective multilateral action, regional action and bilateral collective action all provide fertile and potentially efficient routes to elevating exchange possibilities.[37] Multilateral collective action can establish a minimum set of acceptable and sustainable rules for cooperative exchange among the widest and most diverse group of nations. Collective action among smaller (regional) groupings may promise fuller agreement and more intensive economic ties based on the common interests growing out of proximity, common political associations, or whatever. Bilateral collective action may allow the development of cooperative exchange arrangements further and faster than is possible within a broader regional and multilateral setting.

It is important to note that collective action directed at shaping international economic regimes cannot, of its nature, be 'unilateral' — so that the individual nation state is foreclosed from policy action to secure these important effects — except in the sense that it may be able to implement such policy by exercising hegemony over some other nation or nations, thereby imposing conformity to its preferred rules for economic exchange. In fact, the theory of international relations has given considerable attention to the character and stability of hegemonic systems. It tends to suggest that hegemonies play a crucial role in supplying the collective goods that are necessary to the existence and effectiveness of international regimes (defined as 'sets of implicit or explicit principles, norms, rules and decision-making procedures around which actor expectations converge'). However, as Keohane argues, following Coase's theorem, regimes are also demanded and sustained by incentives to collaborate in the establishment of frameworks for the negotiation of international agreements (thereby reducing transactions costs), and for the coordination of actor expectations (thus improving the quality and quantity of the information available to nation states).[38]

It is significant that agreements at the regional or bilateral level that are consistent with non-discriminatory principles in international trade may well be an effective means of building and extending confidence in international exchange. It is arguable, for example, that the 1957 Agreement on Commerce between Australia and Japan, which incorporated *most-favoured-nation* principles and was non-discriminatory in its thrust, effected the most significant elevation of Australia's specialisation in the international economy in postwar years.[39] However, many bilateral and regional agreements do embody elements of commercial policy discrimination. Some of these agreements may well be effective in serving the objective of promoting and extending confidence in international exchange *despite* their embodying discriminatory elements. It is arguable, for example, that the New Zealand–Australia Closer Economic Relations Trade Agreement (CER) serves that purpose effectively for New Zealand. The efficiency or inefficiency of such discrimination in trade arrangements is a matter that needs separate judgment, although an important conclusion of this book is that discriminatory trade regimes are likely to be damaging to the interests of East Asian and Pacific countries.

THE NATURE OF REGIONAL ECONOMIC COOPERATION

The intensive network of trade and other economic exchange that has grown up within the Pacific region has developed without a firm framework of institutional ties at the regional level and despite the persistence of significant discontinuities between the commodity markets of the national economies involved. There are no comprehensive trade or economic agreements or understandings within the region. Multilateral arrangements and involvements only partially cover the trade and economic exchanges among Pacific countries. High levels of trade protection and other commercial barriers persist.[40] Purposeful action to reduce these barriers and uncertainties associated with trading within the region, even with only vague and tacit commitments to regional economic cooperation, may have the potential to yield important gains to the countries of the Pacific.[41]

The development of overlapping economic relationships and interests among the nations of the Pacific over the past two decades or so can be illustrated by reference to Figure 2.2. Figure 2.2(a) depicts the pattern of economic interaction between North America, Japan and other Western Pacific countries in the earlier postwar period, while Figure 2.2(b) shows the strong three-way interdependence in recent years. In the earlier period the dominance of the bilateral relationships of Japan and the Western Pacific with North America is represented. Japan is now much more important to other Western Pacific countries and the United States, and the shaded areas reflect the vastly enlarged intersection of regional economic interests. The diagram provides a highly stylised but essentially accurate picture of the development of overlapping economic relations within the Pacific, and suggests the interests that might encourage the development of regional cooperative agreements, institutional arrangements and organisations to define and supervise choices within growing spheres of mutual economic interest.

Figure 2.2 Patterns of economic interaction

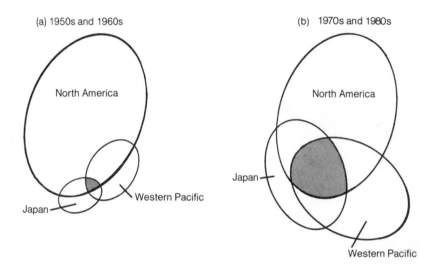

(a) 1950s and 1960s

North America

Western Pacific

Japan

(b) 1970s and 1980s

North America

Japan

Western Pacific

Regional economic cooperation which strengthens the trade regime has a sound basis in such patterns of trade and economic interaction. What form of regional economic cooperation and what structure of economic association might be adopted are matters taken up in detail later in this book. But some of the possibilities, and the characteristics of the more important among alternative forms of economic cooperation, need to be introduced briefly now.

In the field of commercial policy the range of possible commitments to regional economic cooperation include: agreements to consult on commercial policy action; the adoption of codes of trade and investment policy behaviour to maintain open markets; agreements to lower commercial barriers on a *most-favoured-nation* basis; the establishment of a limited or complete free trade area; sectoral agreements to free trade; or the formation of a customs union. The last three forms of economic cooperation involve discrimination against third parties, and are not generally desirable on grounds of economic efficiency.[42] Regional economic cooperation can also take the form of macroeconomic policy coordination; arrangements for partial or complete pooling of foreign exchange reserves; monetary union; or broader economic union, including institutional changes to facilitate integration of the markets for factors of production.[43]

The case for regional economic cooperation which incorporates discrimination against third parties in commercial or other foreign economic policies (as do customs or payments unions) is said to hinge on whether, on balance, the economic 'liberalisation effects' dominate the 'withdrawal effects' of such arrangements for the world as a whole. Johnson, however, has argued that discriminatory arrangements, such as customs unions, should be regarded as devices for the attainment of collective goods such as political alliance, cultural alliance, or higher levels of industrial production than those that would be achieved with the operation of unimpeded market forces.[44] The issue can then be stated in terms of whether a regional grouping that discriminates against third parties (and carries the economic cost of that) is the most efficient means of attaining a given collective aim; and this has to be demonstrated in each specific case, for there is no general presumption that it will be so.[45]

But the argument for regional economic cooperation offered in this book does not depend on whatever case can be made for arrangements which discriminate against third parties (of the kind that are the basis of the European Economic Community, for example). Rather, it identifies the value of regional arrangements which serve collective ends but not at the price of discrimination in commercial policy. The core of economic theory suggests that the optimum integrated area is the world as a whole, since any 'unnatural' interference with the process of equalising international commodity and factor prices (except that designed to eliminate monopoly power or market imperfections) will cause an inefficient allocation of resources.[46] However, the point made earlier in this chapter is that a priority in international economic policy directed at attaining the full benefits from exchange in a world divided by political boundaries has to be the joint securing of the regime within which exchange takes place. It does not follow that multilateral collective action to secure the regime for economic exchange is the only feasible or efficient route to closer economic integration. Regional economic cooperation, within a framework of multilateral economic relations, offers the potential for joint provision of a stronger trade regime — a trade regime which also raises confidence in international economic specialisation and promotes closer world economic integration.[47]

There is another rationale for regional economic cooperation based on the provision of the specific alongside the systemic collective good of rules and agreements governing exchange. While the highest priority is clearly securing the trade regime for countries with sufficiently strong common interests, the objects of collective action can also be a wide array of specific public goods — research and information services, communications systems, health systems and environmental controls, as well as military security.[48] Within nation states the provision of specific collective or public goods is more or less coterminous with the collective action which sustains the regime for exchange itself. This may also be so within associations of nation states, as in Europe. However, the diversity in social preferences within the international community and the different technological considerations for different types of collective goods both suggest that a variety of overlapping jurisdictions — multilateral, regional, bilateral — will serve in the most rational and sensible way the international provision of systemic and specific collective goods.[49]

The shape of international economic cooperation is not just a technical matter; it is also a political question.[50] The determination of an optimal jurisdiction in the realm of international economic policymaking requires, among other ingredients, careful weighing of the political elements in the arrangements that might be considered, since they represent potential constraints on the nature of progress towards, as well as forces which can be mobilised more effectively to achieve, international economic goals. Such linkages in the Pacific are discussed in chapters 8 to 10.

THE LOGIC OF COLLECTIVE CHOICE

It is evident that the domain for international collective action to achieve economic goals is neither single nor disjoint, in the sense that nation states will have an interest in membership of several groups or levels of international organisation.[51] Moreover, the different domains within which collective action sustains a regime for economic exchange or the international provision of specific collective goods have a wide variety of possible origins — economic, geographic, technological, cultural, political and strategic. In turn, these origins shape the choice of regime and the nature of the specific public goods that are provided internationally. If the sovereignty of the nation state is accepted as an initial condition and, by implication, some kind of equality is accorded among nation states, complex questions of collective choice arise within the international economic system.[52]

Diversity among national preferences in respect of regimes for international economic exchange and the provision of other collective goods is an important influence on the feasibility of collective action. Agreement to collective action is likely to be achieved most readily among countries which do not differ greatly in their preferences for the international economic system or for specific public goods.[53] On the other hand, differences in these preferences limit the scope for international economic cooperation and are often the cause of considerable international conflict.

If a pluralist international community is one which accommodates a non-homogeneous set of social preferences among its members — on matters to do with how trade and commerce should be organised, commercial policies managed, monetary arrangements operated, or the whole range of social institutions ordered — a fundamental question is whether and by what principles collective choice can be exercised effectively. Within democratic and pluralistic nation states (which acknowledge the 'equal value' and 'right to differ' principles) more or less satisfactory mechanisms have evolved which allow some measure of reconciliation among divergent positions or some measure of tolerance for collective action which does not have a completely unanimous basis.[54] Between sovereign and independent nation states such mechanisms are by no means fully developed.[55]

A practice of reconciliation and tolerance has built up among some countries in certain fields, and priorities have been established within the international economic community (such as through the GATT, the International Monetary Fund (IMF), within the OECD, and among the Group of Ten, the Group of Seven, and recently the Group of Five); but the basis for this cooperation is only tenuously founded on the principles of *international pluralism*. This question needs to be addressed at some length, since it is at the heart of defining an appropriate framework for economic cooperation among a group of nations such as those within the Pacific community.

The problem of international choice and collective action is complex. It almost always involves multi-dimensional decisions, rather than one-dimensional decisions that can be scaled along a single measure, such as the level of expenditure, without a simultaneous consideration of other values.[56] A group of independent nations about to settle on the nature of a regime for cooperative economic exchange is confronted with just such complexity of choice. The nature and difficulty of this kind of choice can be illustrated by a simple example.[57]

Consider a world in which there are three sovereign nation states whose preferences are accorded equal value. They wish to cooperate to secure an agreement to foster trade under a regime which just sufficiently eliminates arbitrary action that would damage their principal trading interests. Assume that the three countries are an industrial nation, a newly industrialising nation and an agricultural nation. Further, assume that there are three broad classes of commodities: capital-intensive goods, produced most efficiently by the industrial country according to the principle of comparative advantage; labour-intensive goods, produced most efficiently by the newly industrialising country; and land-intensive goods, produced most efficiently by the agricultural nation. Each country harbours feelings of insecurity, which are not totally overcome by the will to cooperate rationally with its partners through economic specialisation. Moreover, these feelings are given effective expression through protectionist pressures, justified on the grounds of national interest and revealed in a national preference for some measure of diversification unattainable under free trade but felt necessary for security's sake.[58]

Preferences for protection in each country are so ordered that the strongest preference for protection is revealed for the good which has the greatest comparative disadvantage, there is a less strong preference for protection of the good of intermediate comparative advantage, and, of course, the weakest preference for protection (zero levels are desired) applies for the good with the greatest comparative advantage. A viable trade regime is taken to require a guarantee of freedom to trade in at least two goods, while allowing arbitrary protection of the third. The choice of trade regime can be styled in terms of the good for which arbitrary protection is allowed. There are three possible trading regimes: one in which arbitrary intervention is allowed against capital-intensive goods (the 'capital protected' regime); one in which arbitrary intervention is allowed against labour-intensive goods (the 'labour protected' regime); and one in which arbitrary intervention is allowed against land-intensive goods (the 'land protected' regime).

Each country's preference for each of these three trade regimes (or states of the world that might be achieved through cooperative agreement) are ranked in Table 2.1.

Table 2.1 Choice of trade regime

	Industrial country	Newly industrialising country	Agricultural country
Land protected	1	2	3
Labour protected	2	3	1
Capital protected	3	1	2

If each country's order of preference counts equally, the logic of collective choice reveals that it is impossible for the group to make a consistent decision by majority rule. Take first the choice between the 'land protected' regime and the 'labour protected' regime. Only the agricultural country prefers the latter, so that majority rule puts the 'land protected' regime ahead. On the next choice, between a 'labour protected' regime and a 'capital protected' regime, only the industrialising country prefers the latter, so that the 'labour protected' is put ahead of the 'capital protected' regime. This would seem to imply that the group preferred a 'land protected' over a 'capital protected' regime, but the reverse turns out to be true! Indeed, the preferences of the group as a whole are cyclically inconsistent. Pairwise choice leads to an endless cycle which cannot be resolved other than arbitrarily.

This is no trivial application of Arrow's insight into the theory of collective choice.[59] Simple as it is, this example typifies the hard choices of international politics and political economy. Indeed, the example is a quite plausible, if partial, representation of the conflicting interests that faced the international community in the establishment of the postwar trade regime. The resolution of such conflicts of choice in international politics is frequently found in the exercise of a decisive role by one or more members of the group. After the Second World War, industrial countries effectively dictated the exclusion of agricultural trading nations from the full benefits of the GATT.[60] The preferences of stronger and larger parties for a choice, such as the one described here, are given fuller rein, and are often allowed to dominate when no independent rules or principles can be addressed to effect a decision.

The question arises whether such problems of collective choice are as readily resolved within nation states as has been assumed thus far. Certainly within nation states there are mechanisms that allow some measure of reconciliation among divergent positions, and these mechanisms have more authority and are more fully developed than any such mechanisms among nation states.

But the contest of preferences or priorities is sometimes open and commonly vigorous. How this contest is resolved in each individual nation state is a matter of considerable interest and importance in the context of trade and foreign economic policy formation. It will affect, for example, whether and how reliably a particular country can deliver a 'cooperative trade strategy' — that is, maintain a commitment to trade without restrictions or penalties.

Indeed, a prolific literature has developed around the analysis of the political market for protection within nation states. It seeks to explain why countries protect domestic production and restrict external trade when trade theory would suggest that the alternative policy approach would improve *national* welfare. In this literature there are some elegant analyses of the determination and structure of tariffs and trade restrictions built upon the presence of competing domestic interests.[61]

These important issues are touched upon in chapters 5 and 6 and again in chapter 9; but here the main purpose is to expose the importance of the international trade regime as an object of policy, and hence the focus of attention is on *international* collective choice and action.

Nonetheless, the conflict in preference ordering or priority setting within nation states suggests that, for any given country, it is important to have information about the domestic collective choice problems of its economic partners, since that information will affect its assessment of the probable pay-off from whatever international strategy it may choose. International consultative institutions provide an effective method of acquiring and disseminating such information. Certainly private traders acting alone are unlikely to be able to undertake adequately the role of acquiring such information. Hence there is an important rationale for the development of consultative mechanisms in the Pacific region, and these mechanisms are discussed in chapter 10.

Conflicts of collective choice are endemic in a genuinely pluralist community. They can be resolved in a number of ways: the exercise of authority by a decisive group member; the weighting of some preferences or priorities over others; and the transformation or shaping of preferences so that they become more homogeneous and consistent. All are possible ways of resolving conflicts of collective choice and attaining cooperative outcomes.[62] In practice pluralist communities incorporate all three solutions, although the exercise of decisive authority would seem compatible with the notion of pluralism only if it were seen to be in some combination with the other two elements — some weighting of priorities and an openness to persuasion. Hence, *agreement to a minimal ordering of priorities* and *the opportunity for communication and persuasion regarding orders of preference* would appear to be two essential conditions to a robust pluralist community.[63] These are evidently two basic requirements for successful economic cooperation among the heterogeneous nations of the Pacific region.

ECONOMIC POWER AND SOVEREIGNTY: COERCIVE OR COLLECTIVE ACTION

One factor already identified as strongly influencing the nature and probable success of international economic cooperation is the structure of economic interdependence. Concepts of interdependence that were formulated with the Atlantic community in mind need to be re-examined in the context of the Pacific.[64] The term 'economic interdependence' is used to stress that mutual benefits of international trade among countries can only derive from their holding shares in each other's markets, and that where there is any vulnerability or weakness deriving from a trade partnership there is commonly, though not always, a mutuality in that vulnerability or weakness. The term is also used to stress the mutual sensitivity of economic partners to policy and general macroeconomic developments in each other's economies.[65]

The central question addressed in Richard Cooper's book, *The Economics of Interdependence: Economic policy in the Atlantic Community*, was 'how to keep the manifold benefits of extensive international economic intercourse free of crippling restrictions while at the same time preserving a maximum degree of freedom for each nation to pursue its legitimate economic objectives'.[66] For Cooper, the crux of this question was the management of imbalances in international payments within the Atlantic community. In this context Japan was yet to play a significant role, and it was accorded only brief acknowledgment as an appendage to the Atlantic economic powers.[67]

Why limit the discussion of this issue to the Atlantic community? Two reasons were put forward. The first was the historical and political interest in Europe and in trans-Atlantic ties. This interest arose from the region's 'industrial might (when taken collectively), its political influence, its diplomatic astuteness and its military potential for good or harm'.[68] The second and more powerful justification, was the

> marked convergence in the economic systems and economic objectives of these countries . . . Knowledge of each other's institutions and practices has increased enormously, and the level of mutual confidence in national economic policies has risen to the point of greatly reducing psychological barriers to movements of capital and the location of production. In short, the major industrial countries are becoming more closely 'integrated'.[69]

The essential message of Cooper's treatise was that the growth of interdependence among the Atlantic economies had so heightened the sensitivity of international transactions to economic changes in the countries of North America and Western Europe that trade was responding much more rapidly to variations in incomes and prices, and capital to differences in yields, in a way which profoundly influenced the ability of countries to manage their economic affairs (particularly their balance of payments policies) independently.[70]

The critical lesson was that, under the prevailing system of fixed exchange rates, the three main instruments that could be brought to bear on the management of international payments imbalances — internal inflation or deflation policies, policies to provide for the financing of payments deficits through increasing international liquidity, and external commercial and taxation policies — had to be reconciled cooperatively for the collective good through the choice of an appropriate and acceptable economic policy.[71]

The successful implementation of each of these instruments of economic policy for managing payments required extensive international cooperation. The use of internal measures required the close coordination of national policies in endeavours to reach a desired combination of policies for the community as a whole, as well as the institutional framework to facilitate such coordination. The provision of adequate financing for adjustment of payments could be based only on cooperative commitments and institutional reform. Even the use of trade and capital restrictions (nowadays exchange rate changes are a feasible alternative) must be premised on a willingness to cooperate to prevent retaliatory measures and minimise the trade and production costs. Whichever way one turns within the coordinates of feasible policy solutions to an imbalance of international payments, a close measure of cooperation and understanding is required among the members of the international economic community.

The choice to be made was a political choice.[72] If something like national empathy is absent from the international economic community, 'the range of possibilities is correspondingly restricted.'[73] In this matter, Cooper observed the history of policy choice and laid out his own prescriptions in order: coordinated and restrained use of external measures (a surrogate for exchange rate changes); increased capability for financing adjustments; and moves towards increased coordination of national policies. Without such cooperation, the Atlantic 'Community', he declared, would not deserve its name.[74]

How were these 'matters of high national importance' to be resolved among the member states of the Atlantic Community, or through what processes of persuasion or coercion were the choice to be made and community priorities set? Paradoxically, these questions were not the subject of Cooper's attention.[75] Perhaps a common need was presumed to prevail over competing national priorities in the construction of an effective system for the adjustment of international payments. Whatever the reason, the mechanisms and institutions that would provide a cooperative solution and allow the Atlantic community to enjoy collectively the benefits of high levels of interdependence were a *sine qua non*, and they were more or less taken for granted in Cooper's argument.

The interaction between the major Pacific economies is now of substantial importance in the choice of a regime for the management of international payments. The imposition of the flexible exchange rate regime and the de facto reform of the international monetary system following the Smithsonian Agreement in 1971 gave prominence to the management of Japan's international payments policies.[76] The continuing problems of exchange rate management are a major economic policy issue for Japan and the United States, and for other countries. The choice of an appropriate international monetary regime is not the focal concern of this book.[77] There are other fundamental questions about the nature of economic interdependence and economic cooperation which need to be explored.

Among countries of similar size and economic structure, dependence is likely to be mutual in the way envisaged in the concept of 'interdependence' introduced by Cooper, so that economic power — the withdrawal of economic advantages through trade, investment or the management of the monetary regime — can, roughly speaking, only be exercised symmetrically.[78] Economic interchange among countries of different sizes and economic structures also produces gains from mutual dependence (the largest gains commonly deriving to the smaller partners), but opens up the possibilities of vulnerability in the structure of economic relations and asymmetry in the use of economic power.[79] In this setting the original meaning of interdependence, which connotes balanced and symmetrical economic relationships, is not germane. Where imbalance and asymmetry are endemic, 'interdependence' appears as an *objective* in the management of economic relations rather than a *condition* given by their nature; the achievement of 'balance and symmetry' through the management of economic relations under rules and institutions which constrain the exercise of economic power becomes the goal of 'interdependence'.[80]

When the structure of economic relations involves a significant degree of asymmetry in the use of economic power in a world unconstrained by reliable rules and institutions, uncertainties about the economic gains from trade dependence become prominent because of the threat from the coercive use of economic power. These uncertainties may be quite pervasive, as they have been in the approaches adopted by many developing countries towards commercial policy and in economic relations between the communist and non-communist countries throughout the postwar period,[81] or they may be focused more sharply on particular trades, like strategic materials, energy goods or foodstuffs.[82] As observed at the beginning of this chapter, these uncertainties will always be present in some degree or other unless there is a strong and universally accepted international code of economic behaviour beyond anything that currently obtains.

Economic power, whether enjoyed symmetrically among equal partners or distributed asymmetrically, introduces the potential for non-coercive influence and cooperation. For instance, the withholding of energy supplies or the rupture of an economic agreement allowing the financing of a development project constitutes the coercive use of economic power, while an agreement to supply energy on a long-term basis or a commitment to development financing, although capable of being used coercively, also provides a basis for cooperation and non-coercive influence.[83]

As noted before, one critical condition of a pluralist international community is that economic, political or social power be exercised under the restraint of agreed rules, procedures or codes of behaviour; otherwise collective choice and benefit might be replaced by coercion or a form of international dictatorship.[84] The nature of collective choice requires a *hierarchy of priorities* in choice. The other essential mechanisms are *forums within which non-coercive influence can be played out* to resolve conflicts of collective interest. The extension of information, persuasion and advice are important sources of such non-coercive influence. For example, one country may have misunderstood what another is seeking to achieve through a new trade agreement, and information can be supplied in order to dispel the misunderstanding. Some international conflicts of interest decrease or disappear once the governments involved are fully informed. Persuasion and advice are related bases of influence. A country may have adequate information on the nature of a new aid arrangement, for instance, but may still misinterpret it. By means of persuasion, its partner may help the relationship to be redefined and the consequences of policy to be evaluated properly. Advice involves suggesting a course of action that will be conducive to the achievement of partner countries' independent goals. It is quite different from a demand which aims to serve exclusively the ends of the country making the demand.[85]

Information, persuasion and advice clarify and enlarge the scope for economic cooperation. Non-coercive influence and cooperation are facilitated when the value preferences of partners converge — when, for instance, they share a common interest in free trade or economic development. But even so, a similar structure of preferences is integrative only if it is characterised by priorities which are susceptible to cooperative solution.[86] The priority accorded to trade growth and economic development among the diverse countries of the Pacific at present might provide the basis for just such cooperative solutions. This question will be explored in chapter 9.

CHALLENGES TO ECONOMIC SOVEREIGNTY

The argument so far has been premised on the assumption that the sovereignty of nation states is both accepted and effective. There are two senses in which closer economic cooperation within the international community presents challenges to national sovereignty, and they now require some discussion.

The first challenge to sovereignty is trivial; but it is sometimes the cause of anxiety and deserves explicit mention. The second raises important policy problems, and will be taken up again later in this book. To return to the first challenge. Consider the case of the Atlantic community. It comprises a group of sovereign states which joined together in various economic, political and strategic associations and agreements of their own volition to pursue some defined collective goods.[87] What has emerged within the Atlantic community, and much more strongly within the European Community, is a system of loosely functioning international federalism around specialised agreements, agencies and organisations (NATO, Euratom, the OECD, the Group of Ten, the Group of Seven, the Group of Five), each with its own sphere of influence, decisionmaking structure and jurisdiction.[88] These associations, while not as strong or as comprehensive as the associations between the states or provinces and other areas of government within federated nation states, serve the same kinds of purposes as such a federation.[89] The specialised international organisations, each established by separate agreement, have their parallels within nation states. When the case is put this way, it is clear that sovereignty is constrained by such associations. If a country surrenders its right to behave in certain ways in respect of commercial policy, for example, by acceding to the provisions of the Treaty of Rome (which established the EEC), it surrenders some sovereignty over its formal ability to make future commercial policy decisions exactly as it wishes. Such concessions hardly represent a fundamental challenge to sovereignty; they merely reflect its exercise in a particular way. If a distinction is made between sovereignty and autonomy (the capacity to execute the objectives of national economic policy), the surrender of some sovereignty in international cooperative agreements may well serve to enhance national autonomy.[90]

The second challenge to national sovereignty needs to be considered more seriously. It assumes particular importance in the discussion of economic relations between large, powerful states and smaller states where the processes of government and administration are less firmly established. But it is important in all international relationships. In relations between powerful and weak states, challenges to sovereignty take the shape of informal, extra-official exchanges and inter-state dealings, which have been common enough throughout history.[91] For nation states with the necessary leverage, available resources and a fluid enough set of supportive values, as well as the means to execute it, transnational corruption can be used as a way of achieving international political or economic objectives. More commonly nowadays, for individuals or corporate entities with similar inclinations and capacities, there are opportunities to pursue self-interested objectives in a way corrosive to the boundaries of the sovereignty of nation states.[92] Such challenges to sovereignty can seriously threaten the independent ordering of social preferences by ostensibly sovereign nation states.

Alternatively, it could be argued that there should be no automatic presumption in favour of sovereignty over bribery since bribery (and corruption) may be an effective, even a necessary, means of tempering rigidities in the 'independent ordering' processes of national governments and bureaucracies. But private bribery and corruption should be distinguished from settlements effected through social and public (government-to-government) side-payments. Such side-payments or 'bribes' are a prominent and legitimate part of linkage diplomacy, and their importance is mentioned in chapter 9. Private bribery and corruption must also be distinguished from transnational influence through persuasion and argument, which are legitimate activities in an open international society and are likely to be supportive of cooperative economic exchange. Unlike these measures, private bribery and corruption pose a fundamental challenge to the integrity of social order and control, whether in the international system or within nation states. This challenge is always likely to be present, but systems of scrutiny and exposure can be developed to keep it in check. Fair dealings among foreign governments and between governments and foreign corporations, and the measures to ensure fair dealings and protect international freedom of association, must therefore be another ingredient in successful economic cooperation among the disparate countries of the Pacific community. This subject will be treated more fully in chapter 7.

The nature of the policy issues confronting the countries of the Pacific is dominated heavily by the structural questions analysed in this chapter. The concern here has not been with how economic variables are equated at the margin or how equilibrium is altered by marginal shifts in conditions such as the removal of particular tariffs or the shift of a supply schedule. Rather it has been with structural questions involving choice among a number of institutional alternatives. The policy issues of importance to Pacific countries revolve around the question of what structural conditions make trade and exchange (or more trade and exchange) both rational and attractive.

The creation of an appropriate framework for closer economic cooperation among the countries of the Pacific is the subject of the remainder of this book, and the principles laid out in this chapter provide the foundations on which the argument of subsequent chapters is constructed. The role of regional economic cooperative institutions has been established. The elements of international pluralism have been defined. Neither are as yet prominent or solid features in the Pacific economy, and the task is to describe why and how they could become so.

NOTES

Chapter 2

1   Richard Cooper presented the first comprehensive statement of this idea in the
     economic literature in his book, *The Economics of Interdependence: Economic Policy
     in the Atlantic Community* New York: McGraw-Hill, 1968. For non-economic
     conceptions of interdependence, see Lester Brown *World Without Borders: The
     Interdependence of Nations* New York: Vintage for Foreign Policy Association,
     1973, and the critical and perceptive analysis in Robert Keohane and Joseph Nye
     Power and Interdependence: World Politics in Transition Boston: Little, Brown &
     Co., 1977.
2   Australian National University, International Economic Data Bank.
3   Karl Deutsch et al. *Political Community and the North Atlantic Area* Princeton, NJ:
     Princeton University Press, 1957; Leon Lindberg *The Political Dynamics of
     European Economic Integration* Stanford: Stanford University Press, 1963; Harold
     Cleveland *The Atlantic Idea and Its European Rivals* New York: McGraw-Hill for
     the Council on Foreign Relations, 1966; and Henry Aubrey *Atlantic Economic
     Cooperation: The Case of the OECD* New York: Praeger for Council on Foreign
     Relations, 1967.
4   Some writings on the Pacific Community have reviewed this aspect in a general
     way. There has been less analysis of the sense of community in the Pacific, and no
     work to rival that which was undertaken early for the Atlantic community, such as
     that by Deutsch et al. in *Political Community*. See Pacific Basin Cooperation Study
     Group *Pacific Basin Cooperation Concept* for a recent synopsis of the character of
     the Pacific Community. See also Hadi Seosastro 'Institutional Aspects of
     ASEAN–Pacific Economic Cooperation' ESCAP Report on ASEAN and Pacific
     Economic Cooperation, Bangkok, June 1982, pp.48–57 and Appendix. J.
     Johansson and R. Moinpour, 'Objective and Perceived Similarity among Pacific
     Rim Countries' *Columbia Journal of World Business* 12, 4, Winter 1977, pp.65–76,
     have attempted a preliminary analysis of characteristic variables to test the
     perception of 'community' within the region.
5   The analysis of international trade specialisation is commonly presented in terms
     of a statement of the welfare effects or policy 'efficiency' of various restrictions on
     trade (tariffs, subsidies, quota restrictions, for example) versus other interventions
     in the market (production subsidies or taxes, consumption taxes or subsidies, for
     example). See W.M. Corden *Trade Policy and Economic Welfare* Oxford: Oxford
     University Press, 1971, pp.2–8, for a characteristically clear statement of this
     interest. The market framework is typically taken for granted in mainstream
     literature (for example, Richard Caves and Ronald Jones *World Trade and
     Payments: An Introduction* Boston: Little, Brown & Co., 1973, pp.2–5). There is a
     somewhat different emphasis, but no alternative statement, in Charles
     Kindleberger *Foreign Trade and the National Economy* New Haven: Yale
     University, 1962, pp.15–20, and Bertil Ohlin 'Some Insufficiencies in the Theories
     of International Economic Relations' *Essays in International Finance* No.34,
     Princeton University, September 1979, pp.7–8.
6   Corden, *Trade Policy*, p.159, provides a concise introduction to the history of the
     literature on monopoly power and the theory of the 'optimum' tariff. Early
     statements of the idea are found in Torrens, John Stuart Mill, and Sidgwick, but
     C. Bickerdike ('The Theory of Incipient Taxes' *Economic Journal* 17, March 1907,

pp.98–102) wrote the first clear presentation of the idea of an 'optimal' trade restriction. It is also found in F. Edgeworth 'The Theory of International Values' *Economic Journal* 4, March 1894, pp.35–50. As Corden observes, there were many contributions on the subject of monopoly power in trade during the 1930s and 1940s; among the most telling is Albert Hirschman *National Power and the Structure of Foreign Trade* Berkeley and Los Angeles: University of California Press, 1945, pp.41–52. H.G. Johnson 'Optimum Tariffs and Retaliation' *Review of Economic Studies* 21, 2, 1953–54, pp. 142–53 is the classic statement of these theoretical propositions.

7   For an excellent survey of the literature on this subject, see Dennis Mueller 'Public Choice: A Survey' *Journal of Economic Literature* 14, 2, June 1976, pp.396–9. See also James Buchanan *The Limits of Liberty: Between Anarchy and Leviathan* Chicago: University of Chicago Press, 1975; W. Bush and L. Mayer 'Some Implications of Anarchy for the Distribution of Property' *Journal of Economic Theory* 8, 4, August 1974, pp.401–12; and for two applications in an international context, see John Harsanyi *Essays on Ethics, Social Behaviour, and Scientific Explanation* Dordrecht: Reidel, ch. VIII (originally published in *Australian Journal of Politics and History* 11, 1965, pp.292–304); and P. Dasgupta and G. Heal *Economic Theory and Exhaustible Resources* Welwyn: Cambridge University Press, 1979 pp.18–21.

8   John von Neumann and Oskar Morgenstern *Theory of Games and Economic Behaviour* Princeton, NJ: Princeton University Press, 1947, p.504; Duncan Luce and Howard Raiffa *Games and Decisions: Introduction and Critical Survey* New York: John Wiley & Sons, 1957, p.115 (who suggest that such games should be treated as cooperative games in an economic context); and Harsanyi *Essays on Ethics* pp.153–6.

9   Mueller 'Public Choice' pp.395–6. 'Coveting' here implies a capacity 'to steal endowments'. In a simple endowment-exchange model this is a more obvious and feasible capacity than in a more complex production-exchange model, where the expression of the propensity to steal requires some form of 'imperialism' and the choice of a 'stealing' strategy is likely to entail large implementation costs. A very much more complex model is required to analyse the benefit–cost of modern imperialism. See Yasuhiro Murota 'Options for a Resource-Poor Developed Country — Japan', and Hugh Patrick 'Options for a Resource-Poor Developed Country, Japan: A Comment' in Lawrence B. Krause and Hugh T. Patrick (eds) *Mineral Resources in the Pacific Area: Papers and Proceedings* 9th Conference on Pacific Trade and Development, San Francisco, 1977, pp.316–58.

10   Harsanyi *Essays on Ethics* pp. 148–53.

11   This analysis incorporates the essence of the well-known *prisoners' dilemma game*, first suggested by A. Tucker (cf. Luce and Raiffa *Games and Decisions* p.95). See Luce and Raiffa *Games and Decisions* pp.94–102; and Harsanyi *Essays on Ethics* pp.154–6. John Harsanyi *Rational Behaviour and Bargaining Equilibrium in Games and Social Situations* Cambridge: Cambridge University Press, 1977, p.122, stressed that the 'dominance principle' is not a postulate of general validity in the sense that it is perfectly rational (where agreements are possible) for partners to use strongly dominated strategies.

12   For a discussion of the standard propositions recommending unilateral pursuit of free trade by a small country, see Paul Wonnacott and Ronald Wonnacott 'Is Unilateral Tariff Reduction Preferable to a Customs Union? The Curious Case of the Missing Foreign Tariffs' *American Economic Review* 71, 4, September 1981, pp.704–14.

13   R. Hawtrey *Economic Aspects of Sovereignty* London: Longmans, Green & Co., 1930, p.27.

14   Hirschman *National Power*, especially pp.1–34.
15   Harsanyi *Essays on Ethics* pp.156–71; and James Buchanan 'Markets, States and the Extent of Morals' *American Economic Review* 68, 2, May 1978, pp.364–8.
16   Hirschman, in *National Power* pp.14–5, quotes from an anti-Napoleon tract of Benjamin Constant:

> War and commerce are but two different means of arriving at the same aim which is to possess what is desired. Trade is nothing but a homage paid to the strength of the possessor by him who aspires to the possession; it is an attempt to obtain by mutual agreement that which one does not hope any longer to obtain by violence. The idea of commerce would never occur to a man who would always be the strongest. It is experience, proving to him that war, that is, the use of his force against the force of others, is exposed to various resistances and various failures, which makes him have recourse to commerce, that is, to a means more subtle and better fitted to induce the interest of others to consent to what is his own interest.

De l'esprit de la conquête et de l'usurpation dans leurs rapports avec la civilisation Européenne, Part 1, ch.II.
17   Mueller 'Public Choice' p.397; Luce and Raiffa *Games and Decisions* p.97; Harsanyi *Essays on Ethics* pp.155–6; and Buchanan 'Markets' p.364.
18   Johnson 'Optimum Tariffs' p.142–53.
19   See Sir John Crawford and Saburō Ōkita (eds) *Raw Materials and Pacific Economic Integration* London: Croom Helm, 1978, pp.44–5 for contemporary illustrations; and Hirschman *National Power* pp.14–24 for an analytic statement of the problem in the more extreme circumstances of the interwar period. Recent developments in international politics, and more easy resort by major traders such as the United States to politically motivated trade embargoes (as distinct from universally agreed economic sanctions within the framework of the United Nations) raise the spectre of increasing use of non-cooperative trade strategies.
20   Anne Krueger 'The Political Economy of the Rent-Seeking Society' *American Economic Review* 64, 3, June 1974; and Bush and Mayer 'Some Implications of Anarchy'.
21   For a recent review of the new literature on the conduct of trade in a 'strategic environment' see Gene M. Grossman and J. David Richardson *Strategic Trade Policy: A Survey of Issues and Early Analysis* Special Papers in International Economics No.15, Princeton, April 1985. John A.C. Conybeare, in 'Public Goods, Prisoners' Dilemmas and the International Political Economy' *International Studies Quarterly* 28, 1984, provides the most thorough exploration of the prisoners' dilemma issue in international trade, but comes to the sanguine conclusion that 'uncooperative prisoners' dilemma elements in international trade have been exaggerated relative to the incentives for some form of cooperation between parties to international trade' (p.5). He takes the interest in agreement formation as a deus ex machina. Here the focus is on the criticality of the formation of agreements.
22   Harsanyi *Essays on Ethics* pp.155–6.
23   Mueller 'Public Choice' p.397.
24   Gerard and Victoria Curzon 'GATT: Traders' Club' in Robert Cox and Harold Jacobson *The Anatomy of Influence: Decision Making in International Organisations* New Haven: Yale University, 1973; Aubrey *Atlantic Economic Cooperation*; Kenneth Dam *The GATT: Law and International Economic Organisation* Chicago: University of Chicago Press, 1970; and Keith Horsefield *The International Monetary Fund, 1945–1965* Washington, DC: International Monetary Fund, 1969.
25   Cooper *Economics of Interdependence* pp. 12–3.
26   See Gerard Curzon *Multilateral Commercial Diplomacy: GATT and Its Impact on*

National Commercial Policies and Technique London: Michael Joseph, 1965, pp.27–33 for a brief but insightful account of the intellectual and policy milieu out of which that commitment grew.

27   Cooper *Economics of Interdependence* p.7.
28   Deutsch et al. *Political Community*. Michael Haas *International Systems: A Behavioural Approach* New York: Chandler, 1974 provides a useful introduction to the literature which analyses this subject, especially in chapters 1 and 8. For the future, Susan Strange observes:

> . . . the shape of the future political relations between states, the areas of administrative management and operative enterprise that states are prepared to abandon or to relinquish to international agencies, the problems on which they will or will not seek international agreement, will depend in the next generation less on the compatibility of their ideologies or on the similarity of their constitutional structures than on the demands of an economic and communications system based on rapidly changing technology.

Susan Strange 'International Economic Relations I: The Need for an Interdisciplinary Approach' in Roger Morgan (ed.) *The Study of International Affairs: Essays in Honour of Kenneth Younger* London: Oxford University Press, 1972.

29   Cooper *Economics of Interdependence* pp.10–11.
30   Drysdale and Garnaut 'Trade Intensities'.
31   ibid., p.67.
32   For a review of the analysis of these issues, see Drysdale and Garnaut 'Trade Intensities'; Ross Garnaut, Australian Trade with Southeast Asia: A Study of Resistances to Bilateral Trade Flows, PhD dissertation, Australian National University, 1972; Charles Wolf and David Weinschrott 'International Transactions and Regionalism: Distinguishing "Insiders" from "Outsiders"' *American Economic Review* 63, 2, May 1973; Maurice Girgis 'Development and Trade Patterns in the Arab World' *Weltwirtschaftliches Archiv* 109, 1973; John Roemer 'The Effect of Sphere of Influence and Economic Distance on the Commodity Composition of Trade in Manufactures' *Review of Economics and Statistics* 59, 3, August 1977; Ephraim Kleiman, 'Trade and the Decline of Colonialism' *Economics Journal* 86, September 1976, and 'Cultural Ties and Trade: Spain's Role in Latin America' *Kyklos* 31, 2, 1978.
33   Drysdale and Garnaut 'Trade Intensities' pp.70–80.
34   Crawford and Ōkita, in *Raw Materials* pp.41–7, justify the strong bilateral policy interest in the Australia–Japan economic relationship on these grounds. See also Drysdale and Garnaut 'Trade Intensities' p.3.
35   Richard Cooper 'Worldwide versus Regional Integration: Is There an Optimal Size of the Integrated Area?' *Yale Economic Growth Center Discussion Paper* 220, November 1974, pp.2–4.
36   ibid., pp.2–3; see also Cooper *Economics of Interdependence* pp.12–13.
37   Mueller 'Public Choice' p.398 reviews the issues which determine the ease of operation and establishment of groups or communities with common interests. The literature on group and alliance formation, to which Mancur Olson, in *The Logic of Collective Action: Public Goods and the Theory of Groups* Cambridge: Harvard University Press, 1965, made the seminal contribution, generally asserts that voluntary alliance or group formation will be limited to a small number and that collective goods will be underprovided. See also Mancur Olson and Richard Zeckhauser 'An Economic Theory of Alliances' *Review of Economics and Statistics* 8, 3, August 1966, pp.266–79; Ernst Haas 'International Integration: The European and the Universal Process' *International Organization* 15, 3, Summer 1961; Bruce Russett (ed.) *Economic Theories of International Politics* Chicago:

Markham, 1968; Bruce Russett and John Sullivan 'Collective Goods and International Organization' *International Organization* 25, 4, Autumn 1971; Mancur Olson 'Increasing Incentives for International Cooperation' *International Organization* 25, 4, Autumn 1971, pp.866–74; John Chamberlin 'Provision of Collective Goods as a Function of Group Size' *American Political Science Review* 68, 2, June 1974, pp.707–16; and Ernst Haas 'Turbulent Fields and the Theory of Regional Integration' *International Organization* 30, 2, Spring 1976, for a critique of Olson's principal conclusions in the case of *pure* collective goods (indivisibility in production or jointness of supply and impossibility of exclusion in consumption) and where there is perfect information about group member reactions.

38   Robert O. Keohane 'The Demand for International Regimes' *International Organization* 36, 2, 1982, pp.325–56; Stephen D. Krasner 'Structural Causes and Regime Consequences: Regimes As Intervening Variables' *International Organization* 36, 2, 1982, pp.185–206; Robert O. Keohane 'The Theory of Hegemonic Stability and Changes in International Economic Regimes; 1967–1977' in Ole R. Holsti, Randolph M. Siverson and Alexander L. George (eds) *Changes in the International System* Boulder: Westview, 1980. I am grateful to Nancy Viviani for drawing this literature in international relations theory to my attention.

39   Crawford and Okita *Raw Materials* pp.47–51; Drysdale 'Australia and Japan in the Pacific and World Economy' in Peter Drysdale and Hironobu Kitaōji (eds) *Japan and Australia: Two Societies and Their Interaction* Canberra: Australian National University, 1981.

40   An indication of how far the vigorous process of economic integration within the Pacific still has to go, in terms merely of commodity market integration, is given in the following comparisons of the prices of important commodities in various countries throughout the region:

	Beef[a]	Crude steel[b]	Aluminium[c]	Automobiles[d]
1980				
New York	100	100	100	100
Manila	76	169	126	117
Tokyo	346	86	149	82
Sydney	109	105	107	114
Seoul	149	164	165	118
Singapore	92	103	129	na
1987				
New York	100	100	100	100
Manila	na	96	103	na
Tokyo	278	132	123	87
Sydney	40	104	98	91
Seoul	80	98	120	56[e]
Singapore	88	93	115	101

Notes: a One kilogram of sirloin; retail.
          b One tonne of 'H' shape angle.
          c One tonne of ingots 99.5 per cent.
          d Toyota Corolla 4-door sedan, manual; price excludes sales tax, import duty, registration fees, etc.
          e Presto AMX 4-door sedan, manual (domestically produced).
Source: Data collected by the Australian government trade representatives in each city shown in April 1980 and October/November 1987. The price data were converted into US dollars using the average exchange rates for the last quarter of 1979 and for the month comprising the last week of October and first 3 weeks of November 1987

41   There is a summary of the major associations to which Pacific nations are partners in Peter Drysdale and Hugh Patrick 'Evaluation of a Proposed Regional Economic Organisation' *Australia-Japan Economic Relations Research Project Paper* No.61, Australian National University, July 1979 (also published by the US

Congressional Research Service as *An Asian–Pacific Regional Economic Organisation: An Exploratory Concept Paper* Washington: US Government Printing Office, July 1979).

42   R. Lipsey 'The Theory of Customs Unions: Trade Diversion and Welfare' *Economica* 24, February 1957, pp.40–6; R. Lipsey 'The Theory of Customs Unions: A General Survey' *Economic Journal* 70, September 1960, pp.498–513; Harry Johnson 'An Economic Theory of Protectionism, Tariff Bargaining, and the Formation of Customs Unions' *Journal of Political Economy* 73, 3, June 1965, pp.256–83; Michael Michaely *Theory of Commercial Policy* Oxford: Philip Allan, 1977, pp.186–230; Peter Robson *The Economics of International Integration* London: George Allen & Unwin, 1980.

43   This is the subject of Cooper's work *Economics of Interdependence*. On the political economy of monetary coordination, perhaps the keenest general insights are provided by Kōichi Hamada 'On the Political Economy of Monetary Integration: A Public Economics Approach' in Robert Aliber (ed.) *The Political Economy of Monetary Reform* London: Macmillan, 1977, pp.13–31, and Kōichi Hamada 'Macroeconomic Strategy and Coordination under Alternative Exchange Rates' in Rudiger Dornbusch and Jacob Frenkel (eds) *International Economic Policy: the Theory and Evidence* Baltimore: Johns Hopkins University Press, 1979, pp.292–324.

44   Albert Breton 'The Economics of Nationalism' *Journal of Political Economy* 72, 4, August 1964, pp.376–86; Harry Johnson 'The Economic Theory of Customs Unions' in *Money, Trade and Economic Growth* London: George Allen & Unwin, 1962; C. Cooper and B. Massell 'A New Look at Customs Union Theory' *Economic Journal* 75, December 1965, pp.742–7; Jagdish Bhagwati *Trade, Tariffs and Growth* Cambridge: MIT Press, 1969, pp.351–5; Harry Johnson (ed.) *Economic Nationalism in Old and New States* London: George Allen & Unwin, 1968, especially pp.1–16. For a recent survey of the customs union literature, see M.B. Krauss 'Recent Developments in Customs Union Theory: An Interpretation Survey' *Journal of Economic Literature* 10, June 1972, pp.413–36. For a critical assessment of this emphasis, see Wonnacott and Wonnacott 'Is Unilateral Tariff Reduction Preferable?' See also Robson *International Integration* ch.4.

45   R. Lipsey and K. Lancaster 'The General Theory of Second Best' *Review of Economic Studies* 24, 1956-57, pp. 11–33.

46   Cooper, in 'Worldwide versus Regional' p.4, makes the point that these allocative issues cannot easily be separated from distributional issues.

47   The relatively new literature on uncertainty and international trade does not tackle the issues raised here, but is largely concerned with establishing, in the presence of randomness, the robustness of the important general propositions of neoclassical trade theory. This literature is surveyed in John Pomery 'Uncertainty and International Trade' in Dornbusch and Frenkel (eds) *International Economic Policy* pp.112–57.

48   For example, see Olson and Zeckhauser 'Economic Theory of Alliances'; Russett and Sullivan 'Collective Goods and International Organisation'; Russett (ed.)' *Economic Theories of International Politics*.

49   The division among different levels of government is discussed in Mancur Olson 'The Principle of "Fiscal Equivalence": The Division of Responsibilities Among Different Levels of Government' *American Economic Review* 59, 2, May 1969, pp.479–87. See also Mueller 'Public Choice' pp.398–9, and Cooper 'Worldwide versus Regional' pp. 10–13.

50   Cooper *Economics of Interdependence* pp.2–13; Richard Cooper 'Prolegomena to the Choice of an International Monetary System' in Fred Bergsten and Lawrence Krause (eds) *World Politics and International Economics* Washington: The

Brookings Institution, 1975, pp.63–97; Hamada 'Political Economy'; Hamada 'Macroeconomic Strategy', and Cooper 'Worldwide versus Regional' pp.10–13.

51   The implications of an assumption of disjointedness in the theory of collective choice are discussed by Dana Stevens and James Foster 'The Possibility of Democratic Pluralism' *Economica* 45, 180, November 1978, pp.40–6. See also Amartya Sen 'Personal Utilities and Public Judgements: Or What's Wrong with Welfare Economies?' *Economic Journal* 89, 355, September 1979, pp.539–58.

52   For an early discussion of the nature of sovereignty in economic affairs see Hawtrey *Economic Aspects of Sovereignty*; he observes that 'sovereignty is not property, but it carries with it important economic rights which are closely related to the rights of property' (p.18). Legalistically a sovereign state is a 'social group that occupies a defined territory and is organized under common political institutions and an effective government' (Jack Plano and Roy Olton *International Relations Dictionary* New York: Holt, Rinehart & Winston, 1969, quoted in Haas *International Systems*) in a way which conveys the ability to make its own decisions, and renounce decisions previously made (Cooper *Economics of Interdependence* p.4).

The kind of equality envisaged here is an equality in the process of collective choice: an equal vote. Other egalitarian principles are also the subject of the theory of collective choice, especially as it touches upon the theory of distributive justice. A rich literature is growing around the discussion of this significant issue, and includes the work of John Rawls *A Theory of Justice* Cambridge: Harvard University, 1972; Robert Nozick *Anarchy, State, and Utopia* Oxford: Basil Blackwell, 1974; Amartya Sen *On Economic Inequality* Oxford: Clarendon Press, 1973. Important aspects are surveyed in E. Phelps (ed.) *Economic Justice* Harmondsworth: Penguin, 1973; Mueller 'Public Choice' pp.415–5; and Sen 'Personal Utilities' pp.537–58. The two dimensions of equality are positively interrelated, as the earlier work of James Buchanan and Gordon Tullock *The Calculus of Consent* Ann Arbor: University of Michigan, 1962 (ch.20 and appendix 1) suggests, but any implications beyond those of the right to an *equal* vote are not relevant here.

53   Cooper *Economics of Interdependence* pp.277–8; and Cooper 'Worldwide versus Regional' pp.9–10. The principles were stated in James Buchanan 'An Economic Theory of Clubs' *Economica* 32, 25, February 1965, pp.1–14. See also Sen 'Personal Utilities' and Stevens and Foster 'The Possibility of Democratic Pluralism'.

54   This question is considered in Robert Dahl and Edward Tufte, *Size and Democracy* Stanford: Stanford University Press, 1973, especially pp.22–25 and 138.

55   See Hedley Bull *The Anarchical Society: A Study of Order in World Politics* London: Macmillan, 1977, pp.8–9 for a crisp statement of the elements of a system of sovereign and independent nation states and *passim* for an elaboration of the imperfect international society.

56   Mueller, in 'Public Choice' pp.403–7, reviews these issues.

57   The modern theory of complex choice was developed by Kenneth Arrow *Social Choice and Individual Values* New York: Witary, 1951. There is now a vast number of papers explaining the Arrowian 'impossibility theorem', of which an example follows. See Amartya Sen *Collective Choice and Social Welfare* San Francisco: Holden–Day, 1970, ch.3. The most recent restatement of its significance and interest is in Sen 'Personal Utilities'.

58   Johnson 'An Economic Theory of Protectionism' . This issue is considered further in chapter 5.

59   ibid.

60   Curzon, in *Multilateral Commercial Diplomacy* pp.166–248, provides one
       perspective on these matters of history. Crawford, *Australian Trade Policy* ch.5,
       provides a complementary perspective.
61   G. Tullock 'The Welfare Cost of Tariffs, Monopolies and Theft' *Western Economic
       Journal* 5, 1967, pp.224–32; Anne O. Krueger 'The Political Economy of the Rent-
       Seeking Society' *American Economic Review* 64, 1974, pp.291–303; J.M. Buchanan,
       R.D. Tollison and G. Tullock (eds) *Towards a Theory of the Rent-Seeking Society*
       College Station: Texas A & M University Press, 1980; R. Findlay and S. Wellisz
       'Some Aspects of the Political Economy of Trade Restrictions' *Kyklos* 36, 1983,
       pp.469–80; J.J. Pincus *Pressure Groups and Politics in Antebellum Tariffs* New
       York: Columbia University Press, 1977; Richard E. Caves 'Economic Models of
       Political Choice: Canada's Tariff Structure' *Canadian Journal of Economics* 9, 1976,
       pp.279–300; G.K. Helleiner 'The Political Economy of Canada's Tariff Structure:
       An Alternative Model' *Canadian Journal of Economics* 10, 1977, pp.318–36; Bruno
       S. Frey 'The Public Choice View of International Political Economy' *International
       Organization* 38, 1, 1984, pp.199-223.
62   Mueller 'Public Choice' pp.403–15; Sen 'Personal Utilities' pp.543–5. For a
       readable and entertaining account of complex social choice, see Robert Mundell
       Man and Economics: the Science of Choice New York: McGraw Hill, 1968,
       pp.153–92.
63   ibid., p.171.
64   Crawford and Ōkita *Raw Materials* p.41.
65   ibid., pp.42–44; Cooper *Economics of Interdependence* pp.54–80.
66   Cooper *Economics of Interdependence* p.5.
67   Cooper's book was published before the current account of Japan's balance of
       payments turned into consistent and substantial surplus.
68   ibid. p.7.
69   ibid. pp.7–8.
70   ibid. p.59.
71   The problem is represented diagrammatically in a triangular coordinate system in
       which the vertices of the triangle specify exclusive use of one or other of the three
       categories of measures: internal measures; financing measures; or external
       measures.
            In Figure 2.3, *G*, for example, (see p.57) represents a gold-standard type regime
       which relies on domestic deflation to eliminate a deficit and inflation to eliminate a
       surplus. Temporary borrowing or limited exchange flexibility within gold points
       comprise a minor external measure element under this regime. *H* represents heavy
       reliance on external measures, such as exchange control, trade restrictions or
       exchange rate changes (which were not allowed under the fixed rate regime
       Cooper analysed). If *MD* represents the limits of financing the economic
       community is prepared to permit, *IN* represents the limit to reliance on external
       measures the integrationists in the community will tolerate, and *OA* the maximum
       intrusion on domestic policies that will be contemplated, the shaded area defines
       the various combinations of internal, financing, and external measures acceptable
       to the community at large (ibid. pp.17–23).
72   2600ibid. p.22.
73   idem.
74   ibid. p.277–78.
75   ibid. p.19.
76   Hugh Patrick 'American Foreign Economic Policy Towards the Western Pacific'
       in Crawford and Ōkita *Raw Materials*.
77   Monetary arrangements among Pacific countries are discussed briefly in chapters
       7 and 8.

Figure 2.3   Measures of international trade imbalances

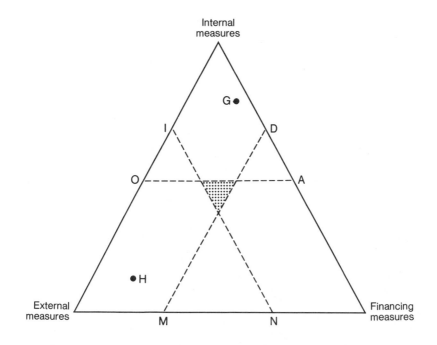

78   Asymmetry here refers to the structure of the interplay between economic
      partners and the possibility that one partner is very much more vulnerable (suffers
      larger relative costs) from any particular withdrawal of economic exchange than
      the other. There is also asymmetry which is a consequence of strategic choice. The
      exchange models presented earlier in this chapter do potentially incorporate these
      asymmetries.
79   This was a major concern in Hirschman *National Power*. The issue is reviewed
      broadly in Charles Kindleberger *Power and Money: The Economics of International
      Politics and the Politics of International Economics* London: Macmillan, 1970, and is
      pervasive in the discussions of economic relations between developed and
      developing countries. See Carlos Diaz–Alejandro 'North–South Relations: The
      Economic Component' in Bergsten and Krause (eds) *World Politics* pp.213–41;
      and Diaz–Alejandro in A. Fishlow, C. Diaz–Alejandro, R. Fagen and R. Hansen
      (eds) *Rich and Poor Nations in the World Economy* New York: McGraw–Hill for
      Council on Foreign Relations, 1978. For some formal statements of the key
      propositions as applied to trade policy and tariff negotiations, see Wolfgang Mayer
      'Theoretical Considerations on Negotiated Tariff Settlements' *Oxford Economic
      Papers* 33, February 1981, pp.135–53; and Conybeare 'Public Goods and the
      International Political Economy', especially pp. 13–19. See also Charles P.
      Kindleberger *Government and International Trade* Princeton, Essays in
      International Finance No.129, July 1978, pp. 1–24.
80   Bull, in *The Anarchical Society* p.280, suggests that
          . . . the term 'interdependence' has become a cant word that serves to

rationalise relations between a dominant power and its dependencies, in which the sensitivity is more one-sided than it is mutual. Appeals to interdependence (among allies in NATO, among rich countries in the OECD, between producers and consumers of resources) have strong political content, and frequently reflect fears that interdependence of one society's decisions and another's will not be recognised, or demands that they should be recognised, rather than the belief that decisions are in fact interdependent . . . The fact of the mutual sensitivity of states and other actors to one another's strategic, economic or ecological decisions can be exploited by each actor for its own purposes and does not in itself determine whether there will be cooperation or conflict.

A fuller analysis of complex interdependence is set out by Keohane and Nye in *Power and Interdependence*. For a clarifying statement of the concept as a target in managing international economic relations, see Lawrence Krause and Joseph Nye 'Reflections on the Economics and Politics of International Economic Organisations' in Bergsten and Krause (eds) *World Politics* pp.232–342.

81   See Diaz–Alejandro in Fishlow et al. *Rich and Poor Nations* on the former; and on the latter, see Richard Gift 'Trading in a Threat System: The US–Soviet Case' *Journal of Conflict Resolution* 13, 4, December 1969.

82   Crawford and Ōkita *Raw Materials* pp.44–45.

83   Klaus Knorr *Power and Wealth: The Political Economy of International Power* London: Macmillan, 1973, pp.22–25; Keohane and Nye *Power and Interdependence* especially ch.8; Kindleberger *Government and Trade*; Conybeare 'Public Goods and the International Political Economy'; and Charles P. Kindleberger 'Dominance and Leadership in the International Economy' *International Studies Quarterly* 25, 1981, pp.242–54.

84   The distinction between 'dictatorship' and 'leadership' is, of course, critical. In the language and structure of the theory of social or collective choice, the distinction does not arise since preferences are given and the dominance of one partner's preferences over other partners', except according to democratic principles, constitutes dictatorship unambiguously. In a dynamic world, the matter is more subtle. Kindleberger suggests that 'If leadership is thought of as the provision of the public good of responsibility, rather than exploitation of followers or the private good of prestige, it remains a positive idea . . . Leadership is necessary in the absence of delegated authority.' (Charles Kindleberger *The World in Depression, 1929–39* Berkeley: University of California Press, 1974, p.307, quoted in Keohane and Nye *Power and Interdependence* p.229.) And where leadership implies action to encourage or induce, not direct and command, or go first, it is consistent with what is called here 'international pluralism'.

85   Knorr *Power and Wealth* p.7. Knorr observes the importance of the development over time of the capacity to cooperate through satisfactory shared experiences.

> Such relationships impede the exercise of coercion and encourage non-coercive influence, whereas settled relations of animosity have the opposite effect. Trust refers to expectations of benevolent behaviour in contrast to suspicion, which feeds on the expectation of malevolence. Although attitudes of respect and friendship may be unrelated to the immediate issues confronting governments, they create an ambience facilitating cooperation. (ibid p.8)

A related perspective on the 'evolutionary' formation of international regimes is presented in Oran R. Young 'Regime Dynamics: The Rise and Fall of International Regimes' *International Organization* 36, 2, 1982, pp.277–98, and Donald J. Puchala and Raymond F. Hopkins 'International Regimes: Lessons from International Analysis' *International Organization* 36, 2, 1982, pp.245–76.

86   Knorr *Power and Wealth* pp.7 ff.

87 Buchanan and Tullock *The Calculus of Consent*, and Olson *The Logic of Collective Action*.

88 For example, as suggested in Olson's 'The Principle of "Fiscal Equivalence"', Russett and Sullivan's 'Collective Goods and International Organisation', and Cooper's 'Worldwide versus Regional' pp.10–13. For a revealing analysis of the structure of power and influence in the major international organisations, see Cox and Jacobson *The Anatomy of Influence*.

89 Cooper 'Worldwide versus Regional' p.12.

90 Cooper *Economics of Interdependence* pp.4–5. Buchanan's *The Limits of Liberty* ch.7 makes the point that the nature of such agreements, which subject behaviour to particular rules, binds the freedom of action of future 'generations'.

91 Victor Le Vine, The Bribe Goes Global: Preliminary Reflections on the New Transnational Aspects of Political Corruption, Edinburgh Congress of the International Studies Association, mimeo, August 1976, pp.1–2.

92 idem. Randall Bartlett *Economic Foundations of Political Power* New York: The Free Press, 1973 provides a general analysis of the use of economic influence within organised social structures which constitutes a useful introduction to the nature of the problem. Charles Lindblom *Politics and Markets: The World's Political-Economic Systems* New York: Basic Books, 1977 provides a grand vision of the economic and political process. For a broad contemporary overview of international trade in extra-legal favours, see Neil Jacoby, Peter Nehemkis and Richard Eells *Bribery and Extortion in World Business: A Study of Corporate Political Payments Abroad* New York: Macmillan, 1977.

3   The Pacific economy

In the past several years there has been considerable discussion of proposals aimed at bringing about closer economic integration among the nations of the 'Pacific community'.[1] This discussion has been generated by the strong rate of economic growth in the countries around the Pacific basin, especially in East Asia; by their rapidly expanding trade, investment and other commercial relations; in response to the entrenchment of the European Community; and in the context of a profound change in the international political environment, particularly the flux in the relationships among the great powers in the area since the Vietnam War.

Central in these developments has been the role of Japan.[2] The initial impetus to growing Pacific economic interdependence came from Japan's postwar recovery, its rapid heavy industrialisation, and its final emergence as a major economic power. And in the past 15 years, vigorous economic development in the other market economies of East Asia, and the cohesion of the Association of Southeast Asian Nations (ASEAN) into an important sub-regional force,[3] have further strengthened regional economic relationships and the idea of 'Pacific economic cooperation'.[4] At the heart of Pacific economic interdependence was a vast new trade in raw materials, reciprocal trade in manufactured goods, and the facilitation of investment flows. The exchange of manufactures between countries at different stages of economic development within the region was also an important but essentially secondary element in the structure of regional interdependence until recent years.

THE SHAPE OF THE PACIFIC ECONOMY

'The Pacific community', 'the Pacific economic community', and 'the Asian–Pacific economic community' are terms used variously to refer to several groups of countries: the five Pacific advanced industrial countries, the United States, Canada, Japan, Australia, and New Zealand; and a wider group, including those five and the developing countries of East Asia (or Northeast Asia and Southeast Asia), and the rest of the Western Pacific. The Western Pacific includes three sub-regional groupings: the ASEAN countries (Brunei, Indonesia, Malaysia, the Philippines, Singapore and Thailand), the Australia–

Income and export growth (percentage average annual growth)				Exports as a share of GNP		Share of trade with Pacific	
Real GNP per capita		Real exports					
1962-70	1970-83	1962-70	1970-83	1962	1983	Exports	Imports
3.7	1.1	7.1	3.3	15.5	15.1	60.4	63.4
9.4	3.4	16.6	10.1	9.6	14.0	60.3	52.9
6.1	3.9	-0.5	7.0	4.7	8.4	74.0	77.0
6.6	6.6	17.0	13.3	30.6	53.4	68.2	69.1
3.4	4.3	6.6	7.8	27.7	32.1	75.2	67.2
6.6	**3.1**	**10.7**	**9.8**	**10.5**	**17.0**	**65.9**	**62.3**
3.0	1.6	7.4	4.6	6.5	9.2	54.4	58.3
1.7	0.1	5.8	4.5	19.6	30.1	60.0	68.0
3.2	**1.8**	**8.3**	**6.7**	**6.9**	**11.9**	**60.4**	**60.3**
3.8	1.9	8.3	5.0	19.2	30.8	13.2	16.0
3.6	2.8	7.9	2.3	15.1	22.1	33.5	27.6
3.1[b]	**1.5[b]**	**8.2[b]**	**4.9[b]**	**11.7[b]**	**19.0[b]**	**34.1**	**35.1**

economy has been high over the past two decades. The share of the Pacific economy in world export trade grew to well over one-third during that period; yet in the mid-1980s Pacific countries were still, on average, one and three-quarter times as important in each others' trade as they were in world trade. The intensity of Pacific trade and its implications for regional trade growth are analysed in detail in chapter 4.[9]

THE EMERGENCE OF PACIFIC COOPERATION

Three factors have stimulated the increased importance of the Pacific in the world economy and the growth of economic interdependence among the East Asian and Pacific economies themselves. One is the growth of Japan's industrial power. As recently as 1967, Japan's per capita income was only about half that of the OECD countries' average, but Japan has now reached average OECD income levels. Rapid growth leading to high per capita incomes, combined with a large population, have meant that for more than a decade Japan has been the second largest economy in the world after the United States. The impact of Japanese growth on the Pacific economy has been pronounced because of the high established intensity of trade with the region. This impact was felt through the huge growth of Japanese demand for minerals and foodstuffs, as well as through the flows of capital and technology that these demands generated throughout the region.

The second factor which has raised the importance of the Pacific economy is the trade and industrial growth of the developing countries of Northeast and Southeast Asia. This was stimulated by two external influences. The first was the effect of Japan's trade and economic growth on the growth of regional trade. Countries such as the resource-rich group in Southeast Asia, alongside Australia, benefited from the opening up of these new trading opportunities.[10] The second influence was the move towards the deliberate adoption of outward-looking, trade-oriented industrialisation strategies to replace earlier protectionist strategies, first in the Northeast Asian market economies, and more recently in some Southeast Asian countries.[11] The rapid industrial growth of South Korea and Taiwan dates from policy initiatives taken between the late 1950s and mid-1960s, and Singapore and Hong Kong had little choice but to follow the same course. Trade orientation in Southeast Asian industrial development strategies came a decade later. Between 1965 and 1973, Singapore was the fastest-growing non-oil-producing economy in the world; South Korea was third; and Taiwan was fifth after Japan — all recording an annual real income growth of more than 10 per cent. Even the Philippines — the slowest-growing developing country in the Pacific basin — enjoyed an annual rate of growth of 5.8 per cent, which was in the top third of the world growth league. What is really significant is the extent to which East Asian growth has been sustained despite the oil crisis in the 1970s and the recessions that followed. The developing countries of East Asia are, on average, the fastest growing and most dynamic economies in the world, OPEC countries included.

A third factor giving prominence to the importance of the Pacific economy is the slide towards slower growth in Western Europe. In the 1950s and 1960s Western Europe enjoyed rapid economic growth and structural change. But since the oil crisis the Western European economies have stagnated, and projections of their future forebode a preoccupation with stabilisation of incomes and economic structures, slower GNP growth, and less relative importance in the world economy.[12]

The steady growth of the East Asian economies continued through the 1970s when the growth of many other industrial economies was slowing down (see Table 3.1).[13] The relatively rapid economic growth in these countries is reflected in their rankings on the international per capita income ladder, and this applies not only to Japan. Incomes in China, too, are now growing rapidly. From 1970 to 1983, China's real GNP per capita grew considerably faster than both the global (see Table 3.1) and the developing country average growth rates, and since 1980, China's growth rate has accelerated.

The economic growth of East Asia has been associated with, and facilitated by, outward-looking trade and industrial development policies. Japan has sustained more than a century of strong economic growth following the opening up of its economy and society late in the 19th century.[14] While Japan has not consistently espoused a liberal trade approach, it is distinguished from many other large industrial countries in the extent to which it has come to view the world as its market place, rather than concentrating on the domestic market, and by its pursuit of a policy of steady trade liberalisation over the past two decades.[15] Hong Kong and Singapore owe much of their economic success to an absence of policies restricting international trade and capital flows into and out of their economies. The economies of Korea and Taiwan grew slowly following their independence from Japan in 1945 and in the shadow of military conflict until the 1960s, when their import-substituting industrial policies were drastically changed and an export-oriented industrialisation strategy, which included liberal policies towards imports of goods, capital and technology, came to dominate. The extraordinary success of these policy changes is widely acknowledged.[16] A number of the ASEAN countries followed the lead of Singapore and the Northeast Asian newly industrialising countries by redirecting their industrial sectors from import substitution towards export-oriented production,[17] and again the benefits of this redirection of development strategy were reflected in high growth rates.

The increased openness of the industrialising countries of East Asia is shown clearly in Table 3.1. Exports are now a relatively high proportion of GNP in almost all these countries, and the growth in their export volumes, especially from 1970 to 1983, has been exceptionally high by world standards. Exports as a share of GNP nearly doubled for Northeast Asia's developing countries between 1962 and 1983, while the share for the ASEAN countries rose from 28 per cent to 32 per cent over the same period. As a result, East Asia's share of world export trade has doubled since 1962, and now represents almost one-fifth of all international trade.

The value of China's exports, as a share of GNP, has until recently been small compared to that of other countries in the region. China's experience with the problems of closed-door policies and its frustration with low standards of living led it in the late 1970s to switch to a more outward-looking policy. The degree of openness in the Chinese economy, and China's share of world trade, have increased dramatically as a consequence. It seems likely that this new course for the Chinese economy is now firmly entrenched, and that modernisation will continue to be accompanied by strong trade growth.[18]

Much of the trade growth resulting from East Asia's outward-looking industrial development has been concentrated in the Pacific region. More than two-thirds of the trade of East Asia (other than Japan) is with other countries in the Pacific region (see Tables 3.1 and 1.2), even though the region accounts for only around two-fifths of world trade. This bias towards intra-regional trade ensures that a disproportionately large share of the benefits of the strong trade growth in East Asia accrues to the Pacific region.

The development of the East Asian and Pacific economy must of course, be seen in the context of a period of unprecedented growth in international exchange, a process to which Japan, through its rise to the status of a great economic power, has contributed significantly. But regional economic growth and its reliance on trade specialisation have brought the Pacific economies together in an intensive network of trade and other economic ties, creating a vast new centre of world economic activity. How have these regional economic links been nurtured?

Typically, as an economy grows, its agricultural sector becomes relatively less important as the production of manufacturing and then services expands. Unless technological change in agriculture is exceptionally fast, or new mineral deposits are found, the share of primary products in exports tends to decline with economic growth. The Pacific economies are no exception to this rule (see Table 3.2). However, there is a corollary to this rule — namely, that high-income countries tend to be exporters mainly of manufactured goods, while exports of low-income countries are dominated by primary products — and some Pacific economies are striking exceptions to this corollary. Primary products are still very important in the exports of the high-income countries of North America and Australasia, while they are now of negligible importance to Northeast Asian countries other than China. The ASEAN economies, with the exception of Singapore, are still exporting mainly primary products, but the growth in their exports of manufactured goods has been much faster than that of the middle-income countries outside East Asia. As a consequence, East Asia (excluding Japan) now accounts for three-quarters of all manufactured exports from developing countries. While its exports account for less than 10 per cent of the world's total manufactured exports, it holds a much higher proportion of labour-intensive products, in which the high-income countries have a strong comparative disadvantage. The East Asian countries (excluding Japan) supplied around one quarter of the world's labour-intensive manufactured exports in 1983.

The economies of the Pacific are evidently highly complementary, and are becoming more so. This is not surprising, given the vast differences in resource-endowment ratios in the region. Japan, Hong Kong, Korea, Singapore and Taiwan are densely populated but extremely poorly endowed with agricultural land and mineral resources. On the other hand, the high-income countries of North America and Australasia have population densities well below the global average of 35 persons per square kilometre; and by world standards they are very well endowed with agricultural land and minerals. Apart from Malaysia, the ASEAN countries and China are three to five times as densely populated as the rest of the world, and so might be expected to have less comparative advantage in primary products (more comparative advantage in manufactured goods) than other countries with similar per capita incomes (see Table 3.2).[19]

Table 3.2　The structure of Pacific production and exports, 1962 and 1983

	Population density (persons per km²)	GDP per capita (US$)	Share of GDP from: Agriculture		Manufacturing		Services		Share of merchandise exports of: Primary products		Manufactured products	
	1983	1983	1962	1983	1962	1983	1962	1983	1962	1983	1962	1983
Australia	2	11 525	11.6	—	28.3a	—	9.6	—	88.7	79.2	11.3	20.8
Canada	3	11 194	5.9	3.1	23.0	16.1	12.7	22.6	66.9	44.9	33.1	55.1
New Zealand	12	8 060	—	—	—	—	—	—	97.1	79.2	2.9	20.8
United States	25	12 502	3.6	2.0	28.2	21.5	6.8	8.5	34.7	30.0	65.4	70.0
Japan	320	10 192	11.2	—	34.0	—	11.7	—	11.7	3.2	88.3	96.8
China	107	312	40.0	37.1	25.7	43.9	6.4	18.2	60.7	49.2	39.3	50.8
Hong Kong	5 106	6 030	3.0	0.6	23.2	21.2	—	—	7.9	3.9	92.1	96.1
Republic of Korea	406	1 987	37.0	13.9	14.4	27.4	7.5	9.0	80.3	9.0	19.7	91.0
Taiwan	520	2 583	25.0	7.0	23.0	42.0	44.0	44.0	54.8	10.3	45.2	89.7
Indonesia	81	585	59.0	26.4	8.0	12.5	6.7	2.2	99.7	92.4	0.3	7.7
Malaysia	45	1 833	35.4	21.4	8.9	19.5	10.9	16.3	94.6	75.1	5.4	25.0
Philippines	174	772	26.1	22.0	21.0	35.9a	16.4	42.1	95.3	49.6	4.7	50.4
Singapore	4 310	6 226	3.3	1.0	12.7	24.0	17.2	11.6	70.6	43.3	29.4	56.7
Thailand	96	807	37.1	23.0	14.1	19.0	9.6	10.6	96.9	68.3	3.1	31.7

Notes:　a　All industry.
　　　　　— denotes missing data.
Sources:　International Economic Data Bank. Research School of Pacific Studies, Australian National University; and *Statistical Yearbook of the Republic of China* 1985

Continued rapid economic growth in Northeast and Southeast Asia will be accompanied by further industrialisation, and by increased demand for, and increased net imports of, industrial raw materials and food, as well as further expansion of manufactured exports. In the lower-income (lower-wage) countries, manufactured exports are dominated by labour-intensive products. As real wages and skills rise, however, countries gradually switch to exporting more skill-intensive and capital-intensive products, leaving the unskilled-labour-intensive market to lower-wage countries. In the Pacific region Japan began this transition in the 1960s, allowing Hong Kong, Korea, Singapore and Taiwan to expand their labour-intensive exports. More recently, the latter countries began their transition from labour-intensive products, so that the other ASEAN countries and China are now finding a place in international markets for their expanding light manufacturing industries.[20] The gap left by Japan's gradual reduction in exports (and increase in imports) of labour-intensive manufactures has been more than filled, first by Hong Kong, Korea and Taiwan, and, more recently, by the ASEAN countries and China. It is noteworthy that while the shares of ASEAN and China in world trade are small, their shares in labour-intensive product markets are sizeable. Indeed, China's increased involvement in world trade has been one of the most important new developments in the 1980s, and will be an important focus of interest in the decades ahead.[21]

The changing economic structure of the East Asian countries associated with rapid income growth and industrialisation has reinforced the strong trade complementarity between the resource-rich countries of the Pacific and the rapidly growing economies of East Asia.[22] The demand for food increases with the growth of population and per capita income, while the demand for industrial raw materials increases with the growth of manufacturing production. The resource-poor, rapidly industrialising countries of Northeast Asia have a strong and increasing comparative disadvantage in foodstuffs and raw materials, whereas resource-rich economies like Australasia and North America have a strong comparative advantage in primary products compared to other countries with similar relative capital and labour endowments. Trade policies frustrate the realisation of trade complementarity to varying degrees, especially when rapid growth, structural change, and declining comparative advantage give rise to effective claims for protection against the pressure of such change.[23] The intensity of raw materials trade within Asia and the Pacific is also strongly reinforced by proximity, and by the effects of transportation costs and other factors which lower resistances to regional trade flows and enhance the penetration of regional markets for resource-related goods.[24]

These new sources of trade and industrial growth in East Asia are creating trading opportunities perhaps much more important than those opened up by the growth of Japan in the two preceding decades. Alongside the established economic weight of Japan in the world economy, the other East Asian economies are beginning to have a noticeable impact in world markets through their success in exporting both primary and, increasingly, manufactured products, as well as through the growth of their import demand. In the period 1967–73, when the world economy was enjoying its strongest postwar growth, trade growth in the newly industrialising countries of Northeast Asia was very high, but it was growth from an extremely low base. However, continued trade growth raised absolute trade levels, and by the 1980s these economies had established a sizeable share in world markets. From 1970 to 1983, Korea's exports grew at 18 per cent a year, Singapore's at 11 per cent, Thailand's at 10 per cent, Taiwan's at 5 per cent, Malaysia's at 8 per cent and Indonesia's at 5 per cent. These growth rates were substantially above those achieved by industrial countries over the same period. As a consequence, East Asian economies are winning larger shares of world markets, and the strength of their competitive challenge is an important issue in international commercial diplomacy.

At the same time these developing countries in East Asia and the Pacific have become significant markets for industrial equipment, foodstuffs, raw materials and intermediate goods such as steel, aluminium and other metals, as well as services; and they also provide growing opportunities for investment from abroad. On the whole their imports have increased even more than their exports, to the extent that, at least until 1984, these countries as a group ran current account deficits amounting in that year to US$2.5 billion.[25] Hence they have been net importers of foreign capital through a mixture of short-term loans, trade credits, longer-term borrowing from international agencies and private capital markets, and in some cases receipts of concessional aid (mainly from Japan, the United States and Australia), as well as direct foreign investment. External debt management has not presented these countries (except the Philippines) with the serious problems that others have had to face, especially the Latin American countries.

Already the combined share of South Korea, Taiwan and Hong Kong in world export trade is almost half of that of Japan, and the share of Northeast and Southeast Asian developing countries together matches Japan's. Most of their trade within the region is with the United States and Japan, although there is a strong trend towards regional trade diversification. Australia, for example, now does almost as much trade with developing countries in East Asia and the Pacific region as its does with Japan. And as it gathers momentum, the movement towards more foreign-trade oriented development strategies in China is reinforcing the dynamism of East Asia's trade and economic growth.[26]

The developing nations of East Asia are unlikely to retreat from their high-growth and foreign-trade-oriented development strategies. This does not mean that trade will always be the leading growth sector; rather, the pursuit of op-portunities in the international marketplace will remain a strategic objective. Growth rates may not continue at around 10 per cent per annum for all these countries, but even a quite conservative judgment suggests that the developing countries of East Asia can achieve an average real GNP growth rate of around 6 per cent or 7 per cent per annum, with imports and exports rising at least as rapidly (more rapidly for some), as a medium-term trend. This is possible despite the continuing fragility of the economic performance of the major industrial economies. By the end of the century the East Asian and Pacific region, already a substantial factor in the world economy, is likely to encompass an immense economy, certainly still far from fully integrated in the European sense, but with very high degrees of interdependence in many spheres.

OTHER PACIFIC ECONOMIC LINKS

Other economic factors link the Pacific basin countries, with foreign investment clearly the most important. Japan is now the largest foreign investor in the less developed countries of Asia and the Pacific: in 1985 Japan had supplied US$19.8 billion of the region's accumulated foreign investment, while America had supplied US$15.3 billion.[27] The rate of growth of Japanese investment has also been very rapid. Japanese investors have extended, and are continuing to extend, their involvement in the manufacturing of electrical goods, machinery, transport equipment, textiles and sundry goods. In the 1970s there was a shift in the direction of investment towards the production of intermediate goods such as petrochemicals (South Korea, Taiwan and Hong Kong), electrical apparatus and transportation machinery (especially in Singapore and Australia). Japanese investment has also been strong in resource-oriented developments, such as forestry and mining, and associated resource processing industries (for example, aluminium refining in Indonesia). Japanese industry is rapidly becoming multinational. The Pacific presently accounts for almost 60 per cent of all Japanese investment abroad, with a huge redirection of direct investment and capital flows towards the United States in the early 1980s. Joint investment projects and joint ventures have always been an important vehicle for Japan's direct foreign investment growth. The Bluff Aluminium Smelter in New Zealand, using Japanese, American and European capital, New Zealand hydroelectric power and Australian bauxite, was an early example of a major joint investment project. The Gladstone aluminium refinery and smelter in Australia, the Sulawesi nickel smelter in Indonesia, and the Asahan aluminium smelter in Indonesia are other examples.

Joint ventures are typical of Japanese manufacturing abroad, with general trading firms often playing a role in the partnerships.[28] Many of these Japanese investments in East Asia originate from small or medium-sized firms: in the mid-1970s almost half Japan's direct foreign investment derived from such firms, although larger firms are becoming increasingly prominent.[29] Japanese corporations are confronting a whole new range of strategic decisions in the mid-1980s about the international relocation of core production-line activities, as Japan-based competitiveness is being eroded by the success of industrialisation elsewhere in the region. These decisions are likely to lead to a more complex and sophisticated pattern of investment, ownership and production ties and intra-industry trade flows in the next phase of East Asian industrialisation.

Until recently the United States was the leading investor in Asia and the Pacific. Although small relative to United States investment elsewhere, investment competition from America and other countries is of great importance to the region.[30] American investment in the region remains considerable, especially direct foreign investment, and accounted for 40 per cent (or US$6.9 billion) of accumulated investment over the years 1976 to 1985, as against the 44 per cent (or US$7.5 billion) supplied by Japan.[31] In 1984 direct investment by the United States was larger than Japanese direct investment in Australia, China, Hong Kong, Singapore and the Philippines, whereas Japan was the largest investor in South Korea, Indonesia, Malaysia (after Singapore), and Thailand.[32] While mining, smelting and petroleum are important areas for American investment in the region, foreign investment has traditionally been in higher technology industries servicing the domestic markets of host countries and in technologically advanced light manufacturing industries, in the form of 'international sourcing' for multinational companies.[33]

Growth in trade, investment and communications has led to a corresponding increase in multinational banking activity in the Pacific. The region is one of the fastest-growing areas of multinational banking, and is becoming the central economic and financial arena of the world, as the Atlantic was in the 1950s and 1960s.[34]

The economic disadvantage of the distances of the Pacific Ocean has been overcome by technological advances in satellite communication and in air and marine transport. The use of jumbo jets, and innovations such as containerised shipping and bulk freighters, are of crucial importance to an area the greater part of whose commerce and travel must cross vast expanses of sea. The revolution in transportation and communications technology over the past two decades has probably been nowhere of more importance than in the Pacific economy. Trans-Pacific tourism and air traffic, although considerably smaller than that across the Atlantic, has grown, and continues to grow, more rapidly than worldwide growth in travel and tourism.[35]

Relations between the Pacific developed and developing countries are also close, not only through the economic links of trade and investment (where regional, especially Japanese, dependence on the developing countries is extensive) but also through the flows of development assistance. Japanese aid, which closely mirrors that country's economic interests, is heavily concentrated in the Asian–Pacific area.[36] Japan's aid commitments in Northeast Asia (especially to China) and to the ASEAN group are large, accounting for 15 per cent and 35 per cent of all bilateral aid in 1985.[37] The Japanese government and the private sector have both been actively engaged in sponsoring regional conferences and organisations in fields such as agriculture, fisheries, industrial productivity, and economic development generally. Japan and the United States are the moving forces behind the Asian Development Bank. The United States, although more deeply committed to aid programs in South Asia, has nevertheless given extensive assistance to South Korea, Taiwan and Thailand as well as to the Philippines and Indonesia, principally in support of security commitments. Australia and New Zealand have focused their aid efforts in Southeast Asia and the South Pacific, with a large Australian grant aid program to Papua New Guinea, a former colony and trust territory.[38] Canadian aid to Asia and the Pacific has been more limited, since its aid program is substantially directed towards Africa and the Caribbean, but Canadian development assistance to Southeast Asian and South Pacific countries is of growing importance.

POLITICAL LINKS AND SHARED PACIFIC INTERESTS

In the first two decades after the Second World War the United States dominated the economy of the Pacific and the 'free' world. American leadership, regionally and globally, was comprehensive and hegemonic, combining military–strategic and political as well as economic interests. For the world economy, the beneficent legacy of a devastating war was the Atlantic Charter and the postwar institutions that facilitated the evolution of a liberal international trade and economic system and orderly international financial markets. Although American foreign policy concerns and priorities came to be focused primarily upon military and security issues, the United States also played an important role as the moral guardian, protector, and exemplar of a liberal international economic system. In this period, the Pacific alliance against communism in the cold war era was also conceived and prosecuted. The GATT-based international trading system and the political–security arrangements centred on the United States came to provide a framework within which Pacific economic partnerships flourished.[39]

The Western Pacific countries had a powerful interest in the development of a liberal international trading system. This followed from their highly skewed resource endowments — Japan and the Northeast Asian countries with deficient material resource endowments; Australia, New Zealand and the principal Southeast Asian countries with abundant natural resources relative to other factors of production. Australia, for example, had suffered badly from the disintegration of the liberal multinational trading system in the 1930s — a disintegration that was helped along by Australia's involvement with imperial preferences and attempts to divert trade from Japan and the United States.[40] In Japan, the breakdown of the international economic system in the 1930s aggravated the tensions that surrounded its embarkation on a disastrous course of aggression and war.

While the GATT made exceptions in the fields of agricultural commodity trade and of Japanese trade, it nonetheless provided a framework of rules within which smaller traders (which included Japan for the first two decades after the war) and even agricultural exporters could negotiate their interests and derive benefit from the widespread trade and economic growth encouraged by the open world economy.[41]

Among the political–security arrangements that evolved across the Pacific, the partnership between the United States and Japan stands out in sheer size and importance. That relationship is an alliance of very broad scope and strategic significance — political, military and economic — between what are now the first and second largest capitalist economies, between the second and third largest political democracies, and between one of the two strongest military powers in the world and the weakest military power among the major industrial nations. For almost 40 years, after the culmination of the Chinese revolution in the Chinese Communist Party's accession to power in 1949, the cornerstone of United States foreign policy in the Pacific was its alliance with Japan.[42]

The alliance with the United States has been the core around which other elements of Japanese foreign policy have had to be manipulated. After regaining independence in 1952 following the traumatic experience of American occupation, democratisation and profound changes in institutions, values, and behaviour, Japan was weak and vulnerable economically, politically, and militarily. In some respects, vulnerable countries have an easy ride: the options are few, choices are simple, the scope for action at the margins is limited. In the early 1950s Japan needed above all else a guardian and patron: the United States was, if not quite the only choice, certainly the most obvious one.[43] Economically Japan has become a very strong nation, although in some respects it remains vulnerable. For Japan the range of options is now wider, the choices are less obvious, and the influence and the opportunities at the margin are substantially enlarged.[44]

The strategic aspect of the United States' alliance with Japan was formalised in the Mutual Security Treaty, first entered into in 1951 and revised in 1960. This treaty, which has been the foundation of Japan's postwar defence and foreign policy, remains a critical element in assessing the political and strategic future of the region. The strategic aspect of the United States' alliance with Australia, New Zealand and the Southeast Asian countries was formalised in the ANZUS (1951) and SEATO (1954) pacts, which were integral to American security policy in East Asia and the Pacific, and formed the cornerstone of Australian and Southeast Asian foreign and defence policies in the 1950s and early 1960s.[45]

Before the end of the Vietnam War these treaties provided a set of political links with the United States which greatly influenced the approach of the smaller partners to the region and the world. To illustrate, the nature of trans-Pacific ties between Japan, Australia and the United States was significant for economic development in the Western Pacific region during the postwar growth period because it brought the political interests of Australia and Japan into closer alignment at the same time as opportunities for bilateral trade were growing. The broader framework of foreign and foreign economic policies of each country facilitated the development of extensive economic ties and the relatively easy acceptance of large-scale economic interdependence. The basis of the rapprochement between Australia and Japan was laid much earlier, in the terms of Australia's accession to the Atlantic Charter (under an Inter-Allied Declaration) and through the terms of the San Francisco Peace Treaty of 1952 after Japan's defeat in the war. In February 1942, Australia entered a Mutual Aid Agreement with the United States, Article 7 of which pledged Australia to the elimination of commercial discrimination and the reduction of other barriers to trade. At this time, the Australian government had little choice but to accede to these principles in return for military aid.[46] The peace treaty, at the insistence of the United States, enjoined the signatories to negotiate these principles with Japan. Digesting these principles and translating them into practical policies was the task of the following decade and a half.

The end of the Vietnam War saw the beginning of some significant changes in the political and strategic relationships in Asia and the Pacific, as well as in relations between the superpowers. Independent forces were also steadily reshaping the world economy, wherein the United States' position was declining in relative terms as Europe and Japan grew strong and the oil producers began to exercise their pricing power. The Pacific region had become far stronger economically, and considerably more complex in terms of its political relationships. Japan was emerging as a major new global and regional power with ever-expanding economic relationships with other nations of the region.[47] Japan's importance to other Pacific countries, including the United States, had increased, but the region's importance to Japan began to decline somewhat.[48] Australia had effected a huge shift in its focus, from the United Kingdom to Asia, and had become a major source of raw materials for Japan.[49] The developing countries of the region, notably South Korea, Taiwan, Hong Kong and Singapore, but also the other ASEAN countries, had achieved rapid growth in national product, industrial output and trade. ASEAN, founded after the Bangkok Declaration of 1967 in the shadow of the Vietnam War, was galvanised into action at the beginning of 1976 'by the security problems which re-unification of Vietnam seemed to present to its members'.[50] The South Pacific territories, most importantly Papua New Guinea, had achieved independence and were beginning to shape their own approach to regional and world affairs.

With Vietnam re-unified; SEATO defunct; ANZUS no longer operational; the replacing of a bipolar with a multipolar set of forces in which Japan and China have become principal actors; the Sino–Soviet split and the reconstruction of a new relationship between these two major communist states; the fundamental changes in China's foreign and domestic policies; and signs of opening in the Soviet Union with all these developments the old assumptions that shaped the political–security relations among Pacific countries in the early postwar period have been brought under increasing scrutiny.[51] And the scrutiny is no less real for its taking place at a time when there is a high degree of political and military stability among the countries of the Asian–Pacific region.[52]

The forces which were reshaping the world economy brought their own challenges to established Pacific interests.[53] The postwar liberal trading system, in which the Pacific countries shared such strong common interests, began to break down from the late 1960s as protection measures against the labour-intensive exports of developing countries (especially textiles, clothing, and footwear) were accepted within the GATT as 'exceptions'. Agricultural trade protection was an 'exception' within the GATT from the outset. These exceptions were particularly damaging to the countries of East Asia and the Western Pacific, to the newly industrialising countries of Northeast Asia and, later, to ASEAN, as well as to the agricultural exporters, Australia and New

Zealand.[54] In agricultural trade they also became a focus of concern in United States commercial diplomacy. 'Voluntary export restraints', not only for labour-intensive exports but for a wide range of Japanese exports, became pervasive.

The GATT had served the international community as the agent of successive postwar tariff reductions and as the channel through which collective solutions were sought for protectionist problems among signatory countries.[55] The commitment of the United States and the major industrial countries to the GATT ensured a liberal international trading environment despite the presence of 'free riders', of which a number of Western Pacific countries have, in different degrees at various times, been conspicuous examples. That commitment, and the GATT system, came under substantial threat in the late 1960s.

CENTRAL POLICY ISSUES

Postwar trade and economic growth flourished within the framework of the GATT-based international trading system under the leadership of the United States. The pay-offs to the Atlantic industrial countries from closer consultation among themselves and with the Pacific industrial countries, especially Japan, grew with closer economic interdependence among the economic powers. Institutionally, these interests were served by the OECD and more recently the Group of Seven in the meetings of heads of states. The growing strength of the European Economic Community (EEC), again with initial support from the United States, sat uncomfortably within these evolving global international economic arrangements, as did UNCTAD (the United Nations Conference for Trade and Development), which aimed, albeit with limited success, to meet the trade and other economic claims of the developing countries. It is questionable whether this global framework now serves effectively the trade growth and development objectives of the growing economies of East Asia and the Pacific.

The vigorous growth of trade and economic interchange among East Asian and Pacific countries has occurred without the framework of special regional institutional arrangements such as those which encouraged the growth of trade within the EEC, or even across the Atlantic, among the original OECD countries. It emerged under the encouragement, leadership and hegemony of the United States, and, more particularly, within the framework provided by the great postwar multilateral institutions.[56] The growth of Pacific economic interdependence and the shift of world economic power away from Europe and the Atlantic towards East Asia and the Pacific has suggested to some observers the need for a new focus in foreign economic policy and a new framework for dealings among the Pacific economies.[57]

Proposals for closer Pacific economic cooperation were given stimulus by the interest in securing trade in raw materials or access to markets for the manufactured goods and primary commodities that are of such importance to Pacific countries. The formation of the EEC at the beginning of the 1960s, and its later expansion to include the United Kingdom and other members of the former European Free Trade Association, posed a threat to world market access. As a focus of interest in Pacific approaches to foreign economic policy, this threat was supplanted in the first half of the 1970s by the risk of economic conflict between suppliers and consumers of raw materials, and later by the intensification of competition among the major industrial countries in a period of unusually prolonged and general recession.[58] An underlying and fundamental interest was always the evolution of a regime within which economic integration among the countries of the Pacific region might be further encouraged by reduction of the very substantial barriers that have been erected to profitable trade and income growth. Such barriers inhibit the confident expansion of regional economic interaction. The discussion of the trading interests of the Pacific area has been premised largely on the judgment that they were best pursued within the framework of global economic arrangements. Regionalism European-style — the formation of a discriminatory economic union or free trade area — was generally eschewed, although the free trade area option was canvassed and rejected as a useful approach in the 1960s.[59] Certainly the United States and Japan (increasingly a global economic power) had much at stake in their global commitments, but the smaller economies, such as Australia and the ASEAN group, also had a powerful interest in not being party to any action that would damage the GATT-based multilateral trading framework.

The weight and structure of established Atlantic and European interests in international economic diplomacy are heavily directed towards the stabilisation of trade shares and reactive protection of the present international order, and against adjustment to dynamic economic growth such as that now taking place in East Asia and the Pacific. The preoccupations of the major European industrial economies in their individual and collective approaches to external adjustment during the 1970s and 1980s have led them further away from automatic support for a free and open international trading environment. The maintenance of a liberal trading system is increasingly being seen by the Western Pacific developing countries as critical to their trade and development ambitions.[60] The main international economic institutions are under extreme test; they no longer provide unequivocal encouragement for the accommodation of trade growth along the lines earlier enjoyed by Japan. The emergence of China and the extension of its economic relations with the market economies in Asia and the Pacific bring an additional complication to fostering Western Pacific trade growth within the framework of the GATT and other global institutions.[61]

A number of related political factors also underline the significance of proposals for a new framework for dealings within the Pacific economy.[62] The United States and Japan have not managed their mutual problems with great sureness in recent years; tension has developed in the economic sphere from American perceptions of unwillingness to rectify balance-of-payments surpluses and trade barriers, and in the security sphere, first from Japanese uncertainty and concern over American policy towards Korea and North Asia more generally, and then over American interest in elevating Japanese defence expenditures and sharing Japanese defence technologies.[63] The established interests of both nations, in bilateral economic relationships and their mutual security arrangements, prevent any abrupt redirection of the United States–Japan alliance in East Asia and the Pacific, but there is more scope now than there has been in the past for refashioning its long-term shape.[64] Any major change in the status of the United States–Japan economic and political alliance would seriously disturb confidence in the East Asian and Pacific economy among the smaller Western Pacific nations, in which there is an active economic and political interest in maintaining the cooperative and competitive involvement of both Japan and America in regional affairs.[65] There is no longer any automatic coincidence of interests in foreign economic policy or foreign policy more generally between Japan and the United States;[66] hence the East Asian and Pacific countries, which are so heavily reliant on these two large economic powers, have a significant interest in the framework within which divergent interests are reconciled so as not to damage confidence in the operation of the regime as it affects regional trade and economic opportunities.

The growth and strength of the Pacific economy in the past three decades were built within the framework of multilateral trading arrangements and ties provided by the GATT, underwritten by the leadership role played by the United States. East Asian and Western Pacific countries have strong interests in ensuring that economic policy efforts are directed towards support for the maintenance of an open, non-discriminatory (GATT-based) trade and economic regime.

These common interests derive from the importance of multilateral and non-discriminatory trade and economic arrangements to the growth and transformation of the East Asian and Pacific economy in the past, and to its prospect for the future.

Defining the character of those interests and the leverage which Pacific economies may be able to develop in the pursuit of their strategic economic policy objectives requires a more detailed analysis of the structure of regional trade interdependence and trade growth. This task is taken up in the next three chapters.

NOTES

Chapter 3

1   A collection of relevant contributions is contained in Sir John Crawford and Greg
     Seow (eds) *Pacific Economic Co-operation: Suggestions for Action* Petaling Jaba,
     Selangor, Malaysia: Heinemann Asia for the Pacific Community Seminar, 1981.
     For an excellent review of the various contributions to this discussion over the
     years, see also Peter Drysdale and Hugh Patrick 'Evaluation of a Proposed Asian-
     Pacific Regional Economic Organisation' *Australia-Japan Economic Relations
     Research Project Research Paper* No.61, Australian National University, July 1979
     (also published by the US Congressional Research Service as *An Asian-Pacific
     Regional Economics Organisation: An Exploratory Concept Paper* Washington: US
     Government Printing Office, July 1979); Japan Pacific Cooperation Study Group
     Report on Pacific Basin Cooperation Concept (Ōhira Study Group Report) Prime
     Minister's Office, Tokyo, 1982; and Hadi Seosastro 'Institutional Aspects of
     ASEAN-Pacific Economic Co-operation' Report on ASEAN and Pacific
     Economic Cooperation, Bangkok, June 1982. For recent reviews of the discussion
     of the Pacific Community idea, see *Asian Survey* XXIII, 12, December 1983, and
     Peter Drysdale 'Building the Foundations of a Pacific Community' in Toshio
     Shishido and Ryuzo Satō (eds) *Economic Policy and Development: New Perspectives*
     Dover: Auburn Publishing House, 1985.
2   Charlotte Williams 'The Pacific Community: A Modest Proposal' *Australia-Japan
     Economic Relations Research Project Research Paper* No.55, Australian National
     University, March 1979, p.1; see also Peter Drysdale 'Australia and Japan in the
     Pacific and World Economy' Peter Drysdale and Hironobu Kitaōji (eds) *Japan
     and Australia: Two Societies and Their Interaction* Canberra: Australian National
     University, 1981, pp.419-39.
3   Ross Garnaut (ed.) *ASEAN in a Changing Pacific and World Economy* Canberra:
     Australian National University Press, 1980; see also Heinz Arndt and Ross
     Garnaut 'ASEAN and the Industrialisation of East Asia' *Journal of Common
     Market Studies* 17, 3, March 1979. For early work on the issue of Southeast Asia's
     economy, see Asian Development Bank *Southeast Asia's Economy in the 1970's*
     New York: Longmans, 1971.
4   Kiichi Saeki (ed.) *The Search for Japan's Comprehensive Guideline in the Changing
     World — National Priorities for the 21st Century* Kamakura: Nomura Research
     Institute, 1978, p.41 [Kokusai kankyō no henka to Nihon no taiō: Nijūichi seiki e
     no teigen]. This point has been stressed by Kiyoshi Kojima in his writing on the
     Pacific economy over the years; for example, in Kiyoshi Kojima *Japan and a
     Pacific Free Trade Area* London: Macmillan, 1971.
5   Drysdale and Patrick 'Evaluation of a Proposed Asian-Pacific Regional Economic
     Organisation'. The question of a definition of the Pacific region is addressed in a
     number of contributions; for example, Williams 'The Pacific Community' pp.1-4;
     also Peter Drysdale 'Organisation for Pacific Trade, Aid and Development:
     Regional Arrangements and the Resource Trade' in Lawrence B. Krause and
     Hugh T. Patrick (eds) *Mineral Resources in the Pacific Area* San Francisco: Federal
     Reserve Bank of San Francisco, 1978; Kiyoshi Kojima 'An Organisation for
     Pacific Trade, Aid and Development: A Proposal' *Australia-Japan Economic
     Relations Research Project Research Paper* No.40, Australian National University,
     September 1976; Crawford and Seow (eds) *Pacific Economic Co-operation*; the

Ōhira Study Group Report; and Soesastro 'Institutional Aspects'. The definition of the Pacific economy used here coincides with the membership of the Pacific Economic Cooperation Conference (PECC), which now includes Australia, Japan, Canada, the United States, the six ASEAN countries, the People's Republic of China, Taiwan, South Korea, and the Pacific Island Nations, with the addition of Hong Kong.

6   Lawrence B. Krause 'The Pacific Economy in an Interdependent World' in Kermit Hanson and Thomas Roehl (eds) *The United States and the Pacific Economy in the 1980s* Seattle: University of Washington, 1980, pp.1–20. The development of Australia's relations with Japan and the Western Pacific region is reviewed in Sir John Crawford and Saburō Ōkita et al. (eds) *Raw Materials and Pacific Economic Integration* London: Croom Helm, 1978, especially Parts II and III. This book grew out of the report presented by Crawford and Ōkita to the Australian and Japanese governments: *Australian, Japan and Western Pacific Economic Relations* Canberra: Australian Government Publishing Service, 1976 (hereafter referred to as *Crawford-Ōkita Report*).

7   Calculated from data in Ōkura-shō (Ministry of Finance), *Kokusai kinyū kyoku nenpō* [Annual Report of Industrial Finance Division] Tokyo, 1986, ch.7, pp.159–60.

8   Kym Anderson 'Intensity of Trade Between Pacific Basin Countries' *Pacific Economic Papers* No.102, Australia–Japan Research Centre, Australian National University, 1983, p.1.

9   The intensity of trade index, devised by Brown, was popularised by Kojima. This and related concepts have been surveyed recently by Drysdale and Garnaut. See A.J. Brown *Applied Economics: Aspects of the World Economy in War and Peace* London: George Allen & Unwin, 1941; Kiyoshi Kojima 'The Pattern of International Trade Among Advanced Countries' *Hitotsubashi Journal of Economics* 5, 1, June 1964, pp.16–36; Peter Drysdale and Ross Garnaut 'Trade Intensities and the Analysis of Bilateral Trade Flows in a Many-Country World' *Hitotsubashi Journal of Economics* 22, 2, February 1982, pp.62–84. The intensity of trade (I_{ij}) is defined for country i's exports to country j as the share of i's exports going to j (x_{ij}/x_i) relative to the share of j's imports (m_j) in world imports net of i's imports ($T - m_i$). That is,

$$I_{ij} = \frac{x_{ij}}{x_i} \Big/ \frac{m_j}{T - m_i}$$

10   Crawford and Ōkita (1978) *Raw Materials*; Ross Garnaut 'The Importance of Industralisation in Southeast and East Asia to an Open Australian Economy' in Peter Drysdale and Kiyoshi Kojima (eds) *Australia-Japan Economic Relations in International Context: Recent Experience and the Prospects Ahead* Australia–Japan Economic Relations Research Project, Australian National University, 1978, pp.95–111; and Kym Anderson and Ben Smith 'Changing Economic Relations between the Asian ADC's and Resource-Exporting Advanced Countries of the Pacific Basin' in Wontack Hong and Lawrence B. Krause (eds) *Trade Growth of the Advanced Developing Countries in the Pacific Basin* Seoul: Korea Development Institute, 1981, pp.293–338.

11   Garnaut 'The Importance of Industrialisation in Southeast and East Asia'; Drysdale 'Australia and Japan in the Pacific and World Economy'; Krause 'The Pacific Economy' pp.7–9.

12   Some projections of European and Pacific trade and economic growth are set out in Kym Anderson, Peter Drysdale, Christopher Findlay, Prue Phillips, Ben Smith and Rodney Tyers 'Pacific Economic Growth and Prospects for Australian Trade' *Pacific Economic Papers* No.122, Australia–Japan Research Centre, Australian National University, May 1985.

13 Further comparative data are provided in Anderson et al. 'Pacific Growth and Australian Trade'.

14 William W. Lockwood, in *The Economic Development of Japan: Growth and Structural Change 1868–1938* Princeton, NJ: Princeton University Press, 1954, provides the most insightful history of Japan's modern economic development.

15 Ryūtarō Komiya and Motoshige Itoh 'International Trade and Trade Policy of Japan: 1955–1984' *Tokyo University Discussion Paper* 85–F–16, January 1986 (based on a paper prepared for the Japan Political Economy Research Conference, East–West Center, Hawaii, August 1984).

16 C.R. Frank, K.S. Kevin and L. Westphal *Foreign Trade Regimes and Economic Development: South Korea* New York: Columbia University Press for the National Bureau of Economic Research, 1975; M.H. Hsing 'Taiwan Industrialisation and Trade Policies' in M.H. Hsing, J.H. Power and G.P. Sicat *Taiwan and the Philippines: Industrialisation and Trade Policies* London: Oxford University Press for the Organisation for Economic Cooperation and Development, 1971; and Wontack Hong and Lawrence B. Krause (eds) *Trade and Growth of the Advanced Developing Countries in the Pacific Basin*. For a general appraisal of East Asian and Pacific growth performance, see S.B. Linder *The Pacific Century: Economic and Political Consequences of Asian–Pacific Dynamism* Stanford: Stanford University Press, 1986.

17 Ross Garnaut (ed.) *ASEAN in a Changing Pacific and World Economy* Canberra: Australian National University Press, 1980. Recent and useful reviews of East Asian trade and industrial policies can be found in Christopher Findlay and Ross Garnaut (eds) *The Political Economy of Manufacturing Protection: Experiences of ASEAN and Australia* Sydney: Allen & Unwin, 1986.

18 Christopher Findlay, Kym Anderson and Peter Drysdale 'China's Trade and Pacific Economic Growth', *Pacific Economic Papers* (forthcoming) Australia–Japan Research Centre, Australian National University, and, for a broader review of the policies of commitment to modernisation, Michel Oksenberg 'China's Confident New Nationalism' *Foreign Affairs* 65, 3, February 1987, pp.502–23.

19 Anderson and Smith 'Changing Economic Relations' pp.293–345.

20 Garnaut *ASEAN and the Pacific* pp.374–412.

21 Shishido and Satō *Economic Policy and Development* p.51.

22 Anderson and Smith 'Changing Economic Relations' pp.293–345.

23 Kym Anderson and Yūjirō Hayami (eds) *The Political Economy of Agricultural Protection* Sydney: Allen & Unwin, 1986.

24 Crawford and Okita *Raw Materials*.

25 World Bank *World Development Report, 1986* Washington: World Bank, Table 14, pp.206–7; and *Statistical Yearbook of the Republic of China, 1985* Supplementary Table 1, p.185.

26 Luo Yuan Zheng 'The Management of China's Modernisation and Its Impact on the Rest of the World' *Australian Journal of Management* 7, 1, June 1982, pp.1–8; Christopher Findlay, Prue Phillips and Rodney Tyers 'China's Merchandise Trade: Composition and Export Growth in the 1980s' *ASEAN–Australia Economic Papers* No.19, Australian National University, 1985; Findlay, Anderson and Drysdale 'China's Trade'; Peter Drysdale 'Australia's Economic Relations with Asia and the Pacific — Past Perspectives and Future Prospects' ch.2 in Hanson and Roehl (eds) *The United States and the Pacific Economy*, and also published in *Current Affairs Bulletin* 55, 11, April 1979.

27 Japan External Trade Organisation (JETRO) *Sekai to Nihon no kaigai chokusetsu tōshi* [World and Japanese direct foreign investment] Tokyo: JETRO, 1987, Table 1 (Japan), pp.17, 376–77; and United States Department of Commerce *Survey of Current Business* 67, 6, June 1987, Table 3, p.43. The Japanese figure is the

cumulative total for fiscal years 1951 to 1985. The American figure is the
cumulative total up to and including calendar 1985 (and excludes investment in
Japan). With Australia and New Zealand included in Asia and the Pacific, the
figures become US$23.7 billion for Japanese investment and US$ 24.3 billion for
American investment.

28   These characteristics of Japanese investment abroad were identified first by
Kiyoshi Kojima *Direct Foreign Investment: A Japanese Model of Multinational
Business Operations* London: Croom Helm, 1978. See also Sueo Sekiguchi and
Lawrence B. Krause 'Direct Foreign Investment in ASEAN by Japan and the
United States' in Ross Garnaut, *ASEAN and the Pacific*; Terutomo Ozawa
Multinationalism Japanese Style: The Political Economy of Outward Dependency
Princeton, NJ: Princeton University Press, 1979; Sueo Sekiguchi *Japanese Direct
Foreign Investment* London: Macmillan, 1979; and Sueo Sekiguchi 'Nihon no
chokusetsu tōshi to Nihon–ASEAN kankei [Japanese direct investment and the
Japan–ASEAN relationship] *Keizai kenkyū* 33, 4, October 1982.

29   Chūshōkigyō-chō *Chūshō kigyō hakusho Shōwa-57 nenban* [White Paper on small-
and medium-sized enterprises, 1982] p.9; Ozawa, *Japanese Multinationals* p.3; and
Sekiguchi *Japanese Foreign Investment* p.54.

30   Peter Drysdale (ed.) *Direct Foreign Investment In Asia and the Pacific* Canberra:
Australian National University Press, 1972, chs 2 and 14; Stephen Kolhagen 'The
Characteristics, Motivations, and Effects of Japanese and United States Direct
Investments in the Pacific Basin' *Explorations in Economic Research* 3, 2, Spring
1976; Kunio Yoshihara *Japanese Investment in Southeast Asia* Kyoto: Kyoto
University, 1978; Thomas Allen 'Direct Investment of United States Enterprises
in Southeast Asia' *ECOCEN Study* No.2, Economic Cooperation Center for the
Asian and Pacific Region, Bangkok, March 1973; and A. Kapoor *Foreign
Investments in Asia* Princeton: Darwin, 1972; Lawrence B. Krause and Sueo
Sekiguchi (eds) *Economic Interaction in the Pacific Basin* Washington, DC: The
Brookings Institution, 1980; Sekiguchi *Japanese Foreign Investment*; Sueo
Sekiguchi *Japanese Direct Foreign Investment in ASEAN* Singapore: Institute of
Southeast Asian Studies, 1982; Sueo Sekiguchi (ed.) *Kantaiheiyōken to Nihon no
chokusetsu tōshi* [The Pacific Basin and Japan's direct foreign investment] Tokyo:
Nihon Keizai Kenkyū Sentā, 1982; and Mari Pangestu 'Japanese and Other
Foreign Investment in the ASEAN Countries' *Australia–Japan Economic Relations
Research Project Research Paper* No. 73, Australian National University, 1980.

31   These are percentages of total direct foreign investment supplied by all developed
advanced countries to Hong Kong, Indonesia, Korea, Malaysia, the Philippines,
Singapore, Taiwan and Thailand; OECD *Geographical Distribution of Financial
Flows* Paris: OECD publications, various.

32   JETRO *Sekai to Nihon no kaigai chokusetsu tōshi* [World and Japanese direct
foreign investment]; and Japan Member Committee, Pacific Basin Economic
Council *Pacific Economic Community Statistics, 1986*.

33   Tsao Yuan 'Capital Flows among Pacific Basin Economies' in Augustine H. Tan
and Basant Kapur (eds) *Pacific Growth and Financial Interdependence* Sydney:
Allen & Unwin, 1986, pp.68–94.

34   Williams 'The Pacific Community' pp.5–6; The Export–Import Bank of Japan
'Business Cooperation Between Asia–Pacific and Japan in the Eighties'
Symposium, Tokyo, May 1980. See also J.R. Hewson 'Offshore Banking in
Singapore: A Case Study in Offshore Banking in Australia' *Commissioned Studies
and Selected Papers* Part II, Canberra: Australian Financial System Enquiry,
Australian Government Publishing Service, 1982. On international bank lending,
see H.W. Arndt 'Financial Development in Asia' *Asian Development Bank Journal*
1, 1, March 1983.

35   John Menadue, paper presented to the session on 'Roles and Problems in Pacific Economic Cooperation' at the Third Symposium on Pacific Cooperation, sponsored by the Pacific Basin Economic Council of Japan, Tokyo, 24 March 1987, p.6.

36   Alan Rix *Japan's Economic Aid* London: Croom Helm, 1980, pp.221-28.

37   Association for the promotion of International Cooperation *Japan's Official Development Assistance, 1986 Annual Report* Tokyo, March 1987.

38   For a discussion of the different emphases in Australian and Japanese aid programs, see Nancy Viviani 'Australia and Japan: Approaches to Development Assistance Policy' *Australia-Japan Economic Relations Research Project Research Paper* No.37, Australian National University, March 1976; and Rix *Japan's Economic Aid*. See also Ross Garnaut and Paul Baxter in consultation with Anne O. Krueger *Exchange Rate and Macro-Economic Policy in Independent Papua New Guinea* Report to the Papua New Guinea Government, Canberra, Development Studies Centre, Australian National University, February 1983.

39   Coral Bell, Hugh Collins and Ross Garnaut 'Conclusion: The Nexus between Economics, Politics and Strategy' in Paul Dibb (ed.) *Australia's External Relations in the 1980s: The Interaction of Economic, Political and Strategic Factors* Canberra: Croom Helm, 1983. See also Charles P. Kindleberger 'International Public Goods without International Government' *Australian Economic Review* March 1986, pp.1-13.

40   ibid.

41   J.G. Crawford *Australian Trade Policy 1942-1966 — A Documentary History* Canberra: ANU Press, 1968, pp.3-95; Peter Drysdale, Japanese-Australian Trade: An Approach to the Study of Bilateral Trade Flows, PhD Thesis, ANU, 1967, ch.VII.

42   Hugh Patrick 'United States-Japan Political Economy: Is the Partnership in Jeopardy?' ch.4 in Hanson and Roehl *The United States and the Pacific Economy*; also circulated as *Australia-Japan Economic Relations Research Project Research Paper* No.59, Australian National University, May 1979 (see p.2).

43   The relevant literature on Japan's communist and socialist alternatives after the Second World War includes: Robert Cole, George Totten and Cecil Uyehara, *Socialist Parties in Postwar Japan* New Haven: Yale University, 1966; Robert Scalapino *The Japanese Communist Movement, 1920-1966* Berkeley: University of California Press, 1967; Rodger Swearingen *Communist Strategy in Japan 1945-1960* Santa Monica: Rand Corporation, 1965, and Toshio Tsukahira *The Postwar Evolution of Communist Strategy in Japan* Cambridge, Mass.: MIT, 1954.

44   Patrick 'United States-Japan Political Economy' p.3.

45   John Welfield 'Australia-Japan in Asian-Pacific International Politics: Some Problems and Projects' in *Australia-Japan Relations Symposium, 1977, Summary of Papers and Discussions*; and John Welfield 'Australia and Japan in the Cold War' in Drysdale and Kitaōji (eds) *Japan and Australia*. See also John Welfield *An Empire in Eclipse: Japan in the Postwar American Alliance System* London: The Athlone Press, 1988 for a comprehensive review of the evolution of Japan's defence and foreign policies in the postwar period.

46   Peter Drysdale 'The Relationship with Japan: Despite the Vicissitudes' in L.T. Evans and J.D.B. Miller (eds) *Policy and Practice: Essays in Honour of Sir John Crawford* Canberra: Australian National University Press, 1987, pp.71-73.

47   The following studies on the interrelationship of political and economic forces are relevant: Donald Hellman (ed.) *China and Japan: A New Balance of Power* Critical Choices for Americans Vol. XII, Lexington: D.C. Heath, 1976; Donald Hellman (ed.) *Southern Asia: The Politics of Poverty and Peace* Critical Choices for Americans, Vol. XIII, Lexington: D.C. Heath, 1976; Bernard Gordon and

Kenneth Rothwell (eds) *The New Political Economy of the Pacific* Cambridge: Ballinger, 1975; and Jagdish Bhagwati and Anne Krueger (eds) *Trade Strategies for Economic Development: The Asian Experience* Manila: Asian Development Bank, 1975. See also Robert A. Scalapino and Jusuf Wanandi (eds) *Economic, Political and Security Issues in Southeast Asia in the 1980s* Berkeley: Institute of East Asian Studies, University of California, 1982; and Peter Drysdale 'The Pacific Basin and Its Economic Vitality' in James W. Morley (ed.) *US Annals of Political Science* New York: Academy of Political Sciences, 36, 1, 1986, p.11-22. For a recent analysis of America's international political and economic problems, see Leonard Silk 'The US and the World Economy' *Foreign Affairs* 65, 3, 1986, pp.458-75.

48   This observation was the theme of a paper by the author prepared in 1970 for the Australian Institute of International Affairs and published as 'Japan in the World Economy: The Decade Ahead' in J.A.A. Stockwin (ed.) *Japan and Australia in the Seventies* Sydney: Angus & Robertson, 1972, pp.10-22.

49   Crawford and Okita *Raw Materials*.

50   Arndt and Garnaut 'ASEAN and the Industrialisation of East Asia'.

51   Drysdale 'Australia's Economic Relations with Asia and the Pacific' pp.12-3. See also Drysdale and Patrick 'Evaluation of a Proposed Asian–Pacific Regional Economic Organisation'.

52   See Robert A. Scalapino 'Introduction' in Scalapino and Wanandi *Economic, Political, and Security Issues*.

53   For an early discussion of this issue, see Peter Drysdale 'Australia, Japan and New Zealand: The Prospects for Western Pacific Economic Integration' *Economic Record* September 1967, pp.321-43; Drysdale 'Australia's Economic Relations with Asia and the Pacific'; Drysdale and Patrick 'Evaluation of a Proposed Asian–Pacific Regional Economic Organisation'; and Han Sung-joo (ed.) *Community-Building in the Pacific Region: Issues and Opportunities* Seoul: The Asiatic Research Center, Korea University, 1981.

54   Bell, Collins and Garnaut 'Conclusion' in Dibb (ed.) *Australia's External Relations*.

55   ibid.

56   Kojima *Japan and a Pacific Free Trade Area* ch.3.

57   Crawford and Seow (eds) *Pacific Economic Co-operation*; Soesastro *Institutional Aspects*.

58   Peter Drysdale 'Organisation for Pacific Trade, Aid and Development'; Soesastro *Institutional Aspects*.

59   Kojima *Japan and a Pacific Free Trade Area*; Kiyoshi Kojima (ed.) *Pacific Trade and Development I*, Tokyo: Japan Economic Research Center 1968. The first Pacific Trade and Development Conference, held in Tokyo in January 1968, reviewed this issue. See also Drysdale 'An Organisation for Pacific Trade, Aid and Development'; Soesastro 'Institutional Aspects'; and Kiyoshi Kojima 'Economic Cooperation in a Pacific Community' *Asia Pacific Community* Spring 1981, pp.1-10. And also Peter Drysdale 'The Proposal for an Organisation for Pacific Trade and Development Revisited' *Asian Survey* XXIII, 12, December 1983; and Drysdale 'Foundations of a Pacific Community'.

60   Crawford and Okita *Raw Materials* pp. 167-77; and Arndt and Garnaut 'ASEAN and the Industrialisation of East Asia' pp.121-212. For early work on the issue, see Asian Development Bank *Southeast Asia's Economy in the 1970's* New York: Longman, 1971.

61   Drysdale 'Australia's Economic Relations with Asia and the Pacific' p.12; Findlay, Anderson and Drysdale 'China and the Pacific'; Oksenberg 'China's Confident Nationalism'.

62   Crawford and Ōkita *Raw Materials* pp.29–31.

63   Takashi Inoguchi 'Trade, Technology and Security: Implications for East Asia and the West: Part II' *Adelphi Paper* No.218, Spring 1987; also published as *Pacific Economic Paper* No.147, Australia–Japan Research Centre, Australian National University, May 1987.

64   Drysdale 'Australia's Economic Relations with Asia and the Pacific' p.13. These interests in stability are probably shared strongly by the main protagonists in the Northeast Asian region, including the Soviet Union and China.

65   Bernard Gordon 'Japan, the United States, and Southeast Asia' *Foreign Affairs* April, 1978.

66   Drysdale and Patrick 'Evaluation of a Proposed Asian–Pacific Regional Economy Organisation'. See also Hugh Patrick 'American Foreign Economic Policy towards the Western Pacific' in Crawford and Ōkita *Raw Materials* ch.2; and I. Destler, H. Sato, P. Clapp and H. Fukui *Managing an Alliance: The Politics of US–Japanese Relations* Washington: The Brookings Institution, 1976; H. Satō and I. Destler *Coping with US–Japanese Economic Conflicts* Lexington: Lexington Books, 1982; C. Fred Bergsten 'Economic Imbalances and World Politics' *Foreign Affairs* 65, 4, Spring 1987, pp. 770–93; and Silk 'US and World Economy' pp.468–75.

4 East Asian and Pacific trade interdependence

The structure of trade interdependence among East Asian and Pacific countries now defines a Pacific domain for trade and other foreign economic policy action. A region in which most countries transact well over half of their trade with each other is either one in which the process of institutional integration has proceeded far, or one in which the forces for market integration are powerful. A more detailed analysis of the intensity of trade among Pacific countries will help to identify the underlying causes of close Pacific trade interdependence and provide the necessary background for assessing alternative policy approaches.

Shifts in the structure of Pacific trade relations have resulted from three broad sets of factors: the relatively rapid growth in the share of Japan and the rest of East Asia in world trade; the extent of complementarity in trade among Pacific countries; and influences related to the geographic, political and historical closeness of the countries in the Pacific basin. These are the principal factors behind the large intra-regional trade growth and very intensive trading relationships among the Pacific economies.

The data in Table 1.1 of chapter 1 show that between 1962 and 1985 the share of Pacific countries in world imports rose from 29.4 per cent to 41.2 per cent, and their share of world exports rose from 32.8 per cent to 37.9 per cent. While North America's share in world trade was actually declining over this period, that of Western Pacific countries grew substantially because of the growth of East Asian trade. In 1962 Western Pacific countries accounted for 12.1 per cent of world import trade and 11.1 per cent of world export trade, but by 1985 these shares had grown to 17.3 per cent and 21.4 per cent. The strength of trade and industrial growth which underlay these changes in East Asia's world trade shares is discussed in chapter 6.

A previous study, which compares trade interdependence in 'Pacific rim' countries and the countries of the European Community, observes that strong Pacific trade growth has not generally been at the expense of third country trade.[1] That study confines its analysis of 'Pacific rim' trade to the trade of the five advanced Pacific countries — the United States, Canada, Japan, Australia, and New Zealand — and does not consider their trade interdependence with the rapidly growing economies of Northeast and Southeast Asia. Employing the methods of transactional analysis,[2] it attempts to establish the extent to which trade growth among Pacific countries can be said to have increased their 'interdependence'; the extent to which the EEC countries show stronger or weaker patterns of 'interdependence' than Pacific basin countries; and the extent to which the growth of 'interdependence' in the Pacific was related negatively to the growth of interdependence in Europe.[3] While the regional focus in that study is narrower than that adopted here, two important subsidiary conclusions emerge alongside the main conclusions above: that the trade growth among Pacific countries and within Europe has been stronger than that between the two regions; and that the Pacific appears to be an 'increasingly important economic area'.[4] While this trend is less pronounced when measured relative to the Pacific region's overall trade growth, it remains quite distinct despite the fact that it is less uniform among Pacific countries than within Europe, and despite the related fact that Japan's trade growth with Europe and other non-Pacific countries has been stronger.[5]

Other studies[6] reinforce this view of Pacific trade growth as a product of the region's global trade growth and a rising Pacific share in world trade. In this respect, the contrast with Europe is notable.

Yet chapter 3 showed that Pacific countries trade intensively with each other, and that trade intensity among them remains high in the 1980s despite their much larger global trade share. In other words, the share of Pacific countries' trade with other Pacific countries is about one and a half times as large as the region's share of all world trade. It is upon an analysis of the determinants and structure of high intensities in trade among Pacific countries that the argument in this chapter is developed.[7]

ANALYSIS OF TRADE INTENSITY

Why, more exactly, do some countries trade more intensively with each other than they do with the rest of the world? One factor affecting trade intensity is evidently whether the trade and economic structures of trading partners are well or badly matched from the standpoint of fostering a large and profitable trade. Another factor is their 'closeness' or 'proximity' and the strength or weakness of 'resistances' to their developing close trading ties. Hence, two countries trade more or less intensively with each other than they do with the rest of the world because of the particular commodity composition of their trade in relation to world trade — this may be called the degree of *complementarity* in bilateral trade — and because of their geographic proximity or special institutional and historical ties — this may be called the degree of *country bias* in trade. Both factors jointly determine the intensity of trade among pairs of countries or trading regions.[8]

'Complementarity' is a term which is often used loosely to describe the extent to which countries have dissimilar resource endowments and structures of production and are therefore likely to trade intensively with each other.

Here the concept is defined in a particular and precise way. It is employed in a relative sense, and measures the extent to which one country's commodity export pattern matches another country's commodity import pattern more closely than it matches the pattern of world imports. An index of *complementarity* in bilateral trade (C_{ij}) can be derived to measure exactly the extent to which country i's exports to country j are relatively large because the commodity composition of i's exports matches that of j's imports more closely than it matches the commodity composition of world trade. It follows that for each pair of countries or regions, in a many-country, many-commodity world, there are two measures of complementarity in bilateral trade, one derived from the flow of i's exports to j, and the other from the flow of j's exports to i. Obviously this measure of complementarity is closely related to the more general usage of the term. But the actual patterns of export and import specialisation in trade, and therefore this measure of complementarity in trade, are affected by many factors other than the structure of resource endowments. Actual trade flows, upon which the measurement of the complementarity index so defined is based, will also be shaped by the pattern of trade interventions and protectionist barriers. This fact assumes considerable importance in the interpretation of trade intensity, and also of trade complementarity indexes.

The concept of *country bias* in trade (B_{ij}) is defined to measure the extent to which, on average, i's exports have more or less favourable access to j's import markets than might be expected simply from both countries' shares of world trade in each commodity. The country bias index indicates the average influence of low or high resistances to individual commodity trade between one country and another relative to their trade with the rest of the world.[9]

Complementarity and *country bias*, together determine *trade intensity*. The intensity of trade (I_{ij}) measures the extent to which country j's share of i's total exports is large or small in relation to j's share in world trade. Thus bilateral trade intensity is influenced by the degree of similarity between the commodity composition of one country's exports and the other's imports, and by the relative strengths of trade resistances across commodities and trading partners. For these indexes a value greater than unity indicates a positive influence or bias, while a value less than unity measures a negative influence, or a relative trade share that is higher or lower than the norm specified.

Because the concepts introduced here are slightly more complex than might appear at first sight, it is probably useful (although not essential) to understanding the key points in the statistical analysis which follows, to set out the definitions of these and related indexes formally.[10]

The trade intensity index measures the relative significance of a particular trade flow independently of the scale of either partner's trade, and is defined for country i's exports to country j as the share of i's exports going to j (x_{ij}/x_i) relative to the share of j's imports (m_j) in world imports (T):

$$I_{ij} = \frac{x_{ij}}{x_i} \Big/ \frac{m_j}{T} \tag{1}$$

Complementarity in bilateral trade is derived from the relation of one partner's export specialisation in trade (R_i) to the other's import specialisation in trade (D_j). R_{ik} is an index of i's specialisation in the export of commodity k:

$$R_{ik} = \frac{x_{ik}}{x_i} \Big/ \frac{T_k}{T} \qquad (2)$$

where x_{ik} is i's exports of commodity k; x_i is i's total exports; T_k is world imports of commodity k; and T is total world imports. This index of export specialisation is essentially the same index as that which Balassa calls an index of 'revealed' comparative advantage.[11]

An index of j's import specialisation in commodity k may be defined analogously:

$$D_{jk} = \frac{m_{jk}}{m_j} \Big/ \frac{T_k}{T} \qquad (3)$$

where m_{jk} is j's imports of commodity k; m_j is j's total imports; and all other terms are as defined above. This index of import specialisation provides a measure of the extent to which country j imports relatively more or less of commodity k than all other importers on average.

Hence C_{ij} provides an index of the degree of complementarity in i's export trade with j:

$$C_{ij} = \sum_{k}^{n} \left(R_{ik} \cdot D_{jk} \cdot \frac{T_k}{T} \right) \qquad (4)$$

or

$$C_{ij} = \sum_{k}^{n} \left(\frac{x_{ik}}{x_i} \cdot \frac{T}{T_k} \cdot \frac{m_{jk}}{m_j} \right) \qquad (5)$$

where all terms are as defined above. This complementarity index provides a measure of the extent to which country i's export trade with j is relatively large or small because of the character of i's export specialisation and j's import specialisation in trade.

Country bias in the trade of a single commodity measures the resistances to trade in that commodity between trading partners:

$$B_{ijk} = \frac{x_{ijk}}{x_{ik}} \Big/ \frac{m_{jk}}{T_k} \qquad (6)$$

where x_{ijk} is i's exports of commodity k to j, and all other terms are as defined above. This index provides a measure of the extent to which i's exports of k have more or less favourable access to j's markets than exports of k from other countries.[12]

These indexes may be weighted and aggregated across commodities to provide an overall measure of bias in bilateral trade:

$$B_{ij} = x_{ij} \Big/ \sum_{k}^{n} \left(\frac{x_{ik} \cdot m_{jk}}{T_k} \right) \qquad (7)$$

where all terms are as previously defined. To calculate this index, all bias indexes for individual commodities are weighted by each commodity's share in i's trade with j when the bias equals unity. The weights are equal to the percentage contribution of commodity k to complementarity in i's exports to j.

It can be shown from (5) and (7) that the intensity of trade in (1) is the product of the degree of complementarity and country bias in trade:

$$I_{ij} = C_{ij}.B_{ij} \qquad (8)$$

Indexes for the intensity of j's export trade to i (I_{ji}) can be constructed analogously.

The results of detailed study of complementarity, bias and intensity in the trade flows of individual Pacific countries for three-year averages around 1965 and 1980 are reported in Tables 4.1 and 4.2. These indexes summarise a vast amount of statistical data on the commodity and country structure of Pacific trade in a useful and instructive way, incorporating analysis of bilateral trade flows among fifteen Pacific economies for 190 commodities.

The methods by which the indexes are calculated, and a brief description of the data upon which the calculations are based, are set out in the notes to these tables and this chapter.[13]

In each table, row c records the degree of complementarity, row b the degree of country bias, and row i the intensity of trade index for each bilateral trade flow. To illustrate the meaning of the analysis, consider Australia's export trade with Japan in 1964–66. The results of the study reveal that, simply because of the character of Australia's export specialisation and Japan's import specialisation in world trade in 1964–66, one might expect Japan's share in Australia's export trade to have been more than one and a half times as large as its share in world exports; further, that Japan's share in Australian exports was around twice as large as might be expected from both countries' shares in world trade for each commodity; and that, therefore, Japan's share in Australia's export trade was around three and a half times as large as might be expected from its overall share in world imports. That is, the degree of complementarity in Australia's export trade with Japan was 1.62, the degree of country bias was 2.16, and the intensity of trade was 3.51. It is interesting to note from Table 4.2 that this picture of the intensity of Australia's export trade with Japan has changed little, although complementarity is somewhat higher and trade bias somewhat lower in the years 1979–81, resulting in a slightly lower trade intensity.

The intensity of trade among these East Asian and Pacific countries is by no means uniform, although it is commonly high. The mean trade intensity in the 1964–66 period was 2.40, and by 1979–81 it had fallen slightly to 2.38. In the 1964–66 period 47 per cent of the intensity coefficients were above unity, and that proportion had grown to 65 per cent by 1979–81.

Trade intensity among Pacific countries has in general increased or remained high and fairly stable over the period studied here. However, there are two important exceptions. The first is Japan, whose trade intensity with the region as a whole has fallen slightly. Japan's average export trade intensity coefficient was 3.43 in the early period, and 2.49 in the later period, whereas the average intensity coefficient for import trade was 2.88 and 2.49 in these years. This reflects the scale of Japan's trade growth relative to world trade growth and the country's increased dependence on Middle East oil over this period. Japan's importance to other Pacific countries, including the United States, has increased; but the region's importance to Japan has declined somewhat, as observed in the preceding chapter. This does not really qualify the fact that Japan remains the centre of the intensive network of trade ties that criss-crosses the Pacific basin.

The second exception is the case of United States trade to Pacific countries. Some American import trade intensities have risen but others have fallen. American export trade intensities to major markets, like Japan, have declined, but American export trade intensities to most other Pacific countries have risen. The North American share in Northeast Asian exports increased steadily from 40 per cent to 45 per cent between 1973 and 1983, and this share is much higher for the newly industrialising countries of East Asia than for Japan. This reflects both the importance of the United States in world imports, and the complementarity and bias in Northeast Asia's export trade with the United States.[14] The fact that the United States exports less intensively to Japan than in the past has important policy consequences which are taken up in chapters 9 and 10.

The net effect of changes in Pacific trade relations over the past decade or so has been to produce less variation in the pattern of Pacific trade intensities, and, gradually, a more fully integrated trading community. The variance in trade intensities among these fifteen Pacific countries in the years 1964–66 was 23.01, but by the 1979–81 period it had fallen to 16.08. Pacific economies are steadily developing intensive trade ties with all the countries in the region, not just the few partners with whom in the earlier period they had special trade relations. Nonetheless, there is more variation in the pattern of Pacific trade intensities than there is among the countries of the European Community, for example.[15]

The development of East Asian and Pacific economic integration must, of course, be seen in the context of unprecedented growth in international exchange, a process to which Japan, through its rapid rise to great economic power status, contributed significantly. Yet the Pacific economy has continued to expand in the period since the mid-1970s, when world trade and economic growth have been uncertain and slow.

COMPLEMENTARITY AND BIAS IN PACIFIC TRADE

The matrix of complementarity in Pacific trade summarises a wealth of detail about the commodity structures of regional trade flows. The data reveal extremely strong complementarity in some Pacific trade flows but only moderate complementarity for trade among these Pacific countries as a whole. Less than half these bilateral trade flows reveal strong complementarity, although this proportion has risen slightly over the years. In 1964–66, 38 per cent of the complementarity coefficients computed were greater than unity, but by 1979–81 this proportion had risen to 42 per cent. The mean complementarity coefficient was 1.01 in the former period and 0.96 in the latter period.

Table 4.1 Complementarity, bias and intensity in Pacific area trade, 1964-66

Exports from		Exports to						
		Australia	Canada	China	Hong Kong	Indonesia	Japan	Korea Rep.
Australia	c	—	0.55	0.63	0.74	0.34	1.62	0.54
	b	—	0.62	9.87	1.90	1.93	2.16	1.03
	i	—	0.34	6.21	1.40	0.66	3.51	0.55
Canada	c	0.86	—	0.52	0.53	0.57	0.95	0.71
	b	0.91	—	4.07	0.39	0.05	0.77	0.28
	i	0.78	—	2.13	0.21	0.03	0.73	0.20
China	c	0.88	0.73	—	2.58	2.66	1.12	0.42
	b	0.98	0.25	—	10.74	4.29	2.59	0.00
	i	0.86	0.19	—	27.67	11.41	2.91	0.00
Hong Kong	c	1.15	0.95	0.20	—	1.74	0.29	0.37
	b	1.16	0.63	2.10	—	2.00	1.86	0.17
	i	1.33	0.60	0.43	—	3.48	0.54	0.06
Indonesia	c	0.89	0.59	2.35	0.40	—	1.50	0.89
	b	4.84	0.01	2.90	3.77	—	2.24	0.18
	i	4.29	0.00	6.84	1.50	—	3.36	0.16
Japan	c	1.23	1.04	0.94	1.31	2.03	—	1.28
	b	1.44	0.50	4.13	2.96	2.30	—	6.03
	i	1.76	0.52	3.90	3.88	4.65	—	7.74
Korea, Republic of	c	0.83	0.78	0.38	1.84	1.53	0.99	—
	b	0.38	0.45	0.00	3.41	0.35	5.52	—
	i	0.31	0.35	0.00	6.27	0.53	5.48	—
Malaysia	c	0.82	0.70	2.93	0.52	0.21	2.35	1.40
	b	1.25	0.71	0.04	2.37	0.66	1.48	1.31
	i	1.03	0.49	0.12	1.24	0.14	3.48	1.83
New Zealand	c	0.21	0.33	0.51	0.78	0.13	1.50	0.39
	b	11.22	0.82	1.85	0.29	0.14	0.81	0.29
	i	2.31	0.27	0.95	0.23	0.02	1.21	0.11
Papua New Guinea	c	0.52	0.70	0.93	0.37	0.04	2.05	0.45
	b	47.89	0.00	0.00	0.02	0.00	0.69	0.00
	i	24.77	0.00	0.00	0.01	0.00	1.41	0.00
Philippines	c	0.41	0.70	0.31	0.59	0.09	3.40	1.70
	b	0.51	0.08	0.00	0.69	0.80	1.72	2.72
	i	0.21	0.06	0.00	0.41	0.07	5.85	4.62
Singapore	c	1.00	0.87	2.16	1.18	1.17	0.99	0.98
	b	1.45	0.23	1.17	4.05	0.00	0.74	0.52
	i	1.44	0.20	2.52	4.80	0.00	0.73	0.51
Taiwan	c	0.57	0.81	0.54	1.81	2.16	0.91	0.78
	b	0.85	0.53	0.00	3.99	0.56	6.32	7.00
	i	0.48	0.42	0.00	7.23	1.20	5.72	5.44
Thailand	c	0.43	0.46	1.28	0.54	0.06	1.29	0.68
	b	0.25	0.08	0.00	13.99	210.74	3.19	0.27
	i	0.11	0.03	0.00	7.49	12.07	4.12	0.19
United States	c	1.18	1.19	1.42	0.80	1.06	0.96	1.05
	b	0.95	3.16	0.00	0.84	0.46	1.38	2.02
	i	1.12	3.76	0.00	0.68	0.48	1.33	2.12

Notes: Row **i** measures the intensity of trade. An index of 1.00 indicates that one country exports (imports) exactly the same proportion of its total exports to (imports from) another country as that country's share in world trade. Row **i** equals row **c**, (complementarity in trade) multiplied by row **b** (country bias in trade). Calculations are based on procedures described in this chapter, using three-digit SITC commodity trade data.

Source: International Economic Data Bank, Research School of Pacific Studies, Australian National University

Malaysia	New Zealand	PNG	Philippines	Singapore	Taiwan	Thailand	USA
0.66	0.46	0.90	0.48	0.49	0.77	0.49	0.87
5.63	21.88	45.06	3.48	1.59	2.19	2.09	1.00
3.74	10.08	40.74	1.66	0.77	1.68	1.03	0.87
0.68	0.71	0.57	0.75	0.58	0.62	0.69	1.26
0.28	0.93	0.00	0.66	0.00	0.39	0.16	3.45
0.19	0.66	0.00	0.49	0.00	0.24	0.11	4.33
1.67	0.95	1.32	1.04	1.49	0.66	0.86	0.99
4.53	0.38	0.00	0.00	4.44	0.09	0.00	0.00
7.57	0.36	0.00	0.00	6.61	0.06	0.00	0.00
1.22	0.99	1.67	0.37	1.37	0.32	1.06	1.37
0.00	2.15	4.45	2.74	2.96	3.85	3.26	1.88
0.00	2.12	7.44	1.00	4.07	1.21	3.45	2.57
1.37	0.66	0.24	0.77	6.24	0.73	0.43	1.16
0.07	0.53	0.00	7.60	0.54	3.28	3.01	1.52
0.09	0.35	0.00	5.86	3.39	2.38	1.29	1.77
0.90	1.36	1.11	1.25	0.91	1.22	1.26	0.97
0.00	0.78	1.90	4.13	2.23	6.17	4.33	2.28
0.00	1.06	2.11	5.18	2.03	7.55	5.44	2.22
1.17	0.80	0.99	0.65	1.10	0.45	0.73	1.54
0.00	0.03	0.00	1.83	1.58	10.82	5.68	1.82
0.00	0.03	0.00	1.19	1.75	4.85	4.17	2.79
—	0.61	0.35	0.76	7.45	1.08	0.27	1.38
—	1.28	0.24	2.61	4.47	1.61	6.89	0.77
—	0.78	0.08	1.97	33.29	1.74	1.85	1.06
0.60	—	0.89	0.49	0.52	0.76	0.37	0.80
1.92	—	0.81	1.91	0.22	0.15	0.27	1.37
1.15	—	0.72	0.93	0.12	0.11	0.10	1.10
0.53	0.29	—	0.47	2.13	1.69	0.19	1.39
0.00	2.88	—	0.00	1.41	0.00	0.00	0.34
0.00	0.84	—	0.00	3.02	0.00	0.00	0.48
0.91	0.42	0.28	—	1.19	1.19	0.11	1.02
0.00	0.20	0.06	—	0.27	2.73	1.22	3.40
0.00	0.08	0.02	—	0.32	5.22	0.13	3.46
1.95	1.02	1.27	0.98	—	0.72	1.17	1.14
0.00	1.70	5.46	0.87	—	2.23	5.05	0.31
0.00	1.74	6.92	0.86	—	1.61	5.89	0.35
1.68	0.83	4.29	0.95	1.40	—	0.60	1.09
0.00	0.74	0.00	3.03	2.11	—	11.32	1.48
0.00	0.61	0.00	2.87	2.96	—	6.75	1.61
0.72	0.33	0.20	0.24	2.81	0.49	—	0.67
0.00	0.28	0.01	14.82	3.40	6.92	—	0.67
0.00	0.09	0.00	3.50	9.56	3.37	—	0.45
0.93	1.05	1.06	1.07	0.83	1.10	1.18	—
0.38	0.54	0.09	1.92	0.09	1.56	0.55	—
0.35	0.57	0.10	2.07	0.07	1.71	0.65	—

Table 4.2 Complementarity, bias and intensity in Pacific area trade, 1979–81

Exports from		Australia	Canada	China	Hong Kong	Indonesia	Japan	Korea Rep.
		Exports to						
Australia	c	—	0.79	2.56	0.70	1.12	1.71	1.46
	b	—	0.57	1.65	1.74	2.50	1.84	1.38
	i	—	0.45	4.22	1.22	2.79	3.14	2.01
Canada	c	0.97	—	1.61	0.61	0.93	1.04	0.81
	b	0.79	—	0.81	0.26	0.29	0.71	0.53
	i	0.77	—	1.30	0.16	0.27	0.74	0.43
China	c	1.03	0.72	—	1.97	0.90	1.10	0.86
	b	1.14	0.37	—	10.12	2.08	2.94	0.01
	i	1.18	0.26	—	19.93	1.88	3.23	0.01
Hong Kong	c	1.39	0.93	0.48	—	0.35	0.52	0.51
	b	1.91	0.87	6.12	—	2.04	0.95	0.46
	i	2.65	0.81	2.93	—	0.72	0.50	0.23
Indonesia	c	0.46	0.49	0.35	0.27	—	2.33	1.38
	b	3.04	0.08	0.05	1.92	—	2.65	0.87
	i	1.39	0.04	0.02	0.51	—	6.19	1.19
Japan	c	1.33	1.39	1.43	1.27	1.34	—	0.97
	b	1.66	0.38	2.81	2.07	2.86	—	3.19
	i	2.21	0.53	4.02	2.63	3.83	—	3.08
Korea, Republic of	c	1.22	0.84	1.20	1.97	0.91	0.64	—
	b	0.88	0.77	0.00	1.87	3.10	3.70	—
	i	1.07	0.65	0.00	3.68	2.81	2.36	—
Malaysia	c	0.70	0.67	1.22	0.66	0.50	1.89	1.73
	b	1.97	0.25	1.34	2.24	1.07	1.54	1.07
	i	1.38	0.17	1.63	1.48	0.53	2.91	1.86
New Zealand	c	0.54	0.54	0.95	1.04	0.52	1.25	1.02
	b	20.36	1.16	3.08	1.11	4.23	1.39	0.97
	i	11.07	0.63	2.93	1.16	2.19	1.74	0.99
Papua New Guinea	c	0.49	0.59	0.51	0.25	0.14	2.69	1.15
	b	14.17	0.15	2.10	0.30	0.02	1.81	1.07
	i	6.99	0.09	1.07	0.08	0.00	4.87	1.24
Philippines	c	0.71	1.08	0.76	0.77	0.95	1.31	0.92
	b	2.33	0.36	1.71	3.62	3.28	2.45	2.70
	i	1.65	0.39	1.31	2.79	3.13	3.22	2.49
Singapore	c	1.22	0.77	1.05	1.25	1.04	0.78	0.94
	b	2.72	0.30	1.36	4.94	0.00	1.53	1.16
	i	3.31	0.23	1.43	6.19	0.00	1.19	1.09
Taiwan	c	1.34	0.97	0.78	2.00	0.79	0.57	0.68
	b	1.77	0.73	0.00	3.12	4.61	2.65	1.33
	i	2.36	0.71	0.00	6.23	3.62	1.53	0.90
Thailand	c	0.59	0.71	0.96	1.16	0.57	1.07	0.88
	b	1.51	0.17	2.63	3.29	8.64	2.03	1.11
	i	0.90	0.12	2.52	3.83	4.92	2.17	0.97
United States	c	1.12	1.27	1.62	0.90	1.18	0.81	1.20
	b	1.35	3.23	0.94	0.87	0.70	1.32	1.15
	i	1.51	4.10	1.53	0.79	0.83	1.07	1.37

Source: International Economic Data Bank, Research School of Pacific Studies, Australian National University.

Malaysia	New Zealand	PNG	Philippines	Singapore	Taiwan	Thailand	USA
0.91	0.75	1.15	1.25	0.47	1.08	0.72	0.66
4.05	18.85	33.37	1.44	3.42	1.57	1.80	0.83
3.70	14.12	38.40	1.80	1.59	1.69	1.30	0.55
0.94	0.88	0.88	0.86	0.64	0.78	0.87	1.05
0.23	0.55	0.29	0.32	0.23	0.30	0.34	4.18
0.22	0.49	0.25	0.27	0.15	0.23	0.29	4.37
0.87	1.04	1.17	0.65	0.94	0.75	0.76	0.90
2.86	0.73	0.44	3.68	2.79	0.00	4.87	0.58
2.50	0.75	0.52	2.39	2.62	0.00	3.69	0.53
0.74	0.73	0.88	0.38	1.02	0.62	0.42	1.21
1.54	1.87	2.15	5.80	1.73	1.79	2.49	1.95
1.13	1.36	1.90	2.21	1.76	1.10	1.05	2.34
0.54	0.55	0.28	0.93	1.51	1.22	0.90	1.27
0.97	3.53	0.01	2.96	5.38	1.22	0.38	1.05
0.52	1.95	0.00	2.74	8.11	1.49	0.34	1.33
1.22	1.22	1.09	0.99	1.12	1.18	0.95	1.00
2.00	1.38	2.01	2.77	1.73	2.76	2.83	1.61
2.44	1.68	2.19	2.73	1.94	3.27	2.70	1.61
1.01	1.04	1.03	0.72	1.12	0.94	0.74	1.04
1.33	0.51	0.30	2.19	0.93	1.12	1.90	1.78
1.34	0.53	0.31	1.56	1.04	1.06	1.41	1.86
—	0.67	0.39	0.70	2.69	1.48	0.79	1.10
—	2.11	1.11	4.32	5.39	1.19	3.58	0.97
—	1.41	0.43	3.02	14.49	1.76	2.83	1.07
0.80	—	1.41	0.66	0.48	0.92	0.55	0.60
2.76	—	11.13	4.39	2.18	0.98	2.19	1.52
2.20	—	15.64	2.90	1.04	0.91	1.21	0.92
1.15	0.34	—	0.24	0.55	0.98	0.22	1.08
0.03	5.61	—	6.78	1.04	0.41	0.05	0.40
0.04	1.89	—	1.61	0.57	0.40	0.01	0.44
0.95	0.49	1.26	—	0.88	0.71	1.24	1.11
2.83	0.55	1.06	—	1.53	2.12	1.02	1.84
2.68	0.27	1.33	—	1.35	1.52	1.27	2.03
1.39	1.29	1.71	1.47	—	1.11	1.28	1.01
18.05	3.64	8.67	2.10	—	1.23	6.31	0.89
25.14	4.71	14.81	3.09	—	1.36	8.07	0.90
0.96	0.88	1.09	0.54	1.01	—	0.61	1.12
1.47	0.71	0.36	4.62	1.94	—	2.97	2.14
1.40	0.63	0.39	2.50	1.96	—	1.81	2.41
0.86	0.62	0.89	0.64	1.37	0.85	—	0.78
8.72	0.56	0.24	0.88	3.93	1.40	—	1.10
7.52	0.35	0.21	0.57	5.39	1.19	—	0.86
1.22	1.08	1.11	1.02	0.90	1.17	0.97	—
0.71	0.84	0.30	1.56	0.92	1.25	0.81	—
0.87	0.91	0.34	1.60	0.83	1.46	0.78	—

There are various reasons for the low proportion of complementarity coefficients higher than unity in Pacific area trade. The first and most obvious reason is that the region includes, broadly, two groups of economies: one which is extremely complementary in economic and trade structures, and one which is competitive. If there were perfect symmetry in terms of size, number and economic structure between two groups of economies within the region (for example, resource-abundant and resource-deficient economies), one would expect only half of these bilateral trade flows to reveal strong complementarity in trade. In fact, in marked contrast with European trade interdependence, the tendency in this direction is an important feature of Pacific trade interdependence; but it does not provide the whole explanation of the low complementarity coefficients that characterise Pacific trade. Complementarity coefficients are lower than even a prediction based upon this only partially valid assumption about the resource base and economic structure of the region would suggest.

The data for 1979–81 reveal strong complementarity in some important Pacific trade flows. Complementarity is strong in Australia's export trade with Japan and Korea; in Japan's with China, Australia, Southeast Asia and Northeast Asia; in the United States' export trade with China, Canada and Northeast Asia; in Southeast Asia's with Japan and the United States; and in Northeast Asia's with Australia and the United States.[16] Complementarity has increased in Northeast Asia's export trade with Australia and Canada; in Southeast Asia's with Northeast Asia; and in Australia's and New Zealand's with China and Northeast Asia. The complementarity in trade of the United States with the region has generally fallen.

Country bias in Pacific trade is commonly very high, even where complementarity in trade is low, especially in the second period under study. Almost 49 per cent of these bilateral trade flows reveal bias coefficients greater than unity in 1964–66, and by 1979–81 this proportion had risen to 67 per cent. Australia's trade with New Zealand, Canada's with the United States, China's with Hong Kong and Japan's with Korea provide good examples of this as a permanent feature, while the growing country bias in trade among the ASEAN countries illustrates the more recent phenomenon. The arithmetic average of trade bias coefficients was 3.41 in 1964–66 and 2.40 in 1979–81.

Careful studies of relative trade resistances, which underlie the structure of country bias in trade, have been undertaken elsewhere.[17] They suggest that the two factors which seem to be particularly important in the evolution of country bias in international trade are distance, and common membership of political blocs, including former membership of imperial trading blocs. Both these factors influence the order in which traders search out and develop international markets, as well as the patterns of multinational investment and transport costs. The decline of the importance of the old imperial blocs within the Pacific region caused relative distance to emerge more powerfully as an important determinant of the high levels of country bias in regional trade.[18] These factors, alongside the influence of the United States after the Second

World War, provide a large part of the explanation of the high country bias in Pacific area trade and of its distinctive pattern.

TRADE INTENSITY AND COMPARATIVE ADVANTAGE

The high intensity of regional trade is not solely the product of the importance of a few extremely intense trading relationships such as those between political groups (ASEAN) or culturally similar neighbours (Australia and New Zealand, Japan and Korea, Canada and the United States).[19] This can be seen from Table 4.3, where 1979–81 trade intensities are calculated for groups of closely integrated economies, each considered as one economy so that trade within

Table 4.3 Intensity of bilateral trade between Pacific basin country groups, 1979–81[a]

	Exports to				
Exports from	Australasia	North America	Japan	Asian NICs[b]	Other ASEAN[c]
Australasia					
Agriculture	—	1.25	1.67	1.26	2.71
Fuel etc.	—	0.19	2.95	1.78	2.82
Light manuf.	—	0.29	6.58	1.82	2.12
Heavy manuf.	—	0.53	1.31	1.84	2.86
Total	—	0.59	2.85	1.50	2.36
North America					
Agriculture	0.88	—	1.33	1.02	0.85
Fuel etc.	0.64	—	0.75	0.61	0.34
Light manuf.	1.08	—	1.28	0.63	0.90
Heavy manuf.	1.18	—	1.60	0.87	0.80
Total	1.16	—	0.94	0.86	0.78
Japan					
Agriculture	2.61	0.82	—	4.20	4.56
Fuel etc.	1.74	0.94	—	6.07	4.95
Light manuf.	1.33	0.82	—	2.79	3.45
Heavy manuf.	1.70	1.56	—	2.62	2.62
Total	2.10	1.40	—	2.70	2.94
Asian NICs					
Agriculture	2.28	0.87	2.37	—	4.94
Fuel etc.	10.67	0.24	1.04	—	12.46
Light manuf.	1.32	2.15	1.99	—	1.87
Heavy manuf.	1.29	1.66	3.49	—	4.22
Total	2.14	1.55	1.40	—	3.85
Other ASEAN					
Agriculture	1.87	0.94	1.94	3.78	—
Fuel etc.	2.12	0.94	3.40	2.58	—
Light manuf.	1.92	1.66	1.43	3.17	—
Heavy manuf.	1.55	1.45	3.92	5.47	—
Total	1.26	1.00	4.65	3.24	—

Notes: a Share of one country group's exports going to another country group relative to the latter's share of world imports (not of the first group's imports). See notes to Table 1.2 for definitions of the four commodity groups.
b Hong Kong, Singapore, South Korea and Taiwan.
c Indonesia, Malaysia, the Philippines and Thailand.
Source: International Economic Data Bank, Research School of Pacific Studies, Australian National University

each group is regarded as internal trade and therefore subtracted from international trade. This table reveals that the intensity of trade among almost all these groups of countries is high. The arithmetic average of these indexes is around 2. They are below unity in about 25 per cent of the cases shown, mostly as a result of the dominance of Middle East petroleum supplies in the fuel trade, or because of Canada's relatively weak integration with the Western Pacific economy.[20]

This can be seen clearly when the commodity structure of trade intensity is broken down, as in Table 4.3. This table also reveals regional trade intensity indexes above unity in almost all the subregional trade flows for each of the four commodity groups shown, with the exception of the fuels, minerals and metals trade. If crude petroleum were included, regional trade intensities would be even higher. The intensities of bilateral trade among groups of countries within the region are as high or higher for agricultural goods and manufactures as they are for total trade. The intensity of fuels, minerals and metals trade within the region, however, tends to be lower and, because of the dominance of petroleum and hence the relatively small volume of other trade in these products, more variable.

Table 4.4 presents indexes of trade complementarity between the main groups of countries within the Pacific region. These indexes are computed from actual trade patterns, not from the patterns of trade that would prevail in the absence of government distortion of trade structure through various policy interventions (including tariffs and other import barriers, as well as export subsidies and industry assistance). Aggregating the important subregions within the Pacific economy, so that countries with close ties but similar resource bases and economic structures (such as Australia and New Zealand or Canada and the United States) are included in the same trading region, allows extension of the analysis of regional trade complementarity of the kind presented in Tables 4.1 and 4.2, which is based on individual country data. Also, the breakdown of trade intensity into four broad commodity categories reveals more clearly the strengths and weaknesses in regional trade complementarity. The picture of trade complementarity presented in Table 4.4 is thus more uniform than that given in Table 4.2, where the trade flows of several 'competitor' economies are analysed separately. Yet the main conclusion to be drawn from both analyses of the Pacific trade data set for the years 1979–81 is that complementarity in regional trade is not particularly high or low. The complementarity indexes shown in Table 4.4 are much more uniform than those shown in Table 4.2, and they tend, with the exception of the complementarity coefficients for exports to resource-poor Japan from resource-rich Australasia and 'other ASEAN' regions, to be clustered around unity. The same generalisation applies within the four commodity groups. Thus the high intensity of trade among Pacific countries is not primarily the result of strong complementarity in actual trade patterns, but of low resistance to trade within the region compared with trade from elsewhere. This is clear from the data presented in Table 4.5 (which may also be compared with the data in Table 4.2 on bias in individual country trade). Almost all the bias indexes exceed unity, except a few involving North America which again are influenced by Canada's position, but also by declining bias in United States export trade with East Asian countries. The bias coefficients are high in all other intra-regional trade flows, except that, because of the nature of the crude oil trade, overall bias in exports from 'other ASEAN' to Australasia is only moderately high.[21]

Table 4.4 Complementarity in bilateral trade between Pacific basin country groups, 1979–81[a]

Exports from	Exports to				
	Australasia	North America	Japan	Asian NICs[b]	Other ASEAN[c]
Australasia					
Agriculture	—	0.71	1.06	0.86	0.98
Fuel etc.	—	0.64	1.47	0.87	0.78
Light manuf.	—	0.77	1.60	1.26	0.91
Heavy manuf.	—	0.95	1.35	0.88	1.07
Total	—	0.67	1.61	0.91	0.92
North America					
Agriculture	0.75	—	1.16	1.08	1.08
Fuel etc.	0.74	—	1.03	0.75	0.69
Light manuf.	1.05	—	1.00	1.06	1.28
Heavy manuf.	1.11	—	1.06	0.94	1.02
Total	1.11	—	0.86	0.96	1.07
Japan					
Agriculture	2.06	0.91	—	1.27	1.92
Fuel etc.	0.81	0.72	—	0.81	0.82
Light manuf.	1.38	0.65	—	1.79	1.75
Heavy manuf.	0.97	1.18	—	1.03	0.98
Total	1.31	1.07	—	1.13	1.15
Asian NICs					
Agriculture	1.55	1.36	1.09	—	0.99
Fuel etc.	2.23	0.83	0.58	—	1.54
Light manuf.	0.93	1.18	1.13	—	0.66
Heavy manuf.	0.94	1.02	1.02	—	0.95
Total	1.24	1.05	0.64	—	0.88
Other ASEAN					
Agriculture	1.18	1.09	1.40	1.77	—
Fuel etc.	0.69	1.12	1.13	0.93	—
Light manuf.	0.83	1.05	1.35	0.83	—
Heavy manuf.	0.84	0.94	1.40	1.63	—
Total	0.56	1.05	1.93	1.27	—

Notes: a The complementarity index measures the extent to which the commodity composition of one country group's exports matches another group's import composition relative to the rest of the world's import composition. The exact formula is given in the text and notes.
b Hong Kong, Singapore, South Korea and Taiwan.
c Indonesia, Malaysia, the Philippines and Thailand.
Source: International Economic Data Bank, Research School of Pacific Studies, Australian National University

An absence of high complementarity in trade between these groups of Pacific economies may, as Anderson has noted,[22] at first seem surprising, given the marked resource endowment differences between them. An appeal to the basic theory of international trade, which stresses the key role of relative resource endowments in determining the structure of comparative advantage, would suggest that the groups of countries comprising the Pacific economy should enjoy extremely strong comparative advantage vis-à-vis each other, and therefore reveal highly complementary trade patterns. Table 4.6 includes data which summarise the nature and strength of regional differences in resource endowment, and which seem to underpin the expectation of very high complementarity in regional trade. Population density and per capita incomes provide approximations of labour/natural resource and capital/labour ratios, and they are set out in the first two rows of this table for each group of countries. The third row reflects the growth of the capital/labour ratio over the past decade or so. Japan and the Asian newly industrialising countries (NICs) are very densely populated and rapidly growing economies, whereas Australasia and North America are lightly populated (especially so in the case of Australasia), and growing less rapidly in terms of per capita output. The 'other ASEAN' countries are moderately densely populated (with the exception of Java in Indonesia), and have also been growing quite rapidly compared with the average rate of growth for all developing countries.

Table 4.5 Bias in bilateral trade between Pacific basin country groups, 1979–81[a]

	Exports to				
Exports from	Australasia	North America	Japan	Asian NICs[b]	Other ASEAN[c]
Australasia					
Agriculture	—	1.76	1.57	1.46	2.77
Fuel etc.	—	0.29	2.01	2.05	3.62
Light manuf.	—	0.38	4.11	1.44	2.32
Heavy manuf.	—	0.56	0.98	2.09	2.68
Total	—	0.89	1.77	1.66	2.57
North America					
Agriculture	1.18	—	1.14	0.94	0.79
Fuel etc.	0.85	—	0.72	0.81	0.50
Light manuf.	1.03	—	1.28	0.60	0.70
Heavy manuf.	1.06	—	1.51	0.93	0.78
Total	1.05	—	1.09	0.89	0.72
Japan					
Agriculture	1.26	0.90	—	3.31	2.38
Fuel etc.	2.14	1.31	—	7.48	6.05
Light manuf.	0.96	1.26	—	1.55	1.97
Heavy manuf.	1.76	1.32	—	2.55	2.67
Total	1.60	1.31	—	2.39	2.56
Asian NICs					
Agriculture	1.47	0.64	2.17	—	4.99
Fuel etc.	4.79	0.29	1.80	—	8.08
Light manuf.	1.41	1.82	1.77	—	2.82
Heavy manuf.	1.37	1.62	3.41	—	4.42
Total	1.72	1.48	2.19	—	4.37
Other ASEAN					
Agriculture	1.59	0.87	1.39	2.13	—
Fuel etc.	3.09	0.84	3.01	2.76	—
Light manuf.	2.31	1.57	1.06	3.82	—
Heavy manuf.	1.84	1.55	2.80	3.36	—
Total	2.25	0.95	2.41	2.55	—

Notes: a The bias index indicates the average influence of relatively low or high resistances to individual commodity trade between one country group and another compared with the latter's trade with the rest of the world. The exact formula is given in the text and notes.
            b Hong Kong, Singapore, South Korea and Taiwan.
            c Indonesia, Malaysia, the Philippines and Thailand.
Source: International Economic Data Bank, Research School of Pacific Studies, Australian National University.

Basic trade theory suggests that countries with higher ratios of labour to natural resources and capital to labour will have a strong comparative advantage in manufactures vis-à-vis primary production and exports, and that comparative advantage in manufactures will grow more rapidly the faster the rate of growth of the capital to labour ratio relative to growth in the rest of the world.[23] A poor country with little capital, despite a high ratio of labour to natural resources, is initially likely to export primary products in exchange for manufactured goods. As capital is accumulated and incomes grow, labour will be attracted into the manufacturing sector and this sector will expand relative to primary production. For any given rate of growth of capital per worker, the reallocation of labour into the manufacturing sector is likely to be faster the lower the initial wage rate, or the smaller the natural resource endowment per worker. A low wage rate will encourage a resource-poor country into having an early comparative advantage in initially labour-intensive, standard-technology manufacturing and to switch from being primarily an agricultural or resource producer to being an exporter of manufactured goods at a low level of capital per worker. As the endowment of capital per worker rises over time, comparative advantage is likely to shift towards more capital-intensive manufacturing activities. A resource-rich country, with an initially high endowment of capital per worker and therefore a relatively high wage rate, will move more slowly towards specialisation in manufacturing, using its accumulation of capital to develop a narrower range of capital-intensive manufacturing activities.[24]

While there are a number of factors which may complicate this picture (such as the effect of proximity on the character of trade specialisation, the role of international capital movements in the determination of comparative advantage, and demand-side influences), it does seem to provide an intuitively sound and powerful interpretation of the likely structure of comparative advantages and disadvantages in the Pacific economy and their relationship to trade complementarities.

Consider the nature of comparative advantages underlying the trade flows analysed in Table 4.4. The resource-poor, rapidly growing economies, such as Japan and the newly industrialising countries of Northeast and Southeast Asia, are likely to have a strong and increasing comparative disadvantage in primary products, while the resource-rich economies (Australasia, Canada, and, to a lesser extent, 'other ASEAN' and the United States) will tend to have a strong comparative advantage in primary products relative to other countries with similar capital to labour ratios or per capita incomes. The data in Table 4.6 confirm these expectations. The Australasian and North American shares of primary exports are well above the average for developed countries and their import shares well below average, whereas the converse is true for Japan. The manufacturing export shares for Asian NICs are much higher than the average for developing countries. The primary commodity export shares of 'other ASEAN' countries were still above the developing country average in the 1970s, but they have been falling rapidly with the sharp rise in capital/labour ratios in these countries over recent years, and they are now close to the developing country average.

Table 4.6 Resource endowments, sectoral shares of total trade and 'revealed' comparative advantage in developed and developing Pacific basin countries, 1983[a]

	Australasia	North America	Japan	China	Asian NICs	Other ASEAN	All developed[b]	All developing[b]
Population density (persons per km²)	2.4	13.6	322.8	106.8	490.4	90.6	23.7	45.7
GNP per capita (US$)	9 987	14 024	9 695	272	2 578	647	10 163	694
Real GNP growth rate per capita, 1970–83 (per cent per annum)	1.1	1.6	3.4	3.9	6.6	4.2	2.0	2.7
Sectoral shares of total trade (per cent)								
Agriculture								
— Exports	44	22	2	23	8	28	14	21
— Imports	8	10	20	26	15	11	15	15
Fuels, minerals and metals								
— Exports	35	12	1	26	10	53	12	32
— Imports	14	23	56	5	26	25	28	26
Light manufactures								
— Exports	3	5	13	34	41	8	11	20
— Imports	14	11	5	8	15	7	10	10
Heavy manufactures								
— Exports	16	58	83	16	39	8	60	25
— Imports	61	53	16	59	42	54	44	47
'Revealed' comparative advantage								
Agriculture	2.8	1.4	0.1	1.5	0.5	1.8	0.9	1.4
Fuels, minerals and metals	2.3	0.8	0.1	1.7	0.6	3.4	0.8	2.0
Light manufactures	0.2	0.4	1.1	2.8	3.3	0.6	0.9	0.8
Heavy manufactures	0.3	1.1	1.5	0.3	0.7	0.2	1.1	0.5

Notes: a Exports and imports refer to export and import shares, respectively. 'Revealed' comparative advantage is defined as the ratio of the share of a commodity group in total exports for a country or group of countries to that commodity group's share of world exports.
b Market economies only.
Sources: International Economic Data Bank, Research School of Pacific Studies, Australian National University; and *Statistical Yearbook of the Republic of China 1985*

These data demonstrate the marked differences in comparative advantage among the economies within the Pacific region. This is also suggested clearly in the last four rows of Table 4.6, which report Balassa's index of 'revealed' comparative advantage for each country group.[25] This index measures the share of each commodity group in an economy's total exports divided by that commodity group's share of world exports, so that the higher the ratio is above (below) unity, the stronger that economy's comparative advantage (disadvantage) in that commodity group, provided that the commodity composition of exports has not been grossly distorted by government policies.[26]

A more detailed indication of the changes as well as the differences in comparative advantage is provided in Table 4.7, which reports these measures of export specialisation (or 'revealed' comparative advantage) over time.[27] Since an economy's export composition is much less likely to be distorted by government policies than its import composition, rankings of the values of this index provide a reasonable indication of comparative advantage relative to the rest of the world.

The indexes in Table 4.7 are calculated for commodity categories which differ slightly from those in Table 4.6, in that they separate metals trade from minerals and fuels. They show the strong comparative advantage of Australasia, ASEAN and China in agriculture; the growing comparative advantage of North America in agriculture; the decreasing comparative advantage of the East Asian economies in agriculture; the very strong comparative advantage of Northeast Asia in labour-intensive manufactured goods, coupled with the dramatic decline in comparative advantage in this field for Japan; the rapid increase in comparative advantage in these products in China and ASEAN; and the gradual movement in the comparative advantage of Japan and, more recently and from a low base, other Northeast Asian economies away from unskilled-labour-intensive manufactures towards other manufactures (capital-intensive, skilled-labour-intensive and technology-intensive).

Table 4.7   Indexes of revealed comparative advantage for the Pacific economies, 1962, 1970 and 1983[a]

	Agricultural products	Minerals	Metals	Labour-intensive manufactures	Other manufactures
Australasia					
1962	2.78	0.44	0.64	0.08	0.11
1970	2.85	1.25	1.26	0.14	0.28
1983	2.75	2.09	2.59	0.18	0.28
North America					
1962	0.98	0.78	1.11	0.58	1.21
1970	1.03	0.78	0.95	0.42	1.21
1983	1.39	0.73	0.82	0.42	1.11
Japan					
1962	0.41	0.20	0.28	3.47	1.15
1970	0.28	0.13	0.45	2.15	1.40
1983	0.12	0.14	0.67	0.92	1.58
China					
1962	1.64	0.82	2.55	2.41	0.26
1970	2.40	0.33	0.21	2.51	0.31
1983	1.46	1.54	0.29	3.03	0.28
Asian NICs					
1962	1.31	0.78	0.15	2.73	0.39
1970	1.14	0.50	0.10	4.11	0.42
1983	0.56	0.61	0.49	3.48	0.72
Other ASEAN					
1962	2.36	1.53	1.86	0.06	0.03
1970	3.05	1.68	1.74	0.08	0.04
1983	1.86	3.09	1.20	0.43	0.15
All developed[b]					
1962	0.78	0.64	0.93	1.14	1.27
1970	0.83	0.59	0.82	1.07	1.22
1983	0.91	0.78	1.06	0.87	1.13
All developing[b]					
1962	1.73	2.17	1.23	0.56	0.10
1970	1.67	2.52	1.71	0.80	0.17
1983	1.40	1.94	0.78	1.65	0.43

Notes: a The index of export specialisation, or 'revealed' comparative advantage, is defined as the share of a particular commodity group in an economy's total exports divided by that commodity group's share of world exports (see equation (2) in this chapter).
          b Market economies only.
Source: International Economic Data Bank, Research School of Pacific Studies, Australian National University

Of course, the main reason why actual trade flows and complementarities do not reflect these underlying comparative advantages as strongly as might be expected is that they are prevented from doing so by government policies and trade restrictions. Most Pacific countries have erected substantial barriers to imports of products in which they have a strong comparative disadvantage. One important example, noted in earlier studies, is the extremely high barriers to food imports other than feedgrains in Japan and South Korea.[28] This results in an index of complementarity below unity for the agricultural trade between Australasia and these countries, and an unexpectedly low complementarity coefficient in their overall bilateral trade.

At the same time, the index of agricultural trade complementarity for the United States (the world's largest feedgrain supplier) is well above unity, despite remaining restrictions on other agricultural trade affecting the United States in these markets. The strength of Australian and New Zealand agricultural export specialisation is in livestock products. As incomes and hence the demand for livestock products have risen in East Asia, farmers have sought to diversify production in order to capture this new market. Since these countries are relatively densely populated and tend not to be low-cost producers of feedgrains, however, they have a comparative disadvantage in producing especially grass-fed and even grain-fed livestock. Domestic producers are therefore able to supply most of this growing demand only with the help of protection from imports of livestock products. Such protection in turn encourages a grain-intensive domestic livestock sector dependent on duty-free imports of feedgrains and soybean. Since the United States is the world's largest supplier of these foodstuffs and is a net importer of meat, it is a beneficiary of livestock protectionism in East Asia, while Australasia, as a major source of red meat and dairy products, loses.[29] The United States' import controls on meat, tariffs on wool, and restrictions on other agricultural imports, including dairy products, similarly limit Australasia's agricultural trade complementarity with North America.

Another important example is the barriers which developed countries in the region have imposed against imports of labour-intensive manufactures, the largest suppliers of which are the Northeast Asian and Southeast Asian NICs.[30] Finally, Australasia and Canada are highly protectionist towards imports of many other manufactured goods, including those which have a significant share in Japan's exports and those which have a growing share in the exports of the Asian NICs.[31] The evolution of comparative advantages within the Pacific economy and their distortion through the intervention of government policies will be elaborated more fully in chapter 5 and subsequent chapters.

PROXIMITY AND REGIONAL TRADE BIAS

The analyses of trade intensity and complementarity in Tables 4.3 and 4.4 show that Pacific country trade is about twice as large as might be expected from regional trade complementarities and world trade share. Regional trade bias also increased considerably over the 1970s, particularly among the countries of Southeast Asia and the newly industrialising countries of Northeast Asia and the rest of the Pacific area. It is important to explain further the origins of this trend towards regional trade concentration in order to understand the character of growing Pacific trade interdependence and its implications for policy. It appears to be a key element in the emergence of a very strong trade network among Pacific countries.[32]

In introducing Table 4.5 it was noted that relative trade resistances are low within the Pacific economy; and in discussing Tables 4.1 and 4.2 it became clear that bias towards trade among the countries within the region has grown. Resistances to trade have not always been low nor trade bias uniformly high, but the trend over time is also clear.

Pacific trade had its origins in geographic proximity, but the causal links are very complex and sometimes quite indirect. It is the *relative*, not the absolute, 'distance' between two countries (or trading regions) that is relevant: the closer pairs of third countries are to each other and the lower the resistances to trade among them, the more they will tend to trade with each other, the less they will trade with each of the focus countries, and the more the two focus countries will trade with each other.[33] Similarly, the lower are the resistances to trade between one of the two focus countries and the rest of the world, the more that country will trade with the rest of the world and the less it will trade with the other focus country. Hence, the growing bias towards Pacific trade has resulted from the intensification of trading ties within other regions such as Europe and from higher resistances to trade between Pacific economies and those regions, as well as from the lowering of resistances to trade among Pacific countries themselves.

In addition to objective trade resistances, which are the product of distance and transport costs or government policies that discriminate between trading partners, traders face various subjective resistances to trade, including imperfect knowledge of trading opportunities and the absence of confident and established business relationships.[34] These objective and subjective resistances to trade interact with each other in complex ways, most importantly through the presence of economies of scale in overcoming some of them, and through the significant external benefits that result from one pioneering trader's efforts to re-shape trading patterns — efforts which reduce the costs to subsequent traders of overcoming these resistances. Economies of scale are important in transport costs and communications, as well as in establishing familiarity with new trading environments.

These effects are similar in nature to the 'agglomeration effects' that concentrate commerce within nation states. Scale factors tend to cause the trade of relatively small economies to agglomerate in comparatively few international trading relationships.[35] The externalities of pioneering new international trading relationships introduce a powerful tendency for large-scale, established trading relationships, associated as they are with lower costs in overcoming resistances to trade because of economies of scale in commerce and communication, to be maintained even after the structure of objective resistances that may have brought them into being has changed. This is one force encouraging the survival of trading empires long after the political basis has corroded.[36] The residue of empires was one factor which earlier inhibited the development of trading ties within the Pacific region.

Relative distance is of considerable importance in transport and communication costs, particularly for countries whose total foreign trade is relatively small. It is also of considerable importance in various subjective resistances. For example, traders tend to look first at the markets of neighbouring countries in searching the international marketplace for trading opportunities. Even large multinational corporations with international communications and trading systems are commonly encouraged to specialise in regional trade by the regional structure in the organisation of the firm.[37] In the long sweep of Japan's commercial history, a common pattern in the development of market shares for new commodity exports was first the penetration of East Asian markets and then expansion to industrial country markets through Australia and North America.

The effect of close political relationships, and conversely political antipathy, on the cost of overcoming resistances in bilateral trading relationships has already been noted. In some circumstances these can have a much more powerful influence in encouraging or discouraging trade than variations in relative distance. Within the great empires that grew out of the industrial revolution, the costs of overcoming government-imposed restrictions and the various subjective resistances to trade were much lower than they were between these imperial blocs. Various studies have shown that common membership of an imperial bloc was a powerful factor in generating high country bias in trade.[38] It has been suggested in another study that

> these tendencies probably reached their peak in the 1930s, before World War II precipitated the dismembering of the European, United States and Japanese empires. Imperial tariff preferences strengthened in the 1930s within the British and Netherlands empires in response to the great depression and increasing competition in light manufactured goods trade from Japan, and led to a further intensification of intra-imperial trade at that time.[39]

These observations about the nature of influences affecting resistances to regional trade and hence regional trade bias are helpful in understanding the growing concentration in Pacific trade. In part the growth of Pacific trade interdependence can be understood in terms of the gradual assertion of the influence of relative proximity over the influence of long-established political blocs in determining the costs of overcoming resistances to trade. In the early postwar period, Australia's trade with Pacific countries, especially those of the Western Pacific, was intense only with those that had British imperial connections — New Zealand, many South Pacific islands, and the British colonies that are now Malaysia and Singapore — and with Indonesia.[40] Australia had imposed discriminatory barriers against trade with Japan and the United States in the celebrated 'trade diversion' episode of the 1930s, and these were continued in the denial of most-favoured-nation treatment to Japan immediately after the War.[41] The trade of post-revolution China was predominantly with the Soviet Union and Eastern Europe until the late 1950s. Cold war politics and military strategy led to strong ties and aid flows between the United States and Taiwan and South Korea, such that from the early 1950s to the late 1960s virtually the only diversion of the latter's trade away from their close neighbour and former imperial power, Japan, had been trade with the United States. United States colonialism in the Philippines had always been associated with preferential trading arrangements that caused the colony's foreign trade to be concentrated almost exclusively with the United States. After Philippines' independence in 1946, highly discriminatory arrangements in favour of trade with the United States were continued under the Laurel–Langley agreement of 1954. The Indochina states, relatively unimportant in foreign trade as a result of the civil war, have concentrated their trade when under communist government with the Soviet bloc, otherwise with the principal military allies of France until 1954 and increasingly the United States between 1954 and 1975.[42]

Trade discrimination within these old imperial blocs was gradually dismantled during the postwar period. Australia ended two decades of discrimination against Japan by extending most-favoured-nation treatment (first conditionally) in 1957.[43] Imperial preferences in Australian import restrictions were substantially modified in the same year and finally eliminated in the 1978 Tokyo Round of multilateral trade negotiations. Japan resumed trade within the GATT framework under United States encouragement. Preferential trade between the United States and the Philippines was phased out during the 1960s and 1970s. The Netherlands' preference in Indonesia ended with independence. Singapore and Malaysia established close ties with their ASEAN neighbours in the process of loosening British connections. The Pacific island nations, notably Papua New Guinea, gained independence and exercised the right not to discriminate in favour of former colonial powers, although Papua New Guinea retains preferential access for some commodities in Australia's markets. In the 1960s Australia also introduced more general preferences for developing countries, which have favoured the intensification of trade ties with Asian–Pacific developing countries.

Long-term technological and political forces built up pressure towards restructuring trading relationships away from historical patterns. But these changes were accelerated by the rapid postwar industrial growth of Japan, where there were strong potential benefits from pioneering new transport and communications networks and rebuilding the old networks in Northeast and Southeast Asia that had been disrupted by war. The scale of Western Pacific growth and complementarity reinforced these trends. The United States' economic relationship with Western Pacific countries was fostered within the framework of postwar political–military alliances in Asia and the Pacific. This was an important precondition of the establishment of close trade and economic ties between Australia and Japan, which, in turn, were fostered through the advantages of relative proximity. The changes to old historical patterns were effected most rapidly through the 1960s and 1970s, between Japan and the whole Western Pacific region, among the neighbouring ASEAN countries, and with Taiwan and South Korea through the 1970s.[44] Relative resistances in the trade of the latter two resource-poor countries with Japan and the United States were low, but as their total trade expanded it became economically efficient to build more intensive trading relationships with a number of other countries in the Pacific, including resource-rich Australia and the ASEAN countries. The emergence of the European Community as an inward-looking trading bloc and the eventual entry of the United Kingdom reduced the relative cost of overcoming trade resistances among countries that were excluded from these arrangements. The way in which this contributed very substantially to the increase in regional trade bias, through a redirection of commercial diplomatic effort by Australia, Japan and other Western Pacific countries, was introduced in chapter 3. Subregional policies which affected the geographic distribution of regional trade and the structure of regional trade bias include the special trading links (sectoral trade agreements) between Canada and the United States,[45] and the New Zealand–Australia Free Trade Agreement and Closer Economic Relations Trade Agreement.[46] There is also preferential trading treatment within ASEAN.[47]

The Pacific economy's increased trade share and underlying trade complementarity have been accompanied by significant regionalisation (or 'bias') in trade growth. The Pacific has emerged as an important element in world trade, and Pacific countries are of much more importance to each other in trade than they are to the world at large. However, the global trading connections of Pacific countries are significant. Regional trade has become a smaller fraction relative to Japan's growing importance in world trade over the years (Japan's intensity of trade with the region having fallen slightly), and the substantial proportion of trade which other countries (including the United States, Australia and, increasingly, Northeast Asian countries other than Japan) have outside the region underlines the importance of the Pacific economy's global trading interests.

The brief analysis in this chapter of the structure of Pacific trade interdependence and the changes that have taken place over the past two decades or so suggests some tentative conclusions for policy, to be explored further in the chapters that follow. The Pacific countries have strong common trading interests, and these have grown stronger over time. There is considerable scope for further expansion of trade by Pacific countries through measures that provide more confident market access and that reduce the trade barriers that limit the realisation of the *potentially* strong complementarity within the region. Given the low resistances to regional trade reflected in extremely high regional trade bias, the reduction of trade barriers on a most-favoured-nation basis in a way which does not offend Pacific countries' global trading interests is likely to mean that most new suppliers of imports will come from within the region rather than from non-Pacific countries. As trade volumes grow it is quite likely that regional trade bias will increase further because of the scale economies in reducing information barriers and other transaction-cost impediments to foreign trade.

The average bias coefficient for Pacific trade in 1979–81 shown in Table 4.5 was 1.8, but these indexes were much higher for the neighbouring countries that this table includes in the sub-regional groups, as can be seen from the data in Table 4.2. The average index of country bias for trade between Australia and New Zealand was 19.6; between the ASEAN countries 3.2; between Japan and South Korea 3.4; and between Canada and the United States 3.7. Discriminatory trade liberalisation of the kind adopted by the European Community is not required as an incentive to regional trade liberalisation by Pacific countries since, if they were to reduce trade barriers on a most-favoured-nation basis, much of the benefit would be reaped within the Pacific region itself. The mutual trading interests among Pacific countries, together with the strong commitment to trade-oriented development strategies among the developing countries within the region, provide a likely springboard for trade and other foreign economic policy measures not only to accommodate the trade and development needs of all the countries within the Pacific economy but also to strengthen the global system of commitments to an open international trade regime.

NOTES

Chapter 4

1   J.K. Johansson and Robert S. Spick 'Trade Interdependence in the Pacific Rim and the E.C.: A Comparative Analysis' *Journal of Common Market Studies* XX, 1, September 1981.
2   Bruce Russett *International Regions and the International System* Chicago: Rand McNally & Co., 1967; Barry Hughes 'Transactional Analysis: The Impact of Operationalization' *International Organization* 25, 1, Winter 1971, pp.143–5; Barry Hughes, 'Transaction Data and Analysis: In Search of Concepts' *International Organization* 25, 3, Summer 1972, pp.657–80; Charles G. Nelson 'European Integration: Trade Data and Measurement Problems' *International Organization* 28, 3, 1974, pp.399–422.
3   Johansson and Spick 'Trade Interdependence' p.42.
4   ibid., p.48.
5   ibid., p.50. This conclusion is consistent with the analysis of trade intensity presented in this chapter.
6   See, for example, B.G. Hickman, Y. Kuroda and L.J. Lau 'The Pacific Basin in World Trade — An Analysis of Changing Trade Patterns 1955–75' *Empirical Economics* 4, 1, 1979, pp.63–85.
7   Anderson 'Intensity of Trade' p.3. The argument in this chapter draws heavily on Anderson's study, which provides an excellent overview of Pacific trade intensities.
8   Trade intensity analysis was pioneered by Brown (Brown *Applied Economics*) and developed and popularised by Kojima (Kiyoshi Kojima *Sekai keizai to Nihon bōeki* [The world economy and Japan's foreign trade] Tokyo: Keisō Shobō, 1962; and 'The Pattern of International Trade' pp.16–36). The decomposition of trade intensity into complementarity and country bias indexes was first presented in the author's doctoral dissertation, Japanese–Australian Trade: An Approach to the Study of Bilateral Trade Flows, Australian National University, 1967. Since then it has been used in several studies of both an analytical and a policy nature. In the latter category, the *Crawford–Ōkita Report* is among the more important. Work following this line of analysis is surveyed in Drysdale and Garnaut 'Trade Intensities' pp.62–84. See also Anderson et al. 'Pacific Growth and Australian Trade' Appendix; and Rod Tyers, Prue Phillips and Peter Drysdale 'Projecting Matrices of International Trade Flows: The Case of Australian and Pacific Basin Trade' (forthcoming in *Journal of Economics and International Relations*).
9   Johnson used this categorisation of 'resistance' influences on geographic trade structure, distinguishing 'geographic distance and the transport cost of overcoming it', 'differences of political and legal systems, culture and language that differentiate nations from one another as market areas', and 'protection', in Harry G. Johnson *Comparative Cost and Commercial Policy Theory for a Developing World Economy* Stockholm: Almqvist and Wicksell, 1968, p.29. See also Drysdale and Garnaut, 'Trade Intensities' p.62 and pp.70–76. Garnaut Australian Trade with Southeast Asia pioneered the analysis of trade resistances using country bias indexes. He used both aggregate and commodity-specific country bias indexes to analyse resistances across the bilateral trade relationships between Australia and each of the (then) five ASEAN countries. His analysis made the important distinction between *objective resistances* and *subjective resistances* to bilateral trade.

10   Drysdale and Garnaut 'Trade Intensities' pp.67–70; Tyers, Drysdale and Phillips 'Pacific and World Trade Flows'. The definitions of the indexes in the text exclude the problem of 'self-trade', in order to simplify the presentation. The relevant international market is that of the world, excluding imports to country **i**. Calculations of trade intensity in the tables use this formulation of the index:

$$I_{ij} = \frac{x_{ij}}{x_i} \Big/ \frac{m_j}{T - m_i} \tag{1a}$$

where world imports are defined to be net of i's imports (m_i) and all other indexes are adjusted analogously. This adjustment is not especially important for most individual country trade flows, but becomes important when indexes are calculated for inter-regional trade flows. See note 12.

11   Bela Balassa 'Trade Liberalisation and "Revealed" Comparative Advantage' *Manchester School of Economic and Social Studies* 33, 2, May 1965, pp.99–124.

12   Alternatively, this index may be written:

$$B_{ijk} = \frac{x_{ijk}}{x_{ik}} \Big/ \frac{m_{ijk}}{T_k - \delta_{ijk} m_{ik}} \tag{6a}$$

where δ_{ijk} is a coefficient governing self-trade. δ_{ijk} is unity when i is a single country unable to export to itself, but some fraction when i is a region or group of countries which may have trade with itself. For some purposes, as in the subsequent argument of this chapter, it may be useful to exclude intra-regional trade from comparative analysis (for example, to treat North America as a single unit and exclude United States–Canada trade from the analysis of Pacific trade intensity), and to impose the restriction $\delta_{ijk} = 1$ for the analysis of inter-regional trade. This restriction is imposed on the calculations of trade intensity, complementarity and bias presented in Tables 4.3 to 4.5.

13   The computations for the intensity of trade analysis presented in this chapter were undertaken by Prue Phillips using the Australian National University's International Economic Data Bank commodity trade data tapes. These are based on United Nations international trade statistics and have been built up from national trade statistics. Commodity trade data used were disaggregated to the three-digit SITC level. Programs for analysing the trade data have been developed by the Data Bank.

14   Anderson et al. 'Pacific Growth and Australia Trade', especially pp.25–41.

15   Johansson and Spick 'Trade Interdependence' p.56.

16   cf. Anderson 'Intensity of Trade' p.5.

17   See Garnaut *Australian Trade with Southeast Asia*, and Drysdale and Garnaut 'Trade Intensities' for a review of the relevant literature.

18   The interaction between transport-cost resistances and other resistances, in their effect on trade intensity and country bias, is discussed later in this chapter. For a fuller discussion of this issue, see Drysdale and Garnaut 'Trade Intensities', pp.70–76; and Drysdale 'Japanese–Australian Trade', ch.8. Additional references on the role of transport costs in shaping the geographic structure of trade may be found included in the Drysdale and Garnaut paper.

19   Anderson 'Intensity of Trade' p.3.

20   idem.

21   Garnaut, Australia's Trade with Southeast Asia; and Garnaut (ed.) *ASEAN*. This is much affected by the nature of Indonesia's crude oil exports and Australia's crude oil imports. Australia produces high-refractory crude oil domestically and has substituted domestic supplies of this commodity for imports previously obtained from Indonesia. Remaining Australian imports are of heavy oils from the Middle East. A full discussion of the effect of the degree of disaggregation of commodity category and commodity definition on the calculation of

complementarity and country bias in trade is contained in Drysdale, Japanese–
Australian Trade, ch.2.

22   Anderson 'Intensity of Trade' p.5.

23   R.G. Garnaut and Kym Anderson 'ASEAN Export Specialisation and the
      Evolution of Comparative Advantage in the Western Pacific Region' ch.13 in
      Garnaut (ed.) ASEAN, which develops an earlier idea introduced by Krueger
      (A.O. Krueger Growth, Distortions and Patterns of Trade Among Many Countries
      Princeton, NJ: International Finance Section, Princeton University, 1977). Kym
      Anderson and Ben Smith 'Changing Economic Relations Between Asian ADCs
      and Resource-Exporting Developed Countries of the Pacific Basin' ch.9 in Hong
      and Krause (eds) Trade and Growth of the Advanced Developing Countries utilises
      the same model. The statement of the model in the present argument is not
      complete, but it incorporates the essential elements. A fuller statement of the
      argument is contained in Findlay, Anderson and Drysdale 'China's Trade and
      Pacific Growth'.

24   ibid., pp.295–6.

25   Balassa '"Revealed" Comparative Advantage'; and also Drysdale, Japanese–
      Australian Trade, ch.2.

26   Drysdale, Japanese–Australian Trade, ch.2; and Drysdale and Garnaut 'Trade
      Intensities' p.70.

27   Anderson et al. 'Pacific Growth and Australian Trade' pp.23–4.

28   Kym Anderson and Aurelia George (eds) Australian Agriculture and Newly
      Industrialising Asia: Issues for Research Australia–Japan Research Centre,
      Australian National University, 1980, especially ch.2; Kym Anderson 'On the
      Gains and Losses from Beef Import Quotas in Japan and Korea' Pacific Economic
      Papers No.90, Australia–Japan Research Centre, Australian National University,
      February 1982; Eric Saxon and Kym Anderson 'Japanese Agricultural Protection
      in Historical Perspective' Pacific Economic Papers No.92, Australia–Japan Research
      Centre, Australian National University, July, 1982; and Anderson and Hayami
      Agricultural Protection, especially chs 1 and 2.

29   Anderson et al. 'Pacific Growth and Australian Trade' pp.60–61; Anderson and
      Hayami Agricultural Protection chs 2 and 5.

30   Kym Anderson and Ross Garnaut 'Australia's Trade Growth with Developing
      Countries' Pacific Economic Papers No.102, Australia–Japan Research Centre,
      Australian National University, July 1983; and D.B. Keesing and M. Wolf Textile
      Quotas Against Developing Countries Thames Essay No.23, Trade Policy Research
      Centre, London, 1980.

31   Garnaut and Anderson 'Australia's Trade with Developing Countries' p.10. For a
      full discussion of this question, see Anderson and Garnaut Australian
      Protectionism, especially chs 2 and 6.

32   Anderson and Garnaut Australian Protectionism ch.7.

33   Garnaut, Australia's Trade with Southeast Asia, ch.2.

34   ibid. ch.2. See also Drysdale, Japanese–Australian Trade, ch.8, for a discussion of
      the importance of this factor in the development of Australia–Japan trade in the
      postwar period.

35   For an early study of concentration in small-country trade, see Michael Michaely
      Concentration in International Trade Amsterdam: North–Holland Publishing Co.,
      1962. This subject is also reported in P. Lamartine Yates Forty Years of Foreign
      Trade London: George Allen & Unwin, 1959. See Drysdale and Garnaut 'Trade
      Intensities' p.79 for a discussion of the values of trade intensity coefficients for
      small trade flows; and Tyers, Phillips and Drysdale 'Analysis of Trade Flows' for a
      report of the statistical testing of these propositions.

36   Ephraim Kleiman 'Trade and the Decline of Colonialism' Economic Journal 86,

343, September 1976, pp.459–80; and Drysdale and Garnaut 'Trade Intensities' pp.72–74.

37　Garnaut, Australia's Trade with Southeast Asia, ch.7. See also Drysdale and Garnaut 'Trade Intensities' p.73.

38　Drysdale, Japanese-Australian Trade, ch.6; Ippei Yamazawa 'Intensity Analysis of World Trade Flows' *Hitotsubashi Journal of Economics* 11, 2, February 1971; Garnaut *Australia's Trade with Southeast Asia*; and Kleiman 'Trade and Colonialism' pp.459–80.

39　Garnaut and Anderson 'Australia's Trade with Developing Countries' pp.24–25.

40　Garnaut, Australia's Trade with Southeast Asia.

41　Drysdale, Japanese-Australian Trade, ch.6.

42　These ideas are drawn from Garnaut, Australia's Trade with Southeast Asia, ch.2.

43　Drysdale, Japanese-Australian Trade, ch.7.

44　Garnaut and Anderson 'Australia's Trade with Developing Countries' p.27.

45　H.E. English 'Canada and Pacific Trade Policy' in Kiyoshi Kojima (ed.) *Pacific Trade and Development I* Tokyo: Japan Economic Research Center, 1968.

46　P.J. Lloyd *Economic Relations between Australia and New Zealand* Department of Economics, Research School of Pacific Studies, Australian National University, 1976; C.F.G. Simkin 'Closer Economic Ties with New Zealand' Discussion Paper No.8, Centre for Economic Policy Research, Australian National University, 1980; Robin Burnett and Alan Burnett *Australia–New Zealand Economic Relations: Issues for the 1980s* Canberra: Australian National University Press, 1981; and Sir Frank Holmes et al. *Closer Economic Relations with Australia: Agenda for Progress* Wellington, NZ: Institute of Policy Studies, 1986.

47　See H.C. Riger 'ASEAN Cooperation and Intra-ASEAN Trade' *Research Notes and Discussions* Paper No.57, Institute of South East Asian Studies, Singapore, 1985; and R.B. Suhartono 'Industrial Cooperation in ASEAN' in H. Mutoh et al. *Industrial Policies for Pacific Economic Growth* Sydney: Allen & Unwin, 1986.

5 Energy and resource trade security

The raw materials trade is at the hub of economic interdependence in the Pacific region. Even trade between the United States and Japan, the two industrial giants among Pacific nations, still has a large vertical component — the exchange of primary goods for manufactures. This contrasts markedly with the character of Western European integration. In 1983 some 35 per cent of imports by the five advanced industrial countries in the Pacific area comprised raw materials, food and fuels. Largely because of Japan's needs, dependence on raw materials trade is extremely high. In 1983 Japan alone accounted for around 30 per cent of world imports of basic ferrous and nonferrous ores and concentrates. Japan and the United States together took 36 per cent of world imports of minerals excluding petroleum, and 28 per cent of crude petroleum imports.[1] The Pacific region as a whole accounted for 28 per cent of world food imports.[2] In no other area of international exchange is the issue of *security* so prominent as in energy and resource trade, including food.[3]

ECONOMIC AND TRADE SECURITY

Economic and trade security[4] are important dimensions of international economic exchange. Historically, energy, raw materials and food have been the trades most associated with the political and economic threats posed by trade dependence.

Throughout the world's history, minerals and their exploitation have been a cause of much conflict and strife.[5] One article of the Atlantic Charter, subsequently endorsed by the United Nations in 1942, enjoined signatories 'to endeavour . . . to further the enjoyment by all States, great or small, victor or vanquished, of access on equal terms, to trade and the raw materials of the world'.[6] It was to avoid a re-emergence of the disruptions, the economic blocs and the cartels of the interwar period, and the monetary practices and other manifestations of economic nationalism, that the economic institutions of the postwar world were developed.[7] These institutions were directed towards building an open, non-discriminatory and multilateral cooperative approach to international trade and monetary problems. The vulnerabilities perceived in the energy and resource goods trade highlight the crucial role of reliable institutions for cooperative exchange as the basis of efficient specialisation in the international economy. It is no coincidence that resource and food security emerged as major issues in international economic diplomacy at the same time in the late 1970s as these institutions were coming under increasing pressure.

Economic security became an important issue at the beginning of the 1970s for several reasons: rapidly escalating oil prices and the success of the OPEC group of oil exporters in raising oil revenues from 1971, and particularly after October 1973; the sway of the Club of Rome's prognosis that world resource supplies were running out;[8] the experience of commodity booms and shortages after a prolonged period of industrial country growth; the application by the United States of export controls on soybeans in order to avoid 'unacceptable' domestic price rises; the scramble for sovereignty over sea resources; and the newly perceived bargaining power between resource-rich developing countries and resource-importing developed countries.[9] The OPEC arrangements for oil, the use of the oil embargo for political bargaining, and the repressed desires of other countries to move in the same direction, all served to dramatise the issue of access to raw materials. The industrial countries, particularly Japan, were, for the first time in the 20 years since the Korean crisis, faced with a high degree of uncertainty about their access to raw materials.

The prospect earlier offered by the Club of Rome has now been heavily discounted and fears about specific commodity shortages have been largely allayed; but the Iran–Iraq war and the United States' contretemps with Iran, and the easy appeal to trade embargoes in the political confrontation with the Soviet Union over the occupation of Afghanistan, have kept resource and food trade security at the forefront of international policy concerns throughout the world. There are now new anxieties about the effects of these disturbances, and the subsequent depression of oil prices, on the adequacy of investment in raw materials production and supplies over the long term.[10]

Within the Pacific economy, Japan's response to these developments is of particular importance. The coincidence of the energy crisis with world food shortages (involving price hikes and also trade embargoes) had a profound effect on the Japanese outlook towards resources and food security.[11] Throughout the 1960s Japan had profited from the generally favourable situation in the global supply of natural resources in a buyer's market. The price of crude oil actually fell between 1948 and 1970, and Japan's heavy industrialisation program was favoured by cheap energy supplies. By the end of the 1960s, the basic change taking place in the world supply and demand equation had become evident in oil bargaining power, and the spectacular increase in world demand for raw materials around this time foreboded future scarcities. The Club of Rome forecasts of long-term resource scarcity made these early concerns about a shortage of resources in Japan plausible. There were some who anticipated the requirements of these changes for Japanese raw material import policy:

. . . Japan's dependence on imports of raw materials, energy and food is so complete that policies attempting self-sufficiency in any of the key items appear unrealistic. Diversifying sources of supply, economising on the use of raw materials and energy, stepping up efforts for increased production from indigenous resources, and building up emergency stocks of energy and food — all these are feasible and should be pursued with seriousness. But the basic character of heavy dependence for key items from overseas will not change.[12]

The Japanese Ministry of International Trade and Industry held the view that the promotion of 'development import' of overseas resources, or subsidisation under the foreign aid program of Japanese direct investment in Japanese import-related resource development projects, would be the key to future resources development policy.[13] Japanese firms were encouraged to seek more active ownership and involvement in the development of foreign resources accorded national priority for supply to Japan. Not unexpectedly, the experience of these years induced a very similar response in the rest of resource-deficient East Asia, especially South Korea. Among all the modern industrial economies, Japan is perhaps the most vulnerable to interruptions in external sources of supply of raw materials and foodstuffs.[14] The United States, Australia, Canada and New Zealand — also within the Pacific economy — are among the least vulnerable. If the potential for industrial development is to be realised in East Asia, policies and conditions which insulate against resource trade vulnerabilities are necessary.

Insurance against the vulnerabilities of resource trade dependence is commonly seen to require one or other of three broad courses of action: greater control over sources of supply; diversification of sources of supply; and stockpiling of needed raw materials.[15] Greater control may be presumed to derive from the development of indigenous supplies of raw materials and substitutes, but availabilities and costs make self-sufficiency policies in many fields quite uneconomic. Moreover, within nation states disruptions may still occur through strike activity or natural disaster, so that there is a measure of resource insecurity, independent of external dependence.[16] Historically, greater control has sometimes been sought through imperialistic aggrandisement or, in more recent times, through political adventurism in support of supposed national commercial interests.[17] But neither imperialism nor neocolonialist adventurism is an acceptable — or for that matter cost-effective — means of securing resources on the scale and complexity demanded by many of the advanced industrial economies' resource links with the rest of the world.

Foreign investment is nowadays frequently perceived as affording control over critical supplies of raw materials. This was a strong emphasis in United States policy in the first decade or two after the Second World War, and has recurring appeal in Japan and Europe, especially West Germany.[18] But, even where private ownership is respected independent of nationality, it is not clear that foreign investment in resource production greatly enhances resource security without the backup of home government support (which would offend against the principles of international pluralism and entail some kind of neo-colonialism) or supportive government-to-government arrangements. This question will be examined more thoroughly later in this chapter and in chapter 7. There is a real possibility that domination of raw materials production by foreign investment from consumer countries may heighten political anxieties in countries that supply raw materials, and may reduce rather than increase resource trade security.[19]

Diversification of sources of supply, or having a range of substitutes readily available, are perhaps more effective means of insuring against the impact of a fracture of any one source of raw materials.[20] This course, which is widely advocated, and not only for Japan, is not without costs, especially given the substantial transportation costs of procuring raw materials. If there are few sources of supply of a particular commodity and substitutability is low in the short term (as with oil), the possibility remains of collective action by suppliers to exert monopoly power. The scope for, and the limitations on, monopolistic behaviour by sellers or monopsonistic behaviour by buyers in minerals markets needs careful assessment, and will be considered later. It can be noted here that, except in the short term, the presence of competitive forces will constrain such behaviour, though it will rarely eliminate it completely.[21]

In the short run, the only way of assuring supplies of raw materials against a wide range of possible interruptions is stockpiling. Stockpiling costs (including the capital charges on the inventory of materials and storage expenses) have to be weighed against the probabilities of a rupture in supplies.[22]

A fourth course of action, which has been notably neglected in the economic literature on resource security, is the voluntary development of private contractual as well as government-to-government arrangements which stress reliable supply and purchase of raw materials and foodstuffs over the long term and can make a major contribution to enhancing resource trade and economic security generally. This is quite distinct and separate from the three courses of action usually identified as the necessary ingredients for increased resource security.[23] It does not involve extending control to a degree that would offend national sovereignty and independence; nor does it necessarily involve the economic burdens inherent in policies of diversification and stockpiling. It relies upon inducing cooperative behaviour within a framework of long-term associations among trading partners as a mechanism for enhancing resource trade security. The prospects for and essential elements of resource trade security built upon *reliable trade arrangements* within the Pacific economy are the subject of the argument that follows in this chapter.

NATURAL RESOURCES AND COMPARATIVE ADVANTAGE

The Pacific interest in the resource trade is very powerful. The regional pattern of natural resource endowments has an important influence upon the structure of comparative advantage, and it is useful here to look in more detail at how it encourages strong resource and food trade ties.

Table 5.1 Natural-resource endowments and economic growth in the Pacific region, 1983

	Pop. (million)	Area (million ha)	GNP (US$ billion)	GNP per capita (US$)	GNP per agricultural hectare (US$)[a]
	(1)	(2)	(3)	(4)	(5)
Resource-rich countries					
Australia	15.4	769	163.5	10 638	324
Canada	24.9	998	314.1	12 608	4 605
New Zealand	3.2	27	22.3	6 954	1 525
United States	234.5	936	3 324.0	14 175	7 768
Resource-poor countries					
Japan	119.3	37	1 156.3	9 695	211 737
Republic of Korea	40.0	10	75.3	1 885	33 565
Hong Kong	5.3	0.1	28.6	5 390	—[b]
Singapore	2.5	0.1	16.5	6 618	—[b]
Taiwan	18.7	4	51.0	2 724	57 048
Other Western Pacific countries					
Indonesia	155.7	192	75.0	482	2 363
Malaysia	14.9	33	27.7	1 863	6 384
Papua New Guinea	3.2	46	2.3	707	4 780
Philippines	52.1	30	34.1	656	3 126
Thailand	49.2	51	39.1	795	2 139
China	1 019.1	956	277.5	272	872

Notes: a Calculated using 1980 agricultural land figures.
  b For Hong Kong and Singapore agricultural land is almost negligible relative to GNP and population.
Sources: International Economic Data Bank, Research School of Pacific Studies, Australian National University; World Bank, *World Tables*, 3rd edn, 1983; Food and Agriculture Organisation of the United Nations *Production Yearbook* 1984; and *Statistical Yearbook of the Republic of China* 1985

Tables 5.1 and 5.2 provide a number of indicators of relative resource endowments and economic growth rates among Pacific countries. Columns (6) to (9) of Table 5.1 show clearly that Australia, Canada, New Zealand, and to a lesser extent the United States, are extremely well endowed with various types of land per head of population. The Northeast Asian industrialising countries and Singapore and Japan have, by contrast, extremely low per capita endowments of land and minerals. Since per capita endowment of land may be taken as a rough proxy for the ratio of agricultural, forest and mineral resources to labour, and also for the structure of comparative advantage in the production of goods based on natural resources, these countries may be expected to have a strong comparative disadvantage in the production of.these goods. Australia, Canada, New Zealand and the United States may be expected to have a strong comparative advantage in producing natural-resource-based goods.[24]

Column (7) of Table 5.1 suggests that Australia and North America are likely to be large suppliers of temperate-zone crops; column (8) suggests that Australia, New Zealand, and to a lesser extent North America, are likely to have large pastoral industries; column (9) suggests that Canada, New Zealand and Papua New Guinea will be relatively large producers of forest products (the Australian woodlands on the whole having lower commercial timber

	Land endowment per capita (ha)			Real GDP growth rate (per cent pa)	Real indust. growth (per cent pa)	Share of GDP exported (per cent)	
Total	Arable	Perm. pasture	Forest/ woods	1970-83	1970-83	1980	1983
(6)	(7)	(8)	(9)	(10)	(11)	(12)	(13)
49.56	3.03	28.95	6.90	2.7	1.0	17.0	17.4
37.02	1.86	0.96	13.09	3.0	2.1	29.3	29.6
8.40	0.15	4.41	3.22	2.1	2.5	29.0	31.2
3.91	0.81	1.03	1.13	2.3	1.6	10.1	8.3
0.31	0.04	0.01	0.21	4.2	5.3	13.9	15.3
0.25	0.05	0.00	0.16	7.4	11.5	33.1	38.0
0.02	—b	—	—	7.9	6.3	87.8	94.5
0.02	—b	—	—	8.2	8.8	208.2	192.2
0.19	0.05	0.00	0.12	8.7	9.8	48.4	49.3
1.16	0.13	0.08	0.78	6.7	6.8	30.5	23.7
2.21	0.29	0.00	1.46	6.9	7.8	59.2	59.7
14.16	0.12	0.03	10.08	1.9	3.0	43.2	45.4
0.57	0.22	0.02	0.23	4.9	6.4	20.2	19.8
1.04	0.39	0.01	0.32	6.1	7.3	24.5	27.5
0.92	0.10	0.28	0.13	5.5	7.6	7.1	7.4

value); and Table 5.2 shows the advantage of Australia, Canada and the United States as regional minerals and energy producers. Table 5.1 shows that other Western Pacific developing countries, including China, retain comparative advantage in agricultural resources vis-à-vis Northeast Asia and Singapore; and Table 5.2 reveals quite large reserves of certain minerals in Southeast Asia in relation to manufacturing output (especially copper, nickel and tin), and hence an ability to achieve strong export specialisation in those minerals. The much higher ratio of GNP to agricultural land in North America than in Australia (column (5) of Table 5.1) suggests Australia's stronger export specialisation in agricultural products. Also, the higher United States output of manufactures and lower endowment of mineral resources in relation to manufacturing output than for Canada or Australia suggest stronger export specialisation in mineral-based products for these two countries. The indicators in Table 5.2 reveal that, among the developing countries in the Pacific, Indonesia, Malaysia and China are relatively well endowed with oil; Indonesia, Malaysia, and Thailand with natural gas (of which Brunei also has large reserves); and China with coal.

It has been pointed out elsewhere[25] that natural-resource endowment is not such a strong determinant of comparative advantage in fishing as it is in other primary goods activities because of access to international waters. Comparative advantage in fisheries products, as in manufactures, depends mainly on other determinants of value added per worker, although a strong demand for fish may produce comparative advantage in production because

Table 5.2 Mineral reserves per capita and per thousand US dollars of industrial output (shown in parentheses) in the Pacific region, 1983

	Copper	Lead	Zinc	Tin	Nickel
Resource-rich countries					
Australia	1 040	1 820	2 530	12	420
	(281)	(492)	(864)	(3)	(114)
Canada	1 330	680	2 240	0	640
	(359)	(184)	(605)	(0)	(173)
New Zealand	—	—	—	—	—
	(—)	(—)	(—)	(—)	(—)
United States	390	110	230	0	10
	(89)	(25)	(52)	(0)	(2)
Resource-poor countries					
Japan	20	—	—	—	—
	(5)	(—)	(—)	(—)	(—)
Republic of Korea	—	—	—	—	—
	(—)	(—)	(—)	(—)	(—)
Taiwan	—	—	—	—	—
	(—)	(—)	(—)	(—)	(—)
Hong Kong	—	—	—	—	—
	(—)	(—)	(—)	(—)	(—)
Singapore	—	—	—	—	—
	(—)	(—)	(—)	(—)	(—)
Other Western Pacific countries					
Indonesia	0	—	—	4	40
	(0)	(—)	(—)	(20)	(200)
Malaysia	40	—	—	74	—
	(57)	(—)	(—)	(106)	(—)
Papua New Guinea	5 020	—	—	—	—
	(26 000)	(—)	(—)	(—)	(—)
Philippines	350	—	—	—	170
	(1 750)	(—)	(—)	(—)	(850)
Thailand	—	—	—	6	—
	(—)	(—)	(—)	(30)	(—)
China	0	0	0	2	0
	(0)	(0)	(0)	(17)	(0)
Pacific total	180	40	80	1	40
	(164)	(36)	(72)	(1)	(36)
World total	110	30	60	1	20
	(115)	(31)	(63)	(1)	(21)
Total Pacific minerals production	4 544	1 422	2 521	115	360
Pacific share of world production (per cent)	55.5	40.6	38.8	59.6	55.6
Total world minerals production	8 192	3 500	6 500	193	647

Notes: All figures are in kilograms except as follows:
- bauxite, iron ore and coal are in tonnes
- oil is in kilolitres
- gas is in thousand cubic metres

All production figures are in thousand tonnes except as follows:
- iron ore, coal and oil are in million tonnes
- gas is in billion cubic metres

0 indicates less than half a unit per capita or industrial output
— indicates no or marginal reserves
u output of centrally planned economies unknown

Sources: US Bureau of Mines *Mineral Commodity Summaries, 1984*; US Bureau of Mines *Commodity Data Summaries, 1984*; Institute of Geological Sciences *World Mineral Statistics 1980-84*; Penwell Publishing Company *International Petroleum Encyclopaedia, 1984*; International Economic Data Bank, Research School of Pacific Studies, Australian National University; Japan Member Committee, Pacific Basin Economic Council *Pacific Economic Community Statistics 1986*; and confidential sources

Cobalt	Bauxite	Iron ore	Coal	Uranium	Oil	Natural gas
6	304.0	1 192	1 752	20.0	17	33
(2)	(82.2)	(322)	(474)	(5.4)	(5)	(9)
11	—	353	67	9.0	42	111
(3)	(—)	(95)	(18)	(2.4)	(11)	(30)
—	—	—	—	—	9	47
(—)	(—)	(—)	(—)	(—)	(4)	(21)
4	0.2	22	471	2.0	19	25
(1)	(5)	(107)	(0.5)	(4)	(6)	
—	—	1	8	0	0	0
(—)	(—)	(0)	(2)	(0)	(0)	(0)
—	—	2	—	0	—	—
(—)	(—)	(2)	(—)	(0)	(—)	(—)
—	—	—	—	—	—	—
(—)	(—)	(—)	(—)	(—)	(—)	(—)
—	—	—	—	—	—	—
(—)	(—)	(—)	(—)	(—)	(—)	(—)
—	—	—	—	—	—	—
(—)	(—)	(—)	(—)	(—)	(—)	(—)
—	4.5	1	0	0	9	5
(—)	(22.5)	(5)	(0)	(0)	(45)	(25)
—	—	6	—	—	36	64
(—)	(—)	(9)	(—)	(—)	(51)	(91)
—	—	—	—	—	—	—
(—)	(—)	(—)	(—)	(—)	(—)	(—)
8	—	2	—	—	0	0
(40)	(—)	(10)	(—)	(—)	(0)	(0)
—	—	—	—	—	0	6
(—)	(—)	(—)	(—)	(—)	(0)	(30)
—	0	6	180	—	3	1
(—)	(0)	(50)	(1500)	(—)	(25)	(8)
2	4.4	25	262	0.5	7	7
(2)	(4.0)	(23)	(238)	(0.5)	(6)	(6)
2	5.0	19	100	0.5	18	15
(2)	(5.2)	(20)	(105)	(0.5)	(19)	(16)
5 330	**45 383**	**373**	**1 680**	**22**	**720**	**590**
28.7	**57.8**	**47.6**	**42.4**	**48.9**u	**27.0**	**36.9**
18 600	**78 563**	**783**	**3 962**	**45**u	**2 662**	**1 600**

assured demand allows economies of scale to be captured. As with agriculture, there is a wide range in the capital intensity of production technologies in the fishing industry, so that even countries with low endowments of capital per worker may enjoy comparative advantage in fisheries production.

The rapid income growth and industrialisation of the resource-poor countries of East Asia suggest growing imports of raw materials for capital-intensive relative to labour-intensive industries, and rising import shares for minerals and metals over agricultural raw materials. In Hong Kong and Singapore, the extreme population densities and relatively high per capita incomes, which indicate

Table 5.3 Pacific trade in minerals and fuels, 1964-66 and 1979-81 (per cent)

	Exports to					
	Australasia		North America		Japan	
Exports from	1964–66	1979–81	1964–66	1979–81	1964–66	1979–81
Australasia						
Oil	33.8	29.8	0.2	3.7	6.6	4.3
Minerals and other fuels	2.0	0.1	0.3	0.2	85.8	71.0
Metals	5.0	3.3	17.4	9.5	17.0	16.7
Total	7.0	3.9	11.8	3.8	32.0	46.0
Intensity	4.1	4.5	0.7	0.2	3.1	3.0
North America						
Oil	2.0	1.1	46.8	59.6	9.3	3.8
Minerals and other fuels	1.7	0.7	45.7	45.6	15.0	16.5
Metals	1.0	0.4	33.4	30.1	7.2	17.4
Total	1.4	0.7	40.3	42.9	10.6	14.4
Intensity	0.7	0.6	1.8	1.7	0.9	0.8
Japan						
Oil	8.1	1.1	9.8	8.1	—	—
Minerals and other fuels	8.8	4.4	15.6	13.5	—	—
Metals	1.0	1.3	39.9	26.4	—	—
Total	2.8	1.8	32.7	22.1	—	—
Intensity	1.5	1.7	1.6	0.9	—	—
China						
Oil	1.6	0.4	0.0	5.6	16.6	60.0
Minerals and other fuels	0.6	0.7	0.0	9.5	65.6	58.2
Metals	0.9	0.7	0.5	21.9	15.7	11.2
Total	0.8	0.4	0.3	7.2	34.9	56.0
Intensity	0.5	0.5	0.0	0.4	3.5	3.6
Asian NICs						
Oil	7.4	11.2	1.7	2.7	9.8	16.4
Minerals and other fuels	0.1	0.2	0.8	0.5	69.6	26.0
Metals	2.7	0.8	4.5	23.6	31.4	17.0
Total	6.0	9.6	2.1	5.0	18.5	16.9
Intensity	3.6	10.7	0.1	0.2	1.8	1.0
Other ASEAN						
Oil	17.5	2.1	13.3	24.1	22.9	47.7
Minerals and other fuels	0.0	4.3	1.2	8.5	95.1	82.0
Metals	1.1	0.1	31.5	16.2	26.4	38.4
Total	7.3	2.1	21.9	20.8	31.0	50.5
Intensity	4.3	2.4	1.2	1.0	3.0	3.2
All Pacific countries						
Oil	7.6	3.7	29.2	25.1	12.5	33.8
Minerals and other fuels	1.7	1.1	40.6	32.4	22.5	33.4
Metals	1.4	0.8	31.1	24.6	11.1	19.6
Total	2.8	2.1	33.7	27.3	15.1	29.9
Intensity	1.1	1.4	1.3	0.8	1.0	1.1
Rest of world						
Oil	1.9	0.8	16.5	19.7	6.1	10.0
Minerals and other fuels	0.4	0.1	9.2	3.1	7.2	12.6
Metals	0.5	0.2	17.4	9.4	4.8	5.3
Total	1.3	0.7	15.7	16.8	5.9	9.8
Intensity	0.3	0.3	0.3	0.4	0.2	0.3

Note: 0.0 indicates figures less than 0.05 per cent.
Source: International Economic Data Bank, Research School of Pacific Studies, Australian National University

China		Asian NICs		Other ASEAN		All Pacific countries		Rest of world	
1964-66	1979-81	1964-66	1979-81	1964-66	1979-81	1964-66	1979-81	1964-66	1979-81
0.0	0.0	6.1	11.4	13.4	13.6	60.1	62.8	39.9	37.2
0.2	1.7	2.5	9.0	2.1	0.7	92.9	82.7	7.1	17.3
0.1	1.6	2.0	5.5	2.7	10.1	44.2	46.7	55.8	53.3
0.1	1.5	2.5	8.0	35	5.2	56.9	68.4	43.1	31.6
0.6	14.6	1.9	1.8	2.6	2.8	1.7	1.6	0.6	0.6
0.0	0.0	1.2	3.5	2.2	1.5	61.5	69.5	38.5	30.5
0.0	0.1	1.1	3.9	0.3	0.5	63.8	67.3	36.2	32.7
0.0	0.5	0.4	2.6	0.4	0.8	42.4	51.8	57.6	48.2
0.0	0.3	0.8	3.4	0.6	0.8	53.7	62.5	46.3	37.5
0.1	1.9	0.5	0.6	0.4	0.3	1.4	1.2	0.6	0.5
0.3	1.3	34.8	41.8	13.9	12.1	66.9	64.4	33.1	35.6
0.4	0.1	32.6	30.9	10.0	10.4	67.4	59.3	32.6	40.7
1.3	2.5	18.8	30.7	12.0	10.5	73.0	71.4	27.0	28.6
1.0	2.0	22.6	32.1	12.2	10.6	71.3	68.6	28.7	31.4
5.1	16.2	15.9	6.1	8.1	5.0	2.0	1.4	0.4	0.5
—	—	1.7	13.2	12.1	10.0	32.0	89.2	68.0	10.8
—	—	8.1	6.7	1.1	3.1	75.4	78.2	24.6	21.8
—	—	2.7	16.3	1.0	3.3	20.8	53.4	79.2	46.6
—	—	4.7	12.8	2.1	8.8	42.8	85.2	57.2	14.8
—	—	3.6	2.9	1.5	4.9	1.3	2.0	0.9	0.3
0.0	0.0	12.1	20.9	11.6	24.4	42.6	75.6	57.4	24.4
0.0	6.2	13.0	26.1	3.2	33.5	86.7	92.5	13.3	7.5
0.1	0.2	5.6	10.8	1.4	8.4	45.7	60.8	54.3	39.2
0.0	0.3	11.2	20.0	9.3	23.0	47.1	74.8	52.9	25.2
0.1	2.8	8.7	4.3	6.8	12.1	1.4	1.7	0.8	0.4
0.0	0.0	20.1	14.5	8.6	3.1	82.4	91.5	17.6	8.5
0.0	0.0	2.7	3.0	0.1	0.5	99.1	98.3	0.9	1.7
0.0	0.4	1.6	10.7	0.4	0.5	61.0	66.3	39.0	33.7
0.0	0.1	8.7	12.4	3.5	2.3	72.4	88.2	27.6	11.8
0.0	0.7	6.7	2.7	2.6	1.3	2.2	2.0	0.4	0.2
0.0	0.0	8.3	13.4	5.9	7.4	63.5	83.4	36.5	16.6
0.0	0.4	1.6	5.3	0.4	1.1	66.8	73.7	33.2	26.3
0.1	0.8	1.5	7.1	1.0	2.9	46.2	55.8	53.8	44.2
0.0	0.4	3.0	9.2	1.8	4.2	56.4	73.1	43.6	26.9
0.1	2.0	1.6	1.2	0.9	1.3	1.2	1.0	0.4	0.3
0.0	0.0	2.0	5.8	0.9	1.8	27.4	38.1	72.6	61.9
0.3	0.1	0.2	0.5	0.2	0.3	17.5	16.7	82.5	83.3
0.7	0.5	0.1	1.0	0.2	0.3	23.7	16.7	76.3	83.3
0.3	0.1	1.2	4.7	0.6	1.5	25.0	33.6	75.0	66.4
0.5	0.3	0.3	0.5	0.1	0.4	0.3	0.3	0.4	0.5

larger endowments of human capital per worker and hence comparative advantage in human-capital-intensive industries such as tradable services, lead to an expectation that these countries' import demand for natural-resource-based goods will be concentrated in foodstuffs rather than in industrial raw materials.

This picture of the structure of regional comparative advantages in natural-resource-based goods viewed from the supply side is reinforced if demand-side factors are also taken into account. Column (5) of Table 5.1 and the data on mineral resources relative to manufacturing output presented in parentheses in Table 5.2 show that the resource-poor countries have high incomes per unit of agricultural land and high manufacturing outputs per unit of mineral resources compared with the resource-rich countries and the rest of the region.

PACIFIC TRADE IN MINERALS AND ENERGY

The dimensions and structure of Pacific trade in natural-resource-based products reflect these underlying regional comparative advantages. About 67 per cent of all the externally derived food and agricultural raw materials needs of the countries of the Pacific are drawn from within the region itself. For minerals and fuels the proportion is 28 per cent. If oil is excluded the share is much higher, at 61 per cent. Indeed, the five advanced industrial countries in the Pacific, with little exception, obtain around half of their basic mineral import requirements from among themselves.[26] Crude petroleum alone is still largely sourced outside the region. Again, 56 per cent of the world's low-cost uranium reserves are located in the Pacific, the only major alternative supplier being South Africa. If uranium, coal and gas are taken as intermediate-term oil substitutes in electricity generation, to a remarkable extent the resource supply problems of Pacific countries have a sharply regional focus.

The *diversity* of raw materials resources, the *scale of reserves* throughout the Pacific and the economics of *proximity* dictate an extremely heavy concentration of raw materials trade within the region itself. The intensity of intra-Pacific trade in minerals is much higher than it is even for commodity trade in general.[27]

Table 5.2 provides an overview of the importance of Pacific countries in world mineral reserves in relation to manufacturing output. The overall picture of Pacific mineral reserves and output reflects the endowments of the three large, resource-rich industrial countries of the region — Australia, Canada and the United States — and, for specific products such as oil, gas, tin, nickel and coal, the endowments of particular countries in Southeast Asia and China. The picture for the trade of the region as a whole is heavily influenced by the Japan's position as by far the largest importer of raw materials in the world and, to a lesser extent, by the trade in raw materials within the highly integrated North American economy. These structural features of Pacific trade in minerals, metals and fuels are set out in Table 5.3.

Three significant general characteristics of the resource economy of the Pacific deserve note. One is that the Pacific region's proportion of world mineral reserves is high in relation to its proportion of world output of minerals. Table 5.2 reveals a relatively high utilisation of tin, nickel and bauxite reserves; but for other minerals utilisation is lower than in other parts of the world. The Pacific region as a whole has a rich endowment of mineral reserves, and there is considerable scope for its further exploitation as industrialisation proceeds within the region. This is not uniformly the case for energy reserves. Although the share of oil reserves is low relative to output, coal, uranium and other energy resources are abundant. In addition to the energy resources quantified in these tables, the Pacific includes a vast tropical belt in which hydro-power and other natural energy sources have a rich potential for further development.

Another significant characteristic is the large Pacific share in world minerals trade relative to its share in world minerals output. Raw materials are a very large component in Pacific economic integration. While Pacific minerals trade dependence is high, the only product for which the region as a whole remains a substantial net importer is crude oil.

Finally, the Pacific region's share in world metals trade is low relative to its share in world trade in unprocessed minerals. This feature of the Pacific resource economy is suggestive of the scope for further economisation in resource use within the region through the transformation of energy and costly-to-transport minerals into larger trades in metal manufactures.

The pattern of resource endowments within the Pacific region is reflected clearly in the geographic structure of minerals and energy trade depicted in Table 5.3. Northeast Asia is deficient in minerals and energy, as well as in agricultural land, relative to its industrial base.[28] Japan stands out from other East Asian countries in the sheer scale of its dependence on imported resources. The United States is both an exporter and an importer of minerals and energy, a consequence of particular resource availabilities and their location within the United States in relation to consumption centres there and the location of alternative supplies across national boundaries and overseas.[29] In Southeast Asia, Singapore alone is obviously deficient in raw materials, and the island nation's trade specialisation is strongly influenced by its role as an oil refining centre. In other respects, the structure of Singapore's trade is much more sophisticated than that of other industrial countries in the region, involving the importation of large quantities of manufactured or processed materials.[30] China's position is ambiguous; it has a large and scattered resource base, and is poised to begin economic modernisation.[31]

Table 5.3 also reveals the ascendancy of Australia as a raw materials supplier over the past 25 years.[32] The extensive raw materials trade between Australia and Japan was a crucial element in facilitating Japan's heavy industrialisation, and it remains a cornerstone in the network of international economic relations upon which Japan's industrial economy is founded. Australia currently provides between 40 per cent and 50 per cent of the raw materials for Japan's key base metals industries. In 1983 Japanese imports accounted for 45 per cent of the value of world market economy trade in iron ore, with Australian exports accounting for 22 per cent. Australia supplied 42 per cent of Japan's total iron ore import requirements. For coal, Japan imported 38 per cent of traded world market economy supplies and Australia exported 28 per cent of those supplies and provided 46 per cent of Japan's import needs. Australia supplied 54 per cent of Japan's import requirements for bauxite and alumina and 33 per cent of world imports. As a result of these developments in Australia–

Japan trade, Australia has emerged as the world's largest producer of bauxite and alumina, the third-largest producer (after the Soviet Union and Brazil) of iron ore (in terms of ferric content), and the third-largest producer of nickel. Although Australia's production of coal is a relatively small part of world production, it is now the world's largest coal exporter. In addition, Australia continues to be an important supplier of products which once dominated its mineral exports (such as copper, lead, zinc, gold and mineral sands), and of recent new discoveries (uranium and natural gas); and opportunities for trade (in steaming coal) offer the prospect of a still larger and more diversified role in world minerals and energy trade.[33]

SECURITY AND THE STRUCTURE OF MINERALS MARKETS

The growth of this vast trade in resources within the Pacific, and between Australia and Japan in particular, was built upon long-term contracting arrangements. The experience of Australia and Japan is of considerable interest in this respect, since it is the operation of these arrangements which has provided the main element of security in market access and supplies that was critical to the development of the trade.[34]

Security of access to sources of raw materials for minerals processors in industrial countries has historically been achieved through direct ownership of 'captive' mines.[35] Processing facilities were located in industrialised countries, so that a substantial international trade in unprocessed or semi-processed minerals developed within vertically integrated operations of the companies involved. Significantly, this has been the dominant pattern for Japan's securing of raw materials from the Pacific to service its rapid heavy industrialisation over the past two decades.[36]

Trade arrangements between independent sellers and buyers characterised the critical resource trade between Australia and Japan, not as a deliberate consequence of policy choice but rather as a result of practical necessity. Rapid industrial growth during the 1960s required Japanese users of basic mineral products to seek large new supplies from overseas sources.[37] Lack of expertise in exploration and mining, a preoccupation with the rapid expansion of processing capacity at home, restrictions on capital export for balance-of-payments reasons, and the immense scale of raw material requirements, led Japanese importers to look for supplies from independent producers rather than attempt to secure them by direct investment.[38] At the same time, large new mineral deposits had been discovered in Australia and opened for development by companies with the expertise and access to capital necessary to permit efficient production.[39] Although many of these companies were subsidiaries of European and North American companies, distance from the Atlantic market and a lack of sufficient demand largely prevented mines from being operated as captive sources of raw materials for their overseas parent companies, so that development depended crucially on sales to independent purchasers in East Asia.[40]

Tying mine development and production to the needs of particular processors may have significant advantages, yet ownership and control of mining by overseas purchasers of minerals creates difficulties for the countries where the mines are located. There is first the question of whether the rate of exploitation of deposits reflects foreign corporation views of what is optimal rather than national views. More importantly, vertically integrated enterprises can transfer profits between mining and processing activities by adjusting the price at which they 'sell' minerals to themselves; and while, in principle, taxation authorities in the host country have the power to deal with this problem, in practice it creates considerable difficulties in the effective collection of natural-resource rents by governments. The assessment for taxation purposes of appropriate transfer prices is made virtually impossible by the general absence of free markets for many basic minerals with which price comparisons could be made, and by the wide divergence in extraction costs governing the value of ore from any given source. For these reasons, governments of resource-rich countries may want ownership and control of mining to be independent of overseas purchases of mine output, even when their general attitude favours foreign investment in the mining sector and in the rest of the economy. Where there is also nationalistic hostility towards foreign investment, it is likely to be particularly strong against foreign investment in resource industries, and to lead to a desire for independent national ownership. In either case, there will be a need to establish trade arrangements between independent sellers and buyers of mineral products to give both sides the security which might otherwise have been provided through vertical integration.[41]

In the absence of ownership ties between Japanese minerals purchasers and the major Australian exporters, long-term supply contracts were negotiated to provide both sides with security of market access. Subsequently, this pattern of trading between independent suppliers and purchasers under long-term contracts has characterised much of both Japan's and Australia's minerals trade with other countries. European purchasers of some minerals also moved towards contractual guarantees as a means of securing access to future sources of supply.[42] And the new mines on the west coast of North America to service the Pacific market have been developed on the same basis.[43]

Most mining operations involve extracting and transporting materials which are of relatively low value to weight. Thus, the capacity to exploit economies of scale in production and transportation is crucial in determining economic viability. The development of mines capable of producing on a large enough scale in turn involves massive capital expenditure, much of which is on assets whose economic value depends wholly on the success of the mine, and there is a lead time of several years before any ore is shipped.

In these circumstances, a free world market for mine output would not provide an efficient mechanism for generating appropriate levels of investment in mining. The uncertainties surrounding a decision to proceed with a new mine, without a defined market and without knowledge of the production plans of potential competitors, would effectively deter new mining investment.

The lumpiness of increments to mine output, and the long lead times involved, require a mechanism which controls the timing and allocation of new investments. Thus consumers of basic mineral products must signal in advance the need for particular mineral deposits to be developed, either by undertaking new mining developments themselves or by guaranteeing to purchase a substantial proportion of the output from those developments. The result is a substantial reduction in the risk associated with investment in mining, and consequently a higher level of output and trade as well as lower prices for mineral raw materials.[44]

The concentration of minerals trade between particular producers and consumers has had the further advantage that it allows the exploitation of economies of scale in shipping and other transactions costs. Shipping costs for basic minerals generally represent a very substantial proportion of their landed value, and the ability to use bulk shipping on a planned long-term basis offers the chance of significant cost savings.[45]

There are also often strong technological reasons for tying processing operations to the output of particular mines. In bauxite processing, for instance, ore from different mines sometimes differs sufficiently to require specific design variations in processing plants which limit or even preclude substitution between alternative sources of supply, especially in the shorter term. In other cases, such as steel production, where the overall characteristics of the feedstock are achieved by blending ores from different sources, some intra-blend substitution is possible; but it is limited, at least to some extent, by the need to keep the characteristics of the feedstock close to those for which the plant is designed.[46]

The effect of these factors is to create a strong incentive for processing and mining to be developed jointly and for their operations to be closely linked thereafter. For most mineral raw materials, therefore, the bulk of world trade is tied up in contractual arrangements of one kind or another, or is conducted within the vertically integrated operations of multinational enterprises.

Once established, this trade structure tends to be self-perpetuating, continuing in some degree independently of the economic and technological factors at its base. The absence of a continuous and free market for most basic minerals means that any enterprise wishing to develop new mining or processing operations or to expand existing operations must also secure a market or supply source for mineral raw materials.[47] Hence, although the levels of investment in exploration, the delineation of deposits and mining feasibility studies are necessarily based on mining company expectations about potential markets, heavy development expenditures are not normally undertaken until contracts covering the bulk of the planned output for a number of years ahead have been concluded. In this situation, the levels of investment in mining, and the sequence of mine development, are determined directly by the requirements of processors. Given the large scale of modern mining, a single processing company may not be capable of contracting to take the full output of a new mine, nor prepared to accept the level of dependence on a single supply source that this would entail. Development will then depend on contracts being written with a number of purchasers at the same time, and consortium purchasing of minerals is commonly organised in these circumstances.[48]

In brief, the structure of international minerals markets is shaped by the special characteristics of minerals products and the technology involved in their production and distribution. The pervasive imperfection in minerals markets is a consequence of imperfect substitutability between the 'same' minerals from different sources, economies of scale in mining and processing, and the associated lumpiness in new capacity. In these conditions, new mining projects or new processing operations cannot commence without the demonstrated availability of a market for, or supply source of, the new mineral raw material. Once a particular pairing of mining and processing operations is established, the two parties to the minerals trade become, to some extent at least, locked into the bilateral trade relationship by technological considerations.

Quite apart from political security aspects, then, a characteristic of the minerals trade generally is its susceptibility to the appearance of some conflict of interests around these elements of monopolistic or monopsonistic power. Effective minerals trade cooperation thus requires contractual institutions which allow the management of these elements with sufficient ease. These characteristics of the minerals and fuels trade, which are purely economic and technological in character, underline the importance of the conclusions of chapter 2 about the role of cooperative arrangements in facilitating efficient trade specialisation. The international political environment within which resource trade is conducted greatly complicates conflicts of interest around 'this trade and adds further weight to these conclusions.

The overwhelming reason for the development of long-term contracts in the minerals trade was the concern for security of market access, coupled with the economic and technological advantages of tying mine production to the requirements of specific processors. The arrangements that have evolved around the Australia–Japan minerals trade now provide the essential security for much of the region's resource trade. The advantages of long-term contracts in this trade were that export quantities were guaranteed within reasonable margins for a relatively long period, and that the price was fixed to ensure the profitability of resource developments. At the same time, Japanese purchasers were guaranteed long-term access to large supplies of highly valued raw materials at prices which allowed them to maintain a competitive position in metals markets. While the adequacy of contractual guarantees was called into question by the effects of exchange-rate changes, by high rates of inflation, and by the difficulties of Japanese purchasers in meeting their contractual commitments during the recessions of the 1970s and 1980s, they continue to provide a broadly cooperative long-term institutional framework for the conduct of the minerals trade.[49] However, the challenges to these purely commercial arrangements — in producer countries in a period of resource market tightness and in consumer countries in a period of prolonged recession

— have raised questions about the adequacy of the policy framework covering these crucial resource trade flows.

The long-term contract relationship provides a degree of quasi-vertical integration between mineral producers and processors. The interdependence of the parties and the long lead times before alternative trade options can be exercised give each a substantial interest in the viability of the other.[50] An important characteristic of the conduct of the Australia–Japan minerals trade has been a willingness to seek compromise solutions when the formal terms of the contract have created significant difficulties for one party. This is an important ingredient for reliability in trades where there is, in the nature of things, some element of bilateral monopoly power, and where shifts in the balance of that power over time might otherwise encourage disruptive market behaviour. The Japanese coal trade with North American partners exhibited some of these problems in the commodity boom of the early 1970s. In the 1980s a fall in the demand for raw materials saw the emergence of buyer pressure to weaken contractual ties. In the 1970s concern about meeting forecast Japanese energy demand encouraged commitments to large-scale new investment in energy projects throughout the Pacific. New coal mines were opened up in Australia, China and North America, and large new gas fields were tapped. Some of these projects (in Canada and China) were heavily subsidised through different forms of Japanese concessional financing.[51] In the event, energy demand forecasts were not realised, and throughout the 1980s there has been intense competition for market share in an oversupplied market for energy (particularly coal). In these circumstances, low-cost established suppliers of coal in Australia and elsewhere have been under intense competitive pressure as Japanese consumers have tried to honour their commitments to new (and often high-cost) project developments. Over-investment in the energy industry over these years certainly adversely affected the terms of trade for energy exporters.

Rightly or not, exporters sometimes suspect that the supply security interest of importers leads then to contract to purchase quantities that will meet their *maximum* possible demand, with the result that excess mine capacity is developed. A view that exporters have thus been placed at a bargaining disadvantage can motivate government intervention in exporting countries.[52] The exercise of export controls, with the implied threat to withhold supplies, will only reinforce the concerns of importers about supply security.

In any case, the cost of Japan's diversification strategy to Japanese taxpayers, and in terms of inefficient resource use, was considerable.[53] Hence greater sharing of information on projections of supply and demand and on the nature of, and motivation for, policies affecting minerals developments and trade is capable of increasing mutual confidence and advantage in minerals and energy trade relations.[54] The reliable-supplier/reliable-buyer feature of long-term contracting in the minerals trade is a key aspect of resource and energy trade security within the Pacific.

To some extent, the integrative nature of long-term contracts and the stable cooperative relationship that they foster between the companies involved also provide a vehicle for rational joint decisions on the efficient location of processing facilities throughout the Pacific region.[55] As Japanese plant needs replacement or as additional capacity is needed, minerals producers can press for processing facilities located outside Japan.[56] It has become increasingly attractive for metals manufacturing to be undertaken, for example, in Australia or Southeast Asia, with Japanese manufacturing industry providing the main market.[57] One avenue to effecting this change in production patterns is expanding the established relations between Japanese, Australian, American and other companies already involved in long-term contracting of raw materials. In the aluminium industry, joint-venture arrangements by multinational consortiums have been a complementary mechanism for the efficient relocation of minerals processing capacity within the Pacific region.[58]

FOOD AND AGRICULTURAL TRADE SECURITY

The distribution of agricultural resources within the Pacific closely parallels that of minerals and energy. The extreme differences in underlying resource endowment provide a strong incentive for heavy specialisation in agricultural production and trade, and are in turn the cause of extreme import-dependence in food and agricultural raw materials among the resource-poor countries of Northeast Asia. Table 5.1 provides a synopsis of the pattern of agricultural resource endowment and the spread of industrialisation in relation to population distribution within the Pacific region.[59] To recapitulate, the per capita endowment of total land, agricultural land and forest land (which can be taken as proxies for the ratios of mineral, agricultural and forest resources to labour on the supply side) and the distribution of GNP per agricultural hectare (which can be taken as indicating the relative strength of demand for agricultural commodities) confirm the strong comparative disadvantage of the rapidly industrialising countries of Northeast Asia and the city states of Hong Kong and Singapore in agricultural and minerals production.[60] The very high population densities of Hong Kong and Singapore and their relatively high per capita incomes (which are an index of human and organisational capital abundance) suggest a concentration of their resource imports in foodstuffs rather than industrial raw materials.[61] The relative growth rates of gross domestic product and industrial output indicate the pressures on resource supplies and the potential for expanding imports of raw materials and food.

Table 5.4 describes the structure of food and agricultural trade within the Pacific region. As with minerals and energy, Japan is a central factor in the agricultural trade in the Pacific. Japan's industrialisation has proceeded further than that of other resource-deficient countries in the region, and its agricultural trade dependence is already large. Japan's overall agricultural self-sufficiency, measured in terms of original calories, stands at 54 per cent.[62] This is lower than the figure for other food-trade-dependent industrial countries: the ratio for the United Kingdom is presently around 60 per cent.[63] South Korea, Taiwan, Hong Kong and, of course, Singapore are also now less able to sustain agricultural self-sufficiency consistently with the pursuit of industrial growth, and their imports of food and other agricultural products have been growing rapidly. South Korea and Taiwan have switched from agricultural exporting to being significant agricultural importers over the past decade.[64]

Table 5.4 reveals trade flows consistent with the predictions of the theory of comparative advantage, although trade intensity is inhibited by agricultural trade barriers, as was pointed out in chapter 4. One striking fact that emerges from the data in this table is the strength of the Pacific as an exporter of food and agricultural raw materials. By 1979–81 Pacific countries accounted for 40 per cent of world exports of these commodities but took only 26 per cent of world imports. The position of the Pacific as a net exporter of food products was very similar.

The weight of Japan in regional food and agricultural imports dominates Pacific agricultural trade flows, but the share of the newly industrialising countries of East Asia, especially in agricultural raw materials trade, is also substantial and increasing. The structure of these trade flows is, of course, greatly influenced by the nature of agricultural trade barriers as well as by natural comparative advantage. A noteworthy feature of the relative shares of resource-exporting countries in the Western Pacific market is the past strength of Australia's position. The share of Australia's resource exports going to resource-poor East Asian countries has been much greater than the share of Canada's or New Zealand's exports going to these countries. While New Zealand is rapidly increasing the share of its export trade with resource-poor East Asian countries as it adjusts to the reality of poor growth prospects in its traditional European markets, the continuing small share of Canada's exports to these countries reflects the high transport-cost resistances to trade across the Pacific as compared with trade into the United States and Europe.

More detailed commodity trade data not presented in this overview table are of interest.[65] In 1980 the Pacific accounted for 14 per cent of world wheat imports; 77 per cent of food grains; 21 per cent of beef; 46 per cent of world timber imports; 24 per cent of wool; and 40 per cent of rubber. The Pacific delivers 75 per cent of world wheat exports; 63 per cent of world rice exports; 70 per cent of coarse grain exports; 28 per cent of beef exports; 46 per cent of world timber exports; 52 per cent of world wool exports; and 72 per cent of world rubber exports.

Over the past few decades world cereal trade has grown at 6.4 per cent a year, almost double the rate of growth of production. Notably, there has been a marked increase in East Asia's net cereal imports, mostly because of the rapid expansion of demand in Japan, China and South Korea.[66] In Japan (the world's largest importer of cereals) and South Korea these cereal imports have met direct consumption needs as well as the rapidly growing demand for livestock feeds which has accompanied industrial development. Until the 1980s, the growth in food trade demand in Asia, combined with growth in imports to Europe, the Soviet Union and Africa, was to a large extent met by expanded North American and Australian supplies. Within the Pacific basin lie the world's most rapidly growing staple grain markets as well as its three lowest-cost cereal exporters.[67] While the net trade of the Southeast Asian countries is not a significant influence on world cereals trade, their share in world exports has also grown somewhat.

The Pacific is a substantial net exporter of food and agricultural raw materials to the rest of the world, and has the agricultural capacity not only to sustain current food consumption but also to support considerably enlarged production of food and agricultural raw materials so long as agricultural trade growth is guaranteed.[68] Security in food and agricultural raw materials is a primary concern for the resource-deficient countries of the region, and reliable access to stable markets is a primary need of the major agricultural exporters of the Pacific. The structure of resource endowments within the Pacific requires that food and agricultural raw materials security be built upon a large agricultural trade.

The collective policy commitments necessary for adequate food and agricultural trade security are not yet strongly entrenched among Pacific countries, as was borne out in the experience of the 1970s. In particular, the United States' embargo on the export of soybean in 1973 had profoundly disturbing effects on Japan and other food importers in Northeast Asia.[69] No account was taken in the policymaking process in the United States (a major agricultural exporter) of the effects of this policy measure on customers almost solely dependent on external supplies of a key food product, nor of the interaction effects of the measure on reliability in agricultural trade relations more generally.[70] The soybean embargo, shortages of food and agricultural raw materials, and the general food price hike in 1972–74 produced sharp trade policy reactions in Japan and other countries, all of which eroded confidence in international sourcing of food and agricultural supplies.

One response in Japan was to ban the importation of beef, ostensibly to stimulate domestic beef production and stabilise domestic prices, following domestic political demands that Japan should aim for lower dependence on outside sources of supply in order to achieve greater security of food supplies.[71] The sharpness of Japan's response to domestic pressures for self-sufficiency created serious problems for agricultural suppliers, especially the pastoral industry in Australia. The developments in agricultural trade in the 1970s gave a fillip to policies directed at inefficient agricultural self-sufficiency, not only in Japan but in other East Asian countries. They underlined the fragility of food security based on trade in an agricultural trade policy environment in which there appeared to be very few constraints on the short-term pursuit of narrow, sectionally directed policy interests.[72] The agricultural trade subsidy war between Europe and the United States, and American concern about market access for agricultural output, have introduced a new element of fragility into the trade of low-cost agricultural producers; but they have also elevated agriculture (not least Japanese agriculture) to the international trade bargaining table.[73]

For Southeast Asia, a critical element in food security is the management of the rice market. A rice export embargo imposed by Thailand on its Southeast Asian trading partners in the 1970s had effects similar to those of the United

Table 5.4   Pacific trade in food and agricultural goods, 1964–66 and 1979–81 (per cent)

Exports from	Exports to Australasia		North America		Japan	
	1964–66	1979–81	1964–66	1979–81	1964–66	1979–81
Australasia						
Food grains	2.6	0.6	0.1	0.0	9.4	11.8
Other foodstuffs	1.2	2.2	22.0	29.7	5.9	19.2
Agricultural raw materials	1.4	3.5	11.0	4.1	22.9	21.4
Total	1.5	2.3	14.2	15.9	14.3	18.5
Intensity	1.5	3.0	0.9	1.3	1.9	1.7
North America						
Food grains	0.0	0.0	4.9	1.2	11.2	13.1
Other foodstuffs	0.7	1.2	32.3	26.5	3.5	17.9
Agricultural raw materials	1.8	1.1	23.4	16.6	14.1	17.4
Total	1.0	0.8	18.8	13.3	11.2	16.1
Intensity	0.9	0.9	1.1	0.9	1.3	1.3
Japan						
Food grains	2.1	0.3	28.4	2.9	—	—
Other foodstuffs	2.7	2.9	36.0	22.2	—	—
Agricultural raw materials	2.8	2.0	21.7	3.8	—	—
Total	2.7	2.2	29.8	11.6	—	—
Intensity	2.6	2.6	1.8	0.8	—	—
China						
Food grains	0.0	0.4	0.0	1.3	29.5	1.7
Other foodstuffs	0.6	1.2	0.8	4.5	12.5	19.9
Agricultural raw materials	1.6	0.6	0.8	8.9	24.1	28.3
Total	0.9	0.9	0.7	6.0	20.0	22.1
Intensity	0.9	1.2	0.0	0.5	2.6	2.0
Asian NICs						
Food grains	0.1	0.8	1.8	5.9	56.7	3.2
Other foodstuffs	1.2	1.5	14.0	13.0	30.3	40.8
Agricultural raw materials	4.1	2.2	11.5	10.2	7.9	12.8
Total	2.5	1.8	12.0	11.6	21.8	27.2
Intensity	2.5	2.3	0.8	0.9	2.8	2.4
Other ASEAN						
Food grains	0.0	0.0	0.0	0.5	21.2	3.2
Other foodstuffs	1.5	2.1	54.9	18.5	6.4	21.3
Agricultural raw materials	1.3	1.3	17.8	10.9	20.3	24.1
Total	1.2	1.4	21.8	12.0	18.1	21.5
Intensity	1.2	1.9	1.4	0.9	2.4	2.0
All Pacific countries						
Food grains	0.3	0.1	4.0	1.1	12.8	12.0
Other foodstuffs	1.1	1.7	27.7	22.2	7.0	21.2
Agricultural raw materials	1.8	1.4	19.0	13.5	16.4	18.6
Total	1.2	1.2	17.6	13.0	13.1	17.8
Intensity	0.9	1.0	0.8	0.7	1.2	1.1
Rest of world						
Food grains	0.1	0.1	1.4	0.8	1.6	0.7
Other foodstuffs	0.8	0.5	20.6	11.9	0.9	2.4
Agricultural raw materials	0.8	0.3	8.5	3.5	3.9	2.4
Total	0.8	0.4	14.4	8.4	2.1	2.2
Intensity	0.2	0.2	0.3	0.2	0.1	0.1

Note: 0.0 indicates figures less than 0.05 per cent.
Source: International Economic Data Bank, Research School of Pacific Studies, Australian National University

States soybean embargo. In the 1980s the threat was from American subsidisation of rice exports. Shortages or rapid changes in the price of rice can be the cause of major political disturbance, and governments are naturally concerned to guard against capricious external determinants of political

China		Asian NICs		Other ASEAN		All Pacific countries		Rest of world	
1964-66	1979-81	1964-66	1979-81	1964-66	1979-81	1964-66	1979-81	1964-66	1979-81
30.5	12.9	3.7	5.6	4.4	8.0	50.7	38.9	49.3	61.1
0.0	1.6	1.2	7.5	4.7	6.0	35.0	66.2	65.0	33.8
1.4	4.8	1.5	7.8	0.4	1.6	38.6	43.2	61.4	56.8
4.3	4.8	1.6	7.2	2.6	5.0	38.5	53.7	61.5	46.3
3.2	2.7	0.6	1.3	1.7	2.7	1.3	1.6	0.9	0.7
3.9	7.7	2.0	6.9	1.5	2.1	23.5	31.0	76.5	69.0
0.0	0.0	2.4	4.5	1.8	1.2	40.7	51.3	59.3	48.7
0.0	3.3	3.2	7.3	1.4	1.9	43.9	47.6	56.1	52.4
1.3	4.2	2.6	6.7	1.5	1.8	36.4	42.9	63.6	57.1
0.8	2.0	0.8	1.0	0.8	0.9	1.1	1.1	0.8	0.8
0.0	0.0	4.3	54.4	2.4	15.5	37.2	73.1	62.8	26.9
0.0	0.0	4.9	18.8	4.5	6.2	48.1	50.1	51.9	49.9
6.2	11.9	15.7	28.3	4.3	10.8	50.7	56.8	49.3	43.2
2.6	5.7	9.5	26.9	4.4	9.3	49.0	55.7	51.0	44.3
1.8	2.8	3.1	4.3	2.7	4.5	1.5	1.5	0.7	0.6
—	—	20.8	49.2	11.4	10.1	61.7	62.7	38.3	37.3
—	—	43.5	36.5	8.5	5.2	65.9	67.3	34.1	32.7
—	—	10.0	19.5	1.9	3.6	38.4	60.9	61.6	39.1
—	—	26.4	30.6	6.3	4.8	54.3	64.4	45.7	35.6
—	—	9.1	5.3	4.1	2.6	1.8	1.9	0.6	0.5
0.0	0.1	4.4	7.7	1.6	47.0	64.6	64.7	35.4	35.3
0.1	0.1	5.7	8.3	1.3	8.1	52.6	71.8	47.4	28.2
4.7	3.1	3.5	10.8	1.1	7.7	32.8	46.8	67.2	53.2
2.2	1.5	4.6	9.4	1.2	9.0	44.3	60.5	55.7	39.5
1.6	0.8	1.6	1.6	0.8	4.6	1.5	1.7	0.8	0.6
0.0	3.3	24.3	16.9	14.0	21.9	59.5	45.8	40.5	54.2
0.4	1.4	11.9	13.7	0.7	3.5	75.8	60.5	24.2	39.5
2.0	2.0	13.1	26.0	0.7	1.8	55.2	66.1	44.8	33.9
1.5	2.0	14.3	22.0	2.3	4.0	59.2	62.9	40.8	37.1
1.1	1.1	4.9	3.8	1.4	2.1	2.0	1.9	0.6	0.6
5.9	7.7	4.2	8.4	2.8	4.5	30.0	33.8	70.0	66.2
0.0	0.6	6.3	10.3	3.2	4.1	45.3	60.1	54.7	39.9
1.0	3.3	5.3	12.1	1.2	2.5	44.7	51.4	55.3	48.6
1.9	3.6	5.3	10.8	2.1	3.4	41.2	49.8	58.8	50.2
1.0	1.3	1.3	1.3	1.0	1.2	1.0	1.0	0.6	0.5
6.2	1.1	0.9	0.5	2.3	0.4	12.5	3.6	87.5	96.4
0.1	0.1	0.5	0.6	0.7	0.5	23.6	16.0	76.4	84.0
1.6	1.6	1.2	1.4	0.3	0.5	16.3	9.7	83.7	90.3
1.2	0.6	0.8	0.8	0.7	0.5	20.0	12.9	80.0	87.1
0.3	0.1	0.1	0.1	0.1	0.1	0.2	0.1	0.4	0.4

instability.[74] Food security in these terms will often be bought at a very high price. The countries of the Association of Southeast Asian Nations (ASEAN) have taken the first steps towards a sub-regional collective approach to emergency food security,[75] but there is still only limited cooperation among these countries and other rice producers in Asia and the Pacific on defining policy directed at stabilising and developing of the regional rice market.

Free trade in food products has never been effectively guaranteed within the GATT multilateral trading system, although the GATT has provided an important measure of support for the growth of food trade in the postwar period. Trade in agricultural raw materials has been much less subject to arbitrary intervention. The common view that food-producing agriculture was in some sense 'special' meant that the major industrial traders and importers of temperate-zone foodstuffs felt more or less free to ignore the rules encouraging trade liberalisation.[76] Substantial waivers were granted on agricultural commodities; breaches of the rules were tolerated; state trading arrangements concealed extensive systems of agricultural protectionism; and in the case of the European Common Agricultural Policy (CAP) ingenious efforts were made to demonstrate the consistency of highly protective import levies within the formal rules, if not the spirit, of the GATT.[77] A number of major food products were covered by international agreements which aimed to underwrite market access to some degree, but international commodity arrangements in various forms were directed mainly at improving trade stability rather than at trade liberalisation. Moreover, there was little room for manoeuvre in bargaining about agricultural trade interests.

Until the Kennedy Round of Multilateral Trade Negotiations (1964–67) introduced agriculture into the general process of trade bargaining, the focus had been confined to bargaining between exporters and importers of the same commodity, and that left little room for progress with agricultural trade liberalisation. The Kennedy Round represented the first attempt to negotiate a package in which concessions within commodity arrangements on market access and prices were to be balanced by concessions given elsewhere, but little advance was made in these negotiations.[78] Agriculture was foreshadowed to be a central factor in the Tokyo Round of Multilateral Trade Negotiations (1973–79), but progress there on general agricultural trade liberalisation was hampered by the play of bilateral bargaining, and the status quo on agricultural trade remained.[79] In fact, the extension of Europe's agricultural trade subsidisation subsequently exacerbated agricultural trade problems. Throughout the postwar period, bilateral arrangements have provided the main security of market access and supply in food trade, and these arrangements have been heavily directed by the interests of industrial importing countries in managing agricultural support schemes. In consequence, international markets for many agricultural commodities assume the character of residual markets, and trade outside established bilateral arrangements is highly volatile.[80]

The product characteristics and market structure of the trade in agricultural commodities, which differ markedly from those of the trade in minerals, make private long-term contracting of food supplies a less convenient instrument for food than for minerals and energy trade security. Long-term contracting is virtually non-existent in the markets for the main food commodities (with the minor exception of grain trade with China and the Middle East), although it has recently emerged as an important mechanism for securing supplies and market access in the sugar trade.[81]

The sugar trade illustrates some of the difficulties, as well as the interest, in long-term contracting in agricultural markets.[82] Historically, world trade in sugar has been heavily regulated by multilateral, bilateral and unilateral arrangements, and only a small proportion of production is traded in the free market. As trade in sugar has grown with rising incomes and consumption in East Asia over the past two decades, the Pacific region has come to comprise an important segment of the free market. The sharp price rises in the early 1970s, however, induced an extension of bilateral agreements between major consumers and overseas suppliers, and government-supported long-term contracts were secured by Australian suppliers throughout the region (at prices which later appeared to have been an overreaction to uncertain world supply conditions in the middle 1970s) to guarantee stable market access and growth. The structural inhibitions on market switching when market circumstances reverse are not as strongly present in agricultural as in mineral trades. Purely private long-term contracting cannot provide the security under these circumstances that it can in minerals, so that government-to-government or government-sponsored arrangements (frequently bilateral) have sought to sustain the stabilising and trade-enlarging roles of long-term contracting in agricultural trades.[83]

The underlying strength and efficiency of agricultural exporters in the Pacific will enable them to take advantage of future market openings where they arise. However, even though new agricultural markets in the Pacific and Asia are likely to emerge and will not initially be bound by the traditional and comprehensive agricultural support arrangements of Europe or even North America, political fears about agricultural trade dependence in these countries make the scale of trade growth and the shape of agricultural protectionism uncertain, and significant matters for negotiation and definition.[84] There is a clear interest in limiting future growth in agricultural protection as regional incomes rise and food consumption and agricultural trade possibilities expand. In 20 years from now, the per capita income for the whole East Asian region could be roughly half the average in industrial economies, on reasonably conservative growth assumptions. These projections imply significant opportunities for growth in agricultural markets.

One approach is for negotiation to take place on a bilateral basis within the Pacific, and to encompass general bargaining across a range of matters in overall bilateral relationships.[85] This has recently been the pattern between the United States and Japan and Australia and Japan, as well as between the less powerful non-temperate-zone agricultural exporters of Southeast Asia and their industrial neighbours.[86] But this is a far from satisfactory solution to the problems of Pacific agricultural trade access, where the overlap of exporter and importer interests in the region is strong and bilateral deals are likely to damage third party interests.[87] For all Pacific food exporters, rising food consumption in East Asia presents promising market opportunities. But the absence of an agreed basis for developing agricultural trade, and arbitrary policy actions of the kind which typified the approach to agricultural trade policy in the 1970s and 1980s, will not encourage their development.

Food and agricultural trade is already too important for the region as a whole for unilateral or bilateral approaches alone to provide a satisfactory means of advancing interests in efficient agricultural specialisation and Pacific food security. An important policy interest, therefore, is to anticipate areas of potential growth and forestall protectionist pressure by negotiating binding agreements on more open agricultural trade consistent with the framework of principles within the GATT system. Such alternative trade policy approaches and arrangements will be canvassed in chapter 9.

COLLECTIVE CHOICE AND THE ENERGY REGIME

The interaction of political and strategic factors in the choice of trade regime is another aspect of the trade security issue that is highlighted by energy trade. Energy security is a very sensitive issue for all countries, even for energy-rich countries like Canada, the United States and Australia, because of the uncertainties surrounding the Middle East oil trade. These uncertainties were abated but not eliminated by the sharp decline in oil prices in the mid-1980s.[88] For Japan and the countries of Northeast Asia, dependence on imported energy takes an extreme form, and energy security involves many aspects aside from security in long-term contracting of energy supplies. Japan is dependent on imports (principally of Middle East oil) for over 90 per cent of its energy requirements, and its vulnerability to breakdown in the energy supply was highlighted during the first oil crisis.[89] Two major objectives for Japan and other Northeast Asian countries are to diversify energy sources (although this can only be achieved slowly) and to improve energy and energy-conserving technologies. Australia, Indonesia, China and the other Pacific resource suppliers will in the years ahead figure more largely in Japan's energy picture, by supplying steaming coal, natural gas and uranium, and participating in the relocation of energy-intensive industry.

One of the most important problems in Pacific economic relations over the next generation will be how to manage adjustment in energy markets and shifts to other energy sources. Each nation within the Pacific will approach the problem from a quite different perspective. The energy issue highlights starkly the complexities of multidimensional collective choice in the management of international economic relations.[90] In the case of oil, for instance, a serious difference between Washington and Tokyo in the first half of the 1970s was the product of divergent perceptions of national and collective interest during the oil crisis, especially from the spring of 1973. For the United States, energy is closely related to concerns about national military security; for Japan the problem is primarily economic. These concerns have to be seen in a global context, especially since it is mainly oil from the Middle East on which the United States seeks to reduce dependence for strategic reasons, but on which Japan must continue to rely for primary energy supplies over the coming decade and beyond. These conditions will not change quickly. Assured Middle Eastern oil supplies will remain vital to Japan for some time. While fears in Japanese officialdom and in the community at large about the unavailability of oil supplies for significant periods in the 1970s proved quite exaggerated, they were a critical factor in Japan's policy response to this and a number of related issues, and they will continue to shape Japanese perceptions of the oil and energy problem.

One observer notes that the differences between the United States and Japan over the oil question are not necessarily competitive:

> Japanese economic and American security interests . . . converge in having the United States develop its own energy reserves. Such an American policy would increase world supplies; alternatively viewed, it would reduce American demand for Middle Eastern or other foreign oil . . . This could leave Japan as the major buyer of Middle Eastern (and perhaps other) oil, providing it with strong bargaining power . . . In addition, to the extent that American energy independence is achieved through extensive, and expensive, research and development efforts, which are economically premature, other countries will benefit in the long run. This technology will become available, and inevitably in substantial part at low cost, to countries able to use it; Japan would be a prime beneficiary.[91]

Access to technology is the nub of negotiations over the nature of the role to be played by nuclear energy in the Pacific and more generally. The complex economic, political, environmental and strategic issues surrounding moves to increase supplies of nuclear energy, not only in Japan but throughout the world, expose in a very pointed fashion the overlapping and different national and collective policy interests among the major Pacific economies — interests which enjoin them to seek more explicit modes of cooperation in decisionmaking on economic policy than have been attempted in the past.

For Japan, the desire to secure energy supplies has meant exploring and developing nuclear technology. Its desire for access to reprocessing technology and for a stake in the development of fast breeder reactors (FBRs) as a means of moving some way towards energy self-sufficiency led Japan to oppose moves by the United States to control international developments in those areas as a means of limiting the proliferation of nuclear weapons. From Japan's viewpoint, the United States' initiatives were likely to lead to increased prices for unenriched uranium, and, more importantly, to prolong extreme reliance on foreign sources of energy. The Japanese government argued that a more appropriate way to approach the proliferation issue was to look at ways of improving safeguards, not to prevent reprocessing or stifle the development of FBRs. In the event, the United States and Japan effectively put conflict over this issue on the back burner by agreeing to proceed with the 'experimental' development of Japanese facilities at Tokai Mura. This resolved, at least temporarily, the underlying conflict between the United States and Japan; but Japan then had to confront the specific restrictions on reprocessing contained in the Nuclear Non Proliferation Act of 1977.[92]

In its commitment to facilitating exports of uranium, the Australian government was caught between its interest in the economic return from uranium and growing concern in the electorate about proliferation of nuclear weapons and environmental issues. The government's support for the nonproliferation objectives of the United States, as well as its appeal to 'moral responsibility' to mine and export uranium, can be interpreted as an attempt to accommodate both these elements of public opinion. The Canadian dilemma is not dissimilar, although it is expressed differently, involves less concern about environmental questions, and has its origins in experience with the administration of safeguards and in a broad consensus on the proliferation question.

What the issue does show is that there are several significantly different positions among the major Pacific economic powers. These differences are most readily summarised in Table 5.5.[93] This table sets out a rough ordering for each national community of the importance attaching to five areas affected by the possibility of a moratorium on reprocessing such as President Carter proposed, and which was among the range of options addressed by the International Nuclear Fuel Cycle Evaluation group. The ordering is purely conjectural, but probably not too inaccurate.

Table 5.5   Rank order of policy areas affected by moratorium on nuclear fuel reprocessing

Policy area	United States	Japan	Australia	Canada
Security	1	5	2	1
Trade	4	3	1	2
Energy	3	1	5	5
Research and development	5	2	4	4
Environment	2	4	3	3

The negotiation of these issues encapsulates, in an extreme and sensitive way, the real interests at stake for these four countries, as well as for South Korea and other nuclear energy users in the Pacific, in regional cooperation, and the potential for political and economic conflict if solutions do not involve collective and commonly held commitments on a nuclear energy regime. In these issues bilateral bargaining, or even arms-length quadrilateral bargaining, is likely to produce less sustainable outcomes. Only some kind of consultative process, on the basis of providing mutual energy security within the Pacific, is likely to be able to advance and coordinate economic and political strategies for effecting energy transformation in the future. Such a framework for the pursuit of common and acceptable objectives seems essential to the resolution of the problems of complex collective choice in energy matters (as well as other matters) among the nations of the Pacific.

POLICY REQUIREMENTS FOR RESOURCE TRADE SECURITY

What are the policy requirements for energy and resource security that emerge from the various constituents of trade relations within the Pacific? A starting point in answering this question has been to establish the importance of the resource trade in Pacific economic integration. A principal factor in economic relations throughout much of the Pacific region is the exchange of raw materials for manufactures. While the Pacific resource and agricultural base is large and rich, it is unevenly dispersed, so that managing a large trade in raw materials and foodstuffs is a central task in the pursuit of economic security and economic development objectives.

While political and economic threats posed by resource trade dependence have not been an explicit feature of Pacific resource interdependence, the underlying insecurities of the resource-dependent nations have had a strong influence on policy and on the shape of Pacific specialisation resource trade. Pacific agricultural and mineral resource endowments are generally under-exploited, and trade in processed resource goods is underdeveloped. The tighter commodity markets and political threats to resource trade security from other parts of the world in the 1970s heightened the Pacific region's sensitivity about the vulnerabilities associated with its large energy and resource trade and encouraged a concentration on regional resource development and trade. This concentration has continued in the 1980s, despite weak commodity markets.

Both the politics of resource trade and the structural characteristics of resource goods markets, particularly for minerals and energy, make confident arrangements between resource trade partners in the Pacific a prime target for policy. *Formal* freeing of trade in resource goods is not necessarily a sufficient guarantee of either an optimal level of specialisation in trade or a reliable flow of trade in resource goods. Resource trade security requires a framework of understandings, institutions and agreements that ensure trade flows and a cooperative process of settlement in trade bargaining at both the private and the national levels. The nature and structure of trade in minerals and energy goods, with its geographic segmentation, the absence of continuous free markets, and rigidities in market links, all imply that the cost of trade conflicts and of the fracture of particular trade links is higher than it is likely to be for commodity trade flows more generally.

Food trade represents another case, in which political uncertainties are more readily mobilised against efficient trade specialisation, and the operation of national agricultural policies exacerbates volatility in the trade so that private as well as national incentives to efficient specialisation are reduced.

Policies directed at resource and food trade security by the industrial countries of the Pacific and elsewhere have usually been defensive, aimed at the extension of national control or self-sufficiency, the diversification of sources of supply, or the accumulation of adequate stockpiling against emergency. Constructive measures for the development of reliable buyer-supplier institutional arrangements and agreements have generally been incidental to one or other of these defensive strategies. Important exceptions to this generalisation are the proposals (which gained some support during the commodity trade confrontations of the 1970s) to establish a common fund with the aim of reducing instability in commodity prices, and the Stabex arrangements for developing countries associated with the European Economic Community (which, however, specifically excluded minerals products from their benefits). In 1984 the scheme was extended to include copper ore and other minerals.[94]

Reliable understandings and agreements between buyers and suppliers are a central element of cooperative resource trade relations. Understandings covering the resource trade could, of course, form a part of overall multilateral commitments to cooperative trading relations. But so far such commitments are limited or one-sided, and their direct application to resource and food trade in the Pacific implicit or weak.

Bilateral agreements provide another avenue to cementing cooperative resource trade relations.[95] Significantly, the resource security aspect of the Australia–Japan relationship was given institutional expression in the Basic Treaty of Friendship and Cooperation, which was signed after a period of uncertainty in the resource trade relations between the two countries. Seen by both countries as an important foreign policy initiative, the Treaty places a bilateral relationship in the context of multilateral and regional obligations, and enunciates a bilateral policy framework which stresses Japan's role as a 'reliable market' and Australia's responsibility as a 'stable supplier' of raw materials and agricultural commodities.[96] This agreement is an instrument for encouraging confidence in reliable access to and supply of resource goods within a bilateral framework, and for imposing restraints on arbitrary policy action. The extension of similar undertakings, which encourage confidence in the resource trade, consultation on resource and agricultural policies and restraint on the exercise of trade restrictions among the nations of the Pacific, could enhance the regional framework for resource trade security consistently with multilateral trading interests.

To be successful, reliable buyer–seller agreements between governments covering the resource and food trades must be underpinned by appropriate institutional arrangements for private or state trading and must incorporate liberal commercial policies. In the minerals and energy trades, long-term contracting has provided an appropriate private institutional form. Less reliance on vertical integration in the private organisation of the Pacific resource trade has allowed more effective reflection of different national objectives consistently with resource trade cooperation, and has served the purposes of *international pluralism*. Government policy approaches need to support long-term contracting institutions and their adaptation to a changing international economic environment. Long-term contracting, joint-venture arrangements and multinational consortium investment, as well as direct foreign investment in resource development and trade, all have the potential to contribute to efficient organisation of trade in minerals, energy and some agricultural raw materials.

In the food trade long-term contracting has been important in sugar, but not without government support in organising national industry coordination in bilateral agreements. While long-term contracting could have potential for other food trades, such as meat, it has yet to be tested more widely. An initial and useful step towards opening up markets in the food trade could be commodity-by-commodity agreements among governments, with minimal undertakings not to increase the protection embodied in agricultural support arrangements, and scheduled commitments to more comprehensive trade liberalisation. Cooperative action to direct stockpiling policies to the needs of food security rather than the interests of agricultural protectionism is another requirement. Regional or sub-regional (for example, ASEAN) arrangements for insuring against food shortages could be effective in reducing the insecurity associated with food trade dependence. Remarkably, the exchange of information about opportunities for trade specialisation remains an important policy yet to be systematically implemented.[97]

In processed minerals and metals, information exchange and the development of intergovernmental understandings on trading opportunities through joint study programs are also important requirements, alongside the reduction of conventional commercial barriers to trade.[98] The scope for closer integration within the metal manufacturing sectors of Pacific economies is great. National policies combined with autarchic business institutions and practices frustrate the optimal regional location of resource processing and metal manufacturing capacity, from the viewpoint of minimising transport costs, utilising scale economies, and using high-quality and low-cost resources specific to particular parts of the region. Tariffs and import restrictions are the most important of the national policies that have this effect. Autarchic business institutions and purchase agreements work in the same direction. Imperfect knowledge in the business or government sectors about opportunities for profitable investment and trade also frustrates the efficient location of production capacity.[99]

One important set of defensive measures for resource security favoured by industrial countries aims to extend the operations and privileges of national investors. Bilateral investment agreements, national investment insurance schemes and special foreign investment subsidiary credit facilities have all been directed at strengthening the role of resource purchaser-investors, particularly in developing countries. It is not clear that these measures, or the objectives pursued, satisfactorily serve the interest in resource security. This question is taken up again in chapter 7.

Resource and energy security issues also reveal, in sharp relief, the problems of complex international choice, beyond the economic choice of an appropriate commercial or trade policy framework. The political aspect of international economic policy choice is always present, whether tacitly or more overtly, as it has been in recent times. Arranging the oil trade involves strategic-military elements in the international ordering of preferences, as well as, more narrowly, economic preferences. The nuclear fuel cycle in the Pacific involves a complex international ordering of preferences in which there is no easy or automatic consistency. Cooperative resource trade arrangements within a pluralistic international community, around such issues as these, require as an essential prerequisite the establishment of strong consultative processes and forums so that there may be an effective and acceptable resolution of these complexities of collective international choice.

NOTES

Chapter 5

1   See appendix 1, Tables M1, M2, M3, M4, in Drysdale and Patrick *Evaluation of a
      Proposed Asian–Pacific Regional Organisation* pp.45–48 for additional data on the
      position of the Pacific in world minerals trade and production. See also Peter
      Drysdale 'An Organisation for Pacific Trade, Aid and Development'. Data here
      exclude communist bloc trade, and are drawn from the International Economic
      Data Bank, Australian National University. For a review of minerals, energy and
      resource trade issues, four volumes from the Pacific Trade and Development
      Conference series are of particular interest: Krause and Patrick *Mineral Resources*;
      Harry Edward English and Anthony Scott (eds) *Renewable Resources in the Pacific*
      Proceedings of the 12th Pacific Trade and Development Conference, held in
      Vancouver, Canada, 7–11 September 1981, International Development Research
      Centre, Ottawa, 1982; Romeo Bautista and Seiji Naya (eds) *Energy and Structural
      Change in the Asia–Pacific Region* Manila: Asian Development Bank and Philippine
      Institute for Development Studies, 1983; and Pacific Minerals and Energy Forum
      (MEF) *PECC Forum on Minerals and Energy Papers and Report, Jakarta, 6–8 July
      1986*, Australian National University, October 1987.
2   International Economic Data Bank, Research School of Pacific Studies, Australian
      National University.
3   Richard Cooper 'Natural Resources and National Security' *Resources Policy* 1, 4,
      June 1975, pp.192–203; Crawford and Ōkita *Raw Materials* pp.42–44.
4   These are concepts unfamiliar in the language of international economic theory
      but prevalent in the literature of international relations. See Keohane and Nye
      Power and Interdependence; Krause and Nye 'Reflections on the Economics and
      Politics of International Economic Organisations'; Cooper 'Natural Resources';
      David Bigman and Shlomo Reutlinger 'National and International Policies
      Toward Food Security and Price Stabilisation' *American Economic Review, Papers
      and Proceedings* 69, May 1979, pp.159–63; J.S. Hillman, D.G. Johnson and R.
      Gray 'Food Reserve Policies for World Food Security: A Consultant Study on
      Alternative Approaches' United Nations, FAO, ESC/72/2, January 1975; Rodney
      Tyers (ed.) *Food Security in Asia and the Pacific: Issues for Research* Report of the
      First Meeting of the Food Security Working Group, June 18–30, 1979, East–West
      Resource Systems Institute, Hawaii, 1979.
5   Adam Smith *The Wealth of Nations* (1778) is much concerned with these forces
      and their influence on the nature of contact with the New World (see for examples
      book IV, ch.VII). In more recent times, W.K. Hancock *Survey of British
      Commonwealth Affairs* II, London: Oxford University Press, 1940 provides a rich
      and full account of these influences in the 'Great Imperial' phase of world history.
      For insights into the economic aspects of interwar strife, see Hirschman *National
      Power*, and Hawtrey *Economic Aspects of Sovereignty*. For examples of conflictive
      and cooperative experience in raw materials exploitation by foreign enterprise, see
      Raymond F. Mikesell (ed.) *Foreign Investment in the Petroleum and Mineral
      Industries* Baltimore: Johns Hopkins Press, 1971. There are now a number of
      classic studies of particular experience; for example, Theodore Moran
      Multinational Corporations and the Politics of Dependence: Copper in Chile
      Princeton, NJ: Princeton University Press, 1974; Robert Baldwin *Economic
      Development and Export Growth: A Study of Northern Rhodesia, 1920–1960*

Berkeley: University of California Press, 1966; Edith Penrose 'Profit Sharing between Producing Countries and Oil Companies in the Middle East' *Economic Journal* June 1959, pp.238–4; Phillip Connelly and Robert Pelman *The Politics of Scarcity; Resource Conflicts in International Relations* London: Oxford University Press, 1975; and Mason Willrich *Energy and World Politics* New York: Free Press, 1975. These issues are also addressed in a study by Stuart Harris for the Royal Institute of International Affairs, Chatham House, entitled *Energy in the Asia-Pacific Region* London: Gower, 1983.

6   Clause 4 of the Atlantic Charter of 14 August 1941 (Julius Stone *The Atlantic Charter* Sydney: Angus & Robertson, 1943, appendix 1); this Charter became embodied in the United Nations Declaration of 1942 (United Nations, Department of Public Information, A Guide to the United Nations Charter, 1947, p.5). For a more recent discussion of the need to ensure access to trade, see, for example, Richard Gardner 'The Hard Road to World Order' *Foreign Affairs* 52, 3, April 1974, pp.556–76; Guy Erb 'Controlling Export Controls' *Foreign Policy* Winter 1974, pp.79–4; and Robert Hormats 'The World Economy Under Stress' *Foreign Affairs* 64, 3, 1986, pp.455–78.

7   Stuart Harris 'Australian Security and Resources Diplomacy: An Economic Viewpoint' Paper presented to ANZAAS Conference, Canberra, January 1975, p.3.

8   D.H. Meadows et al. *The Limits of Growth* London: Earth Island, 1972. The MIT research team concluded that the interaction of exponential growth of population and capital with depletion of non-renewable resources, pollution and famine would result in world growth reaching an absolute limit in the next hundred years. Technological advances or discovery of new resources would merely delay, not prevent, the limits being reached.

9   For an account of these developments, see C. Fred Bergsten 'The Threat from the Third World' *Foreign Policy* 11, Summer 1973, pp.102–4; Bergsten 'The Response to the Third World' *Foreign Policy* 17, Winter 1974–75, pp.3–4; Crawford and Ōkita *Raw Materials* ch. 8; Cooper 'Natural Resources'; Cooper 'A New International Economic Order for Mutual Gain' *Foreign Policy* 26, Spring 1977, pp.66–120; Werner Feld 'Atlantic Interdependence and Competition for Raw Materials in the Third World' *The Atlantic Community Quarterly* 14, 3, Fall 1976, pp.369–77; Yoichi Itagaki 'Economic Nationalism and the Problem of National Resources' *The Developing Economies* 11, 3, September 1973, pp.217–30; Geoffrey Kemp 'Scarcity and Strategy' *Foreign Affairs* 56, 2, January 1978, pp.396–414; Henry Kissinger, Address to the Fourth Ministerial Meeting of the United Nations Conference on Trade and Development, Nairobi, 6 May 1976, in *Atlantic Community Quarterly* 14, 2, Summer 1976, pp. 253–72; Hollis Chenery 'Restructuring the World Economy' *Foreign Affairs* 53, 2, January 1975, pp.242–3. See also Yuan-li Wei *Japan's Search for Oil: A Case Study of Economic Nationalism and International Security* Stanford: Hoover Institution Press, 1977; Raymond Vernon *Two Hungry Giants: The United States and Japan in the Quest for Oil and Ores* Cambridge: Harvard University Press, 1983; R.A. Morse (ed.) *The Politics of Japan's Energy Strategy* Berkeley: Institute of East Asian Studies, University of California, 1981; and D.A. Deese and Joseph S. Nye (eds) *Energy and Security* Cambridge: Ballinger (with Harper & Row), 1981. The interaction between economic and political bargaining is considered in Stuart Harris 'International Practice and Mores in Resources Policy' *Australian Outlook* 35, 3, December 1981, pp. 262–73.

10   Kissinger 'Address to UNCTAD IV'; 'Raw Materials and Political Risk' submission by European mining companies to the Commission of the European Communities, 1976. See also Drysdale 'An Organisation for Pacific Trade, Aid and Development' pp. 635–38.

11   Shinichi Ichimura 'Japan: The Rising Sun or Sinking Ship: the Energy Problem
      and the Food Shortage' *Center for South-East Asian Studies Discussion Paper* 74,
      Kyoto, July 1974, p.1; Geoff George 'Japan's Oil Import Policies in the Age of
      "Multipolar Diplomacy"' *Australia-Japan Economic Relations Research Project
      Research Paper* No. 8, Australian National University, April 1974, pp.27-62;
      Yuan-li Wei *Japan's Search for Oil*; and Morse *Japan's Energy Strategy*.
12   Saburo Ōkita 'Natural Resources Dependency and Japanese Foreign Policy'
      Foreign Affairs 52, 4, July 1974, p.723.
13   Literally translated from *kaihatsu yunyū*. For a discussion of official Japanese
      thinking about resources policy at this time, see Ministry of International Trade
      and Industry 'Resources Development and Imports of Japan' *Modern Government
      and National Development* July 1970, pp.39-45; Ministry of International Trade
      and Industry *Outlook on Resources Problems* Tokyo, 4 October 1971.
14   Cooper 'Natural Resources' p.196. This issue is addressed in Stuart Harris and
      Keichi Ōshima (eds) *Australia and Japan: Nuclear Energy Issues in the Pacific*
      Canberra and Tokyo: Australia-Japan Research Centre, 1980; Stuart Harris and
      Toyoaki Ikuta *Australia, Japan and the Energy Coal Trade* Canberra and Tokyo:
      Australia-Japan Research Centre, 1982; and Peter Drysdale and Hirofumi Shibata
      (eds) *Federalism and Resource Development* Sydney: Allen & Unwin, 1986.
15   Cooper 'Natural Resources' pp.196-68. See especially the prescription offered as a
      remedy to Japan's resource trade security (note 15).
16   The United States coal strike of 1977-78, for example, lasted for 110 days, and,
      but for the fact that a number of power utilities had stockpiled coal following an
      earlier series of 'wildcat' strikes, its impact would have been considerably greater
      (*Forbes Magazine* 15 May 1978). See Cooper 'Natural Resources' p.197 for a
      comment on the 1974 British coal strike.
17   The Chilean copper industry since the 1950s has experienced three separate
      episodes aimed at restructuring: the Nuevo Trato legislation of 1955, intended to
      create a good investment climate; the 'Chileanisation' program of the Frei regime;
      and, in 1970, nationalisation by the Allende government. See Moran *Copper in
      Chile*, and Stefan de Vylder *Allende's Chile* Cambridge: Cambridge University
      Press, 1974. Subsequently Pinochet's government has attempted to promote
      foreign investment in the industry.
18   Ministry of International Trade and Industry *Resources Problems*; Drysdale 'An
      Organisation for Pacific Trade, Aid and Development' p.625; Ben Smith 'The
      Japanese Connection' in Peter Hastings and Andrew Farran (eds) *Australia's
      Resources Future; Threats, Myths and Realities in the 1980s* Melbourne: Nelson,
      1978, pp.108-43.
19   Crawford and Ōkita *Raw Materials* pp.136-38; Kiyoshi Kojima 'Japan's Resource
      Security and Foreign Investment in the Pacific: A Case Study of Bilateral Devices
      between Advanced Countries' in Krause and Patrick *Mineral Resources*.
20   Cooper 'Natural Resources' p.198.
21   Ben Smith and Peter Drysdale 'Stabilisation and the Reduction of Uncertainty in
      Bilateral Minerals Trade Arrangements' *Australia-Japan Economic Relations
      Research Project Research Paper* No.65, Australian National University, December,
      1979. See also Ben Smith 'Long-Term Contracts for the Supply of Raw Materials'
      in Crawford and Ōkita *Raw Materials*.
22   Stuart Harris, Mark Salmon and Ben Smith 'Analysis of Commodity Markets for
      Policy Purposes' *Thames Essay* No.17, London: Trade Policy Research Centre,
      1978, pp.58-59; Gershon Felder et al. 'Storage with Price Uncertainty in
      International Trade' *International Economic Review* 18, 3, October 1977, pp.553-68.
23   There is virtually no discussion of the rationale for it or interest in it in the
      economic literature. In policy approaches it is reflected in some bilateral

arrangements, and there was an unsuccessful attempt to incorporate into the Tokyo Round of Trade Negotiations multilateral undertakings inhibiting embargoes on raw materials exports. See Peter Lloyd 'Japan and Australia in the Multilateral Trade Negotiations' *Australia-Japan Economic Relations Research Project Research Paper* No.20, Australian National University, March 1975; and Crawford and Ōkita *Raw Materials* ch.8. In the policy discussion of this route to resource security in the 1970s, the contribution of economists is ambiguous. See, for instance, Cooper 'Natural Resources', and Cooper 'A New International Economic Order'.

24   The argument here draws on the insights of Garnaut's work on trade and industrialisation in Southeast and Northeast Asia. See Garnaut *ASEAN*; Anderson and Garnaut *Australian Protectionism*; and Anderson and Smith 'Changing Economic Relations'.

25   Garnaut *ASEAN* p.306.

26   International Economic Data Bank, Research School of Pacific Studies, Australian National University.

27   Drysdale 'An Organisation for Pacific Trade, Aid and Development'.

28   Ross Garnaut and Kym Anderson 'ASEAN Export Specialisation and the Evolution of Comparative Advantage in the Western Pacific Region' in Garnaut (ed.) *ASEAN* pp.374–413.

29   Irving Kravis '"Availability" and Other Influences on the Commodity Composition of Trade' *Journal of Political Economy* 64, 2, April 1956, pp.143–55; Krueger 'Growth, Distortions and Patterns of Trade'.

30   Garnaut and Anderson 'ASEAN Export Specialisation'.

31   Findlay, Anderson and Drysdale 'China's Trade and Pacific Growth'; see especially pp.3–7.

32   Australia's growth as a raw materials supplier is summarised in Peter Drysdale and Alan Rix 'Australia's Trading Patterns' *Current Affairs Bulletin* 55, 11, April 1979, p.8. For a fuller discussion, see Crawford and Ōkita *Raw Materials* Chs 1, 4 and 6.

33   Smith 'The Japanese Connection'.

34   Smith 'Long-Term Contracts'; Crawford and Ōkita *Raw Materials* ch.6; Ben Smith 'Security and Stability in Minerals Markets: The Role of Long-Term Contracts' *The World Economy* 2, 1, January 1979, pp. 65–78; Smith and Drysdale 'Stabilisation and the Reduction of Uncertainty'; Kiyoshi Kojima 'Japan's Resource Security' pp. 506–22. Smith's is the seminal work on long-term contracts, and the ensuing argument draws heavily on his contributions. Smith, Christopher Findlay and the author are engaged on a continuing study at the Australia–Japan Research Centre of the development of long-term contracting institutions in the minerals trades.

35   Ben Smith 'Security and Stability' p.65; also discussed in Smith 'Long-Term Contracts' p.231. The following argument draws directly on Smith's excellent analysis of these developments in this work.

36   ibid. Also Kiyoshi Kojima 'Japan's Resource Security'.

37   Crawford and Ōkita *Raw Materials* ch.4; Smith 'Long-Term Contracts'; Smith 'Security and Stability'.

38   Kojima 'Japan's Resource Security'.

39   Smith 'Long-Term Contracts'; Smith 'Australian Minerals Development, Future Prospects for the Mining Industry and Effects on the Australian Economy' in Wolfgang Kasper and Thomas Parry (eds) *Growth, Trade and Structural Change in an Open Australian Economy* Sydney: Centre for Applied Economic Research, University of New South Wales, 1978, pp.130–5; R.B. McKern *Multinational Enterprise and Natural Resources* Sydney: McGraw-Hill, 1976; and Ben Smith

'The Role of Resource Development in Australian Economic Growth' Discussion Paper No.167, Centre for Economic Policy Research, Australian National University, May 1987.

40   The pattern was different in some developing countries throughout the region where there was a larger Japanese investment presence in resource activities. See Kōichi Hamada 'Japanese Investment Abroad' in Drysdale (ed.) *Direct Foreign Investment in Asia and the Pacific* Canberra: Australian National University Press, 1972, pp. 173–96; Kojima *Direct Foreign Investment*.

41   Smith 'Security and Stability' pp.65–66. On the question of appropriate taxation of resource projects, see Ross Garnaut and Anthony Clunies-Ross *The Taxation of Mineral Rents* Oxford: Oxford University Press, 1983.

42   The announcement by Coal and Allied Industries of two major steaming coal contracts with West German interests, one for 5 years and one for 12, was seen as marking a major change in European coal sales (*Australian Financial Review* 27 April 1978). Since 1978 an increasingly large proportion of Australia's steaming coal sales have been directed to markets outside Japan, to elsewhere in East Asia and in Europe. In 1984 Japan's share of Australia's steaming coal exports was 40 per cent. For an overview of earlier sales to Europe and shorter term contracts, see Joint Coal Board *Annual Report 1976–77* pp.134–35 and *Annual Report 1977–78* p.12.

43   A full review of issues in minerals and energy trade and development in the Pacific has been undertaken in connection with the work of the Pacific Economic Cooperation Conference Task Force on Minerals and Energy, based at the Australian National University and instigated by the Second Pacific Cooperation Conference held under the auspices of ESCAP, Bangkok, June 1982 (*Report of the Task Force on Minerals and Energy* Canberra: Australia–Japan Research Centre, July 1983). This work led to the organisation of the first Pacific Minerals and Energy Forum in Jakarta in July 1986; see MEF *PECC Forum on Minerals and Energy*. The background to this study is discussed in chapter 8.

44   Smith 'Security and Stability' p.67. This is a particular and important illustration of the general importance of the argument of chapter 2 about the gains from firm contractual arrangements for international trade.

45   Kojima 'Japan's Resource Security'; T. Hamada 'The Steel Industry and Japan — Its Role in the Japanese Economy' address to the American Chamber of Commerce in Japan, Tokyo, 13 March 1969; J.M. Finger and A.J. Yeats 'Effective Protection by Transportation Costs and Tariffs: A Comparison of Magnitudes' *Quarterly Journal of Economics* 90, February 1976, pp.169–76; Gary Sampson and Alexander Yeats 'Tariff and Transport Barriers Facing Australian Exports' *Journal of Transport Economics and Policy* 11, 2, May 1977, pp.141–44.

46   The data and information upon which this argument is based were assembled through the project on long-term contracting in the resource trade between Australia and Japan completed by Smith, Findlay and the author. Smith surveys the issues in 'Security and Stability'.

47   Crawford and Okita *Raw Materials* p.138.

48   In the raw materials trade with the Japanese iron and steel industry, such arrangements have been coordinated by the trading steel producer, Nippon Steel.

49   Drysdale and Kojima *Australia-Japan Economic Relations* pp.24–28.

50   ibid. Long-term contracts give each side a commitment to trade with the other, and the contract terms indicate the basis on which that trade will be conducted for the foreseeable future. In the face of unforeseen changes in circumstances, experience has been that both sides have shown readiness to discuss possible revision of the terms on which the trade is conducted, even though no explicit allowance for this may have been made in the original contract. Flexibility is an

important component of the security which each party seeks, since neither has an interest in seeing the viability of the other threatened. Thus, for example, Australian exporters have sometimes been able to negotiate significant price increases outside the formal provisions of contracts, and in return have accepted, more or less philosophically, the inability of Japanese purchasers to take full deliveries during recession.

51   Josephine Au Yeong, Financing of Japanese Direct Foreign Investment, PhD dissertation, Australian National University, 1987, ch.6.
52   Ben Smith 'Bilateral Commercial Arrangements in the Energy Coal Trade' in S. Harris and T. Ikuta (eds) *Australia, Japan and the Energy Coal Trade*.
53   Au Yeong, Japanese Foreign Investment, pp.174–79.
54   Anderson et al. 'Pacific Growth and Australia's Trade' p.62.
55   Smith 'Long-Term Contracts'; Crawford and Ōkita *Raw Materials* chs 6, 8 and 9.
56   Hence the relocation of capacity may well be in Western Pacific countries. For example, the attraction of cheap hydro-electricity led Japanese processors and Australian raw materials suppliers to establish aluminium smelters in New Zealand in the late 1960s, in one of the earlier important steps in this direction. See Drysdale 'Australia, Japan and New Zealand'.
57   Ben Smith and Alistair Ulph 'The Impact of Developed Country Environmental Policy on the Trade of Developing Countries in the ESCAP Region' paper prepared for the UNEP/ESCAP Project on Environment and Development and released as *CRES Report* R/R5, Australian National University, 1979, pp.46–60.
58   John Stuckey 'Joint Ventures in the Aluminium Industry' *Australia-Japan Economic Relations Research Project Research Paper* No. 67, Australian National University, December 1979. For a fuller discussion see John Stuckey *Vertical Integration in the Aluminium Trade* Cambridge: Harvard University Press, 1983.
59   Garnaut and Anderson 'ASEAN Export Specialisation' p.384; Anderson et al. 'Australia and the Pacific' section 2.
60   Garnaut and Anderson 'ASEAN Export Specialisation' pp.388–9; Kym Anderson et al. 'Australia's Agricultural Trade with Northeast Asia' *Australia-Japan Economic Relations Research Project Research Paper* No.63, Australian National University, December 1979, pp.10–11 and Table 2 (p.26); Kym Anderson and Rod Tyers 'Agricultural Policies of Western Europe and East Asia and their Effects on Traditional Food Exporters' Figure 3.4 (p.53) in Kym Anderson (ed.) 'East Asian and West European Agricultural Policies: Implications for Australia' *Pacific Economic Papers* No.143, Australia–Japan Research Centre, Australian National University, January 1987.
61   The supply factors (population densities) indicate that Australia has a strong comparative advantage, at least in mineral and agricultural products. On the demand side Australia has extremely low, and Northeast Asia very high, incomes per hectare and manufacturing output per hectare. To the extent that land area is a useful proxy for national resource endowment, it follows from dynamic comparative cost theory that high densities of manufacturing production per hectare are likely to be negatively related to strong export specialisation in natural-resource-based goods, as domestic demand for natural resources will tend to be large relative to domestic supply. However actual trade flows need not correspond to the revealed pattern of comparative advantage, due to factors such as protective trade policies, trade intensity, and special country bias (Garnaut and Anderson 'ASEAN Export Specialisation' pp.380–87; Anderson and George *Australian Agriculture*; and Anderson and Hayami *Agricultural Protection*).
62   Estimate for 1980; calculated from *2000 nen no Nihon (kakuron)* — *tajuteki na keizai shakai no anzen o motomete* [Japan in the year 2000 (detailed discussion) — in search of security for a diverse economic society] Tokyo: Economic Planning

Agency, 1982, Table IV–4, p.204. When calculating self-sufficiency measured by original calories, calories of livestock products are counted in terms of calories of animal feed needed, and for self-supply only that part of livestock and poultry production fed by domestic feed. See also Saburō Okita 'Japan's High Dependence on Import of Raw Materials' in Crawford and Okita *Raw Materials* pp.219–22.

63   Okita 'Japan's Dependence' p.222. Different bases for calculating the ratios produce different relative orderings. Another common basis of calculation is aggregate value, but the ratios derived present difficulties in international comparisons, because they reflect not only different production and consumption structures but also differences in the relative prices of commodities. Because rice and beef are much higher priced relative to other agricultural commodities than they are in other countries, Japan has a higher self-sufficiency ratio in value terms even when its actual degree of self-sufficiency in rice or beef is roughly the same as in other countries.

64   Eric Saxon and Kym Anderson 'Japanese Agricultural Protection in Historical Perspective' *Pacific Economic Papers* No.92, Australia–Japan Research Centre, Australian National University, July 1982; Anderson and Hayami *Agricultural Protection* chs 1 and 2 and appendix 1; Anderson 'East Asian Agricultural Policies'.

65   Figures are derived from United Nations trade data in the International Economic Data Bank, Australian National University.

66   Rod Tyers 'Effects on ASEAN of Food Trade Liberalisation in Industrial Countries' paper presented to the second Western Pacific Food Trade Workshop, Jakarta, 22–23 August 1982, pp. 10–11; Anderson and Hayami *Agricultural Protection* ch.5.

67   Tyers 'ASEAN Food Trade' p.11.

68   Some preliminary projections by Rodney Tyers and Suthad Setboonsarng, Some Aggregate Trends in the Structure and Stability of Staple Food Markets in the Asia–Pacific Region, mimeo (paper presented at the third biennial meeting of the Agricultural Economic Society of Southeast Asia, Kuala Lumpur, 27–29 November 1979), suggest that until 1990 more than 12 per cent of additional food consumption for the Asian–Pacific region (including South Asia) as a whole will be met through trade. Food trade dependence for all major food commodities except wheat must rise substantially. These are estimates of tonnages consumed and trade, and do not weight properly the rapid growth of trade in high-value foodstuffs such as meat. See also projections in Tyers 'ASEAN Food Trade' pp.16–33.

69   Crawford and Okita *Raw Materials* pp.169–70; Kenzō Hemmi 'Japanese Agricultural Policy and Australian Trade Prospects' in Kenzō Hemmi and G.C. Allen 'Structural Adjustment of Japanese Agriculture' *Australia–Japan Economic Relations Research Project Research Paper* No.11, Australian National University, May 1974; J.G. Crawford et al. 'Australian Agriculture and Trade with Japan' *Australia–Japan Economic Relations Research Project Research Paper* No.27, Australian National University, July 1975.

70   Krause 'The Pacific Economy'.

71   See Crawford and Okita *Raw Materials*; Hemmi 'Japanese Agriculture'; Keizō Tsuchiya 'Japanese Agriculture and Problems in Importing Farm Products' in Anderson et al. Agricultural Trade; Aurelia George, The Strategies of Influence: Japan's Agricultural Cooperative (Nōkyō) as a Pressure Group, PhD dissertation, Australian National University, 1980; Aurelia George 'The Changing Patterns of Japan's Agricultural Import Trade: Implications for Australia' *Pacific Economic Papers* No.100, Australia–Japan Research Centre, Australian National University,

January 1983; Aurelia George 'The Comparative Study of Interest Groups in Japan: An International Framework' *Pacific Economic Papers* No.95, Australia–Japan Research Centre, Australian National University, December 1982; and Aurelia George 'Agricultural Politics and Policymaking' in Haruo Fukui (ed.) *Public Policies and Policymaking in Post-Oil Crisis Japan* Berkeley: University of California Press (forthcoming).

72   Australia did take the issue of Japan's beef import embargo to the GATT. There was also intensive bilateral negotiation, but leverage in this framework is limited. Subsequently agricultural issues were the subject of negotiation in the Tokyo Round of Multilateral Trade Negotiations (see Australia, Department of Trade and Resources *Multilateral Trade Negotiations: Australia–Japan Bilateral Settlement* Canberra, November 1979 and *Multilateral Trade Negotiations: Australia–European Economic Community Bilateral Settlement* Canberra, November 1979). However, the agricultural trade settlements under the Tokyo Round involved no substantial trade liberalisation, merely the adjustment of existing arrangements. The agreement to proceed to a New Round of Multilateral Trade Negotiations in September 1986 does involve the inclusion of agricultural trade as a substantial issue for negotiation. For a discussion of political bargaining, including food, see Peter Wallensteen 'Scarce Goods as Political Weapons: The Case of Food' *Journal of Peace Research* XIII, 4, 1976, pp.277–98.

73   NPCC (National Pacific Cooperation Committee, Australia) *Australia and Pacific Economic Cooperation* Australian National University, July, 1987.

74   See Peter McCawley and Christopher Manning 'Survey of Recent Developments' *Bulletin of Indonesian Economic Studies* XII, 3, November 1976, pp.3–7, and the survey articles in subsequent issues, for the Indonesian experience. See also Christopher Manning 'Labour Surplus to Labour Scarcity? — The Impact of Rapid Economic Growth and the Green Revolution on Labour Markets in Rural Java' paper presented to the 31st Annual Conference of the Australian Agriculture Society, Adelaide, 9–12 February 1987.

75   The ASEAN countries have agreed to give each other first right of refusal to accept exported rice under emergency circumstances, and have agreed to establish a rice reserve among themselves.

76   Curzon and Curzon 'GATT: Traders' Club'; Gardner 'World Order'; Crawford *Australia's Trade Policy, 1942–1966.*

77   Stuart Harris 'Australian Agriculture and World Commodity Trading Arrangements' paper presented to the Annual Conference of the Australian Agricultural Economics Society, University of Adelaide, February 1980, p.4.

78   Stuart Harris 'Agricultural Trade and Its International Trade Policy Context' *CRES Working Paper* R/WP 37, Australian National University, 1979, p.17.

79   Robert Baldwin 'Beyond the Tokyo Round Negotiations' *Thames Essay* No.22, London: Trade Policy Research Centre, 1979; Harris 'Agricultural Trade' pp.28–29; T.E. Josling 'Agriculture in the Tokyo Round Negotiations' London: Trade Policy Research Centre, 1977.

80   US Senate Committee on Finance, MTN Studies: 1. 'Results for US Agriculture' Washington, June 1979, and 2. 'Tokyo–Geneva Round: Its Relation to US Agriculture' Washington, June 1979; D. Gale Johnson 'Impact of Farm Support Policies on International Trade' in Hugh Corbet and Robert Jackson (eds) *In Search of a New World Economic Order* London: Croom Helm/Trade Policy Research Centre, 1974; Harold Malmgren 'International Order for Public Subsidies' *Thames Essay* No. 11, London: Trade Policy Research·Centre, 1977; *Trends in International Trade: A Report by a Panel of Experts* (the Haberler Report) Geneva: General Agreement on Tariffs and Trade, 1958; Stuart Harris 'Commodity Problems and the International Economic Order: What Rules of

What Game?' in Peter Oppenheimer (ed.) *Issues in International Economics*
London: Oriel Press, 1980; Anderson and Hayami *Agricultural Protection*; and
Rodney Tyers 'Distortions in World Food Markets: A Quantitive Assessment'
background paper prepared for the World Bank's *World Development Report 1986*
Washington, DC: World Bank, 1986.

81   Wheat contracts with China have the feature that price is negotiated with
reference to the 'free' market. There are a number of minor agricultural
commodity trades in Asia and the Pacific that have incorporated the contracting of
agricultural supplies from new development projects, such as the Japanese maize
trade with Thailand and later Indonesia. On contracting of major agricultural
commodities, see Smith 'Long-Term Contracts' pp. 263–68.

82   Smith 'Long-Term Contracts'; Kojima 'Japan's Resource Security' pp. 517–18;
Drysdale and Kojima *Australia-Japan Economic Relations* pp. 23–31; Robert M.
March 'The Australia-Japan Sugar Negotiations' *Australia-Japan Economic
Relations Research Project Research Paper* No. 56, Australian National University,
March 1979.

83   Crawford and Okita, in *Raw Materials* p. 134–35, advocate the expansion of long-
term contracting for the beef trade.

84   Harris 'Australian Agriculture' pp. 21–22. See Crawford and Okita *Raw Materials*
pp. 44–45, for a discussion of Japan's fears about agricultural trade dependence.
Japanese agricultural self-sufficiency policies have in the past been legitimised by
claims that there are no reliably friendly agricultural supplier nations close to
Japan (Yasuo Takeyama 'Don't Take Japan for Granted' in Richard Cooper (ed.)
A Re-Ordered World: Emerging International Economic Problems Washington:
Potomac Association, 1973; and Ryūtarō Komiya 'Commentary on Economic
Assumptions of the Case for Liberal Trade' in C. Fred Bergsten *Toward a New
World Trade Policy: The Maidenhead Papers* Lexington: Lexington Books, 1975,
pp.33–35).

85   Harris 'Australian Agriculture' p.20.

86   The dangers of unilateral settlements as they affect third parties were revealed in
the settlements on beef and other matters which the United States pressed upon
Japan during 1977–78. See Hugh Patrick 'United States-Japan Political Economy:
Is the Partnership in Jeopardy?' in Hanson and Roehl *The United States and the
Pacific Economy in the 1980s*; and Drysdale and Kojima *Australia-Japan Economic
Relations* pp.16–18.

87   Aurelia George 'Japan's Beef Import Policies, 1978–84: The Growth of Bilateralism'
Pacific Economic Papers No.113, Australia-Japan Research Centre, Australian
National University, July, 1984; Anderson et al. 'Australia and the Pacific'; Peter
Drysdale, Ben Smith, Kym Anderson and Christopher Findlay 'Australia and the
Pacific Economy' *Economic Record* 62, 176, March 1986, pp.60–66.

88   Forum on Minerals and Energy *Report of the Fifth Pacific Economic Cooperation
Conference, Vancouver, November 16–19, 1986* Ottawa: Canadian Chamber of
Commerce, 1987, pp.89–102.

89   Okita 'Japan's Dependence' p.218; George 'Japan's Oil Import Policies'; Morse
Japan's Energy Strategy; and *MEF Report* July 1986.

90   For an interesting first-brush approach to the Arab oil embargo in these terms, see
Richard B. Lillich 'Economic Coercion and the International Legal Order'
International Affairs 51, 3, July 1975, pp.358–71.

91   Hugh Patrick 'United States Foreign Economic Policy Towards Japan and the
Pacific' *Australia-Japan Economic Relations Research Project Research Paper* No.32,
Australian National University, November 1975, p.19; Patrick 'American Foreign
Economic Policy Towards the Western Pacific' in Crawford and Okita *Raw
Materials* pp.36–37.

92   Drysdale 'An Organisation for Pacific Trade, Aid and Development'.
93   An approach suggested by Richard Suttmeier in 'Japanese Reactions to United
      States Nuclear Policy: Domestic Origins of An International Negotiating Position'
      Orbis 22, 3, 1978, pp.651-80. The orderings set out in Table 5.5 are those
      currently thought to have dominant effective political expression. There will be
      other orderings expressed in each country: see also Harris and Oshima *Nuclear
      Energy Issues*.
94   Under the Stabex arrangements, a country deriving a certain minimum share of its
      export earnings from a listed commodity and whose proceeds from sales of that
      commodity to the European Community are a specified percentage below the
      reference level may request a compensatory transfer from the fund. In principle
      the loans are to be repaid over five years, provided that both the unit value and the
      quantity exported of the particular commodity then exceed the reference unit
      value and quantity (see Hugo Hasenpflug 'The Stabilization of Export Earnings in
      the Lome Convention: A Model Case?' in K.P. Suvant and H. Hasenpflug (eds)
      *The New International Economic Order — Confrontation or Co-operation between
      North and South* Frankfurt: Campus Verlag, 1977, pp.165-74).
          For details of all claims and transfers in a given year, see the Report of the
      Commission of the European Community on the operation during 1975 of the
      system set up by the Lome Convention for stabilising export earnings (Brussels).
      The Lome III convention of 1984 left the scheme essentially unchanged, but with
      three new agricultural products included and dependence and fluctuation
      thresholds reduced. Mineral products, including copper ore, were also brought in
      under the SYSMIN (mining products: special financing facility) scheme, which
      operates along similar lines to Stabex. However, some copper producers have
      expressed concern that the support measures will favour inefficient producers.
95   Either in the form of comprehensive bilateral trade agreements or commodity-
      specific agreements. The former are more likely to be inconsistent with most-
      favoured-nation principles.
96   *Basic Treaty of Friendship and Co-operation between Australia and Japan* Articles V
      and VI.
97   This is particularly important in this development of trade with the 'new' food
      importers of Northeast and Southeast Asia, including China. The information-
      gathering and monitoring capacity of the agricultural policy management divisions
      of governments in these countries have few links with the established agricultural
      exporters, and a top policy priority in the development of efficient and confident
      food trade specialisation is to develop such links.
98   Drysdale 'Minerals and Metals in Japanese–Australian Trade' *The Developing
      Economies* 18, 2, June 1970, pp. 211-12; Crawford and Ōkita *Raw Materials* pp.134
      and 139-141.
99   Drysdale 'Minerals and Metals' p.212. The three types of benefit which would
      derive from closer regional integration within the minerals and metals industries are
      clear in principle. First, protection of basic treatment processes that require large
      inputs of low value-to-weight raw materials prevents treatment closer to resource
      deposits, and high transport costs are needlessly added to the cost of the product. Pig
      iron production, alumina refining, or nickel refining are all examples of industries
      which thrive on being located close to the source of raw materials. Second, in
      industries with access to significant economies of scale, high protective barriers made
      secure by government support can lead to the duplication of plants of suboptimal
      scale. All stages of aluminium production can give rise to this inefficiency. Finally,
      protective barriers can lead to the establishment of industries outside countries, with
      important advantages in the quality and cost of inputs. The aluminium smelting
      industry, which requires large volumes of electricity, is one such case.

6 Outward-looking development strategies

The countries of Northeast and Southeast Asia are among the fastest-growing, most rapidly industrialising and open economies in the developing world.[1] These newly industrialising countries in the Western Pacific represent another dynamic dimension of the Pacific economy. They have been styled the 'second and third generation Japans' because their growth experience and industrial transformation in the past two decades has, more or less, followed that of Japan in the two decades before.[2] South Korea, Taiwan, Hong Kong and Singapore have other features in common with Japan. All four have very high population densities and very low natural resource endowments in terms of land and mineral reserves per capita. They also began the process of industrialisation from very low levels of income per head, either as agricultural exporters in the cases of South Korea and Taiwan, or as entrepôt traders in the cases of Hong Kong and Singapore. Now they have become significant exporters of manufactured goods and, alongside Japan, important purchasers of agricultural goods and raw materials, so that their trade and growth prospects are more and more intimately linked with those of the resource-rich countries of the Pacific.

The newly industrialising countries of Asia are outstanding examples of the success of outward-looking strategies for economic development. Rapid growth in manufacturing output and incomes has been closely tied to rapid trade growth. As observed in chapters 4 and 5, resource endowment has dictated an obvious and binding rationale for outward-looking development strategies for the resource-poor countries of Northeast and Southeast Asia; but other Western Pacific developing countries have adopted the same policy course. While China's resource base is large in absolute terms, its population density is on average high, and its commitment to modernisation has also involved substantially increased trade dependence.

This course of industrialisation has not only had a profound effect on the structure of the East Asian economies themselves; it has also impacted dramatically on regional and world trade flows, adding weight to the effect of Japan's rise as an industrial power in shifting the structure of the international economy towards the Pacific.

What are the bases of export-oriented East Asian industrialisation, and what are the requirements for its continued success? The ambitions of East Asian countries for economic modernisation parallel those of Japan in an earlier era, and their accommodation constitutes a legitimate claim, especially on neighbouring industrial countries in the Pacific, but also upon the wider international community. The experience of the newly industrialising countries of East Asia in pursuing outward-looking economic development and the nature of *their* interests in Pacific economic policy are the focus of attention in this chapter.

EAST ASIAN INDUSTRIALISATION AND TRADE SHARE

The East Asian developing countries now enjoy a share in world trade almost equal to that of Japan. In the 1960s Japan's world trade share grew to 6.6 per cent, almost double that of all other East Asian counties at 4.1 per cent. In 1985 the newly industrialising countries of East Asia accounted for 9.8 per cent of world exports, while Japan's share in world exports was 10.0 per cent.

The East Asian developing countries have been responsible for almost all the growth in developing countries' share in world exports, excluding oil, over the past decade. Table 3.1 highlights the two factors behind their growing world trade share: their very high rates of GNP growth, and the significant increase in the share of external trade in their GNPs. The economies of these countries have been growing much more rapidly than the world economy as a whole, and the ratio of exports to gross domestic product has risen more noticeably for East Asian developing countries than it has for developing countries as a whole. For much of the past two decades international trade has grown faster than world output, but for East Asian countries the increasing dependence on world markets has been particularly striking.

The main thrust of East Asian trade growth in the past few decades has come from the manufacturing sector. The contribution of manufactures to export growth has been substantial even for Southeast Asian countries other than Singapore over the past decade or so. Table 6.1 presents data on exports of manufactures as a proportion of total exports for the Pacific countries and the world as a whole from 1962 to 1985. By the middle of the 1980s manufactured goods represented around 65 per cent of world trade, as against 55 per cent in the early 1960s. The share of manufactured goods in the exports of industrial countries was higher, at around 76 per cent, while the share of manufactures in the exports of all developing countries was around 36 per cent. Japan and the East Asian newly industrialising countries stand out because of their large and rapidly growing shares of manufactured exports. Australia, New Zealand and, to a lesser extent, Canada are exceptional among industrial countries in the large proportions of their exports which are still primary based.[3] Even the United States has a significantly larger primary-based export share than the average for industrial countries.

Table 6.1   Share of manufactured goods in Pacific and world exports, 1962–85 (per cent)

	1962	1965	1970	1975	1980	1985
Australasia	9.2	12.3	17.2	18.0	25.1	19.7
North America	58.3	58.8	64.9	63.5	63.4	70.3
Japan	88.3	91.1	93.3	95.7	95.7	97.3
Pacific industrial countries[a]	58.2	60.7	68.2	69.1	70.7	77.1
China	39.3	45.2	45.2	42.3	46.8	51.6
Asian NICs	49.4	58.4	71.0	74.9	80.7	81.8
Other ASEAN countries	3.5	4.8	6.0	9.4	13.4	25.2
European industrial countries	73.8	74.8	77.5	78.1	74.9	75.4
All industrial countries	68.2	69.8	74.2	75.0	73.6	76.1
All developing countries	13.5	14.9	20.9	18.5	27.1	35.8
World	55.2	56.4	62.8	60.1	60.0	65.2

Note: a Australia, Japan, Canada, the United States and New Zealand.
Source: International Economic Data Bank, Australian National University

Much of the growth of the East Asian manufactured goods trade has been concentrated, at least initially, within the Pacific market. Table 6.2 details Pacific trade in manufactured goods, classified into two broad commodity categories, namely labour-intensive and capital- and technology-intensive products, and compares the Pacific market shares for these commodities in the mid-1960s and early 1980s. The concentration of East Asia's exports of manufactures within the region, especially in the North American market, is strong. However, the region has become steadily less important as a destination for exports of manufactured goods from Japan (a pattern subsequently followed by the newly industrialising countries of Northeast Asia), although regional trade intensity in these goods remains high. It has also maintained its relative importance as a destination for North American exports of manufactured goods.

THE DYNAMICS OF OUTWARD-LOOKING GROWTH

There is now a substantial literature on the connection between trade growth and rapid industrialisation in East Asia.[4] The rapid growth of South Korea and Taiwan dates from deliberate policy changes, including credit policy reforms and a shift towards export-oriented industrialisation, in the early 1960s. The city states of Hong Kong and Singapore maintained virtually free trade. The acceleration of Southeast Asian economic growth a decade later was also associated with the liberalisation of trade and investment policies, particularly in Indonesia.[5] Some interpretations of the East Asian industrialisation experience have stressed the link between trade liberalisation and strong growth.[6] However, though this was clearly an important factor, it was by no means the only one.[7]

Neither the newly industrialising countries of Northeast Asia nor the countries of Southeast Asia (including Singapore) pursued non-interventionist economic policies over this period, but there was a significant tilt towards less discrimination between home and foreign production. Indeed, in South

Korea and Taiwan the balance perhaps actually tipped in favour of subsidising export production — complex systems of intervention persisted even in commodity markets, and their effects are difficult to disentangle completely.[8] Reasons have been put forward to suggest how, through the nature of competition, the exchange of market information, technological progress, and scale effects in the international marketplace, the presumed bias towards industrial export subsidisation promoted industrial and income growth.[9] The important point is that the direction of policy change in these countries was clearly towards two objectives: the removal of major distortions inhibiting trade growth, and the fostering of closer integration of the domestic with the international economy.[10] This twofold objective is one of the linchpins of industrialisation strategy throughout the region, and constitutes an important assumption upon which future development ambitions are based.[11]

Quite apart from the beneficial allocative and productivity effects[12] of outward-looking development strategies, another factor, based on trade expansion, favoured East Asian growth over these years.[13] The 1960s and early 1970s were decades of very strong growth in industrial countries, much of it concentrated in neighbouring Japan, and this growth was associated with some liberalisation of trade policy, which opened up markets for labour-intensive manufactures as structural adjustment took place in high-wage countries. The growth effects interacted powerfully with improved competitiveness, so that when world trade growth slowed later, in the 1970s and 1980s, East Asian and Western Pacific developing countries continued to enjoy more rapid trade growth as their exports of relatively labour-intensive commodities — a comparatively slow-growth category in world trade even during the high-growth phase — made big inroads into the market shares of established industrial exporters.

Japan's market share in exports of relatively labour-intensive commodities declined sharply at this time. Despite the increased competitiveness of its capital- and technology-intensive industries throughout the 1960s, Japan had continued to dominate world markets for many of the more sophisticated labour-intensive commodities until the early 1970s. A huge adjustment took place in trade in labour-intensive commodities over these years; a change that in some respects paralleled the change that took place in the 1920s and 1930s, when Japan emerged to challenge British pre-eminence in world textile markets. In the 1950s and early 1960s Japan had re-established its position in world markets for textiles and other labour-intensive commodities, and was beginning to build up a share in the markets for capital- and technology-intensive commodities. The steady reduction of discrimination against Japanese goods negotiated under the umbrella of the GATT and general trade liberalisation facilitated a huge transformation in the structure and growth of Japan's trade at this time. By the 1970s Japan had switched dramatically from being a leading exporter to being a significant importer of textiles and other labour-intensive goods.[14] In recent years a similar process of adjustment has begun to take place as the newly industrialising countries of Northeast Asia have started to give way to the lower-wage countries of ASEAN and

Table 6.2 Pacific trade in manufactured goods, 1964–66 and 1979–81 (per cent)

| | Exports to | | | | | |
| | Australasia | | North America | | Japan | |
Exports from	1964–66	1979–81	1964–66	1979–81	1964–66	1979–81
Australasia						
Labour-intensive	34.8	33.3	7.0	7.5	3.1	8.0
Capital-intensive	36.0	18.2	9.5	10.0	3.8	2.5
Total	35.9	20.1	9.3	9.7	3.8	3.2
Intensity	9.8	9.4	0.5	0.5	2.1	1.2
North America						
Labour-intensive	2.6	3.1	18.8	18.3	1.5	4.0
Capital-intensive	3.8	2.9	32.5	31.3	3.7	4.8
Total	3.7	2.9	31.1	30.3	3.5	4.8
Intensity	0.9	1.1	1.5	1.3	1.6	1.5
Japan						
Labour-intensive	4.2	3.0	28.0	13.6	—	—
Capital-intensive	4.3	3.5	33.6	29.7	—	—
Total	4.3	3.4	31.5	27.8	—	—
Intensity	1.2	1.6	1.8	1.5	—	—
China						
Labour-intensive	4.3	3.4	1.9	13.2	2.2	11.9
Capital-intensive	1.6	1.4	0.5	7.5	3.2	8.3
Total	3.4	2.8	1.4	11.2	2.6	10.7
Intensity	0.9	1.3	0.1	0.6	1.5	4.1
Asian NICs						
Labour-intensive	3.7	3.1	35.6	36.8	0.9	8.5
Capital-intensive	1.1	2.6	15.3	33.3	1.8	8.7
Total	2.9	2.9	29.3	35.1	1.2	8.6
Intensity	0.8	1.3	1.7	1.8	0.7	3.1
Other ASEAN countries						
Labour-intensive	3.1	5.1	20.8	26.1	4.7	5.9
Capital-intensive	1.8	3.0	5.0	30.2	3.0	7.8
Total	2.3	3.8	11.8	28.5	3.7	7.0
Intensity	0.6	1.8	0.7	1.5	2.1	2.6
All Pacific countries						
Labour-intensive	3.8	3.4	24.1	25.0	0.8	5.9
Capital-intensive	4.3	3.3	31.7	30.3	3.0	3.4
Total	4.2	3.3	30.1	29.4	2.5	3.9
Intensity	0.9	1.1	1.3	1.1	1.0	1.0
Rest of World						
Labour-intensive	2.2	0.8	12.1	6.4	0.5	1.3
Capital-intensive	2.8	1.0	9.9	7.6	1.1	1.2
Total	2.7	1.0	10.3	7.4	1.0	1.2
Intensity	0.2	0.2	0.2	0.1	0.2	0.2

Notes: a These figures are less than 0.05 per cent.
Source: International Economic Data Bank, Australian National University

China in the competition for world markets in simple manufactured goods.[15]

One very succinct yet comprehensive statement[16] of the origins of recent East Asian industrialisation experience identifies a number of important factors in the contemporary Asian economic environment which have promoted rapid growth: the international and regional economic climate favouring trade expansion and the timely adoption of both trade policies and economic policies that facilitated exploitation of the opportunities for international specialisation; the opportunities provided by 'dualistic' economic structures for transferring labour and other resources from low-productivity traditional activities to high-

China		Asian NICs		Other ASEAN		All Pacific		Rest of world	
1964–66	1979–81	1964–66	1979–81	1964–66	1979–81	1964–66	1979–81	1964–66	1979–81
0.1	1.8	7.9	14.7	9.4	3.6	62.3	68.9	37.7	31.1
0.3	2.2	3.7	9.0	9.5	7.8	62.8	49.7	37.2	50.3
0.3	2.2	4.0	9.7	9.5	7.3	62.8	52.2	37.2	47.8
0.5	2.2	1.7	1.8	3.5	2.9	2.2	1.6	0.5	0.7
0.0[a]	1.3	1.4	3.3	2.3	1.2	26.6	31.2	73.4	68.8
0.0	0.6	1.4	5.2	2.1	2.6	43.5	47.4	56.5	52.6
0.0	0.6	1.4	5.1	2.1	2.5	41.8	46.2	58.2	53.8
0.0	0.5	0.5	0.8	0.7	0.8	1.2	1.2	0.7	0.6
0.5	3.2	8.6	16.4	5.8	4.4	47.1	40.6	53.0	59.4
4.6	3.6	11.2	13.6	9.3	7.3	63.0	57.7	37.0	42.3
3.0	3.6	10.2	13.9	8.0	7.0	57.0	55.7	43.0	44.3
5.0	3.6	4.5	2.6	3.0	2.7	2.0	1.7	0.6	0.6
—	—	37.1	33.9	12.6	2.2	58.1	64.6	41.9	35.4
—	—	25.2	31.9	19.3	10.4	49.8	59.5	50.2	40.5
—	—	32.9	33.2	14.9	5.0	55.2	62.9	44.8	37.1
—	—	14.7	6.3	5.6	2.0	2.0	2.0	0.6	0.5
0.2	0.6	5.0	6.6	3.6	2.8	49.0	58.4	51.0	41.6
0.1	0.9	6.0	8.7	8.5	12.3	32.8	66.5	67.2	33.5
0.2	0.7	5.3	7.6	5.1	7.4	44.0	62.3	56.0	37.7
0.3	0.7	2.3	1.4	1.9	2.8	1.5	1.9	0.8	0.5
3.1	0.5	37.8	14.2	7.0	2.4	76.5	54.2	23.5	45.8
0.1	0.6	61.6	31.7	15.3	6.9	86.8	80.2	13.2	19.8
1.4	0.6	51.4	24.4	11.7	5.0	82.3	69.3	17.7	30.7
2.2	0.6	22.5	4.6	4.3	1.9	2.9	2.1	0.2	0.4
0.3	1.3	7.6	10.8	4.7	2.8	41.3	49.2	58.7	50.8
0.9	1.7	3.7	9.1	3.9	5.3	47.5	53.1	52.5	46.9
0.8	1.7	4.5	9.4	4.0	4.9	46.1	52.6	53.9	47.4
0.9	1.2	1.5	1.2	1.1	1.3	1.2	1.1	0.5	0.5
0.2	0.2	0.8	1.2	0.7	0.6	16.5	10.5	83.5	89.5
0.6	0.6	0.7	1.5	1.5	1.0	16.6	12.9	83.4	87.1
0.5	0.5	0.8	1.4	1.3	0.9	16.6	12.4	83.4	87.6
0.2	0.2	0.1	0.1	0.2	0.1	0.2	0.1	0.3	0.4

productivity 'modern' employment; the presence of scale economies in the production and distribution of both traded and non-traded goods within rapidly growing middle-income countries; high rates of investment from high savings ratios, supplemented in some countries by the constructive use of large net capital inflows; demographic structures which were and remain favourable to high growth; and abundant human capital in the form of high literacy rates and widespread general education which, in combination with the openness of most of these economies, has facilitated the rapid absorption of technology from abroad.[17] These factors were more prevalent in Northeast Asia and Singapore than in Southeast Asia. In the late 1970s, however,

Indonesian growth received a significant fillip from the growth of oil revenues.[18]

The same analysis rightly stresses that standard economic argument provides only a partial explanation of the East Asian industrialisation experience, and emphasises the variation in growth performance across countries in East Asia. A critical factor has been the political and social commitment to high growth and the acceptance of the associated inevitable social and economic changes.

> The political acceptance of structural change is associated with wide agreement within society that growth is advantageous, and this agreement is more readily forthcoming where the distribution of incomes and wealth is less unequal (Japan, Taiwan, and South Korea) or where the benefits of growth are widely distributed in the form of rising real wages or increased provision of widely-accessible public goods (Malaysia and Singapore). The social and political cohesion and the positive attitude to hard work directed at material advancement that are conducive to rapid growth and which are present to a relatively high degree in Japan, South Korea, Singapore and China (both mainland and Taiwan) also owe something to historical and cultural traditions. In the garrison states of Taiwan and South Korea, and to some extent the People's Republic of China and Singapore, perceptions of external military threats have reinforced social and political cohesion.[19]

Repression has also been a factor in the maintenance of political stability in some countries in Northeast Asia and Southeast Asia. It is not clear that the tensions repressed were closely related to the process of high economic growth — other political, ethnic and social issues were at the root of many of these conflicts. Indeed, the principal lesson from the East Asian experience seems to be that political repression is not capable of creating an environment within which growth can be maintained over long periods.[20] No appeal to external threat could smother the stark choice which emerged clearly in the aftermath of the assassination of President Park in South Korea in 1977 and the disturbances that followed in 1980 — the choice between retreating from 'democratisation' towards greater repression, and fracturing the economic growth process together with the basis of political cohesion it provided. Moreover, the East Asian experience confirms that there is no single cultural, social or institutional route to economic modernisation and industrialisation: beyond the political and social commitment to these goals, a variety of paths may successfully be followed.[21]

THE TRANSFORMATION OF PACIFIC TRADE STRUCTURE

Economic growth and the growth of manufactured goods exports from East Asian developing countries were achieved by a radical transformation in the structure of regional production and trade. Following the pattern in Japan, the composition of each country's manufacturing exports underwent more or less constant change.

By the early 1960s Japan's specialisation in manufactures had been well established for more than four decades. On the other hand, an important part of the entrepôt trade of Hong Kong and Singapore was still in agricultural commodities and raw materials, and Korea and Taiwan remained at that time substantial exporters of raw materials.[22] All this underwent spectacular change in the following decade, and by the end of the 1960s Korea and Taiwan had also become strong exporters of manufactures. Moreover, the combination of Northeast Asian productivity and wage growth and the accumulation of manufacturing skills in Southeast Asia had encouraged the emergence of manufactured exports from Southeast Asian countries, as well as from Singapore.[23] Table 6.3 reveals that, among the Southeast Asian countries, average hourly wages in manufacturing were lowest for Indonesia. However, until the mid-1980s Indonesia's comparative advantage was dominated by the availability of oil.[24] For other Southeast Asian countries and, significantly, for China, rising wages in the newly industrialising countries of Northeast Asia opened up the possibility of competitive exports of manufactured goods.

Table 6.3 Average hourly wages in manufacturing: selected Pacific countries, 1975–84 (current US$)

	1975	1976	1977	1978	1979	1980	1984[a]
Australia	2.93	2.38	3.76	4.03	4.34	4.79	—
Canada	5.30	6.03	6.68	7.16	7.79	8.57	8.50
China	—	—	—	—	—	—	0.26
Hong Kong	0.52	0.61	0.67	0.76	0.89	1.01	1.65
Indonesia[b]	0.11	-	0.21	—	—	—	—
Japan	4.60	5.16	5.65	6.04	6.41	6.88	6.30
Malaysia	0.58	—	0.67	—	—	—	—
New Zealand	2.15	2.46	2.83	3.24	3.74	4.45	—
Philippines	0.23	—	—	—	—	—	—
Singapore	0.89	0.93	0.98	1.04	1.15	1.30	—
South Korea	0.27	0.36	0.48	0.65	0.83	1.02	1.90
Taiwan[b]	0.49	—	0.65	0.76	0.96	—	—
Thailand	0.17	—	—	—	—	—	—
United States	4.83	5.22	5.68	6.69	6.70	7.27	8.60

Notes: a The figures in 1984 are total hourly wages in the spinning and weaving industry.
   b These figures have been calculated using 1979 exchange rates.
Sources: United Nations *Statistical Yearbook* New York. 1982; *Werner International Survey of Labour Costs*, from Aweave, Submission No. 134

An analysis of the changing composition of East Asian manufactured exports and imports, using value added per worker as a proxy for the labour intensity of manufacturing activity, provides useful insights into the changes that have taken place in these countries' industrial competitiveness.[25] Here again, manufactures ranked by value added per worker are divided into two broad categories: labour-intensive goods (produced by relatively unskilled labour using fairly standard and widely known technologies), and capital-intensive goods (produced by more highly skilled labour using more expensive equipment and more sophisticated and less accessible technologies and resources). Of course, the goods within each group embody, in varying degrees, other factors of production such as natural resources, machine technology and process technology and human capital; but the focus here is on changing relative labour availabilities and the structure of manufacturing trade specialisation, so that the labour-intensive and capital-intensive dichotomy is an appropriate device.[26] Classified in this way, labour-intensive goods accounted for 18.6 per cent of world trade in manufactured goods in the early 1980s, a fall from over 20 per cent in the early 1960s.

Pacific exports of manufactures broken down into these two categories are set out in Table 6.4 for the period 1962–84. The table also includes data for the same categories of imports of manufactures by the advanced industrial countries of Japan, North America and Australasia.

Except in the case of Japan, exports from all the industrial countries in the Pacific have been heavily concentrated in the capital-intensive group of goods for the entire period. United States exports of manufactures are overwhelmingly capital-intensive and also involve high technology and human-capital intensity.[27] Japan's exports now closely mirror the North American structure, although the structure was significantly different at the beginning of this period. The share of manufactures in total Australasian exports is small, but they are largely capital-intensive. Disaggregation of the Australasian and North American data would show that both New Zealand and Canadian manufactured exports are rather more heavily concentrated in labour-intensive goods than might be expected from their per capita incomes and relative wage levels (shown in Table 6.3). This results from the very low resistances to trade with Australia in the case of New Zealand, and with the United States in the case of Canada, reflecting close political and institutional associations, as well as geographic proximity and cultural factors which cause comparative advantage in the smaller partners to be determined, to an extent, bilaterally vis-à-vis their higher-income and higher-wage neighbours and partners.[28] More than half of New Zealand's manufactured exports are destined for Australia, and the share is even larger for Canadian exports to the United States.

Labour-intensive goods were still a big component of Japan's port trade at the beginning of the 1960s, accounting for over 40 per cent of Japanese manufactured exports at this time, double their share in world trade. Since that time a substantial change has taken place. By the early 1980s labour-intensive manufactures constituted only 14 per cent of Japan's manufactured exports. Moreover, Japan had become a significant importer of these goods, their share having climbed from less than 10 per cent to 24 per cent over these two decades, although manufactures remain a relatively small component of Japan's total imports. The structure of Japan's trade specialisation underwent particularly rapid adjustment in the 1970s in response to the concentrated pressures of trade liberalisation, domestic expansion, yen revaluation, and the promotion of capital outflow. Though these adjustments slowed down in the subsequent recession years, they resumed with the re-emergence of payments surpluses and further revaluations in the late 1970s and the mid-1980s.

Table 6.4 Shares of labour-intensive and capital-intensive goods[a] in East Asian exports and Pacific industrial country imports and exports of manufactured goods (per cent)

	1962-64	1964-66	1967-69	1970-72	1973-75	1976-78	1979-81	1982-84
Developing countries								
Hong Kong								
Labour-intensive[a]	83.0	81.4	77.8	74.8	68.9	65.6	60.4	58.8
Capital-intensive	17.0	18.6	22.2	25.2	31.1	34.4	39.6	41.2
Taiwan								
Labour-intensive	57.1	55.1	57.2	59.9	60.2	59.2	56.5	56.4
Capital-intensive	42.9	44.9	42.8	40.1	39.8	40.8	43.5	43.6
Korea								
Labour-intensive	69.1	79.7	85.7	76.8	62.9	62.8	53.8	56.9
Capital-intensive	30.9	20.3	14.3	23.2	37.1	37.2	46.2	43.1
Singapore								
Labour-intensive	28.4	28.8	34.3	33.3	26.3	27.5	23.8	23.5
Capital-intensive	71.6	71.2	65.7	66.7	73.7	72.5	76.2	76.5
Indonesia								
Labour-intensive	59.4	88.7	29.8	25.4	22.2	25.2	47.9	65.0
Capital-intensive	40.6	11.3	70.2	74.6	77.8	74.8	52.1	35.0
Malaysia								
Labour-intensive	23.5	25.4	37.7	49.7	43.7	42.7	29.1	23.1
Capital-intensive	76.5	74.6	62.3	50.3	56.3	57.3	70.9	76.8
Philippines								
Labour-intensive	89.6	89.5	83.6	68.4	72.2	69.3	69.0	65.7
Capital-intensive	10.4	10.5	16.4	31.6	27.8	30.7	31.0	34.3
Thailand								
Labour-intensive	34.6	38.9	47.0	50.8	57.8	68.6	68.4	67.3
Capital-intensive	65.4	61.1	53.0	49.2	42.2	31.4	31.6	32.7
China								
Labour-intensive	84.7	82.3	86.5	84.9	85.6	85.9	81.4	80.1
Capital-intensive	15.3	17.7	13.5	15.1	14.4	14.1	18.6	19.9
Industrial countries								
Japan								
Labour-intensive								
— exports	41.9	38.2	33.1	26.4	22.7	20.0	14.1	13.8
— imports	10.2	12.3	14.1	20.6	27.5	28.8	27.4	24.2
Capital-intensive								
— exports	58.1	61.8	66.9	73.6	77.3	80.0	85.9	86.2
— imports	89.9	87.7	85.9	79.4	72.5	71.2	72.6	75.8
North America								
Labour-intensive								
— exports	11.8	10.0	7.7	7.5	8.2	8.2	8.5	7.6
— imports	23.0	20.7	18.2	18.5	16.2	17.0	16.5	17.6
Capital-intensive								
— exports	88.2	90.0	92.3	92.5	91.8	91.8	91.5	92.4
— imports	77.0	79.3	81.8	81.5	83.8	83.0	83.5	82.4
Australasia								
Labour-intensive								
— exports	13.9	11.1	10.2	10.4	12.9	13.0	16.2	16.0
— imports	22.7	19.9	19.9	19.5	19.6	19.6	19.1	18.9
Capital-intensive								
— exports	86.1	88.9	89.8	89.6	87.1	87.0	83.8	84.0
— imports	77.3	80.1	80.1	80.5	80.4	80.4	80.9	81.1
World								
Labour-intensive								
— exports	21.7	21.0	20.1	20.2	19.5	19.6	18.3	18.2
— imports	21.1	20.5	19.5	19.4	18.7	19.3	18.6	18.9
Capital-intensive								
— exports	78.3	79.0	79.9	79.8	80.5	80.4	81.7	81.8
— imports	78.9	79.5	80.5	80.6	81.3	80.7	81.4	81.1

Note: a For commodity categories. see Anderson (ed) 'Pacific Economic Growth and the Prospects for Australian Trade' *Pacific Economic Papers* No. 122, Australian National University, Table A2.

Source: International Economic Data Bank, Australian National University

Labour-intensive manufactures have been the pre-eminent constituent of exports from the newly industrialising countries in East Asia since the early 1960s. However, as productivity, incomes and wages have risen, these countries have followed Japan, after a lag of several years, with growing specialisation in more capital-intensive exports. Labour-intensive exports still accounted for 59 per cent of Hong Kong's manufactured exports, 57 per cent of South Korea's and 56 per cent of Taiwan's in the early 1980s. The share of these commodities had risen steadily under conditions of labour surplus and more or less stable real wages through to 1968, after which South Korea and Taiwan moved into a period of rapid adjustment to increased capital availability and labour scarcities. The adjustments in both countries in the early 1970s paralleled those in Japan, although on a different plane. Exports of labour-intensive goods were at the base of Northeast Asian manufacturing performance throughout the 1960s, and they remain a critical factor in the prosperity of these countries despite the upsurge of increasingly sophisticated capital- and technology-intensive exports in recent years.

Singapore presents a rather different picture. Labour-intensive goods comprised 34 per cent of Singapore's manufactured exports at their peak in the late 1960s. Singapore began industrialisation with much higher per capita incomes and accumulations of human capital, and moved more quickly into capital- and technology-intensive exports, as well as trade in a wide range of services.

The timing and pattern of the trend towards stronger export specialisation in manufactures among the other Southeast Asian countries has been very different. The Philippines followed the Northeast Asian pattern most closely; its labour-intensive exports were around 70 per cent of its manufactured exports by 1970. Falling relative wages noticeably strengthened its comparative advantage vis-à-vis Northeast Asian competitors in the 1970s. Indonesia, Thailand and Malaysia have also enjoyed strong growth in labour-intensive manufactured goods exports but, especially in the case of Malaysia, capital-intensive manufactured exports (usually embodying high resource intensity) have also been important, as might be expected from the resource endowments and initial income levels and distributions in these countries.

China has the strongest comparative advantage in exports of labour-intensive commodities among all the countries of East Asia, with extremely low wage levels and rapidly rising productivity. In the early 1980s, these products held an 80 per cent share in China's total exports of manufactured goods.

Other studies have noted that the evolution of manufacturing towards more capital-intensive production proceeds through the 'upgrading' of output in terms of the final product, as well as through changes in the composition of output.[29] Textiles, which are generally included in the labour-intensive product group, encompass some highly sophisticated products (in terms of production technology and design characteristics).

The textile industry in Japan, for example, has steadily increased production and export specialisation at this end of the product range. This process occurs over a wide range of manufacturing activities, so that analysis of changing comparative advantage in industrial production in terms only of changes in the commodity composition of production and trade understates the extent of the industrial transformation that has in fact taken place in the Western Pacific economy.

In brief, the process of capital accumulation in manufacturing around the East Asian and Pacific economy has induced quite remarkable changes in the structure and direction of trade in manufactured goods. Variations in factor endowment and wage growth opened up the potential for the growth of the new trade flows. The potential for trade growth based upon differences in labour costs remains strong, as reflected in the wage variation among Northeast and Southeast Asian countries and the opportunities it presents for intra-regional trade growth as well as further trade growth with industrial countries in the Pacific and elsewhere. The persistence of protectionism in industrial countries and high levels of protection among the developing countries themselves, as within the ASEAN group, frustrates trade expansion and income growth. The relative stability in the shares of labour-intensive manufactured imports by Australasia and North America over a period of rapidly declining competitiveness for their labour-intensive import competing industries provides some indication of the opportunities for trade expansion that have not been realised.

Two important concerns have emerged about the overall effect of East Asian industrialisation and trade growth on competition in regional and international markets for manufactured goods, especially labour-intensive manufactures. One concern of powerful and vocal lobbies in industrial countries is the strength of competition in the markets for imported goods.[30] Another is whether this large trade growth has 'saturated' international markets and 'crowded out' latecomers, such as the ASEAN countries and China, from the process of rapid industrialisation.[31] An important conclusion here is that *the very success of established exporters of labour-intensive commodities weakened their comparative advantage* and left their competitive position in export markets open to corrosion by newcomers as they moved on to specialise in more complex and capital-intensive manufactures. This sequence can be observed in the data presented in Table 6.4. It is even more clearly evident in Table 6.5.

In the course of East Asia's rapid economic growth and industrialisation, textiles and other labour-intensive manufactures have been the leading export sector after the transition from primary production and export. In the lower-income (lower-wage) countries, manufactured exports are dominated by labour-intensive products. As real wages and skills rise, however, countries gradually switch to exporting more skill-intensive and capital-intensive products, leaving the unskilled-labour-intensive market to lower-wage countries. Japan began this transition in the 1960s, allowing Hong Kong, Korea, Singapore and Taiwan to export their labour-intensive products. More recently these countries began their own transition away from labour-intensive products, so that the other ASEAN countries and China are now finding a place in international markets for the products of their expanding light manufacturing industries. The gap left by Japan's gradual reduction in exports (and increase in imports) of labour-intensive manufactures has been more than filled, first by Hong Kong, Korea and Taiwan and also, more recently, by the ASEAN countries and China.[32] China's share of total world trade is small, and even its share in the markets for labour-intensive products is still very small (see Table 6.5). However, China's increased involvement in world trade is likely to lead to a huge restructuring of trade in labour-intensive goods over the coming decades.[33]

Table 6.5 East Asia's share in world exports of textiles and other labour-intensive products (per cent)

	1962-64	1964-66	1967-69	1970-72	1973-75	1976-78	1979-81	1982-84
Japan								
Textiles	14.4	14.0	13.7	11.6	8.0	6.9	5.9	6.6
Other	12.6	16.3	18.0	17.9	18.8	18.4	13.3	15.4
Total	13.6	15.0	15.7	14.5	13.3	12.9	9.6	11.1
Northeast Asia[a]								
Textiles	5.0	5.7	7.9	10.8	13.9	18.1	18.4	19.8
Other	2.1	2.8	4.6	5.5	5.3	7.6	10.0	12.7
Total	3.7	4.4	6.4	8.3	9.6	12.6	14.3	16.2
ASEAN								
Textiles	0.9	0.7	0.7	0.8	1.3	1.9	2.5	2.9
Other	0.8	1.0	0.8	1.0	1.5	1.9	2.8	3.6
Total	0.8	0.9	0.8	0.9	1.4	1.9	2.7	3.3
China								
Textiles	2.2	3.0	2.6	2.0	2.7	2.7	4.2	6.3
Other	0.5	1.0	1.2	0.9	1.1	1.1	1.5	1.8
Total	1.4	2.1	1.9	1.5	1.9	1.9	2.9	4.0
All East Asia								
Textiles	22.5	23.4	24.9	25.2	25.9	29.6	31.0	35.6
Other	16.0	21.1	24.6	25.3	26.7	29.0	27.7	33.5
Total	19.5	22.4	24.8	25.2	26.2	29.3	29.4	34.6
Rest of World								
Textiles	77.5	76.6	75.1	74.8	74.1	70.4	69.0	64.4
Other	84.0	78.9	75.4	74.7	73.3	71.0	71.0	66.5
Total	80.5	77.6	75.2	74.8	73.8	70.7	70.6	65.4

Note: a Does not include Japan and China.
Source: International Economic Data Bank, Australian National University

Table 6.6 reveals the importance of the North American market for East Asian exporters of textiles and other labour-intensive commodities. In the early 1960s North America alone accounted for 19 per cent of world textile imports and 19 per cent of world imports of all labour-intensive products. At the beginning of the 1980s these shares were even higher, at 25 per cent and 24 per cent respectively. At the same time, the importance of Western Europe as a market for labour-intensive goods has risen slightly for textiles and fallen for other labour-intensive products. However, much of that market is the preserve of other European suppliers and of developing countries with special links with the European Community. The share of East Asian countries in the European market has risen from 6 per cent to 14 per cent over these 20 years, but, despite competition from Latin American suppliers, East Asian exporters hold a very large share of the North American market. Among

Table 6.6 Pacific share in world markets for textiles and other labour-intensive products (per cent)

	1962-64	1964-66	1967-69	1970-72	1973-75	1976-78	1979-81	1982-84
Imports								
North America								
Textiles	18.9	17.5	19.5	20.9	16.0	17.7	16.7	24.8
Other	18.9	18.6	20.7	19.6	15.6	14.8	16.2	23.1
Total	18.9	18.0	20.0	20.3	15.8	16.3	16.5	24.0
Japan								
Textiles	0.5	0.6	1.2	1.9	4.2	3.6	4.0	4.0
Other	1.7	1.9	2.4	3.7	4.0	3.4	4.1	4.1
Total	1.0	1.2	1.7	2.7	4.1	3.5	4.1	4.1
Australasia								
Textiles	3.6	3.6	2.9	2.5	2.8	2.3	2.1	2.2
Other	2.2	3.1	2.8	2.2	2.3	1.9	2.2	2.6
Total	3.1	3.4	2.9	2.4	2.6	2.1	2.1	2.4
Pacific industrial countries[a]								
Textiles	23.0	21.6	23.6	25.3	23.0	23.6	22.8	31.0
Other	22.9	23.7	25.9	25.5	21.9	20.2	22.5	29.8
Total	22.9	22.5	24.6	25.4	22.5	21.9	22.7	30.5
Western Europe								
Textiles	49.8	50.0	51.4	54.0	56.8	56.8	58.1	53.4
Other	55.0	54.0	53.0	55.0	56.4	52.2	50.7	46.2
Total	52.0	51.7	52.1	54.5	56.6	54.6	54.6	49.9
Exports								
Share of East Asia[b] in Pacific markets								
Textiles	32.3	35.8	41.6	45.0	47.6	56.6	59.1	64.2
Other	32.7	32.7	35.7	36.5	34.7	39.9	42.5	47.8
Total	32.4	34.4	38.9	41.2	41.8	49.0	51.2	56.5
Share of East Asia in North American market								
Textiles	33.2	36.5	41.6	44.0	43.1	54.4	58.2	64.3
Other	36.8	38.0	40.7	42.0	36.8	43.8	46.9	51.5
Total	34.7	37.2	41.2	43.1	40.2	49.6	52.8	58.4
Share of East Asia in European markets								
Textiles	8.2	8.8	8.2	6.7	10.7	12.2	13.4	14.3
Other	4.2	7.4	9.1	8.8	10.0	13.4	12.9	14.2
Total	6.4	8.2	8.6	8.7	10.4	12.8	13.2	14.2

Notes: a Includes Australia, Japan. Canada. the United States and New Zealand.
 b Includes Japan.
Source: International Economic Data Bank. Australian National University

East Asian exporters, Japan's competitive position in all major markets has declined sharply, as can be seen from Table 6.5. By the early 1980s Japan was itself beginning to emerge as a significant import market for labour-intensive goods.[34] Australasia, while it is a small market in absolute terms, draws an overwhelming proportion of its labour-intensive imports from East Asia. Both the Pacific and the world markets grew larger, although some East Asian suppliers had limited access to European markets and the growth of trade in labour-intensive products was slower than the total trade growth in industrial goods. A critical element allowing rapid growth of exports from East Asian developing countries was the retreat of Japan from these markets. This finding is particularly valid[35] when account is taken of the scope to shift production towards more capital-intensive products within this

Table 6.7 The penetration[a] of manufactured goods imports into Pacific and other industrial country markets (per cent)

	1970	1971	1972	1973	1974	1975
North America						
Textiles, clothing, footwear						
— East Asian[b] exporting	1.45	1.89	1.65	2.43	2.76	3.18
— other developing	0.89	1.01	1.79	1.47	1.84	1.64
— total	7.11	7.95	8.49	8.76	9.17	9.16
Other labour-intensive						
— East Asian exporting	1.33	1.51	1.28	2.62	3.08	2.61
— other developing	0.39	0.43	1.26	0.72	1.00	0.91
— total	8.81	9.82	11.13	12.26	12.63	11.64
Japan						
Textiles, clothing, footwear						
— East Asian exporting	1.77	2.20	2.69	4.86	5.22	3.88
— other developing	0.55	0.63	0.64	1.01	0.76	0.50
— total	4.19	4.54	5.10	8.59	9.08	6.80
Other labour-intensive						
— East Asian exporting	0.63	0.55	0.62	1.35	1.51	1.21
— other developing	0.06	0.16	0.14	0.08	0.12	0.14
— total	3.64	3.63	3.84	4.30	5.35	4.90
Australia						
Textiles, clothing, footwear						
— East Asian exporting	4.71	5.71	5.32	6.76	9.16	8.60
— other developing	2.53	2.05	3.19	4.44	6.18	3.55
— total	26.33	27.16	26.63	29.07	35.88	29.25
Other labour-intensive						
— East Asian exporting	2.27	2.27	1.69	2.60	3.69	2.38
— other developing	0.44	0.59	0.91	1.40	1.66	1.32
— total	25.02	22.27	22.22	23.78	28.21	29.86
Pacific industrial[c]						
Textiles. clothing, footwear						
— East Asian exporting	1.58	2.03	1.95	3.21	3.57	3.51
— other developing	0.87	0.96	1.58	1.43	1.71	1.41
— total	7.03	7.77	8.19	9.26	10.02	9.16
Other labour-intensive						
— East Asian exporting	1.15	1.26	1.10	2.19	2.60	2.16
— other developing	0.30	0.36	0.92	0.52	0.74	0.68
— total	7.73	8.38	9.21	9.82	10.75	10.08
Western Europe[d]						
Textiles, clothing, footwear						
— East Asian exporting	1.40	1.60	1.92	2.46	2.89	3.35
— other developing	1.66	1.83	2.25	2.88	2.97	2.99
— total	22.01	23.79	26.36	29.59	31.91	32.74
Other labour-intensive						
— East Asian exporting	0.79	0.78	0.97	1.67	1.50	1.59
— other developing	0.84	1.09	1.02	1.28	1.00	0.91
— total	24.22	24.20	25.37	29.99	30.38	29.85

Notes: a Penetration is defined as imports from a country divided by apparent consumption, where apparent consumption is production *plus* imports *minus* exports.
b East Asia includes China, Korea, Taiwan, Hong Kong, and the ASEAN countries. Japan is not included.
c Pacific industrial is North America, Australia and Japan.
d Western Europe is Belgium, Luxembourg, Finland, France, West Germany, Italy, the Netherlands, Norway, Sweden and the United Kingdom

Source: OECD compatible trade and production data base, International Economic Data Bank, Australian National University

1976	1977	1978	1979	1980	1981	1982	1983
4.53	4.43	5.99	6.09	6.77	7.55	8.09	8.85
1.83	1.69	2.20	2.38	2.27	2.42	2.13	2.34
10.86	10.39	13.08	13.36	13.28	14.30	14.28	15.44
3.40	3.57	4.16	4.63	4.83	5.08	5.50	5.96
0.96	0.38	1.00	1.13	1.09	1.14	1.22	1.45
14.29	13.74	15.13	15.15	14.74	15.68	15.87	17.90
4.58	4.30	5.20	6.38	5.40	5.97	6.09	5.22
0.57	0.43	0.57	0.83	0.59	0.66	0.82	0.72
7.54	7.30	8.46	10.84	9.53	10.10	10.50	8.94
1.51	1.27	1.15	1.65	1.60	1.51	1.48	1.45
0.23	0.11	0.16	0.21	0.29	0.26	0.12	0.12
5.46	4.80	5.00	5.82	6.49	5.71	5.30	5.22
10.11	10.42	10.66	11.28	11.59	16.34	17.76	15.84
4.73	6.32	7.00	7.58	7.69	3.49	3.29	2.93
35.38	37.38	37.94	39.21	38.51	38.11	39.30	35.20
3.57	4.58	3.87	4.84	4.66	7.51	7.23	5.75
1.82	1.89	2.09	2.61	3.14	0.44	0.64	0.39
29.92	32.11	30.86	35.01	33.65	37.90	38.93	33.99
4.70	4.54	5.87	6.30	6.52	7.38	7.83	8.14
1.60	1.49	1.84	2.05	1.95	2.00	1.83	1.97
10.71	10.27	12.33	13.24	12.92	13.86	13.97	14.34
2.83	2.90	3.17	3.67	3.76	3.99	4.32	4.59
0.76	0.64	0.75	0.86	0.87	0.84	0.87	1.03
12.01	11.48	12.14	12.54	12.41	13.00	13.24	14.40
4.10	4.20	4.29	4.76	5.43	6.96	6.87	6.81
3.93	4.28	4.43	5.02	5.13	5.38	5.53	5.77
36.64	38.09	40.84	43.18	44.35	47.38	48.64	50.00
2.35	2.73	2.88	3.80	3.78	2.26	4.34	5.33
0.99	1.11	1.09	1.29	1.15	0.59	1.13	1.22
34.01	35.18	34.88	35.77	34.62	20.11	38.84	41.38

commodity group, and of the fact that in part the evolution of trade specialisation by established industrial producers took this form.[36]

There was a net expansion of international markets for textiles and other labour-intensive commodities throughout the 1970s, although this came to a halt, at least momentarily, in the mid-1980s. Import penetration of industrial country markets, particularly in the Pacific, grew steadily over these years, from 7 per cent to 14 per cent for textiles, and from 8 per cent to 14 per cent for other labour-intensive manufactures, as shown in Table 6.7. Details of the proportions of Pacific and other industrial country consumption of labour-intensive manufactured goods supplied by imports from East Asia and other sources are set out in this table.[37] These statistics reveal that a large proportion of consumption is still supplied by domestic producers (usually under various. forms of protection) to most industrial country markets for these commodities. Import penetration is much higher for Western European than for Pacific countries on average, but developing countries supplied less than one-quarter of imports to Europe, most of which were drawn from within the region. Nonetheless, access, first to Pacific and then to European markets, has been critical to East Asian trade growth and industrialisation, partly because of the expansion of the total market but mainly because of the sharp decline in Japan's competitiveness in these markets in the early 1970s, under the influence of rising costs, the strong yen, and trade regulation. The newly industrialising countries of East Asia were substantially more important suppliers of labour-intensive manufactures in the early 1980s than they had been in the early 1970s, largely at the expense of Japan, and much more for Pacific markets than for other industrial countries.

ACCESS FOR PACIFIC INDUSTRIAL EXPORTS

The success of development strategies such as those that have been embraced by East Asian developing countries clearly depends on reasonable access to international markets. Trade growth is partly just a function of growth in international incomes and the opportunity which market growth provides to new suppliers. But it also comes at the expense of established domestic suppliers in foreign markets or established suppliers to export markets. How easily it comes is conditioned in turn by the international trading and trade policy environment. Earlier, the importance of a favourable international trading and trade policy environment to the success of the development strategies of the newly industrialising countries in Asia was stressed. A few decades before, Japan's postwar trade and industrial recovery was favoured by the same conditions.

The postwar trade liberalisation of industrial countries, under the auspices of the GATT, favoured trade expansion generally.[38] While commodities of direct interest to developing countries were not a major part of this process, it was nonetheless critical to their interests. Two aspects are worthy of note. Importantly, trade liberalisation among the stronger industrial countries facilitated the evolution of new specialisations in international trade and the vacation of international markets as developing countries established their competitive strength, particularly in the exportation of labour-intensive products.[39] Additionally, Japan was gradually accorded non-discriminatory (most-favoured-nation) treatment under the GATT, and the opportunity to re-establish and extend its position in world markets for light manufactured goods. There was also some general liberalisation of trade in these products, but that appears unimportant alongside the opportunities provided by the shedding of the import markets held by industrial countries. This pattern is reflected in the story of East Asian and Pacific trade and industrial transformation recounted above.

Table 6.8 Selected Pacific and industrial country tariffs against industrial goods exports, 1980 (per cent)

	Pacific					Other industrial			
	Australia	United States		Japan		EEC		Sweden	
	Tariff average[a]	Tariff average[b]	Standard deviation	Tariff average[b]	Standard deviation	Tariff average[b]	Standard deviation	Tariff average[b]	Standard deviation
Rubber	18.6	4.5	3.2	2.7	4.5	2.2	3.4	5.1	4.4
Raw hides and skins, leather	29.4[c]	10.6	2.7	5.8	6.5	5.1	4.1	7.9	2.6
Furs	—	1.6	2.4	15.7	5.5	1.6	2.5	3.1	3.0
Wood and cork	8.1	1.0	1.9	0.6	1.5	2.5	2.3	1.6	1.6
Textiles	20.3	18.2	6.6	5.4	5.6	8.5	5.2	20.2	3.4
Mineral products and fertiliser	8.8	4.3	4.1	1.1	1.6	3.0	3.2	2.9	3.0
Precious stones and precious metals	—	1.3	2.5	3.0	1.5	0.2	0.5	1.1	3.2
Ores and metals	11.2	3.0	1.8	1.5	3.4	2.2	2.4	2.2	1.8
Chemicals	—	4.1	1.8	5.2	0.9	5.6	2.4	2.9	3.1
Machinery, transport equipment and scientific instruments	11.8[d]	3.3	1.2	4.4	0.6	5.9	1.7	3.0	0.9
Miscellaneous manufactures	—	4.9	1.3	4.9	0.3	6.6	0.4	3.1	0.6
Other products not elsewhere specified in CCN chs 25-99 (excluding petroleum)	—	1.0	—[e]	1.2	—[e]	2.0	—[e]	0.9	—[e]
All industrial products (excluding petroleum)	11.5	4.3	1.8	2.7	2.5	4.6	2.7	4.0	1.5

Notes: a MFN duty weighted average as of 1981 based on imports in 1980/81 from MFN and GSP sources. Subdivisions for calculating standard deviations are not available.
b Tariff average of the post-Tokyo-Round MFN tariff weighted by values of 1977 imports of MFN origin for the country concerned. Standard deviation measures the disparity of tariff rates across subdivisions, determined by the degree of processing, about the tariff average.
c Leather manufactures only.
d Electric machines and apparatus.
e Subdivisions not available.

Source: Compiled from the General Agreement on Tariffs and Trade *Tariff Escalation: Note by the Secretariat* document prepared for the Committee on Trade and Development, Forty-First Session, 10-11 July 1980, COM.TD/w-/315, July 1980 and *Part Four Consultations: Background information Australia, Note by the Secretariat,* Committee on Trade and Development, Fifty-Seventh Session, 14-16 October 1985

But, despite the significant trend towards trade liberalisation in the postwar period, protection against labour-intensive imports (and agricultural imports, as noted in chapter 5) remains deeply entrenched in industrial countries. In addition, a wide array of special agreements and arrangements, beginning with the United States–Japan Cotton Textile Agreement of the late 1950s,[40] governs and limits access for these commodities to the world's main markets.[41]

High tariffs are only one aspect of the protection system that limits import penetration in most industrial countries. However, tariff structures provide an indication of the overall impact of protection systems. Table 6.8 details average tariff levels and standard deviations across commodity categories for manufactured imports into the principal Pacific and other industrial countries at the end of the Tokyo Round of Multilateral Trade Negotiations (the last successful GATT initiative) in 1975 to 1979.[42]

Labour-intensive goods attract by far the highest tariff rates, and the large variation in tariffs on these commodities suggests a tariff structure specially targeted to cushion the impact of trade competition and restrict market penetration.[43]

High tariff levels in industrial countries help to explain why industrial country imports of labour-intensive goods have retained such a stable share in overall imports and why import penetration was so limited and unchanging until the mid-1970s.

The pattern of protection against labour-intensive imports across industrial countries is partly a reflection simply of the pattern of comparative disadvantage among these countries in the production of these goods. If the tariff data in Table 6.8 are compared with the data in Table 6.7 on import penetration ratios, it can be seen that the highest tariff rates and the highest variation in tariff rates are also associated with high levels of import penetration, or strong comparative disadvantage in the production of labour-intensive goods. An outstanding example is Australia, where, despite high tariff rates, import penetration ratios were generally higher than average import penetration ratios for industrial countries. Moreover, developing countries, principally in East Asia and the Pacific, were responsible for most of the growth of import penetration in the case of Australia, unlike the case for other industrial countries (except Sweden).

Caution needs to be taken when using tariff data alone to compare protection levels for the textiles, clothing and footwear industries across countries because of the widespread use of quantitative restrictions on trade in these commodities. Quantitative restrictions are ubiquitous and include so-called 'voluntary export restraints' (VERs), negotiated on a country-by-country basis. Non-tariff trade barriers became increasingly prevalent after the mid-1970s. One estimate suggests that no less than 75 per cent of world trade in these commodities is subject to quota restrictions or special agreements.[44] Typically, 'orderly marketing arrangements' (OMAs) or 'voluntary export restraints' (VERs) were initially negotiated with Japan outside the framework of the GATT.[45] In the mid-1950s, textile trade restrictions in the United States took the form of an agreement with Japan in 32 categories of cotton products.[46] By the beginning of the 1980s the United States had agreements with more than 20 countries, covering hundreds of product categories for labour-intensive manufactures alone. They have also extended to an ever-increasing range of industrial product categories and have been widely emulated by European importers, both on a national and an industry-specific level. The incidence of these restrictions falls particularly heavily upon the fast-growing exporters of manufactured goods from the newly industrialising East Asian countries. Not only do they limit market access generally; because they entail country and industry-specific deals, they also involve discrimination against new suppliers in the process of transforming international trade specialisation.

The effect of these specific deals and non-tariff trade barriers is large. One estimate suggests that 43 per cent of United States imports are now covered by special non-tariff trade barriers, many of these emanating from the precedent of bilateral arrangements with Japan.[47] Some data on non-tariff trade barriers for other countries, including import restrictions, voluntary export restraints, and negotiated arrangements in labour-intensive exports of importance to developing countries are assembled in Table 6.9. These data give only an imprecise measure of the scope and impact of non-tariff trade barriers, but they reveal them to be now quite pervasive.

Table 6.9 Non-tariff protection in the Asian-Pacific region (controlled trade by country, as a percentage of total trade)

	All goods				Manufactures			
	1974	1979	1980	1983[a]	1974	1979	1980	1983[a]
Australia	17.9	34.8	34.8	34.1	7.8	30.0	30.0	23.6
Canada	22.4	18.3	18.3	—	11.4	5.8	5.8	—
Japan	56.1	59.4	59.4		0.0	4.3	4.3	7.7
United States	36.2	44.4	45.8	43.0	5.6	18.4	21.0	—
Non-oil developing countries	49.8	46.8	46.9	—	25.0	22.7	22.8	17.1
OECD	36.3	43.8	44.3	—	4.0	16.8	17.4	—
All industrial country markets	—	—	—	27.1	—	—	—	16.1
World	40.1	47.5	47.8	—	12.9	23.0	23.6	—

Note: a Figures in 1983 are non-tariff barrier coverage percentages using 1983 own-country imports for weighting purposes.
Sources: S.A.B. Page 'The Revival of Protectionism and its Consequences for Europe' *Journal of Common Market Studies* XX, 1, September 1981, table 1: Saxonhouse and Stern 'An Analytical Survey of Formal and Informal Barriers to International Trade and Investment in the United States, Canada, and Japan' paper presented to a Conference on United States-Canadian Trade and Investment Relations with Japan, Ann Arbor, Michigan, 2-3 April 1987, table 3

The most fully developed of such arrangements is the Multi-Fibre Agreement (MFA) for textiles, under which industrial countries impose commodity- and country-specific quotas on the whole range of natural and synthetic yarns, cloth and garments from developing countries.[48] This agreement has evolved out of 'a series of broadening actions [from] a simple United States–Japan bilateral "voluntary export restraint" arrangement in 1957 to limit United States imports of Japanese "dollar blouses" and imprinted cotton cloth'.[49] Japan–United States and Japan–Europe trade in steel, automobiles, VCRs and semiconductors has also become subject to 'management' in this way.

'Managed' trading has slowed, but not completely blocked, the trade and industrial transformation of the newly industrialising countries of East Asia. New exporters have been able to adjust their trade structure or circumvent restrictions, thus avoiding some of the damaging effects of these arrangements.[50]

Throughout the 1970s and early 1980s, trade restructuring continued apace. Successful trade transformation in this period was accomplished partly by East Asian countries exploiting the weaknesses and administrative 'inefficiencies' in the 'new' protectionism (coupled with the sheer strength of their growing competitive power),[51] and partly by the safety net which reference to the non-discriminatory trading principles of the GATT continued to provide, however imperfectly. Neither condition is necessarily permanent. The 'management' of trade restrictions has become more comprehensive and administratively 'efficient'. The GATT system has become so compromised by these (and other) exceptions to its principles that it now provides less and less insurance against the politics of protectionism in industrial countries, notably in the United States, which heretofore had provided the ideological and political bulwark of the open GATT-based international trading system.[52]

The second aspect of market access relates to that held by established export suppliers. An important conclusion here is that access to established export markets and the shedding of these markets by more mature industrial countries has been critical to the success of East Asian trade and industrial adjustment. Japan's entry into international markets in the years between the wars took place in quite a different climate, in which there was extensive discrimination in trade policy, and growing bilateralism was heavily directed against new entrants and encouraged the protection of established trade shares in old imperial markets. In this kind of policy environment, the scope for effective and smooth trade and industrial transformation was seriously handicapped. If new competitors are sufficiently determined adjustment may nonetheless take place, but it is likely to exacerbate economic and political tensions of the sort that were experienced in prewar years. One disturbing feature of the data laid out in Table 6.9 is that such discrimination in trade policies appears to have become a much more prevalent feature of restrictions on world trade over the past decade. The principle of most-favoured-nation treatment is being seriously eroded as restrictions are increasingly negotiated or applied on a bilateral basis. The very nature of 'voluntary export restraints', for example, is that they discriminate among suppliers.[53] In assessing the future of Pacific industrialisation and trade growth, and international economic policy strategy, this development is a serious concern.

TRADE PROSPECTS AND POLICY COMMITMENTS

In large measure, Japan can be regarded as the 'leading edge' of East Asian growth, developing industries and markets which are subsequently taken over by the newly industrialising countries of the region. Importantly, this process depends on access for newer Japanese products in European and North American markets and on continued access to those markets for 'older' products as competitiveness in their production shifts from Japan to other countries in East Asia.

A further issue which merits attention is related to the opportunities for growth of trade within the region itself. Thus far, the largest element in Pacific trade growth has been vertical trade, commonly the exchange of manufactures for raw materials and food. As chapter 5 and this chapter make clear, the large differences in factor endowment within the region provide a strong incentive for continuing and steady growth of vertical trade in the

Pacific economy. But a new force in regional trade and industrialisation is now emerging around Japan's economic success, and around the appearance of competing industrial economies in East Asia and the commercial networks that have been built upon the established trade in raw materials and manufactures. The next phase of East Asian industrialisation is likely to involve substantial growth in intra-industry trade within the region, the potential for which is as yet largely unexploited.[54]

As Table 6.10a demonstrates, the degree of intra-industry trade in the Pacific economy is very low compared with that within Europe, or even that within the Atlantic economy. In all categories of manufactured goods trade, the index of intra-industry trade for the Pacific is much lower than that for Europe and the Atlantic. However, the index of intra-industry trade for Pacific countries rose from 14.24 per cent to 17.19 per cent between the mid-1970s and the early 1980s, and it is likely that the gap between the levels of intra-industry trade in the Pacific and Europe will continue to narrow. Intra-industry trade within the Western Pacific is exceptionally low, but also rose considerably between 1975 and 1982. Table 6.10b reveals that levels of intra-industry trade for each region's trade into the world as whole are higher than intra-regional intra-industry trade. This reflects the advantages of proximity in food and resource trade specialisation and the global scope of industrial goods markets. This table also reveals more strongly increasing world intra-industry trade for Pacific countries between 1975 and 1982. At the same time, the large difference between indexes of intra-industry for Western Pacific and Atlantic countries remains. These differences of degree and trend in intra-industry trade reflect the underlying structure of resource endowment within each regional economy, its overall stage of economic development, and differences in intra-regional variation in stages of economic development. In turn, these factors affect the trade and foreign investment climate as it shapes opportunities for intra-industry trade growth.[55]

Intra-industry trade growth is in part based on close investment cooperation. American and Japanese direct foreign investment in East Asia and the Pacific has been quite substantial, as outlined in chapter 3. However, direct foreign investment, especially by large Japanese corporate investors, has been relatively modest. These corporations have been attracted towards investment in North America and Australia in establishing offshore production capacity in recent years, but they have few large, integrated production systems throughout East Asia and the Pacific. Small-scale Japanese investors have been more ambitious in terms of the relocation of production capacity elsewhere in East Asia as Japan-based production has become increasingly uncompetitive. In consequence, the structure of trade and international industrial activities that has developed in East Asia and the Pacific has not supported, from the Japanese industrial base, extensive intra-industry trade in manufactured goods in the past. However, this is changing, especially because of the sharp currency, cost and trade adjustments in the mid-1980s.[56] Offshore operations based on locational, resource, energy or marketing advantages still appear somewhat risky to large Japanese investors, despite the significant cost changes that

Table 6.10a   Intra-industry trade indexes[a] for intra-regional trade in the Pacific, Europe and the Atlantic (per cent)

	North America		Western Pacific		Pacific		Europe		Atlant c	
	1975	1985	1975	1985	1975	1985	1975	1985	1975	1985
All manufactures[b]	67.28	70.68	26.91	43.99	64.00	68.17	67.06	71.10	67.64	70.24
Labour-intensive manufactures	40.70	56.01	37.40	42.63	40.15	54.77	68.79	65.39	66.44	62.98
Capital-intensive manufactures	69.02	71.79	24.65	45.29	65.69	69.25	69.51	72.47	68.13	71.64
All commodities	54.27	61.47	18.86	33.51	51.42	59.17	62.42	64.29	59.81	63.29

Table 6.10b   Intra-industry trade indexes[a] for all Pacific, European and Atlantic trade (per cent)

	North America		Western Pacific		Pacific		Europe		Atlantic	
	1975	1985	1975	1985	1975	1985	1975	1985	1975	1985
All manufactures[b]	61.86	62.96	25.98	22.19	59.00	60.72	66.32	70.28	65.21	67.97
Labour-intensive manufactures	45.63	30.15	17.06	22.21	42.33	29.63	66.28	62.55	62.91	54.39
Capital-intensive manufactures	63.43	68.01	26.93	21.29	60.75	65.55	65.83	71.76	65.18	70.51
All commodities	48.69	54.69	18.19	21.49	45.69	52.15	55.35	61.68	53.57	59.52

Notes: a Weighted average calculated at SITC 3-digit level.
             b Commodity categories defined as above.
Source: International Economic Data Bank. Australian National University

have emerged in this period, but less and less so.

For example, the growth of intra-industry trade in motor vehicles and components has been rapid, although from a low base. Japanese corporations, notably the Mitsubishi Motor Corporation, are now following American producers in establishing integrated regional production and marketing systems. Regional production systems in this industry, and in electronics and other industries, quickened the pace of intra-industry trade growth in the mid-1980s.[57] Even the textile and other labour-intensive industries witnessed sizeable intra-industry trade growth in this period, as revealed in the indexes for intra-industry trade in labour-intensive manufactures shown in Table 6.10.[58]

An important component of intra-industry trade is critically linked to foreign investment and international corporate strategies. Intra-industry trade is certainly not uniquely dependent on the operations of multinational corporations, but international corporate activities and networks[59] (including those of multinational corporations) are one important ingredient in the growth of intra-industry trade. The future growth of this trade will therefore be closely related to the encouragement of multinational corporate operations, joint ventures or other forms of international corporate association to exploit the advantages of multinational production within East Asia and the Pacific. Active support, in the form not only of open trade policies but also of open investment policies and commercial policies affecting the freedom to trade a range of services, is required to facilitate these trade and international industrial activities.

The rapid industrialisation experience of the developing countries of East Asia contains five main lessons. These will be taken up again in chapters 8 and 9, where policy problems and approaches are reviewed more fully.

First, these countries shared a *common commitment to outward-looking development strategies*, by way of strong development ambitions and a pragmatic openness in international economic relations. While the countries of the Western Pacific may be extremely different in many respects (not only in their social, cultural and political characteristics, but also in their economic and resource characteristics), they have this common feature, which constitutes a basis for cooperative collective action. Second, the distribution of resources among the countries of East Asia is such that realisation of industrialisation ambitions would be impossible without trade growth. *Increased trade dependence* and integration into the regional and international economy *was a necessary condition of successful industrialisation*, most obviously for the resource-deficient countries of Northeast Asia and Singapore, but equally significantly for Malaysia, Thailand, and Indonesia. Initially small, poor economies, deficient in either natural resources or capital and industrial technology, have gained enormously in productivity and income from trade growth. Third, the industrial transformation that has taken place in the Pacific economy required *the acceptance of major structural adjustments by established international traders*, first the United States and then Japan, and future growth in industrialisation and trade requires the continued acceptance of similar adjustments. Much of the cost of adjustment to East Asian industrialisation was first borne in domestic American markets. The initial cost of adjustment by Japan to other East Asian industrialisation was first borne in its international markets, although domestic market adjustments are now the issue. Northeast Asian countries are already dependent on access to international markets for more sophisticated manufactures, and Japan on access to worldwide markets for products which are more capital-intensive and use advanced technology.[60] Failure at any point in this chain of international market access will damage, in some measure, the process of industrial transformation in Pacific countries. Fourth, the success of East Asian industrialisation has opened up *opportunities for intra-industry trade growth* supported by international industrial and commercial activities and networks. Finally, an international trade and economic policy environment where a substantial measure of *international trade competition* is tolerated, if not always welcomed, and where the principle of *non-discrimination* holds firmly enough to allow continued access for newcomers to markets for manufactures, seems to have been a sine qua non for East Asian development and industrialisation over the past few decades.

These five conditions are not necessarily permanent or in any sense inevitable. They are rather objectives of policy as much as they are the conditions upon which successful trade and development strategy can be based.

NOTES

Chapter 6

1   OECD *The Impact of the Newly Industrialising Countries on Production and Trade in Manufactures* Paris: OECD, June 1979; Garnaut *ASEAN*, especially chs 1 and 13; and Anderson and Garnaut *Australian Protectionism*.
2   Garnaut *ASEAN* chs 1 and 13.
3   Anderson and Garnaut *Australian Protectionism* ch. 3.
4   D.B. Keesing 'Outward-Looking Policies and Economic Development' *Economic Journal* 77, June 1967, pp.303-20; Ian Little, Tibor Scitovsky and Maurice Scott *Industry and Trade in Some Developing Countries* London: Oxford University Press, 1970; Asian Development Bank *Southeast Asia's Economy: Development Policies in the 1970s* Harmondsworth: Penguin, 1972 (the first important policy recommendation along these lines); Charles R. Frank, Kwang Suk Kim and Larry E. Westphal *Foreign Trade Regimes and Economic Development: South Korea* New York: Columbia University Press, 1975; Bela Balassa 'Export Incentives and Export Performance in Developing Countries: A Comparative Analysis' *Weltwirtschaftliches Archiv* 114, 1, 1978, pp.24-61; Jagdish Bhagwati, *Foreign Trade Regimes and Economic Development: Anatomy and Consequences of Exchange Control Regimes* Cambridge, Mass.: Ballinger 1978; Anne O. Krueger *Foreign Trade Regimes and Economic Development: Liberalisation Attempts and Consequences* Cambridge, Mass.: Ballinger 1978; Ronald I. McKinnon 'Foreign Trade Regimes and Economic Development: A Review Article' *Journal of International Economics* 9, 1979, pp.429-52; Garnaut *ASEAN*; Anne O. Krueger, Hal B. Lary, Terry Monson and Narongchai Akrasanee (eds) *Trade and Employment in Developing Countries 1: Individual Studies* Chicago: University of Chicago Press, 1981; Hong and Krause *Pacific ADCs*; Lawrence B. Krause US *Economic Policy toward the Association of Southeast Asian Nations: Meeting the Japanese Challenge* Washington, DC: The Brookings Institution, 1982; Bela Balassa *Developing Strategies in Semi-Industrial Economies* Baltimore: Johns Hopkins Press, 1982; World Bank *World Development Report* 1983 New York: Oxford University Press, 1983.
5   Asian Development Bank *Southeast Asia's Economy*; Peter Drysdale *Direct Foreign Investment*.
6   Bhagwati *Foreign Trade Regimes*.
7   Ronald Findlay 'Comments on Export-led Industrialisation' in Hong and Krause *Pacific ADCs* pp.30-33.
8   ibid., p.30.
9   Keesing 'Outward-Looking Policies'; Findlay 'Comments'.
10   Anderson and Garnaut *Australian Protectionism* ch.3.
11   For a review of policy interests, see Crawford and Seow *Pacific Economic Cooperation*.
12   This terminology, and the distinction between allocation and productivity effects, was first introduced by John Stuart Mill in *Principles of Political Economy with Some of Their Applications to Social Philosophy* London: The Standard Library Company, 1848, book III, ch. 17, p.394. Productivity effects might be thought of as related to the idea of 'X-efficiency' introduced by Harvey Leibenstein *General X-Efficiency Theory and Economic Development* New York: Oxford University Press, 1978.
13   This was behind the thinking that went into the preparation of the Asian

Development Bank's report on *Southeast Asia's Economy in the 1970s* published in the series Penguin Modern Economics Texts. H. Myint *Southeast Asia's Economy: Development Policies in the 1970s* Harmondsworth: Penguin Books, 1972.

14 Garnaut *ASEAN* pp.378–402.
15 ibid., p.402.
16 Anderson and Garnaut *Australian Protectionism* ch.3.
17 Edward E. Denison and William K. Chung *How Japan's Economy Grew So Fast: The Source of Postwar Expansion* Washington, DC: The Brookings Institution, 1976, ch.8.
18 Ross Garnaut 'Survey of Recent Developments' *Bulletin of Indonesian Economic Studies* 15, 3, November 1979, pp.1–42.
19 Garnaut and Anderson 'Australia's Trade with Developing Countries' pp.13–14.
20 See Bruce Cummings 'The Origins and Development of the Northeast Asian Political Economy: Industrialisation, Product Cycles, and Political Consequences' *International Organization* 38, Winter 1984, pp.1–40, for an interesting and provocative analysis of the political economy of industrialisation in Northeast Asia. On the specific point made in the text here, Cummings' interpretation of these events is ambiguous (see pp.29–30).
21 Linder *Pacific Challenge*, especially pp.21–69; see the author's review of Linder's book in *Journal of Asian Pacific Economic Literature* 1, 1, May 1986.
22 Hong and Krause *Trade and Growth in the Pacific* ch.9.
23 Garnaut *ASEAN* pp.386–87; Krause *US Economic Policy and ASEAN* ch.4.
24 Anne Booth and Peter McCawley (eds) *The Indonesian Economy During the Soeharto Era* Kuala Lumpur: Oxford University Press, 1981; R.G. Garnaut 'General Repercussions of the Resources Boom in the Segmented Indonesian Economy' in J.J. Fox et al. (eds) *Indonesia: Australian Perspectives* Canberra: Research School of Pacific Studies, Australian National University, 1980.
25 Garnaut *ASEAN* chs 1 and 13, pp.388–97; Krause *US Economic Policy and ASEAN* ch.4 and appendix; Anderson and Garnaut *Australian Protectionism* ch.3.
26 William Branson 'Trends in United States International Trade and Comparative Advantage: Analysis and Prospects' in National Science Foundation *International Economic Policy Research* Papers and Proceedings of a Colloquium held in Washington, DC, 3–4 October 1980 (NSF 1980), pp.22–48; Robert M. Stern 'Changes in US Comparative Advantage: Issues for Research and Policy' ibid., pp.81–105; Bela Balassa 'The Changing Pattern of Comparative Advantage in Manufactured Goods' *Review of Economics and Statistics* 61, 2, 1979, pp.259–66; Krause *US Economic Policy and ASEAN* ch.4 and appendix.
27 Krause *US Economic Policy and ASEAN* pp.38–55.
28 Drysdale and Garnaut 'Trade Intensities'; Garnaut and Anderson 'Australia's Trade With Developing Countries'.
29 Wontack Hong 'Capital Accumulation, Factor Substitution, and the Changing Factor Intensity of Trade: The Case of Korea (1966-72)' in Wontack Hong and Anne O. Krueger (eds) *Trade and Development in Korea*, Seoul: Korea Development Institute, 1975.
30 Robert E. Baldwin 'US Political Pressures Against Adjustment to Greater Imports' in Hong and Krause *Trade and Growth in the Pacific*; Kym Anderson and Robert E. Baldwin 'The Political Market for Protection in Industrial Countries' in A.M. El-Agraa (ed.) *Protection, Cooperation, Development and Integration: Essays in Honour of Hiroshi Kitamura* London: Macmillan, 1987, ch.2; Anderson and Garnaut *Australian Protectionism* chs 4 and 5.
31 Garnaut *ASEAN* p.398; see also Gustav Ranis 'Challenges and Opportunities Posed by Asia's Super Exporters: Implications for Manufactured Exports from Latin America' *Quarterly Review of Economics and Business* 21, 2, Summer 1981.

32   Findlay, Anderson and Drysdale 'China and the Pacific'.
33   Garnaut *ASEAN* pp.398–401.
34   ibid., p.400.
35   ibid., p.401.
36   Ippei Yamazawa 'Renewal of Textile Industry in Developed Countries and World
      Textile Trade' *Hitotsubashi Journal of Economics* 24, 1 June 1983.
37   Anderson and Garnaut *Australian Protectionism* ch. 3.
38   Gerard Curzon *Multilateral Commercial Diplomacy: The General Agreement on
      Tariffs and Trade and Its Impact on National Commercial Policies and Techniques*
      London: Michael Joseph, 1965; Richard N. Gardner *Sterling–Dollar Diplomacy:
      The Origins and the Prospects of Our International Economic Order* New York:
      McGraw–Hill, 1969; John W. Evans *The Kennedy Round in American Trade
      Policy: The Twilight of the GATT?* Cambridge, Mass.: Harvard University Press,
      1971.
39   Hong and Krause *Trade and Growth in the Pacific* ch.9; Garnaut *ASEAN* ch. 13.
40   Warren Hunsberger *Japan and the United States in World Trade* New York:
      Harper & Row for the Council on Foreign Relations, 1964, ch.9.
41   Ingo Walter 'Nontariff Barriers and the Export Performance of Developing
      Economies' *American Economic Review* 61, Papers and Proceedings 1971,
      pp.195–205; Hirofumi Shibata 'A Note on the Equivalence of Tariffs and Quotas'
      American Economic Review 58, 1968, pp.137–41; Murray, Schmidt and Walter
      'Alternative Forms of Protection'; Chris Farrands 'Textiles Diplomacy: The
      Making and Implementation of European Textile Policy 1974–1978' *Journal of
      Common Market Studies* 18, 1, September 1979; David B. Yoffie 'Orderly
      Marketing Agreements as an Industrial Policy' *Public Policy*, 29, 1, Winter 1981,
      pp.92–99.
42   C.F. Teese 'A View from the Dress Circle in the Theatre of Trade Disputes' *The
      World Economy* 5, 1, March 1982, pp.43–60; and Patrizio Merciai 'Safeguard
      Measures in GATT' *Journal of World Trade Law* 15, 1, Jan/Feb 1981. See Gary
      R. Saxonhouse and Robert M. Stern 'An Analytical Survey of Formal and
      Informal Barriers to International Trade and Investment in the United States,
      Canada and Japan' paper presented to a Conference on United States–Canadian
      Trade and Investment Relations with Japan, Ann Arbor, Michigan, 2–3 April
      1987, tables 2 and 3 and footnote 4. Saxonhouse and Stern evaluate studies by
      B. Balassa, C. Bergsten and W. Cline, E. Leamer, M. Noland, G. Saxonhouse,
      and R. Staiger et al. of average industrial country protection.
43   Anderson and Garnaut *Australian Protectionism* ch.2.
44   Tracy Murray, Wilson Schmidt and Ingo Walter 'Alternative Forms of Protection
      Against Market Disruption' *Kyklos* 31, 4, 1978, pp.624–37.
45   Hugh Patrick, 'The Management of the United States–Japan Trade Relationship
      and Its Implications for the Pacific Basin Economies', background paper for
      project on the impact of Japan–US economic relations on other Pacific Basin
      nations, United States National Committee for Pacific Economic Cooperation
      (mimeo), Columbia University, May 1987, p.27.
46   David Yoffie 'The Newly Industrialising Countries and the Political Economy of
      Protectionism' *International Studies Quarterly* 25, 4, December 1981, pp.569–99
      (especially pp.594–95); see also Hunsberger *Japan and the United States*.
47   Hugh Patrick 'Management of the United States–Japan Relationship' p.27.
48   idem.
49   ibid., pp.27–28.
50   Yoffie 'Political Economy of Protectionism', especially pp.575–85.
51   ibid., pp.594–96.
52   See Stephen D. Krasner 'The Tokyo Round: Particularistic Interests and

Prospects for Stability in the Global Trading System' *International Studies Quarterly* 23, 4, December 1979, pp.495–531 (for the first point); and Jock A. Finlayson and Mark W. Zacher 'The GATT and the Regulation of Trade Barriers: Regime Dynamics and Functions' *International Organization* 35, 4, Autumn 1981, pp.561–602 (for the second).

53 Shibata 'Equivalence of Tariffs and Quotas'; Murray, Schmidt and Walker 'Alternative Forms of Protection'.

54 Don Gunasekera, Intra-industry Trade in East Asia, PhD thesis, Australian National University, 1987, chs 3.4 and 9.

55 ibid., ch.3.

56 Tōru Nakakita 'The World Economy in the 1990s' *Look Japan* January 1987, pp.9–11.

57 Konosuke Odaka *Motor Vehicle Industry in Asia: A Study of Ancillary Firm Development* Singapore: Singapore University Press, 1983, ch.7.

58 Kym Anderson and Young-il Park 'China and the International Relocation of World Textile and Clothing Activity' paper prepared for a pre-AAES Conference Workshop on 'Developments in China's Food and Fibre Markets: Their International Significance' held at the University of Adelaide, 9 February 1987, (also published as *Pacific Economic Papers* No. 158, Australia–Japan Research Centre, Australian National University); Young-il Park 'The Changing Pattern of Textile Trade in Northeast Asia' paper presented to the Australian–Japan Research Centre Workshop on Northeast Asian Trade, 25 March 1987, at the Australian National University, Canberra.

59 Ikuo Kaneko and Kenichi Imai 'A Network View of the Firm' paper prepared for the First Hitotsubashi–Stanford Conference, Stanford 29 March to 1 April 1987, and a background paper for the Australia–Japan Research Centre Workshop on Corporate Organisation and Trade in Technology and Services, 27 February 1987, at the Australian National University. These issues are being explored in an Australia–Japan Research Centre research program, from which a volume will shortly appear on corporate organisation and international adjustment.

60 Garnaut *ASEAN* p.398.

7 Financing Pacific development

The rapid growth of the Pacific economies has been associated with an even more rapid expansion of international trade flows and economic interdependence. Economic growth has been financed not only through a huge mobilisation of domestic savings but also through reliance on international capital. The mobilisation of capital for regional development has also been associated with significant changes in the structure of capital markets, financial institutions and financial instruments.[1]

The financing of Pacific development has been no less impressive than the transformation of Pacific trade and industrial structures. Nonetheless, the success in financing industrial and trade growth has not always been smooth, either for the region as a whole or for individual countries within it. While the Pacific economies adjusted more rapidly than the rest of the world to the oil crises, inflation and recessions of the 1970s and 1980s, the effect of these disturbances was profound.

This period was one of fundamental structural change in the international financial system. It witnessed the adoption of flexible exchange rates, the development of a large, bank-lending-based international capital market, and the accumulation of large foreign debts.[2] These changes put pressure on national financial institutions and on the direction of financial policy management in many countries. The reaction to the pressures differed among countries, in a way reflective of particular national circumstances; but in many Pacific countries the longer term response has been to generate new approaches to financial policy management, involving more policy flexibility and financial liberalisation and deregulation.[3]

In short, the net effect of these changes in the international financial environment upon Pacific capital markets has been to strengthen still further the region's growing role as an international financial arena. While there are residual uncertainties about the vulnerability and structure of international capital markets,[4] to which Pacific countries (with the exception of the Philippines) have not generally exposed themselves,[5] the Pacific region as a whole continues to accumulate financial strength. This is the result of its fundamental investment potential; of the emergence of new centres of international finance within the region; of the rapid evolution of more open capital markets; and of a generally stable environment within which foreign investors can contribute to regional development.[6]

180

THE STRUCTURE OF PACIFIC CAPITAL FLOWS

There have been three major structural changes in Pacific capital flows in the past decade. First, the United States has been toppled from its position as the pre-eminent capital exporter, and is now a massive net capital importer (Table 7.1). As a consequence the whole Pacific region, including North America, has become a net capital importer.[7] This is a product of misalignment in international macroeconomic policies in a world of flexible exchange rates and a high degree of capital mobility, rather than a reflection of the underlying strength and long-term lending capacity of the United States; but it is a circumstance that is likely to persist until the United States budget deficit is reduced relative to national product.

Table 7.1 Long-term capital flows to Pacific countries[a] (US$ million)

	1970		1985	
	Direct investment (net)	Other long-term capital (net)	Direct investment (net)	Other long-term capital (net)
Western Pacific developing countries	**375**	**1 034**	**3 539**	**12 137**
China	na	na	1 031	3 407
Fiji	6	9	33	−25
Indonesia	83	207	256	1 266
Korea	66	430	197	2 095
Malaysia	94	2	685	887
Papua New Guinea	19	113	113	121
Philippines	−29	159	−11	3 102
Singapore	93	47	1 075	−160
Thailand	43	67	160	1 444
Pacific developed countries	**−5 039**	**−1 684**	**−11 653**	**23 553**
Australia	785	280	−283	6 221
Canada	566	386	−5 344	5 984
Japan	−260	−1 200	−5 808	−57 121
New Zealand	na	na	97[b]	−2 186[b]
United States	−6 130	−1 150	−315	70 655

Notes: a Negative sign indicates a net outflow.
        b Figures are for fiscal 1984.
        na Data not available.
Sources: World Bank *World Tables* 3rd edn, I, 1983; International Monetary Fund *Balance of Payments Statistics* 37, Yearbook, Part I, 1986

Second, Japan has emerged as a significant net long-term capital exporter.[8] Earlier, Japan's exports of capital were concentrated more or less exclusively on direct foreign investment and closely related concessionary financing for developing countries. The strength of Japan's savings base and the progressive liberalisation of the Japanese capital market have encouraged the diversification of Japanese capital exports across the entire range of international financial instruments.[9] Japan is now established as far and away the single most important source of capital to other Asian–Pacific countries, and is also a significant investor in the United States. Japan's role in this respect was more prominent in the mid-1980s because of the imbalances in the international macroeconomy which led to high United States interest rates, first creating a strong US dollar and later a strong yen. But Japan's position as the most substantial source of foreign capital for East Asian and Pacific countries will not be threatened by lower interest rates in the United States and a weakening US dollar in the foreseeable future. Japan's capital exports are very heavily concentrated upon East Asian and Pacific countries, and any restoration of the United States' role as a net capital exporter is unlikely to overwhelm the growing scale and entrenched concentration of Japanese capital flows in the region.[10]

The third significant change in the structure of international capital flows has been the large-scale growth of international bank lending.[11] The growth of bank lending, following the development of the Eurodollar market and the recent growth of Asian-dollar markets, initially improved the efficiency of the international capital market and provided a new pool of development capital. However, the extension of bank lending towards general balance-of-payments support and the exposure of bank creditors to high risks of general default in recent years have been sources of serious weakness in the international financial system. The effects of this weakness have been concentrated heavily in Latin America, although of course concern focuses on its systemic dimension. The ratio of investment to foreign indebtedness of Latin American borrowing countries has risen more than thirtyfold over the past 10 years. Experience with borrowing varies in East Asia and the Western Pacific, but overall the growth of direct foreign investment has been somewhat more rapid than the growth of other long-term borrowing. Bank lending has been project-related, primarily to the private sector. Public sector borrowing from the international private capital market grew as a proportion of total public borrowings, from 33 per cent to 62 per cent between 1979 and 1982; in 1982 around 54 per cent of the outstanding debt of East Asian developing countries was with private creditors.[12]

The pattern of financial flows in the Pacific region has therefore changed dramatically over the past decade. At the beginning of the 1970s the Pacific was a net exporter of long-term capital to the extent of about US$5.3 billion, but by the middle of the 1980s it had become a net importer of long-term capital to the tune of over US$28 billion (see Table 7.1). Of total net inflows of long-term capital (including direct foreign investment), US$16 billion went to the developing countries of East Asia and the Western Pacific.

By 1981 the United States already had an annual net capital inflow of US$26 billion, almost twice the amount destined for developing Western Pacific countries. In the first half of the 1980s net capital inflow into the United States continued to rise and Americans acquired fewer foreign assets. Between 1982 and 1983 alone, international lending by United States banks dropped from US$109 billion to US$25 billion and purchases of foreign securities fell from US$8 billion to US$7 billion. In 1982 the disinvestment of American firms abroad amounted to US$3 billion, although there was investment of US$8 billion overseas the following year. In 1985 the United States' long-term capital inflow exceeded US$70 billion.

These developments have been viewed with some concern. Why was a large industrial economy like the United States soaking up international investible funds in the 1980s instead of providing them to the rest of the region and the world, as it had done over the previous 70 years on such a large scale? Would not these 'perverse' capital flows, from the poor to the rich so it seemed, seriously retard economic growth in the developing Western Pacific if they continued?[13]

MANAGING PACIFIC FINANCIAL INTERDEPENDENCE

These concerns about the movement of capital into the United States in the early 1980s were, at least in the first instance, largely misplaced. The huge reversal of United States net capital flows was at that time induced by successful reflation and the powerful financial stimulus that fuelled it. Under a regime of free capital movement and flexible exchange rates, the capital inflow into the United States was the inevitable product of American budget deficits, a buoyant economy, the accompanying tight monetary control and high investment yields.[14] Moreover, the consequence of these capital movements — especially given the exchange rate appreciation which they set in motion — was a massive import expansion and trade deficit which fed strong export growth and economic recovery in other countries, most particularly in the strongly competitive industrial countries of East Asia, including Japan. What Western Pacific economies may have lost in terms of the flow of investible funds into North America, they regained in large measure through trade recovery and the stimulus it gave to economic growth potential. Between 1983 and 1984 United States imports of manufactured goods jumped by 36.2 per cent, and exports of manufactured goods from Japan and the newly industrialising countries of East Asia to the United States grew by an impressive 36.4 per cent in nominal terms.[15] The trade expansion induced by the United States significantly boosted regional economic growth, even that of Japan.

It is important to review the macroeconomic interaction of the United States with the Western Pacific economies, especially with Japan, in the first half of the 1980s because it illustrates some of the more permanent structural features which now have to be taken into account in the management of Pacific financial interdependence. The interaction between the United States and Japan dominates developments in Pacific financial markets. It is useful to turn attention to Japan in discussing this problem.

Two other prisms through which the capital inflow into the United States can be viewed reflect concerns about misalignment of the yen/dollar exchange rate and the sharp rise in the Japanese current account surplus. Both issues are, of course, part of the mirror image of the United States' problems with its dollar and its current account deficit. In 1984 Japan's current account surplus was running at more than US$30 billion, or nearly 3 per cent of GNP. The United States current account deficit stood at over US$80 billion (and about the same share of a larger GNP) in that year.[16] Tax cuts, strong government expenditure, a mounting budget deficit and tight monetary control in the United States had been mismatched with curbs on the growth of the budget deficit and loose monetary policy in Japan. There was some change in the direction of monetary policy in both the United States and Japan after 1983, but the implicit coordination in monetary targeting that evolved during this period was certainly not sufficient to take the pressure off the United States–Japan economic relationship. Bilateral economic tensions which emerged as a by-product focused on trade policy issues and constantly threatened to erupt into uncontrollable political problems.[17]

The interaction between macroeconomic financial interdependence and management of the international trading relationships is an important issue here.[18] Growing surpluses in Japan's current account involved large bilateral trade imbalances with the United States. The strong dollar weakened the ability of the United States manufacturing industry (and the farm sector) to compete internationally. A large-scale industrial adjustment had to be effected. At the same time protectionist sentiment strengthened. While the Reagan Administration resisted protectionist pressures, the bilateral trade imbalance again became the trigger-point for action on trade and exchange-rate problems. Inexorably, bilateral trade concessions were sought as the 'side-payment' for Japan's trade and payments 'misbehaviour'. Japan acquiesced in this process, a disturbing aspect of which was the drift away from multilateral trade settlement towards an approach that is perhaps most accurately described as 'veiled bilateralism'.[19] This is a central policy issue for Pacific countries generally, and will be taken up more fully in chapter 9.

Japan's current account surplus is no transitory phenomenon. Despite the particular vulnerability of its external accounts to the oil crises of the 1970s, Japan established its position as an international creditor with the emergence of persistent current account surpluses in the late 1960s. In the decade after 1973 the expansion of exports accounted for 9 per cent of GNP growth, and caused considerable conflict in international trade diplomacy between Japan and her main trading partners in Europe and North America. Table 7.2 records the steady progress in Japan's capacity to serve as an international creditor. Only temporarily, in the years of the two oil crises, were there deficits in Japan's current account after 1965. Japanese savings remained high while the rate of domestic capital formation slowed. Savings were high enough to accommodate the growth of both government deficits and current account surpluses. By the mid-1980s Japan's new role as the world's largest exporter of capital had dovetailed with its transformation into an industrial power, rich in technology and managerial skills which could be combined with capital in the flow of direct investment abroad.[20]

Japan's new status as an international creditor has led to its performing the function of a centre of financial intermediation by providing savings to borrowers in both the regional and the international economies. This normally involves borrowing at the short end of the international market in financial assets through making domestic-currency-denominated liquid assets (for example, treasury bills) available to non-residents and providing long-term capital in the form of direct foreign investment, portfolio investment, syndicated loans and foreign aid. The capacity of a potential creditor country to create international liquidity in this way and to offer the whole range of long-term credit facilities is, of course, circumscribed by the degree of liberalisation and internationalisation of its own financial markets.

Table 7.2   Japan's current account balance (three-yearly averages)

	Current account balance (US$ million)	Current account balance as a proportion of GNP (per cent)
1965–67	665	0.6
1968–70	1 712	1.0
1971–73	4 095	1.3
1974–76	-1 695	-0.3
1977–79	6 233	0.7
1980–82	291	0.0
1983–85	34 990	2.8

Sources: Statistics Bureau. Prime Minister's Office *Japan Statistical Yearbook* (various issues); International Economic Data Bank, Australian National University

The regulation of Japan's financial markets has in the past limited its capacity to assume the role of a fully fledged participant in the international capital market. It also had the effect of channelling Japanese lending very narrowly into direct foreign investment. Excessive concentration on direct foreign investment attracted political and other difficulties and distorted the portfolio of Japanese lending away from a more efficient pattern.[21]

The problem of Japanese financial regulation and the question of internationalisation of the Japanese capital market therefore attracted much policy attention, both inside and outside the country. Inside Japan, the growth and management of public debt increased the breadth and depth of the market in government bonds, so that it became increasingly difficult to sustain controls on the issue of, and the trade in, short-term securities in the primary market.[22] At the same time, competitive financial institutions (commercial banks, long-term credit banks, securities houses, and so on) are chafing against regulations that maintain segmentation of financial markets and limit market growth.[23] These forces have produced significant deregulation in Japanese capital markets in a direction which makes them better able to play a significant international role.[24] On the international front, deregulation of foreign exchange markets, de facto in the late 1970s and formally in December 1980, was the main step towards the internationalisation of Tokyo's capital market. The freer use of the euroyen bond market by residents and non-residents and the gradual opening of a yen-dominated foreign bond market (samurai bonds) for non-residents provided wider access for foreigners to the Japanese capital market.[25] However, the Treasury Bill market was still not open in 1987, and until that step is taken Japan will remain a limited, and to some extent destabilising, source of international liquidity.

The process of Japanese financial market deregulation — which has involved a shift from a highly regulated market with administratively determined interest rates, combined with extensive control over international capital transactions, towards market determination of interest rates and freer international capital movements — has two important implications.

First, the integration of Japanese financial markets into international financial markets gave investors the opportunity for freer portfolio selection and the potential for more efficient resource allocation, and this should enhance the prospects for Pacific economic development. Second, deeper international financial integration increasingly limited independence in the conduct of monetary policy, which became more closely tied to developments and disturbances overseas, particularly in the United States.[26]

Mundell and Fleming[27] demonstrated in their celebrated work more than 20 years ago that once international movements of capital are introduced there is no effective mechanism which allows complete insulation from foreign economic disturbances, even under flexible exchange rates. So it was with the fiscal expansion through which the United States led the world from recession in the first half of the 1980s. The convergence of real interest rates in Japan towards the high rates that prevailed in the United States during this period is one manifestation of the highly integrated Pacific capital market; the 'misalignment' of the yen/dollar exchange rate in this period is another. The power and nature of these financial and exchange rate interactions between the two major Pacific economic powers, and between them and Europe, are permanent factors that have to be taken into account by policymakers on both sides of the Pacific.

It is worth noting that, had Japan been emboldened to take the initiative of a large-scale fiscal expansion ahead of the United States in the 1980s, the course of exchange rate, capital flow and trade balance interaction with the United States economy would probably have been quite different. The structure of the interaction would have been precisely the same. But the effect of capital flows on the exchange rate and the current account balance would probably have been less dominant: indeed, the yen may well have depreciated, not appreciated, as did the dollar[28] after the United States fiscal expansion.

These features of the Pacific capital market, and the consequences of growing financial interdependence for economic management in Japan and the United States, suggest a strong interest in the development of a framework for macroeconomic policy coordination within the Pacific region. More explicit consultation in shaping monetary targets could be one element of fruitful policy coordination.[29] Another, of particular value to smaller third parties, could be a monitoring and consultation process on adjustment pressures felt through the trade and current account balance. Such pressures have the potential for letting loose protectionist forces and narrowly focused trade policy diplomacy damaging to the broader interest in a healthy international trading system. Focus on bilateral trade and payments issues, in the course of dealing with the effects of financial and economic interactions through the experiences of 1982–85 and after, seduced United States and Japanese policymakers to move in two ill-considered directions. One was towards seeking bilateral trade settlements (in beef, coal, automobiles, steel, semiconductors) to redress the 'imbalance' in bilateral trade and payments, a direction in which they had strayed on earlier occasions.[30] The other was towards contemplating the introduction of an interest-equalisation tax directed at stemming the tide of capital flows and relieving the exchange-rate adjustment. Both directions took scant account of the harm that their implementation would have caused to other countries, especially trading partners in the Pacific, or to the efficiency and strength of the international trading and financial system as a whole.

In addition, the mismatch in macroeconomic policy approach between the United States and its industrial country partners (including Japan) persisted. American reflation was not followed closely by expansion in Japan or Europe, and external funding of the American deficit became a 'structural' problem.[31] Policymakers in the United States, Japan and the major industrial countries then fixed on the course of encouraging depreciation of the dollar against the yen and European currencies, under the Group of Five (G–5) arrangements in September 1985. Concern about the diversion of international capital flows away from developing countries into the United States became increasingly valid as economic growth faltered and trade problems multiplied. While Japan hesitated to undertake domestic expansion, attention was focused on new schemes to subsidise the flow of Japanese lending towards developing countries and away from industrial countries, such as the United States.[32]

FOREIGN CAPITAL AND EAST ASIAN DEVELOPMENT

These changes in the structure of Pacific capital flows and features of the management of Pacific financial interdependence provide the context in which the important role played by external capital in the growth and development of East Asian and Pacific economies can be explored. One special interest, from the viewpoint of assessing the scope for Pacific economic cooperation arrangements, is in the regional concentration of Pacific capital flows and, in particular, the relatively large contributions made by direct foreign investment and concessionary financial flows from Japan.

Here the focus of discussion is upon the mobilisation of external resources for investment in the developing countries of East Asia, and on the role played by the Pacific industrial countries, most importantly the United States and Japan, as sources of external capital.[33]

The East Asian developing countries are all major recipients of external capital, and in the early 1980s annual capital inflow into the region as a whole amounted to over US$11 billion. Capital inflow into each East Asian country (except Taiwan and Indonesia) averaged over US$1 billion annually (Table 7.3).

The structure of capital inflow differed greatly from country to country, depending on the stage of economic development, the structure of resource endowments, and the approach to the management of financial and macroeconomic policies.[34] Direct foreign investment played a very much more important role for Hong Kong, Singapore and Taiwan, accounting for between half and two-thirds of all capital inflow. Official sources of external capital

Table 7.3   Total net capital flows to East Asian developing countries, 1969-84[a]

	1969-71	1972-76	1977-80[b]	1981-84
Northeast Asia				
China (US$m)			226.3	1 056.6
— official (%)			116.2	68.7
— private (%)			−16.2	31.3
— (direct investment) (%)			(5.2)	(2.4)
Hong Kong (US$m)	229.1	213.2	597.2	1 327.0
— official (%)	30.8	27.0	2.0	1.3
— private (%)	69.2	73.0	98.0	98.7
— (direct investment) (%)	(11.7)	(54.0)	(46.1)	(57.0)
Korea (US$m)	547.2	846.3	1 328.5	1 579.1
— official (%)	73.2	66.1	56.5	56.0
— private (%)	26.8	33.9	43.5	44.0
— (direct investment) (%)	(3.1)	(12.8)	(0.1)	(8.7)
Taiwan (US$m)	186.2	255.1	234.9	250.6
— official (%)	47.0	41.6	74.5	18.3
— private (%)	53.0	58.4	25.5	81.7
— (direct investment) (%)	(10.1)	(8.3)	(29.3)	(50.3)
Southeast Asia				
Indonesia (US$m)	521.4	1 647.6	1 136.0	3 445.4
— official (%)	90.6	47.1	88.2	44.6
— private (%)	9.4	52.9	11.8	55.4
— (direct investment) (%)	(13.7)	(32.2)	(5.5)	(27.9)
Malaysia (US$m)	80.4	245.5	446.5	1 213.2
— official (%)	71.3	49.7	44.0	27.5
— private (%)	28.7	50.3	56.0	72.5
— (direct investment) (%)	(31.3)	(36.7)	(21.4)	(3.0)
Philippines (US$m)	225.8	469.8	974.7	1 159.2
— official (%)	64.1	57.6	48.9	76.4
— private (%)	35.9	42.4	51.1	23.6
— (direct investment) (%)	(12.4)	(20.5)	(18.3)	(4.3)
Singapore (US$m)	81.3	165.5	444.7	894.1
— official (%)	55.3	34.4	14.0	2.5
— private (%)	44.7	65.6	86.0	97.5
— (direct investment) (%)	(19.4)	(42.8)	(65.1)	(64.7)
Thailand (US$m)	208.7	142.3	746.6	1 380.7
— official (%)	53.4	74.9	68.0	63.4
— private (%)	46.6	25.1	32.0	36.6
— (direct investment) (%)	(6.1)	(16.8)	(11.3)	(15.7)
Total[c] (US$m)	2 080.1	3 985.3	5 909.1	11 249.3
— official (%)	66.8	51.6	53.9	40.9
— private (%)	33.2	48.4	46.1	59.1
— (direct investment) (%)	(10.4)	(26.5)	(17.9)	(25.5)

Notes: a Yearly averages, US$ million in every first line, per cent of total thereafter.
b 1979-80 only for China: earlier data not available.
c Excludes China.
Sources: H. Hill and B. Johns 'The Role of Direct Foreign Investment in Developing East Asian countries' *Weltwirtschaftliches Archiv* 121, 1985; updated and expanded from OECD *Geographical Distribution of Financial Flows* (various issues), Paris: OECD

are more important for the rest of the region. Private loan capital has also become more important generally. In the past decade or so, direct foreign investment averaged between 10 per cent and 30 per cent of capital inflow for all East Asian developing countries, although the share was considerably higher for Malaysia and Indonesia in the periods of commodity boom, as well as for Hong Kong and Singapore. An important trend has been an overall rise in the share of direct foreign investment in capital inflow over the period (see Table 7.3). This trend reflects the rapid industrialisation of the region as a whole, and the increasingly confident climate for foreign investors in all these countries except the Philippines in the second half of the 1970s and the early 1980s.[35]

The process of economic and financial development in the East Asian countries has by and large been very successful. Increasingly sophisticated financial markets have been associated with high levels of domestic savings, as well as the effective mobilisation of external funds for investment purposes. Hong Kong and Singapore have emerged as significant offshore currency markets.[36] While domestic savings are certainly the principal source of investment funds for the countries of East Asia, external capital has played a very important role, especially through the growth in direct foreign investment.

In the early 1980s the contribution of external capital flows to gross domestic capital formation in East Asia ranged between a low 6 per cent (for Taiwan) to a high 19 per cent (for Indonesia), and averaged around 13 per cent. The share of direct foreign investment in gross domestic capital formation averaged 4 per cent for the region in this period.[37]

These measures understate the importance of external capital and direct foreign investment to the developing countries of the Western Pacific in two ways. First, while the ratios of direct foreign investment and aggregate capital inflow to gross domestic capital formation may not appear high in absolute terms, they represent a large mobilisation of external resources for investment compared with the experience of other countries at this stage of industrial development. Second, the relationship between the financial flows measured in these statistics (particularly those for direct foreign investment) and other financial and non-financial resources needs to be taken into account in assessing their importance to regional growth and industrialisation. Direct investment is often associated with domestic borrowing, and also generates profits which are ploughed back into the host country; and both contributions add to its weight in the process of capital formation. More importantly, it is associated with the mobilisation of other non-financial resources, such as technology and management services, which may contribute independently to the process of industrialisation and economic development. Foreign investment tends to be very heavily concentrated in key sectors of the economy at successive stages of industrialisation, and thereby provides a critical link with international technology and management services. In the course of East Asian industrialisation, direct foreign investment has provided management skills, international market links and technology in resource development projects, and technology, management skills and sometimes international market links in manufacturing activities, as well as the transfer of financial capital.[38]

The growth of foreign investment in East Asian manufacturing, and the adoption of export-oriented industrialisation strategies by the governments of East Asian countries, raise the questions of the role of foreign firms in promoting manufactured goods exports and the transformation of foreign trade structure. Some commentators question whether foreign investment in manufacturing is consistent with export-oriented industrialisation, since foreign investors may restrict the access of overseas subsidiaries to international markets. Some countries impose export requirements on foreign investors or joint ventures for this and other reasons. China is a prominent case, imposing export requirements on foreign investors and joint ventures with the object of boosting foreign exchange earnings and (so it is argued) covering foreign exchange outlays under a complex system of foreign exchange controls.[39] This question is, however, somewhat misdirected, since foreign investment in manufacturing may well yield substantial benefits in terms of productivity gain and income without the requirement of export orientation.[40] But in so far as international market links are among the potential benefits from direct foreign investment, it is of some interest to examine what evidence is available on foreign-investment-related exportation of manufactured goods. The evidence is limited but suggestive.[41] United States imports from United-States-affiliated firms in Asia and the Pacific account for only a small proportion (6–7 per cent) of all imports of manufactured goods from the region. For Japan this proportion is very much higher (around 30 per cent).[42] Yet data on the destination of sales from American and Japanese affiliates in East Asia reveal that United States firms ship a very large share of their output to overseas markets, whereas Japanese firms concentrate their sales very heavily on host-country markets. United States imports of manufactured goods from East Asia are, of course, very much larger than Japanese imports of manufactured goods from the region (see Table 6.6). Hence, an interesting issue is whether foreign investment plays a critical role in the development of international market links more generally. A careful analysis of this issue would require study of the involvement of foreign firms and their corporate strategies in the international market over time. It is difficult to draw any clear conclusions from a comparison of the export performances of United States and Japanese affiliates at a single point in time, since the history of their operations differs markedly.[43] There is some indirect evidence to suggest a strong but complex association between geographic trade patterns and direct investment links, not only between host and home country but also with third countries, in both import and export trade.[44]

On balance, foreign investment can be seen as a very important catalyst in the process of the trade and industrial transformation of the East Asian economies. But the role of foreign investment, joint ventures and international corporate links is likely to become more important as the East Asian economy moves into more complex manufacturing activity and industrial procurement systems in the next round of industrialisation. Pacific countries have a common interest in building a foreign investment and commercial policy environment which will encourage the development of intra-industry trade specialisation in the way suggested in chapter 6.

JAPAN AND PACIFIC SOURCES OF CAPITAL

What has been the role of Pacific industrial countries as sources of external capital to the developing countries of East Asia? The United States has been a huge provider of capital to the rest of the world in years past, but the question is whether American capital outflow is more heavily concentrated in East Asian countries than in other capital-importing developing country regions. Japan has emerged as a substantial net exporter of capital to the rest of the world, but once again the question is whether these new capital flows are directed more heavily to the Pacific region than elsewhere. The small Pacific industrial countries (Australia, Canada and New Zealand) are commonly net capital importers, but there is also the question of whether their exports of capital are destined primarily for countries in East Asia and the Pacific.

Two recent studies reveal that the industrial countries of the Pacific (the Pacific Five) have indeed forged exceptionally strong investment links, alongside their trade links, within East Asia and the Pacific.[45] It is to be expected that, since the Pacific Five includes Japan and the United States (the world's two largest capital exporters), capital exports from that region to East Asia will be large. But it turns out that the share of the Pacific Five in the capital inflows of East Asia is from one-and-a-half to almost two times the share of the Pacific Five in the capital inflow of all developing countries. Moreover, the concentration of Pacific Five capital exports within the Asian–Pacific region has increased over the past decade (Table 7.4). The same tendency is revealed for all forms of capital flow, although the concentration of official development assistance flows within the region may have peaked in 1981. The extent of regional concentration in capital flows is stronger for Japan than for the United States, so that the growing importance of Japan as a source of capital to the region has reinforced the overall tendency towards stronger regional financial linkages.

Around 60 per cent of East Asia's external capital has come from the Pacific Five since 1970. Of this, about 60 per cent originated in Japan and around 35 per cent in the United States. Europe accounts for just over one-fifth of East Asia's supply of foreign capital, a share which has come to be matched by the contribution of the multilateral agencies. Japan's share of official development assistance (and the scale of its development assistance effort) has grown, while the reverse is true for development assistance from the United States. Japan also dominates net private-sector capital flows from the Pacific Five to East Asia (with a 54 per cent share, compared to the United States share of 43 per cent), but the United States is the larger direct foreign investor.

Japan is an important source of foreign capital to East Asia, but East Asia is also an important element in Japan's total capital outflows to developing countries. Around 43 per cent of all Japan's capital exports to developing countries went to East Asia at the beginning of the 1980s. For the United States the figure was just over 12 per cent; and for the Pacific Five as a group, East Asia was the destination of 19 per cent of their capital exports.[46] The concentration of Japanese direct foreign investment within East Asia is exceptionally marked: East Asia ranks with North America as an outlet for Japanese direct foreign investment, each accounting for just under 28 per cent of all Japan's direct investment abroad.[47]

Table 7.4   The relative concentration[a] of financial flows from Pacific industrial countries to East Asian developing countries, 1970-84

	1970	1971	1972	1973	1974	1975
Official development assistance (ODA)	1.49	1.42	1.56	1.91	2.06	2.37
Other official flows (OOF)						
Private sector flows						
Private export credits						
Direct foreign investment						
Total financial flows	1.48	1.35	1.35	1.34	1.37	1.67
Value of total flows (US$ million)	1397	1456	1643	2456	1724	3605
Share of East Asia in Pacific flows to all developing countries (per cent)	20.4	17.3	17.4	18.6	13.0	19.6

Notes: All flows are net except for private export credit which is gross.
Blanks appear for earlier years because disaggregated data are not available.
a Relative concentration ratios are calculated by dividing the share of East Asian countries' financial flows from the five Pacific industrial countries in their flows to all developing countries by the share of East Asian countries' financial flows from all sources to all developing countries. (See Tsao Yuan 'Capital Flows Among Pacific Basin Countries' pp.70-71 for a formal description.)
b No breakdown by destination is available for Canadian direct investment, so Canada is excluded from Pacific industrial country flows.

Sources: Adapted from Tsao Yuan 'Capital Flows Among Pacific Basin Countries' in Tan and Kapur (eds) *Pacific Growth and Financial Interdependence* Sydney: Allen & Unwin, 1985, pp.72-75; updated from OECD *Geographical Distribution of Financial Flows 1982/1985* Paris: OECD Publications, 1987

Another feature of the interdependence of capital markets in Asia and the Pacific is the growth of investment flows, and especially of direct foreign investment flows, within the East Asian region itself. The network of 'overseas Chinese' capital flows and investment links has traditionally been important in intra-regional capital movement. Alongside these traditional networks, Singapore, Hong Kong, Taiwan and Korea have all become sizeable sources of direct foreign investment and other capital flows within the East Asian region.[48]

The growth of Asian offshore currency centres in Singapore and Hong Kong has added a new dimension to international financial intermediation in the East Asian region. East Asian and Pacific developing countries are commonly net borrowers from these markets, while Europe and North America provide the loanable funds. Significantly, the two largest borrowers from Hong Kong have been the Philippines and Korea. The presence of United States and Japanese banks in the East Asian region has also grown enormously; in 1983 the United States banking system had claims amounting to over US$6 billion in East Asian developing countries.[49]

The liberalisation of the Japanese capital market will certainly strengthen Japan's position as a source of foreign capital and a centre for financial intermediation. It is less clear, however, whether the intensity of Japan's capital market flows within the region will grow or weaken in consequence of further moves in this direction. The structure of Japan's capital outflow to date, with its emphases upon direct foreign investment, export credits, and official development assistance closely related to trade and investment flows, has probably encouraged a special regional concentration in its capital exports. Diversification in the portfolio of Japan's capital outflows may well be accompanied by diversification in the geographic distribution of its capital

1976	1977	1978	1979	1980	1981	1982	1983	1984
2.28	2.31	2.61	2.37	2.24	2.56	1.85	1.85	1.83
	1.33	1.06	1.50	1.58	1.05	0.78	2.38	1.15
	0.59	2.05	1.41	1.79	1.34	1.43	1.46	1.33
			1.86	1.53	1.20	1.94	1.81	1.66
			1.04	1.58	1.46	1.43	2.74[b]	1.64[b]
1.52	1.22	1.89	1.57	1.93	1.56	1.41	1.52	1.44
3240	3878	3377	3477	3499	8173	5630	5539	7248
21.2	8.6	13.5	13.0	17.4	22.2	16.9	21.5	18.4

exports. But another factor will have the converse effect. The liberalisation of capital markets and the internationalisation of financial services in the Pacific region (not only in Japan, but also in Australia, Korea and New Zealand) will further enhance the capacity to exploit opportunities for regional trade and international specialisation within the region. Since the growth potential of the Pacific economy seems so large in relation to what can be expected in the rest of the world, there will be strong forces working towards the continuing growth of financial flows among East Asian and Pacific countries.

The explanation of regional concentration in capital flows in terms of the growing importance of Japan as a capital exporter is important to understanding the link between investment and trade flows in the next phase of East Asian industrialisation, as well as in the management of foreign investment, technology and related policy cooperation. These subjects need more detailed and careful investigation, but some preliminary observations may help to identify the common policy interests of Pacific countries in foreign investment, trade and industrialisation linkages.

The evidence so far assembled suggests that the factors encouraging regional concentration in investment flows parallel those encouraging regional concentration in trade flows, as set out in the analysis of regional trade intensities in chapter 4. Indeed, the geographic distribution of investment appears to be affected by many of the same 'bias' factors which play such a prominent role in determining the geographic distribution of trade. Geographic proximity, close communications and political ties ease the coordination of investment links and enhance the flow of direct investment. Cultural, linguistic and ideological similarities, common institutional settings, and close historical associations also help to foster close investment ties.[50] These factors interact with the advantages of proximity to affect investors' perceptions of the investment climate in particular host countries. The structure of investment flows by sector is also a potentially important determinant of the strength or intensity of investment ties, in a way analogous to the role of complementarity in determining the geographic structure of trade. Whether the direct foreign investment from one country is from specific sectors which are the main users of foreign capital in a host country will open up or limit the development of strong investment ties between particular source and host countries. But the evidence so far gives much greater weight to the role of 'distance' (in all its dimensions) or resistance factors in explaining the regional concentration of direct investment flows.[51]

As noted in chapter 3, Japan is the largest direct foreign investor in South Korea, Indonesia, Thailand and Malaysia (after Singapore), while the United States is larger in Hong Kong, Singapore, the Philippines and China (after Hong Kong). This pattern of investment in the region shapes the opportunities for developing trade and other economic ties, and reflects underlying investment opportunities as well as investor perceptions of the investment climate in particular countries. So investment links also have a prominent political dimension which can become a source of tension, thereby reducing investor confidence. Investment relations are particularly susceptible to such tension if they are managed bilaterally, without a framework of commonly accepted principles, rules and procedures. Japan's exposure to this problem has been significant in its relations with Indonesia and Thailand in the 1970s, and with China and other Northeast Asian countries in more recent years. The existence of these close links in the East Asian and Pacific capital market, and the strong intra-Pacific concentration in direct foreign investment flows, therefore suggest a powerful common interest in regional codes of investment behaviour which serve to husband and further develop confidence in the regional investment climate.

CONCESSIONARY DEVELOPMENT FINANCE

Concessionary development finance is a diminishing component of capital flows to Western Pacific countries, but it continues to play a significant role in the less developed countries of Southeast Asia and the Southwest Pacific, and in some sectors of the regional economy whose development is of importance to donor countries and, to some extent, to the international agencies through which development assistance funds are increasingly being channelled.[52] At the beginning of the 1970s, about two-thirds of public external borrowing by Western Pacific countries came from official sources; that is, both bilateral and multilateral official development assistance. By the beginning of the 1980s, only about one-third came from these sources. This decline was due to a significant reduction in bilateral official development assistance from most sources (Japan being a major exception), and was only partly compensated by increases in funds from multilateral institutions. 'Aid fatigue' was one of the factors which led to a reduced supply of official funds and increased reliance on private sources for public-sector borrowing.

Among the official sources of external public debt, multilateral agencies have become a vastly more important source of funds. At the same time, more than 80 per cent of bilateral disbursements of official development assistance to Western Pacific developing countries originate from the Pacific Five.[53] This reinforces the close financial interdependence within the East Asian and Pacific economy and recommends a brief review of some of the issues that have arisen in the concessionary financing of regional development in the past, as well as some of the changes that are likely to shape its course in the future. A major interest in this latter regard is in the financing of development projects in the modernisation of China.

There are many mechanisms through which foreign governments and international agencies make funds available on economical terms to project investments in developing countries. The general effect of the provision of these funds is to reduce the supply price of investment directly, or to reduce the opportunity cost to host governments of funds allocated to projects. One objective, on the part of a donor country, may be to increase supplies of particular commodities (for example, minerals and energy resources) in the quest for economic security. Other objectives, apart from seeking political goodwill through the provision of development assistance, may be to promote sales of equipment or managerial expertise, or to facilitate industrial adjustment.

Much concessionary development finance in the decade up to the early 1980s, especially from Japan, was directed towards large resource development projects.[54] Although the availability of capital for large-scale project developments from foreign official sources provides opportunities for strong income and resource growth in recipient countries, it raises complex problems for economic policymaking and administration. It also raises the question of effective national sovereignty over development priorities, and that of its antithesis, the problem of 'neo-colonialism'.

The worst problems of economic policy administration in developing countries are associated with difficulties in determining the true opportunity cost of public expenditure on projects that are financed with foreign assistance. Aid for resource developments, for example, has posed all the usual problems of tied aid and project aid, although often in an extreme and politically prominent form because of the scale and impact of the projects involved. Such aid is likely to be better than nothing (possibly very much better than nothing) when its availability reduces the supply price of investment and increases government revenues from project development. However, there are circumstances in which it can be worse than nothing, and it is always difficult for a recipient government to judge whether the alternative really is nothing, or whether some less restrictive kind of aid can be negotiated.

There are three circumstances in which the acceptance of aid to fund development projects can bring negative net benefits to a recipient country. The first is where the availability of concessionary funds from a particular source leads to inefficient use of a valuable resource. This will occur only where the host country's administration is inefficient, but unfortunately there are many examples of inefficient administrative systems in developing countries. The second circumstance is where the recipient government's financial commitments to a project exceed the concessionary element in the foreign funding, and where the taxation of the rents generated by the investment is less than this shortfall. The third circumstance is where the development project itself brings positive net benefits, but where the acceptance of aid specific to one kind of investment reduces the amount of aid available from the same source for purposes with higher priority. It is always difficult for a recipient of aid to identify the third circumstance in practice, and high orders of political judgment are required in the administration of policy in this area. Recipients of large quantities of concessional assistance may soon be left with very little control over the directions of national development effort if the terms upon which aid is provided by all donors deteriorate to the lowest common denominator among existing forms of aid.

These may not have been considered significant problems for Western Pacific developing countries in the receipt of assistance for development projects in the past. However, they are problems endemic in the structure of concessionary financial flows, not only for resource development projects but also for industrial projects or infrastructural developments financed under bilateral assistance programs. And they could well become a more important issue in the future.[55] They are problems which are amenable to solution through policy cooperation, and they will be less important where aid programs are delivered through multilateral agencies, or are subject to multilateral procedures and scrutiny. Working together, Pacific countries will be able to manage these problems more successfully than have individual countries in the past.

Consider the experience with the 'development–import' strategy favoured by Japanese policymakers from the late 1960s, which aimed to foster resource project developments embodying Japanese direct foreign investment and concessionary finance in order to secure Japan's resource import requirements. This approach involved concessionary financing to national investors and pervasive aid-tying in a way that could have entailed serious costs for recipient countries; and it tended to corrode, through political processes, stable and long-term trade, investment and assistance relationships between Japan and these countries. While Japan is not the only nation whose aid relationships have been perceived as exploitative, it did become dangerously exposed to this perception in Southeast Asia in the 1970s as its trade, investment and development assistance presence grew rapidly.[56] The United States and Australia (in the southeast Pacific) have had problems of the same character. Aid administrators and policymakers in Japan responded to the effects of these practices on economic and political relations with recipient countries by beginning to formulate alternative development assistance strategies, both towards Southeast Asia and more generally.

In this respect Japan took a very important initiative in promoting a development assistance, investment and economic cooperation relationship with China at the beginning of the 1980s. Japan moved decisively to untie the assistance for project development and procurements provided through the Export–Import Bank of Japan, an important agency through which concessionary finance has been available to China. This step has had many beneficial effects for Japan, for China, and for the efficient allocation of resources and specialisation within the regional economy. China, relieved of the real constraints of aid-tying, has been less reluctant to develop substantial financial and economic relationships with Japan. At the same time Japan, a competitive supplier of a range of industrial equipment and supplies which China needs, has expanded its trade with China enormously. Third countries such as Australia (an efficient supplier of raw materials to Japanese-financed industrial projects in China) have expanded their trade through these new China-Japan arrangements — arrangements which provide an economically and politically sound basis for China's integration into the Pacific economy.

Indeed, one of the most exciting and challenging developments in East Asia and the Pacific in the years ahead will be the growing trade and investment relationship with China. The United States has embraced the investment opportunity quickly and is by far the largest foreign investor in joint ventures in China to date, while Japan has played a cautious role in direct investment.[57] But Japan's initiative in financing trade growth and project development involves a bold and successful break with the past, and Japanese investors are also heavily committed in the field of offshore petroleum exploration and development. China is Japan's largest aid recipient, taking around 15 per cent of all Japan's bilateral aid disbursements.[58]

China's industrial growth in the first half of the 1980s and the Chinese commitment to opening up economic development towards the rest of the world presage that China will have a sizeable impact on regional trade and investment flows in the years ahead. Economic reform (of commodity markets, financial markets and the foreign exchange market) is at a relatively early stage, and how reforms in China are managed and sequenced will determine in part how easily Chinese trade and industrial expansion can be accommodated without putting undue economic and political strain on countries in the region and on the international trade regime, itself in a process of testing and transition. Japan's initiative in untying an important component of its development assistance to China is one step which will ease the pressures attendant on China's coming out. China's initiative in seeking to fulfil the conditions for membership of the GATT is another. More basically, China's willingness to participate in regional and international consultative processes on foreign economic policy formulation will increase the chances of its successful accommodation within the regional and international economy.[59] This is a major task for Pacific economic cooperation, and it will be discussed further in chapter 10.

THE GROWTH OF BANK LENDING

The large flows of private funds to Western Pacific countries over the past decade have been associated with the accumulation of external debt. Not only were banks big lenders in traditional areas for development projects and trade finance, but governments also sought to fund adjustment to the changes in the international economy wrought by the oil crises, inflation and recession, through extensive public borrowing from these private sources. Public sector (and publicly guaranteed) debt has increased relative to private debt. The composition of public debt has shifted from public to private sources.[60] With the exception of the Philippines, Western Pacific countries have avoided major debt problems through successful adjustment to the oil crises and the slump in commodity prices, sustained growth and industrial transformation, and the purposeful correction of macroeconomic imbalances.

The growth in the activity of international banks in East Asia and the Pacific is one of the most visible manifestations of the region's growing financial interdependence. Yet the vulnerability of the international banking system and its developing country customers to the international debt problem has led to some reconsideration of the role of commercial banks in development financing. This reassessment deserves attention here, since it provides a clue to future trends.

Foreign banks have been active and effective participants in the Western Pacific economy in the development of more efficient financial intermediation (in regional currency markets, for example) and in fostering financial innovation (foreign-exchange-risk insurance is a prominent example). There is no question that these banks will continue to play an active role in economic development and restructuring. However, the financing role of the banks may be more circumscribed in the future because of reluctance to increase exposure since the debt crisis in Latin America. There is also likely to be a return to concentration on more traditional international banking business, such as trade and project financing, rather than extension of general-purpose or balance-of-payments financing. By focusing on business where a clear source of repayment can be specified and where possibilities for organising collateral exist, bankers can reduce the impact of debt-service problems. Co-financing with multilateral institutions appears increasingly attractive. Banks are also focusing attention on the provision of services that can contribute to earnings without jeopardising their balance sheets or assets. Foreign exchange trading, forecasting, investment and treasury management are areas where the international banks are strongly placed.

McKinnon[61] makes the point that the fragility of international banking in the past decade has arisen fundamentally because the commercial banks have sought to operate in foreign currency markets abroad, outside the regulatory environment which provides their domestic credit backing. Herein lies an inherent risk to the system. The initial effect of the development of the Eurodollar market on the world economy was undoubtedly positive, since the international financial system was hamstrung by exchange controls and regulated interest rates. The negative effects began to emerge in the 1970s with the growth of high-risk, long-term bank loans, with few or no safeguards, to developing country governments. The dual system of banking regulation became unbalanced. Regulated national operations encouraged excessive exposure in non-regulated markets abroad. McKinnon notes that in the past (at the turn of the century) this kind of lending function was serviced by a highly developed long-term bond market, and that crises in that market did not threaten the whole banking and monetary system.[62] McKinnon believes that this system would encourage the development of a healthier international capital market based mainly on bonds and equities. Any international movement towards the kinds of rules embodied in the Glass–Steagall Act would, of course, have to be applied more or less uniformly internationally and nationally by the major financial powers — the United

States, Japan and Europe.

Whether so radical an institutional reform is possible or not, the interest in the development of rules to govern the management of the international banking system emphasises the importance that must be attached to sustaining the regime within which international financial markets operate. Even without formal accord, much can be done to shape and direct the operation of international financial markets and the practices and institutional forms that evolve with it. In the Pacific region there is clearly a powerful interest in monitoring financial market behaviour and sharing information on developments in the Pacific international banking arena. The commitment in a number of countries to financial market liberalisation also suggests the wisdom of sharing experience on progress in this area.

The Asian Development Bank can play a useful role in further assisting the development of East Asian and Pacific financial interdependence, alongside the growth of its role as a multilateral fund disbursement agency. In its early years the Bank, commissioned to review economic strategies towards the 1970s, played the role of catalyst in policy discussion and policy development for ASEAN. The Bank can now play a central part, in the second half of the 1980s, in fostering cooperative activity of the kind that is suggested here, and that is required to monitor and shape an institutional environment within which regional financial markets can continue to expand. The Bank's organisational and support function can be effectively married to national policy and research capacities throughout the region, and, if mobilised, can constructively influence the management of financial interdependence in the region and the shape of the East Asian and Pacific economy, and economic policy more broadly.

While the ADB's disbursement capacity is still rather limited (about US$4 billion in 1984), there is also scope for, and an obvious interest in, innovation in disbursement policy. This would most likely involve closer integration of the Bank's lending programs with private lending activity, a positive view of equity investment, and a role as guarantor of some developing country government borrowings in developed country capital markets.

But the major influence on Pacific financial markets in the coming several decades will be developments in the financial market and in financial management in Japan. United States–Japanese macroeconomic interaction is one dimension.[63] Another is the successful management of Western Pacific financial interdependence with Japan.[64] Western Pacific policy authorities have a particularly strong interest in closer consultation and cooperation with Tokyo in seeking to manage financial and other economic policies within the region around the fact of ever-stronger financial, as well as trade, ties with Japan.

NOTES

Chapter 7

1   David C. Cole and Hugh Patrick 'Financial Development in the Pacific Basin
     Market Economies' in Augustine Tan and Basant Kapur (eds) *Pacific Growth and
     Financial Interdependence* Sydney: Allen & Unwin, 1985, pp.39–67; H. W. Arndt
     'Financial Development in Asia' *Asian Development Review* 1, 1, 1983, pp.86–100.
2   Cole and Patrick 'Financial Development'; Tsao Yuan 'Capital Flows Among
     Pacific Basin Countries' in Tan and Kapur (eds) *Pacific Growth and Financial
     Interdependence*; Ronald McKinnon 'Issues and Perspectives: An Overview of
     Banking Regulation and Monetary Control' in Tan and Kapur *Pacific Growth and
     Financial Interdependence* (also published as *Pacific Economic Papers* No.117,
     Australia–Japan Research Centre, Australian National University, December
     1984).
3   Cole and Patrick 'Financial Development' p.39.
4   Seiji Maya and William James 'External Shocks, Policy Responses and External
     Debt of Asian Developing Countries' in Tan and Kapur *Pacific Growth and
     Financial Interdependence*; Shinichi Ichimura 'Debt Problems of Developing
     Countries: The Asian Perspectives' *Pacific Economic Papers* Special Paper,
     Australia–Japan Research Centre, Australian National University, November
     1984.
5   The Philippines has had particular problems, associated not only with the
     approach to financial management but also with the political uncertainties created
     by the growth of opposition to and the collapse of the regime of President Marcos
     after the assassination of Benigno Aquino. Korea's high levels of indebtedness also
     attracted attention, but were of different origin.
6   For an earlier review of the foreign investment climate in Asia and the Pacific,
     see Drysdale *Direct Foreign Investment in Asia and the Pacific*. The most recent
     survey is by Hal Hill and Brian Johns 'The Role of Direct Foreign Investment
     in Developing East Asian Countries' *Weltwirtschaftliches Archiv* 121, 1985,
     pp.355–81.
7   *Report of the Pacific Economic Cooperation Conference Task Force on Capital Flows*
     Fourth Pacific Economic Cooperation Conference, Seoul, April–May 1985; Naya
     'External Shocks'.
8   Yuan 'Capital Flows' pp.68–98.
9   *Task Force on Capital Flows*; for a full review of factors influencing the direction of
     liberalisation in the Japanese capital market, see James Horne *Japan's Financial
     Markets: Conflict and Consensus in Policymaking* Sydney: Allen & Unwin, 1985;
     Eisuke Sakakibara 'The Internationalisation of Tokyo's Financial Markets' in Tan
     and Kapur *Pacific Growth and Financial Interdependence*. For earlier assessments of
     developments in the Japanese financial market, see Export–Import Bank of Japan
     Business Cooperation Between Asia–Pacific and Japan in the Eighties Final Report of
     Symposium held in Tokyo, 26–7 May 1980, pp.66–8 and 165–240; and Eric
     W. Hayden 'Internationalisation of Japan's Financial System' *Occasional Paper of
     the Northeast Asia–United States Forum on International Policy* December 1980,
     pp.1–29.
10   Yuan 'Capital Flows' pp.68–94; Hill and Johns 'Role of Direct Investment'
     pp.12–17; Makoto Sakurai 'Japanese Direct Investment: Studies on its Growth in
     the 1970s' *Discussion Paper* No. 397, Economic Growth Center, Yale University,

1982; Sueo Sekiguchi *Japanese Direct Foreign Investment* Montclair: Allenheld & Osmen & Co., 1979.

11 Yuan 'Capital Flows' pp.68–94; McKinnon 'Issues and Perspectives' pp.319–36; Ichimura 'Debt Problems' pp.8–9; John Hewson 'The Internationalisation of Banking' in Tan and Kapur *Pacific Growth and Financial Interdependence*.

12 *Task Force on Capital Flows*.

13 ibid.

14 Masaru Yoshitomi 'Recent US–Japan Financial Interactions Under Flexible Exchange Rates' in Tan and Kapur *Pacific Growth and Financial Interdependence* pp.263–76; and Sakakibara 'Internationalisation' pp.237–46. See also Masaru Yoshitomi and the Japanese Economic Planning Agency World Model Group 'The Insulation and Transmission Mechanisms of Floating Exchange Rates Analysed by the EPA World Econometric Model' Economic Planning Agency, Tokyo, March 1984 for a simulation of these interactions; Stephen E. Haynes, Michael M. Hutchinson and Raymond F. Mikesell 'Japanese Financial Policies and the US Trade Deficit' *Essays in International Finance* No.162, Princeton, April 1986, pp.1–25.

15 International Economic Data Bank, Australian National University.

16 Yoshitomi 'US–Japan Financial Interactions' p.271.

17 McKinnon 'Issues and Perspectives' pp.319–36.

18 For an excellent review of these issues, see Patrick 'The United States–Japan Relationship', and papers presented to a Conference on United States–Canadian Trade and investment Relations with Japan, University of Michigan, Ann Arbor, 2–3 April 1987. For earlier views of the structural character of this interaction, see Peter Drysdale and Kiyoshi Kojima 'Australia–Japan Economic Relations in the International Context: Recent Experiences and the Prospects Ahead' in Drysdale and Kojima (eds) *Australia–Japan Prospects* pp.13–18; and Hugh Patrick 'United States–Japan Political Economy'.

19 ibid. p.17; and Aurelia George 'Japan's Beef Import Policies 1978–84: the Growth of Bilateralism' *Pacific Economic Papers* No.113, Australia–Japan Research Centre, Australian National University, July 1984.

20 Hill and Johns 'Role of Direct Investment'; and for an overview of the growth of Japanese direct foreign investment activities, see Michael Yoshino *Japan's Multinational Enterprises* Cambridge: Harvard University Press, 1976; Yoshihiro Tsurumi *The Japanese Are Coming: a Multinational Interaction of Firms and Politics* Cambridge: Ballinger, 1976; Kiyoshi Kojima *Direct Foreign Investment: A Japanese Model of Multinational Business Operations* London: Croom Helm, 1978; Terutomo Ozawa *Multinationalism, Japanese Style* Princeton, NJ: Princeton University Press, 1979; Sekiguchi and Krause 'Direct Foreign Investment in ASEAN' ; Kunio Yoshihara *Sōgo Shōsha: Vanguard of the Japanese Economy* Kuala Lumpur: Oxford University Press, 1983; and Sekiguchi *Japan's Direct Foreign Investment*.

21 Export–Import Bank of Japan *Asia–Pacific Cooperation* pp.66–8; and Peter Drysdale 'An Organisation for Pacific Trade, Aid and Development: Regional Arrangements and the Resource Trade' in Laurence B. Krause and Hugh Patrick (eds) *Mineral Resources in the Pacific Area* San Francisco: Federal Reserve Bank of San Francisco, 1978, pp.611–60.

22 Horne *Japan's Financial Markets*; Sakakibara 'Internationalisation'; Yoshitomi 'US–Japan Financial Interactions' pp.274–75.

23 ibid.

24 See especially Yoshitomi 'US–Japan Financial Interactions'.

25 Horne *Japan's Financial Markets*; and James Horne 'National, International and Sectional Interests in Policymaking: The Evaluation of the Yen Bond Market, 1970–82' *Pacific Economic Papers* No.98, Australia–Japan Research Centre,

Australian National University, December 1982.

26   Yoshitomi 'US-Japan Financial Interactions' p.275; and McKinnon 'Issues and
       Perspectives' pp.319–36.

27   J. M. Fleming 'Domestic Financial Policies under Fixed and Floating Exchange
       Rates' *IMF Staff Papers* November 1962, pp.369–80; and R.A. Mundell
       International Economics New York: Macmillan, 1968.

28   Theoretically it cannot be predicted in advance, without empirical knowledge of
       the relevant parameters, whether a fiscal expansion at home will cause the
       exchange rate of the home currency to appreciate or depreciate. Nor can it be
       known, from theory, whether the current account deficit induced by the fiscal
       policy expansion will outweigh the capital account surplus induced by the higher
       interest rates which will be a consequence of unaccommodated expansionary fiscal
       policy. See Yoshitomi 'US-Japan Financial Interactions' pp.265–68 for an
       empirical investigation of this question in the United States–Japan context.

29   McKinnon 'Issues and Perspectives' p.331.

30   Drysdale and Kojima 'Australia–Japan Economic Relations in the International
       Context' pp.16–17; I. Destler, H. Satō, P. Clapp and H. Fukui *Managing the
       Alliance: The Politics of US–Japanese Relations* Washington, DC: The Brookings
       Institution, 1976; H. Satō and I. Destler *Coping with US–Japanese Economic
       Conflicts* Lexington: Lexington Books, 1982; Stephen D. Krasner, 'Trade
       Conflicts and the Common Defence: The United States and Japan' *Political
       Science Quarterly* 101, 5, 1986; Patrick 'The United States–Japan Relationship'.

31   Patrick, in 'The United States–Japan Relationship' p.26, refers to 'Japan's lost
       opportunity . . . between 1982–1985 when its exports were growing rapidly and
       adjustment would have been less difficult'.

32   Discussion of this in Japan was initiated by Saburō Ōkita. See WIDER
       'Mobilising International Surpluses for World Development: a WIDER plan for a
       Japanese Initiative' World Institute for Development Economics Research
       (WIDER), Helsinki and Tokyo, 7 May 1987.

33   The smaller developed countries, such as Australia, Canada and New Zealand, are
       among the most important net capital importers in the region.

34   Hill and Johns 'Direct Foreign Investment'; *Task Force on Capital Flows*.

35   Naya and James 'External Shocks' pp.292–316.

36   Arndt 'Financial Development in Asia'; Hewson 'Internationalisation of Banking'
       and Lee Sheng Yi 'Developing Asian Financial Centres' in Tan and Kapur
       Pacific Growth and Financial Interdependence.

37   Hill and Johns 'Direct Foreign Investment' Table 2; and estimates calculated from
       data in this paper by the author.

38   Drysdale *Direct Foreign Investment*, especially ch.1.

39   See Oksenberg 'China's Confident Nationalism'; Findlay, Anderson and Drysdale
       'China and the Pacific Economy'.

40   Hill and Johns, 'Direct Foreign Investment' pp.12–18; H.W. Arndt 'Professor
       Kojima on the Macro-economics of Foreign Direct Investment' *Hitotsubashi
       Journal of Economics* 15, 11, 1974, pp.26–35.

41   Hill and Johns 'Direct Foreign Investment' pp.24–29.

42   ibid. These statistics on Japan were derived from data made available to the
       Australia–Japan Research Centre by the Japanese Ministry of International Trade
       and Industry.

43   Sekiguchi and Krause 'Direct Foreign Investment in ASEAN'.

44   ibid.; Mari Pangestu 'Japanese and Other Foreign Investment in the ASEAN
       Countries' *Australia-Japan Economic Relations Research Project Research Paper*
       No.73, Australia-Japan Research Centre, Australian National University,
       December 1980.

45 Yuan 'Capital Flows'; Pangestu 'Japanese Investment in ASEAN'.
46 Yuan 'Capital Flows' pp.72–73. See also ESCAP Secretariat 'ASEAN Foreign Investments from Pacific Sources' in United Nations ESCAP 'ASEAN and Pacific Economic Co-operation' *Development Papers* No. 2, 1983, pp.179–230.
47 Yuan 'Capital Flows' pp.72–73.
48 ibid.
49 Yuan 'Capital Flows' pp.90–91.
50 Pangestu 'Japanese Investment in ASEAN' pp. 101–105.
51 ibid.
52 *Task Force on Capital Flows*.
53 Yuan 'Capital Flows' pp.72–73.
54 Drysdale 'Organisation for Pacific Trade, Aid and Development' pp.626–36.
55 This is a sensitive issue in Japanese aid and business relations with the Philippines, Indonesia and China. There is also the problem of corruption, as evidenced by the suspected misuse of Japanese aid to the Philippines by ex-president Marcos, involving Japanese corporations, officials and politicians. See Manila correspondent Jose Marte Abueg 'Investigation could cause Tokyo scandal' *Australian Financial Review* 9 May 1986.
56 Alan Rix *Japan's Economic Aid* London: Croom–Helm, 1980.
57 Yuan 'Capital Flows' p.78.
58 *Japan's Official Development Assistance* Tokyo: Ministry of Foreign Affairs, 1986, p.9.
59 China joined the Pacific Economic Co-operation Conference at that organisation's fifth conference, held in Vancouver in November 1986.
60 *Task Force on Capital Flows*; Yuan 'Capital Flows' pp.91–94.
61 McKinnon 'Issues and Perspectives' pp.333–35.
62 ibid. p.334. It is interesting to note that it was this bond market to which Takahashi (later to become Japanese Finance Minister at the beginning of the Great Depression and to formulate a Keynesian approach to Japanese macroeconomic policy at that time, before the General Theory had been published) also went in order to raise funds to finance Japanese involvement in the Russo–Japanese War. McKinnon mentions that when Russia defaulted on the Czarist bonds, the banking system as a whole was not threatened.
63 Yoshitomi 'US–Japan Financial Interactions'.
64 See Colin McKenzie and Michael Stutchbury (eds) *Japan's Money Markets and the Future of the Yen* (forthcoming).

8   Integration European style?

Vigorous expansion of trade, investment and other economic ties within the East Asian and Pacific economy has taken place without the framework of formal regional institutional arrangements that fostered European integration in the form of the European Economic Community, or even of the type that fostered integration across the Atlantic among the original OECD countries.[1] The growth of Pacific economic integration represents an impressive example of 'market integration' around significant institutional and legal barriers to trade, capital movements and other forms of economic interchange.[2]

But institutional and market integration involve an important two-way interaction wherein close ties and common economic problems set the requirements for institutional arrangements which, once in place, influence the degree of economic and political cohesion among countries. Hence, the growth of the East Asian economy and of Pacific economic interdependence, the shift of world economic power away from Europe and the Atlantic towards Asia and the Pacific, and the changed status of Japan and the United States in world affairs have all encouraged suggestions of the need for a new focus in foreign economic policy and a new institutional framework for dealings among Pacific economies.[3] Prominent in this discussion has been the notion of a developing Pacific community; but the debate about what forms of institution-building might best serve the interests of Pacific countries in managing and further developing their already substantial economic interrelationship has notably eschewed the idea of integration European style.

ALTERNATIVE ROUTES TO INTEGRATION

While the growth of East Asian and Pacific economic interdependence did not originate in the establishment of formal regional institutional arrangements, two important elements in the nexus of political and commercial history in which it took place can be identified fairly easily. The first is the role played by the GATT in the postwar recovery; the second is the dominance of the United States during this formative period.

First, postwar trade and economic growth flourished within the framework of the GATT-based international trading system under the leadership of the

United States. The GATT-based trade regime[4] grew out of the Atlantic Charter and the Mutual Aid Agreements of the wartime period,[5] and served well the cause of reconstruction and liberalisation of trade and economic activity for the first two decades or so after the Second World War. It provided the essentials of a global trade regime,[6] far from comprehensive in its coverage of commodities or commercial interests (as the aborted plan for an International Trade Organisation might have been), yet hugely supportive of trade expansion and world economic recovery and growth generally.[7] This was critical to countries in East Asia and the Western Pacific which were not immediate or direct beneficiaries under the initial rules and terms of the GATT. But it also directed and limited trade and economic growth in some areas, as the following argument suggests.

Second, the United States dominated the Pacific economy during that period. American leadership, regional as well as global, was comprehensive and hegemonic, combining military–strategic, political and economic interests. In this period the Pacific alliance against communism in the Cold War era was conceived and executed.[8]

It is instructive to recall how these factors influenced the development of the significant economic relationship between Australia and Japan.[9] The Australian alliance with the United States, formalised in the ANZUS (1951) and SEATO (1954) pacts, was integral to American security policy in East Asia and the Pacific, and formed the cornerstone of Australian foreign and defence policies in the 1950s.[10] Japan was linked with the United States through a mutual security pact, first entered into in 1951 and revised in 1960. The United States Japanese Mutual Security Treaty, itself the foundation of postwar Japanese defence and foreign policy, remains a critical element in assessing the political and strategic future of the region. Even though the continued effectiveness of ANZUS was questioned after the Vietnam war and, more recently, the exclusion of New Zealand over the port visits issue, it remained part of a broader set of political and economic links with the United States which greatly influenced Australia's approach to the region and the world. The trans-Pacific ties between Japan, Australia and the United States (as well as similar ties with the other countries of non-communist Northeast and Southeast Asia) were significant for economic development in the Western Pacific region during the postwar period because they brought Australia and Japan into closer alignment in their political interests at the same time as opportunities for bilateral trade were growing. The broader framework of the foreign and foreign economic policies of each country facilitated the extensive economic ties which developed and the relatively easy acceptance of extensive economic interdependence.

The signing of the Australia–Japan Agreement on Commerce on 6 July 1957, which accorded both parties most-favoured-nation trading treatment, marked a watershed in the nature and terms of the relationship.[11] In 1956 Australia had renegotiated the trade agreement with the United Kingdom which dated back to the Ottawa Agreement of 1932, under the dual pressures of, first Great Britain's diminishing role in Australia's trade and the need to improve access for some exports in British markets, and second the search for new markets (notably in Japan) as long-run payments prospects seemed less and less consistent with national growth ambitions. This revised agreement required the lowering of preferential trading margins for British imports, and therefore provided room for manoeuvre in trade negotiations with other countries.[12]

The 1957 Agreement on Commerce with Japan, negotiated in an atmosphere of 'ambivalence',[13] political sensitivity and criticism, was renewed in 1960 and revised in 1963, when Article V (which had given Australia the right to invoke Article XXXV of the GATT against Japan) was abrogated. The growth of bilateral trade since the early 1960s testifies to the rapid acceptance of formal trading arrangements with Japan and the reflection of this in the marketplace.[14] The application of GATT principles in the arrangements between Australia and Japan fostered faster growth of their bilateral trade than was then typical of regional trade growth, so that Australia soon became Japan's largest import supplier after the United States, and Japan Australia's largest trading partner.[15]

While Japan and Australia shared none of the cultural, political or sentimental links that had once supported the trading relationship between Australia and the United Kingdom,[16] there was a long and colourful history of commercial contact.[17] Japan had become an important trade partner for Australia in the 1920s and early 1930s, and extensive commercial links were forged during those years.[18] But the *trade diversion* dispute during the Great Depression and the bitterness of the Pacific war inhibited any easy resumption of trade growth after the war.[19] Nevertheless, following the Agreement on Commerce, Australia's trade with Japan rapidly outstripped and supplanted its trade with its traditional trading partners, and the Australia–Japan relationship became one of the key elements in East Asian and Pacific economic interdependence.[20]

The GATT framework (more importantly, Japan's accommodation within it under the aegis of the United States) and the framework of the Pacific security alliances provided the underpinnings for this achievement, and for the confident development of other trading links within the East Asian and Pacific economy.

The idea of a community associated in some form of regional arrangement began to emerge in the middle of the 1960s, principally in business and academic circles, and later, tentatively, in official quarters.[21] The spectacular increase in economic power in the region and the striking growth in trade among the Pacific countries themselves were the principal reasons for the interest in this idea.

Within the Pacific region Australia and Japan were already at that time developing a bilateral economic relationship of considerable international significance, which had grown out of the commercial policy initiatives of the mid-1950s. In their subsequent reactions to the changing international economic environment both countries moved towards closer involvement with each other. There is no better illustration of this than their response to the emergence of the EEC and the problems of global market access in the middle of the 1960s.[22]

Australia's response to the damaging effects of the European Common Agricultural Policy on the prospects for Australian economic growth based on the expansion of its traditional markets for agricultural exports was to intensify the development of new markets in Japan, the Pacific and East Asia.[23] Japan's response to the emergence of a discriminatory bloc in Western Europe was to encourage closer economic relations with its main Pacific trading partners and pursue a line of commercial diplomacy designed to counter the effects of intensified European protectionism by developing an alignment of interests within the Pacific economy.[24] These policy responses were in part a product of established trading intensities between Australia and Japan and their Pacific neighbours. Unprecedented developments in the minerals trade brought the two countries even closer together.[25] But in the early stages they were conditioned in important ways by events in Europe, as well as by perceptions of the development and potential of Pacific economic growth and interdependence.[26]

THE FREE TRADE AREA PROPOSAL

In the climate of these policy developments in Europe, it was not surprising that the birth of the first detailed proposal for a Pacific regional economic association took the form of a free trade area scheme. Kojima's original paper on the idea of a Pacific free trade area (PAFTA) was prepared in 1965 and revised and extended in 1968.[27] The rationale advanced for institutional integration, involving *discriminatory* treatment in international trade, was based upon analysis of the effects of the formation of the European Economic Community upon the Pacific Five advanced industrial countries and upon the relations between them and the developing countries of Asia and the Pacific (the 'extended Pacific area').[28] The starting point in his argument was that '[e]ach time a shock was felt from outside the five Pacific countries, the necessity for closer Pacific integration was felt more seriously.'[29]

The proposal for a Pacific free trade area, consisting of the Pacific Five as full members and incorporating Asian–Pacific developing countries as associate members enjoying non-reciprocated tariff concessions, was primarily a reaction to the establishment of the European Economic Community.[30] The EEC was destined, it was felt, not only to have a huge impact on international trade and investment flows but also to influence profoundly the balance of world economic power. The completion of the EEC's internal tariff elimination in 1968 added to fears of an increasingly inward-looking and self-sufficient European bloc damaging to Pacific interests in global market access.[31] Kojima urged the logic of Pacific economic integration, both in response to the threat of institutional integration in Europe and as a vehicle for realising the potential of the East Asian and Pacific region. The completion of the Kennedy Round of negotiations in June 1967 gave tactical point to Kojima's PAFTA proposal.[32] A further round of global tariff reductions seemed unlikely for a decade or so; under these circumstances, the formation of a Pacific free trade area could prove the most effective means of expanding trade among the Pacific Five and contributing to the momentum of world trade liberalisation. While Kojima's analysis suggested that a Pacific free trade area would result in a sizeable expansion of trade among countries within the area, the distribution of gains was very likely to be uneven and, he acknowledged, this would make it difficult to obtain the consensus necessary to proceed in this direction.[33] This judgment proved right, for that and more fundamental reasons.

The most important factor working against the Pacific free trade area proposal was the global interest in United States commercial diplomacy. The United States could not easily or sensibly participate in discriminatory regional trading arrangements through a grouping of either European or Pacific countries; this course would have been quite incompatible with its stature in world trade at that time, and contrary to the main thrust of its approach to international trade policy.[34] Moreover, even the Pacific Five included countries of disparate industrial size, and lacked the degree of integration required to make the dismantling of protective measures within the group politically or economically feasible.[35]

The Pacific free trade area idea proved both politically and economically unacceptable. Inside Japan there were those who drew parallels between the Asian–Pacific area proposals and the discredited concept of a Greater East Asia Co-prosperity Sphere of the interwar and wartime period.[36] There were in fact no such simple parallels. It is true that in Japanese attitudes towards relations with Asian and Pacific countries there is historically an ambivalence between the nationalist-expansionist position and the internationalist position, with pan-Asianism incorporating large doses of the former emphasis as well as the latter.[37] But the Pacific free trade area idea was motivated by an interest in meeting the challenge from European integration, in straightening out increasingly important relationships among the Pacific Five, and in correcting a growing disparity in the development of their economic relations with neighbouring countries.[38] The PAFTA proposals derived principally from a concern to maintain and extend Japan's links with the rest of the world, not to confine and restrict its economic partnerships to the region. Outside Japan, the reaction to this specific proposal was not enthusiastic. In the smaller countries, such as Australia, Canada and New Zealand,[39] there were fears of Japanese economic domination. The potential economic gains (wrongly conceived by Japanese proponents and foreign critics alike as measurable in country-by-country balance-of-trade movements) were seen as heavily weighted in Japan's favour. And all this Japanese gain was to be achieved at substantial adjustment cost to the smaller partners, or so it was argued.[40]

Nonetheless, the foreign economic policy interest which underlay the Pacific free trade area proposal, while perhaps overambitious and of limited direct policy relevance, contained the seeds of a useful approach to important problems which were emerging in the growing economic and other relations among the diverse economies and societies of the Asian–Pacific region.[41] The huge growth of trade, investment and aid relationships among the countries of East Asia and the Pacific was spawning not only opportunities but quite predictable policy problems that would be managed less and less well within established bilateral arrangements or by individual countries unilaterally. In this context the Pacific free trade area proposal provided a useful starting point for the evaluation of other ideas, the most prominent of which was the proposal for the establishment of an Organisation for Pacific Trade and Development (OPTAD).

REGIONAL ORGANISATION

The proposal for an Organisation for Pacific Trade and Development has been around in different forms for quite a long time,[42] but it was not until 1979, with the publication of a paper entitled *Evaluation of a Proposed Asian-Pacific Regional Economic Organization* for the United States Congressional Research Service, that it received any serious attention in North America.[43]

The paper was called for at the initiative of the office of Senator John Glenn, then Chairman of the United States Senate Foreign Relations Committee's Subcommittee on Asia and the Pacific, in July 1978. The paper was commissioned to:

— review the nature and origins of the current proposal for a regional association in the form of an organisation for Pacific trade, aid and development;

— propose a role the United States Congress might play in the evolving situation; and

— suggest whether that role should take the form of legislation, congressional resolution, sponsoring of a major conference, or some other action.

The paper was prepared in response to new interest in the idea of a regional economic association among Asian–Pacific nations, especially with the elevation of Ōhira to the prime ministership of Japan in November 1978; its inspiration extended back to the discussion of regionalism among political, official, business and academic leaders in Shimoda, Japan, late in 1977 in the context of problems in the United States–Japan relationship.[44] Interest in a Pacific regional organisation went back further still, and was particularly associated with discussion in academic circles at the Pacific Trade and Development Conferences, and among business and political leaders in the Western Pacific countries, notably Japan and Australia.[45]

It is not surprising that the idea of a formal Pacific association was first articulated by the business, political and intellectual leadership in Japan.[46] No nation is more central to the substantial number of interests that have come to be shared by the countries of the Pacific region. In the mid-1960s the concept of a burgeoning Asian–Pacific community of nations became a commonplace in the rhetoric of Japanese of stature as they talked of world affairs.[47] The idea of a formal Pacific association was first espoused by the Japanese at an official level in 1967, when the then foreign minister, Takeo

Miki, outlined his ideas for an 'Asian Pacific policy' based on an 'awareness of common principles', regional cooperation in Asia, cooperation among the advanced nations in the Pacific area, and more extensive aid programs.[48]

Although there were no major policy initiatives while Miki was foreign minister, the Pacific Trade and Development Conference series was launched, with the support of the Japanese Foreign Ministry, to consider Kojima's Pacific free trade area proposal;[49] and it has continued to involve a wider and wider group of policy-interested economists in the discussion of regional foreign economic policy issues over the ensuing decade and a half.[50] Each conference has involved the definition of a research program on a particular theme, the discussion of research results and their implications for policy, and the publication of research findings. The purpose, from the very beginning, was not primarily to originate specific policy proposals — although that does sometimes happen — but to delineate issues and consider policy options, to present basic and relevant empirical evidence, to explicate national and regional interests and points of view, and generally to provide a more informed basis for policy discussion of these issues among East Asian and Pacific nations.[51] The development of thinking about Pacific economic cooperation this forum was a critical element in heightening official interest in the idea at the end of the 1970s.

One question which inevitably required consideration was whether existing arrangements and organisations within East Asia and the Pacific were perfectly adequate for managing and fostering economic integration on the scale envisaged for the region. Alongside bilateral economic, political and security arrangements (such as the United States–Japan Mutual Security Treaty, the Australia–Japan Treaty of Friendship and Co-operation, and the Japan–China Treaty of Friendship, among many others) there are a number of existing regional institutions with which any new regional organisation might seem to be competing. In fact none of the established regional institutions served the purposes that the proposed new regional economic association was designed to promote.[52]

The Economic and Social Commission for Asia and the Pacific (ESCAP), a United Nations regional organisation, is the most comprehensive of the existing regional organisations in membership and interest, but its weakness lies in its very comprehensiveness and its remoteness from policy influence in its diverse membership. While it (in its predecessor form, ECAFE) served as a contact point in the establishment of the Asian Development Bank, ESCAP was not designed to serve the functions that a regional association of the kind suggested in this study would fulfil. Equally importantly, it was unlikely to be remodelled for that end.

The Asian Development Bank is, of course, a functionally specific organisation devoted to development financing within the region. Like the World Bank and the other regional development banks, it mobilises soft and commercial funds for financing specific development projects. To date it has only on occasion served extensively as a focus for comprehensive discussion or exchange of ideas on regional trade and other regional economic issues, although it has a substantial capacity to assist the development of such discussion.[53]

The most important regional organisation with a trade and development focus is ASEAN, which also has an important political role. There is also the free trade arrangement between Australia and New Zealand, earlier limited under the NAFTA arrangements but renegotiated in the early 1980s into a more expansive Closer Economic Relationship (CER). The South Pacific Bureau for Economic Cooperation facilitates economic cooperation among the smaller economies of the Southwest Pacific and Papua New Guinea. The Ministerial Conference on Southeast Asia, which involved Australia, Japan and the Northeast and Southeast Asian non-communist economies (and which no longer convenes), was a very low-key consultative meeting at foreign ministry level without specific functions.

ASEAN represents the boldest attempt to date by a group of Asian–Pacific countries to develop common approaches to foreign economic policy.[54] However, it includes only the six non-communist Southeast Asian nations, and therefore does not represent the broader economic interests of the Pacific area as a whole. The ASEAN countries have been engaged in much more than just managing their own economic interdependence, which is as yet quite modest for the majority of them. Thus, while ASEAN could not readily be extended to take in other Pacific partners, because of its interest in presenting a common front to the Pacific and the rest of the world, it was destined to become an important group in the response to the advocation of a framework for wider Pacific economic association.

Indeed, the need for a wide, flexible and non-bureaucratic institutional association for East Asian and Pacific economies committed to outward-looking trade and development seemed to be typified in the experience of both the ASEAN group and the independent Northeast Asian developing economies such as South Korea in their attempts to deal with the bigger Pacific partners — the United States and Japan — on a bilateral level. Common regional and global interests have been sensitised because, when the overlap among regional economic interests is strong, movement on a bilateral front can damage the interest of third countries. Japanese policymakers, for example, were made newly aware of United States, Australian and Southeast Asian sensitivities when they sought to take initiatives with the ASEAN group and in the evolution of economic relations with China. In both areas, the tying of Japanese credit, development assistance programs and projects to procurement of Japanese goods was an early concern. This concern was not limited to competing suppliers of the Southeast Asian and Chinese markets; it also complicated the economics and politics of managing external funding and development assistance for the ASEAN countries and China, in ways already outlined in chapter 7. Moreover, as Japan directed concessional funds and markets towards China, ASEAN countries became fearful about whether they would have equal access to resources and markets in Japan. The management of bilateral dealings within a framework which protects third country and multilateral interests has become a steadily more serious issue in trade policy, as the extension of bilateral settlements and arrangements between the United States and Japan has begun to affect the interests of third countries (for example, Korea, Australia, Thailand) in the Pacific and elsewhere.

In 1967, businessmen, bankers and industrialists from the five advanced Pacific nations formed the Pacific Basin Economic Council (PBEC), a body designed to promote consideration of issues in regional trade and investment and greater cooperation between public and private interests. As a private organisation the PBEC has been useful, if low-key, in promoting Pacific business interests; but it has had neither the representation nor the prerogative to influence the broad framework of Asian–Pacific foreign economic policy.[55]

The PBEC grew out of bilateral bodies such as the Australian–Japan Business Cooperation Committee, which was founded in 1962, and now has a membership of more than 400 major companies from the five industrially advanced Pacific nations and from many developing countries throughout the Pacific region. Alongside the research community, the business community, through the PBEC, came to promote actively the idea of closer Pacific economic cooperation.

The advocacy of an Organisation for Pacific Trade and Development grew out of the debate over the desirability of a Pacific free trade area in the Pacific Trade and Development Conference.[56] While it was generally agreed at the first and subsequent conferences that a free trade area was not consistent with United States or regional foreign economic policy interests, there seemed a real need and ample scope for institutional innovation and policy initiatives directed towards the broad objective of securing and extending Pacific economic cooperation.

This and other concepts of regional economic association were first widely discussed in Japan and Australia.[57] The OPTAD proposal was endorsed in the Crawford–Okita *Report to the Governments of Australia and Japan* in 1976.[58] In 1982, in an important paper reviewing the history of thinking about Pacific economic cooperation and ASEAN responses to it, Soesastro observed that Japanese and Australian interest in these proposals was a quite natural outgrowth of thinking about the development of their regional economic interests.[59]

The discussion of the OPTAD proposal, both within the context of the Pacific Trade and Development Conference series and more widely over the years, reveals four broad goals. First, it was conceived as a more effective safety valve, given high existing levels of economic interdependence, through which trade and economic grievances among Pacific countries might be discussed in a rational and cooperative atmosphere, calculated to make third-country interests transparent and to safeguard profitable national trading interests. Second, it aimed to provide both a stimulus to investment and aid flows within the region, and a framework for improving the structure and quality of their aid, investment and trade relations with the developed countries in the Pacific. Third, it was to provide a forum for consultation and discussion about measures to promote the longer term developments in, and economic transformation of, the region. A final but nonetheless fundamental consideration was the role envisaged for OPTAD in providing a more secure framework of economic alliance among the countries of Asia and the Pacific, an alliance within which participants could feel free to develop closer economic integration in smaller groupings and through which participants could play a more constructive role in the expansion of relations with China, the Soviet Union and Indochina following the Vietnam War, as well as in global economic forums.

The establishment of an Organisation for Pacific Trade and Development which served these aims could, it was felt, effectively weld together the three main strands in relationships among East Asian and Pacific countries: the crucial economic links with Japan and the United States; the political, diplomatic and economic involvements with the developing countries, both non-communist and communist, in the Western Pacific region; and the strategic interest in stable and constructive relationships among the major powers in East Asia and the Pacific.

OPTAD AND OPTAD REVISITED

The fullest statement to date of the OPTAD proposal and the discussion leading up to it is still to be found in the United States Congressional Research Service paper prepared by Drysdale and Patrick. The proposal had antecedents in the work of both Drysdale and Kojima, but there were important differences in emphasis among the Kojima proposal put forward in 1968, Drysdale's earlier ideas, and the 1979 proposal. As Soesastro[60] has explained, Kojima's emphasis had initially been on events outside the region (that is, on the development of the European Community) and their impact on Pacific countries. This was also an element in Drysdale's thinking: Australia was in the process of redirecting its economic relationships away from Europe towards Asia and the Pacific;[61] but the challenge of economic development in Southeast Asia and the Western Pacific and the participation of these countries was also a central feature from the beginning.[62] Kojima

> originally thought that OPTAD would be an intermediate step and would constitute a steering body to realise a Pacific free trade area. [Later he looked] . . . to changes in the present multilateral approaches and negotiations through OPTAD, so as to give much closer attention and priority to the promotion of functional economic integration and development in the Pacific, Asian and Latin American region.[63]

Drysdale stressed the potential of OPTAD, even in the absence of a comprehensive movement towards regional trade liberalisation on a most-favoured-nation or a preferred basis, for encouraging trade expansion and investment flows which would serve the development objective. OPTAD was assigned the important role of '. . . promoting and directing capital movement into less industrialised partners.'[64] By 1979 the focus was very much on the internal dynamics of the East Asian and Pacific economy and the challenges and opportunities which East Asian trade and industrial growth presented for the formulation of foreign economic policy.

The Drysdale and Patrick paper identified three factors which had given a major impetus to the growth, of the East Asian economies and the increased importance of the Pacific within the world economy. The first was the growth of Japan's industrial power, which had been felt through increased demand for minerals and foodstuffs, as well as through the flows of capital generated throughout the region by these demands. The second was the trade and industrial growth achievements of the developing economies of East Asia, which had been stimulated by the effects of Japan's trade and economic growth on the regional economy, as well as by the adoption of outward-looking, trade-oriented industrialisation strategies in place of earlier protectionist strategies by other Northeast and Southeast Asian countries and by the success of these national development efforts. The third was the slide towards slower growth in Western Europe, as a consequence of which opportunities in the European market seemed relatively limited.[65]

The study suggested that the emergence of Pacific economic power required a new regional reference point to facilitate the pursuit of common trade and development objectives within the Pacific economy and overcome conflicting ones. It was also argued that existing regional and international institutions, and the focus of government policy attention, were inadequately directed to meet that need in full.

The recommended structure of OPTAD was as follows:

— that OPTAD be a governmental organisation, with its members the constituent governments;
— that membership include, in the first instance, Australia, Japan, the United States, Canada, South Korea, the market economies of Southeast Asia and other Pacific basin countries;
— that the administrative apparatus be small and not heavily bureaucratic;
— that issues be handled by specific functional task forces with specified policy-oriented assignments, initiated through a high-level political consultative mechanism;
— that the style of operations be consultative, informal and communicative. An important function would be the exchange of information and ideas, as well as the initiation of negotiations on policy issues.[66]

The main work of OPTAD would be undertaken by functional task forces established ad hoc to treat specific policy issues.[67] Among the substantial issues on the agenda for task force activity were: the Pacific interest in trade liberalisation and the resolution of regional trade conflicts; trade and industrial restructuring; the financing of regional development; foreign investment policies; resource and energy security; and trade and economic relations with the non-market economies of East Asia and the Pacific. The delicate question of participation by the People's Republic of China and other communist states was raised, and a selective functional participation in relevant task forces was suggested.[68]

The OPTAD proposal addressed a central requirement in the development of closer Pacific economic cooperation, in that it sought to engage government and official-level attention in meeting the challenges of Pacific growth. There was no established inter-governmental mechanism through which this could readily occur at that time. The research and intellectual base had been established within the Pacific Trade and Development Conference series and elsewhere, and the PBEC had mobilised the interests of the business community. The OPTAD proposal focused quite properly on the need to involve governments in the promotion and discussion of Pacific economic cooperation. But the idea of developing a mechanism such as OPTAD, wherein separate government-to-government consultations would take place, was premature. The particular characteristics of the Pacific economy and polity made that step impractical in the immediate term, and suggested the need for continuing support from the business and research communities in the next practical steps that could be taken.

The United States Senate report was, nonetheless, an important catalyst in the refinement of ideas about Pacific cooperation arrangements. Soon after the report was published, in 1979, the Ōhira government in Japan established a Study Group on the Pacific Basin Cooperation Concept,[69] the report from which became an important background document for an international seminar at the Australian National University in September 1980, sponsored by the Australian government, to discuss what was involved in the idea of a Pacific community and how it might be translated into action.[70]

ECONOMIC DIPLOMACY AND THE PRACTICE OF COOPERATION

What is different about these and subsequent developments in the 1980s, in Australia and throughout the Pacific region, is that there was a significant quickening of political interest in the exploration of new arrangements for Pacific economic cooperation. This really signified that political leaders were coming to agree with the view that economic and political power is shifting from the Atlantic towards the Pacific and that the trend is likely to continue for many years to come. It was against this broad economic and political background that the then Prime Minister of Australia, Mr Fraser, and the late Prime Minister of Japan, Mr Ōhira, agreed to convene a seminar at the Australian National University in Canberra in September 1980 to survey interest in the idea of a Pacific community.

An important feature of the Canberra meeting was that it included participants from government, the business sector and the research community. It recommended the setting up of a Pacific Cooperation Committee, with members appointed by governments to represent their countries in a non-official capacity. Governments were thus to be drawn into the discussion of Pacific economic cooperation issues without having to take a leading role. The Committee was to direct task force work on substantial issues for cooperation in fields including trade, investment, marine resources and communications.[71]

The discussions at the Canberra seminar highlighted a number of features that have since conditioned the exploration of economic cooperation arrangements in the region. The view that emerged from this meeting was that the particular circumstances facing the Pacific community would not permit reliance on models of cooperation applying elsewhere in the world. A new approach was required, as were a new set of objectives and 'rules of the game'. Some issues identified as important to the Pacific community were:

— the need to avoid military–security issues in order to create a sense of community without creating a sense of threat;
— that EEC-style discriminatory trading arrangements were inappropriate in the Pacific;
— the need to 'hasten slowly', to see the full blossoming of the Pacific Community idea as a longer term objective and to proceed towards long-term goals step by step, with each intermediate step being useful in itself and not dependent for success on further steps being taken;
— the need to ensure that existing bilateral, regional and global mechanisms for cooperation are not undermined by any wider regional arrangement and that it be complementary to them;
— the need to ensure that it is an outward-looking arrangement;
— the need for an 'organic approach' building up private arrangements already in existence in the Pacific, including such bodies as the Pacific Basin Economic Council and the Pacific Trade and Development Conferences and other privately based activities;
— the need to involve academics, businessmen and governments jointly in this cooperative enterprise;
— the need to avoid unnecessarily bureaucratic structures;
— the need for a fairly loose and as far as possible non-institutionalized structure recognising that, while disputes settlement may prove difficult in sensitive areas, discussion of problems may contribute towards ameliorating them;
— the need for all members to be placed on an equal footing (that is, no EEC-style associate membership);
— the need to concentrate attention on areas of mutual regional interest;
— the need to make substantive progress in improving upon the benefits emanating from existing bilateral, global and regional arrangements.[72]

The Canberra recommendations did not receive immediate acceptance in ASEAN, largely because they implied that each government would have to recognise the activity officially and become involved in carrying it forward. Crawford, who had guided the meeting to its conclusion, had extensive consultations with ASEAN governments to clarify these issues, and within ASEAN Indonesia's Centre for Strategic and International Studies (CSIS) set in motion a study of the issues from an ASEAN perspective. The CSIS-sponsored study endorsed the thrust of the Canberra proposal. A follow-up study under the auspices of ESCAP provided background material for a Second Pacific Economic Cooperation Conference, held in Bangkok in June 1982.[73]

The Bangkok Conference saw the formation of a Standing Committee (rather like the committee that had been proposed in Canberra) to guide the work of four task forces based at institutions in Australia, Korea, Japan and Thailand. These task forces and the Standing Committee reported to a third conference, in the same format, held in Indonesia in November 1983.[74] The Indonesian conference achieved a substantial consolidation of the Pacific Economic Cooperation Conference process and the task force activities, and its outcome was a significant elevation in the profile of government support for developing the practice of regional cooperation.[75]

This third conference came to three main conclusions: that Pacific countries should participate, and take a leading role, in a new round of multilateral trade negotiations; that the governments concerned should also give full consideration to a set of specific measures for regional cooperation, which were identified by the task forces in trade and other areas such as fisheries management, minerals and energy matters, foreign investment, and technology transfer; and that consultation, involving the private sector, research institutions and governments, should be pursued in the areas covered by the task forces to increase mutual understanding of national policies and market conditions. The issues to be explored in the following round of task force activities were specific opportunities for Pacific economic cooperation in trade negotiations, fisheries development, minerals and energy consultation, technology transfer through foreign investment, and capital flows.[76]

The Standing Committee of the conference and its individual members began, with the help of a coordinating group, to play a more active role in giving effect to the conclusions of the conference.[77] Two important initiatives at government level flowed directly from the Indonesian conference in this way. The first was that taken by the Australian government in encouraging the establishment of informal consultations among senior trade officials of Western Pacific countries on multilateral trade negotiations and trade policy questions.[78] This initiative followed consultations between the Australian delegation to the Indonesian conference and Australian Prime Minister Hawke; it was the first time regional trade consultations had taken place in this way.[79]

The second initiative was that taken by the ASEAN countries in establishing a new dialogue with their five Pacific partner countries in September 1984.[80] The ASEAN–Pacific Dialogue meeting led to an agreement to explore ways of strengthening the development of human resources through cooperative technical exchange programs within the region.[81] The ASEAN initiative followed discussions at the Bali conference of the broad issue of technical exchange and training programs. Though it did not embrace all the countries with strong interests in regional cooperation, this ASEAN–Pacific Dialogue represented the first significant inter-governmental association within the Pacific, and signalled that ASEAN was seeking to take an initiative in shaping developments in regional cooperation at this level.[82]

The work of the Pacific Economic Cooperation Conference task forces confirmed that both the regional focus of external relations and the common outward orientation of the individual Pacific countries provide a broad basis for concrete and substantive multilateral cooperation in many areas. It also suggested that the case for regional economic cooperation was becoming more compelling as the economies of Asia and the Pacific grew and developed. Perhaps it is of particular significance that the tripartite mechanism of government, industry and research participation (the defining characteristic of the Pacific Economic Cooperation Conference — the PECC) came to provide an extremely effective channel through which to develop the practice of Pacific economic cooperation.[83]

The importance and value of the process of informal association and consultation that has developed through the Pacific Economic Cooperation Conferences lies in the contribution it makes both to widening the channels of communication between the disparate nation states of the Pacific region on economic policy issues and problems and to providing a useful mechanism for consultation and feedback on these matters. The practice of regional dialogue on economic policy questions that this process has encouraged has created a climate in which specific issues of common concern can be identified and addressed. This has brought concrete results in the development of a regional approach to economic policy (on trade issues) and economic problems (on human resource development issues). Other consultative mechanisms (in the areas of minerals and energy, fisheries and trade) have already been established.

Since the Indonesian conference, a fourth conference has been held in Seoul and a fifth in Vancouver. The sixth conference is being held in Osaka, Japan in May 1988. The fourth conference was the instrument for establishing a Pacific Trade Policy Forum and a Pacific Minerals and Energy Forum, as well as for taking some useful initiatives in fisheries training exchange between the South Pacific and the ASEAN countries. The fifth conference saw the entry of China and Taipei to full participation in the PECC.

The essential features of this process were defined at the Canberra seminar, in discussion at the conference that followed, and in a Pacific Declaration endorsed at the Vancouver conference. Their character was born of the nature of the Pacific region itself: its economic and political heterogeneity, and its embryonic cohesion in terms of the varied structure of the diplomatic, political and economic associations among the sovereign nation states that are its constituents.

As Cooper observed in another connection,[84] if something akin to international empathy is missing the range of possibilities in international exchange will be restricted. Hence, that arm of international policy which relates the pursuit of national economic interest to the choice of an appropriate framework within which to foster confident exchange in the international community has very special significance in this setting. Therefore, Pacific economic cooperation interests have come to focus heavily on building institutions that may be functionally oriented to the economic interests of individual Pacific countries and to the region as a whole, and on the evolution of an international regime within which the Pacific countries can continue their economic expansion. It is not easy for institution-building either to precede or to follow the integration of economic markets; and the policy challenge for Pacific nations collectively is to match the pace and structure of institution-building to the requirements and potential of market integration.

The evolution of this approach to building institutions within which the potential of Pacific economic interdependence can be fully realised underlines, as essential ingredients in the development of a confident regime for international economic exchange, pluralistic mechanisms wherein common policy priorities and bases for policy action towards integration, Pacific-style, can be gradually developed. Without these ingredients, mutually beneficial exchange is always at risk.

A pluralistic community is one which accommodates heterogeneity and in which there is a measure of equality among the members as they engage in the process of seeking and settling upon common understandings and come to collective agreements. It also requires effective mechanisms for representing different policy and institutional preferences, the reconciliation of divergent positions, the identification of common approaches, and some measure of tolerance for collective action which does not have a completely unanimous basis. Divided by religion, culture, ethnic composition, ideology, security interests, political systems and, importantly, levels of economic development, the Pacific nations are a pluralistic group with a strong and growing community of interests around their extensive economic interdependence. The development of effective cooperation mechanisms has become an evident priority for continuing and successful economic cooperation among this heterogeneous group of nations, and it is an important aspect of policy.

Purposeful collective action to reduce the level of uncertainty associated with international economic exchange can yield important gains to the countries in the Pacific. A necessary condition for collective agreement and action on cooperative exchange is the establishment of a common basis of understanding of the issues and options and the pursuit of common policy goals. The process of consultation and cooperation in the Pacific region is clearly still in a very early stage, but the emergence of broad common interests in the approach to economic policy has been a feature of the dialogues that have already supported its development at various levels. Existing institutions have been used in this process of exploration, but new institutions, distinctive to the region, are also emerging to provide the basis for a regional grouping and a more comprehensive attempt at Pacific cooperation than has existed in the past.

Heterogeneity among the nations of the Pacific also shapes the substance of common policy interests, for it limits the appeal of comprehensive and discriminatory economic union, European-style. An additional and powerful argument recommends to Pacific countries that they stress non-discrimination in the approach they adopt towards international economic policy. An open and non-discriminatory trading and economic system remains fundamental to the trade and development aspirations of the industrialising nations within the region, and a critical influence upon the thrust towards economic integration, Pacific-style. A heterogeneous group of countries that are nevertheless highly complementary in terms of economic activity can develop an intensive pattern of economic relations fostered by proximity, common political associations and a strong coalition of interests which both encourages and requires closer policy coordination and economic association; and this is occurring steadily among the countries of the Pacific. It is worth underlining that collective agreements and understandings which secure the framework for exchange at the regional level among such countries can be seen as quite effective, even when they do not embody elements of commercial policy discrimination. Indeed, an underlying notion in the exploration of Pacific economic association is that such regional economic cooperation, within a framework of multilateral economic relations, offers the potential for joint provision of a stronger trade regime — a regime which also raises confidence in international economic specialisation more generally and builds closer world economic integration.

GOALS FOR PACIFIC COOPERATION

The goals for Pacific economic cooperation have been to a considerable extent defined in the discussion and developments around the Pacific Economic Cooperation Conference process. But the meaning of the term 'economic cooperation' should be clarified. Sometimes this term simply refers to trade or other forms of economic exchanges, and sometimes more specifically to development assistance arrangements. It is obviously being used here in a broader sense, and relates to international cooperation on, or coordination of approaches towards, various economic policy matters. Policy coordination is commonly conceived in macroeconomic terms — the international coordination of monetary and fiscal policy, or the management of the exchange rate and the international monetary system. This is one important aspect of economic cooperation among the major industrial powers, but it has not yet been an important focus of interest in economic policy cooperation among East Asian and Pacific economies (although it is likely to become so in the future, as the argument in chapter 7 suggests). Economic cooperation interests in the Pacific are targeted on the development of common or mutually consistent approaches to such matters as trade policy, foreign investment policy, aid policy, structural adjustment policy and commercial policy generally. It is to these areas that priority has been given in the development of common Pacific policy approaches.[85]

Trade policy is a key interest. The Seoul meeting pressed Pacific governments to take a leading role in developing a comprehensive program of trade negotiations.[86] It commended the Australian government's initiative in establishing a Western Pacific perspective on the multilateral negotiation of trade liberalisation by instigating official talks in January 1984. It urged Pacific countries to seek progress through trade liberalisation on a regional basis, concurrently with efforts through the GATT. And a Pacific Trade Policy

Forum was conceived to debate and promote these trade policy interests.

No countries have a bigger stake in a confident trade regime than those of East Asia and the Pacific. In the earlier postwar period Western Pacific countries might have been able to operate to some extent on the assumption that the international trade regime was firmly in place and that other countries' protection systems were data in the formulation of their own approach to international economic policy. This was the luxury of the period in which the United States was large enough and rich enough relative to every other country to be able to sustain the trade rules and system, and in which Western Pacific countries were relatively unimportant. Neither Japan nor the other East Asian and Pacific countries collectively are any longer in that position.

Perhaps no countries have a bigger interest in efforts to sustain and extend the GATT trade rules, and in becoming the exemplars of a liberal international trade regime, than do the Pacific countries. Japan, of course, has a peculiarly crucial role to play in these matters. The question is whether the Japanese community and its political leadership are prepared for this responsibility, and for the effort of building an international partnership and constituency in the Pacific that will make it manageable. This will not be an easy burden to carry unless there is a more explicit Pacific economic alliance in these matters, as well as in the important collective development objective of raising the incomes of the poorer countries of the region. A purposeful effort towards the development of a strong Pacific voice in international commercial diplomacy, and a stronger voice for Pacific development, are important Pacific cooperation objectives, if only around a coalition of national self-interests.

In the context of regional economic development and trade growth, there are important mutual interests among Pacific countries in the creation of a new climate in their own approaches to commercial policy. In the course of industrialisation and trade growth, such as that being witnessed in the Western Pacific region, some industries prosper and expand while others become inefficient and should be allowed to contract. Often, as inefficient industries face increasing trade competition from neighbouring countries, they are inclined to demand — and secure — protection. Since protection damages the interests of trade partners and limits the scope for growth, Pacific countries can sensibly cooperate to limit the extension of their own protectionism in the course of further industrialisation.

Pacific cooperation can be directed towards building a stronger global trade regime and *binding* protection to promote regional industrialisation. A regional approach which combines both these elements, it should be repeated, does not imply discriminatory trade policy action or a discriminatory trade policy regime:[87] quite the reverse. The interest here is in the scope for Pacific collective action to strengthen the most-favoured-nation rules and the global trading system. Given their industrialisation and trade growth ambitions, there is a major interest for East Asian and Pacific countries in most-favoured-nation trade liberalisation and in entering into arrangements to *bind* their own protectionism, especially while Atlantic countries remain reluctant to maintain liberal trade. The important conclusion is that collective action is necessary to strengthen the regional and multilateral trade and development regime under current international economic policy circumstances; and there is a long-term interest in the Pacific as an effective domain for promoting this kind of collective action.

These are long-term tasks and objectives in the trade policy arena. Other policy issues accorded priority in Pacific economic cooperation discussions include: fisheries resource training and management; consultations on minerals and energy trade and development issues; agricultural trade access; the development of 'ground rules' on foreign investment and programs to facilitate technical and professional exchanges; and measures to liberalise financial markets and enhance capital flows. There will be a need for continuing discussion and thinking about the development of a consensus on regional policy priorities and their relation to global interests and commitments, but already progress has been made in this direction.

The work of the Pacific Economic Cooperation Conferences has been important in defining the goals for Pacific cooperation.[88] It is being steadily complemented by more widely based national efforts and by the work of established institutions, such as the Asian Development Bank, ESCAP, PBEC and the Pacific Trade and Development Conference series. These efforts constitute the necessary preparation for any action at the political level on closer Pacific economic cooperation involving different groups of countries within the region. It may be some time before a comprehensive inter-governmental mechanism for consultation among Pacific countries on foreign economic policy issues comes into being, such are the constraints of Pacific diplomacy. Basic diplomatic channels are not open between ASEAN and Korea, between Korea and China, or between China and Korea and ASEAN. But the common interests are powerful, and much is being achieved through three-sector discussion (research, industry and government) of the kind that has been fostered through the Pacific Economic Cooperation Conference process. Indeed, there is evidence that effective movement towards cooperation requires officials to be involved in international economic policy development in a less formal role than politically sanctioned government-to-government arrangements would allow. The evolution of the bodies which support the Pacific Economic Cooperation Conference activity (the International Standing Committee, the member Pacific Cooperation Committees, the International Coordinating Group, and the task force coordinators and secretariats) was a large step forward in terms of Pacific institution-building. The question is not so much whether there will be a formal inter-governmental association among the countries of the Pacific; rather it is when, and how actively, regional governments will use the mechanism that is already in place as a launching pad for promoting Pacific cooperation in international economic policy, and which governments will take the leading role in this process.

NOTES

Chapter 8

1   John Crawford and Saburō Ōkita *Australia, Japan and the Western Pacific Economic Relations* a report to the Governments of Australia and Japan, Canberra: Australian Government Publishing Service, 1976, p.34.

2   See Crawford and Ōkita (eds) *Raw Materials* Parts I and II. A useful collection of papers is contained in Paul F. Hooper (ed.) *Building a Pacific Community* Honolulu: University of Hawaii Press, 1982; another is contained in Crawford and Seow *Pacific Economic Cooperation*; and, most recently, issues in Pacific economic cooperation have been reviewed in *Asian Survey* XXIII, 12, December 1983 (a special issue on 'Perspectives on the Pacific Community Concept').

3   A good review of the wellsprings of this discussion is provided in Hadi Soesastro 'Institutional Aspects of Pacific Economic Cooperation' in Hadi Soesastro and Sung-joo Han (eds) *Pacific Economic Cooperation: The Next Phase* Jakarta: Centre for Strategic and International Studies, 1983, pp.3–53 (prepared originally as ESCAP Report on ASEAN and Pacific Economic Cooperation, Bangkok, June 1982, entitled *Institutional Aspects of ASEAN–Pacific Economic Cooperation*).

4   See J.G. Crawford *Australian Trade Policy, 1942–1966* Canberra: Australian National University Press, 1968, p.10 for a useful review of the documents and issues affecting the establishment of the GATT system, and for an account of its impact on one Pacific trader. For an early history and analysis, see Gerard Curzon *Multilateral Commercial Diplomacy* London: Michael Joseph, 1965.

5   Crawford *Australian Trade Policy* pp.9–10.

6   Jock Finlayson and Mark Zacher 'The GATT and the Regulation of Trade Barriers: Regime Dynamics and Functions' *International Organization* 35, 4, Autumn 1981.

7   Robert Keohane and Joseph Nye *Power and Interdependence: World Politics in Transition* Boston: Little, Brown & Company, 1977.

8   Drysdale and Patrick 'An Evaluation of a Proposed Asian–Pacific Regional Economic Organisation' p.1.

9   Peter Drysdale 'Australia and Japan in the Pacific and World Economy' in Drysdale and Kitaōji *Japan and Australia* pp.420–21.

10   ibid.

11   Peter Drysdale 'Japan, Australia, and New Zealand: The Prospect for Western Pacific Economic Integration' *Economic Record* 45, 111, September 1969, pp.321–42.

12   Crawford *Australian Trade Policy* ch.9.

13   ibid., p.332.

14   Peter Drysdale 'Japanese–Australian Trade' in D.C.S. Sissons *Papers on Modern Japan* Canberra: Australian National University Press, 1965, pp.83–98; and Japanese–Australian Trade: A Study in the Analysis of Bilateral Trade Flows, unpublished PhD dissertation, Australian National University, 1967, ch.1.

15   ibid.

16   Crawford and Ōkita *Pacific Economic Integration* p.49.

17   Drysdale, Japanese–Australian Trade, pp.2–8.

18   ibid.; and W.A. Purcell 'The Nature and Extent of Japanese Commercial and Economic Interests in Australia 1932–1941' *Australia–Japan Economic Relations Research Project Research Paper* No. 53, Australian National University, 1978, pp.3–5.

19   Drysdale, Japanese–Australian Trade, p.90.
20   Crawford and Ōkita *Pacific Economic Relations* ch.1.
21   Drysdale and Patrick 'Regional Organisation' pp.18–21.
22   Peter Drysdale 'An Organization for Pacific Trade, Aid and Development' in Krause and Patrick *Mineral Resources in the Pacific Area* pp.613–14.
23   Crawford and Ōkita *Pacific Economic Relations* pp.25–30.
24   Kiyoshi Kojima *Japan and a Pacific Free Trade Area* London: Macmillan, 1971, chs 1 and 3.
25   Crawford and Ōkita *Pacific Economic Relations* chs 2, 5 and 6.
26   Soesastro 'Institutional Aspects' pp.28–32.
27   ibid., p.28.
28   ibid.
29   ibid., p.28; and Kiyoshi Kojima *Japan and a New World Economic Order* Tokyo: Charles Tuttle & Co., 1977, p.180.
30   Soesastro 'Institutional Aspects' pp.28–31.
31   The original contribution to this discussion was made in Kiyoshi Kojima and Hiroshi Kurimoto 'A Pacific Economic Community and Asian Developing Countries' in *Measures for Trade Expansion of Developing Countries* Tokyo: Japan Economic Research Center, October 1966, pp.93–134 (also published in *Hitotsubashi Journal of Economics* 7, 1, June 1966, pp.17–37).
32   Soesastro 'Institutional Aspects' p.28.
33   See, for example, H.W. Arndt 'PAFTA: An Australian Assessment' *Intereconomics* 10, 1967, pp.271–6. There is an extensive review and critique of the Pacific free trade area proposal in the papers from the first two Pacific Trade and Development Conferences. See Kiyoshi Kojima (ed.) *Pacific Trade and Development* Tokyo: Japan Economic Research Center, 1968; and Kiyoshi Kojima (ed.) *Pacific Trade and Development II* Tokyo: Japan Economic Research Center, 1969.
34   Richard N. Cooper, in 'Financial Aspects of Economic Cooperation Around the Pacific' in Kojima *Pacific Trade and Development* pp.283–306, introduced the first cautionary note.
35   Arndt 'PAFTA'; Bruce W. Wilkinson 'A Re-estimation of the Effects of the Formation of a Pacific Free Trade Area' in Kojima *Pacific Trade and Development II* pp. 53–102.
36   Tessa Morris-Suzuki 'Japan and the Pacific Basin Community' *The World Today* December 1981, pp.454–61; Soesastro 'Institutional Aspects' pp.16–7; Drysdale 'Organisation' p.619; Sir John Crawford 'The Pacific Basin Cooperative Concept' speech to the Thirteenth Annual Meeting of the Pacific Basin Economic Council, Sydney, 6 May 1980.
37   Drysdale 'Organisation' p.619. For a brilliant interpretation of Japanese foreign policy and attitudes towards the outside world, see Junji Banno 'Foreign Policy and Attitudes to the Outside World 1868–1945' in Drysdale and Kitaōji *Japan and Australia* pp.11–32.
38   Drysdale 'Organisation' p.619.
39   Arndt 'PAFTA'.
40   ibid.; I.A. McDougall 'Prospects for the Economic Integration of Japan, Australia and New Zealand' in Kojima *Pacific Trade and Development II*.
41   Drysdale 'Western Pacific Economic Integration'.
42   The first two variants were put forward by Kiyoshi Kojima and myself at the first Pacific Trade and Development Conference; see Kiyoshi Kojima 'Japan's Interest in Pacific Trade Expansion' and Peter Drysdale 'Pacific Economic Integration: An Australian View' in Kojima *Pacific Trade and Development*. Kojima and I had discussed these ideas since 1965 in the context of his advocacy of a Pacific free

trade area. The acronym OPTAD in Kojima's paper stood for Organization for Pacific Trade and Development; in my paper it stood for Organization for Pacific Trade, Aid and Development. This distinction was highlighted in the reporting of the conference in the Japanese-language daily newspaper *Nihon Keizai Shimbun* on 13 January 1968. Although development aid remains an important focus of interest in Pacific economic cooperation, in recent years I have tended to subsume the aid interest under the 'development' title in using Kojima's form of the acronym. See also Peter Drysdale 'Japan, Australia and Pacific Economic Integration' *Australia's Neighbours* November–December, 1967; and Peter Drysdale 'Pacific Economic Integration: The Evolution of a New Approach to Regional Trade and Development Policies' *Australia's Neighbours* October–December, 1968.

43 Drysdale and Patrick 'Regional Organisation'.

44 Soesastro 'Institutional Aspects' reports the background to this study as follows:

> The second important event in 1978 was the official support for a 'Pan-Pacific Association', announced by the then newly elected Prime Minister of Japan, Masayoshi Ohira in December. Senator John Glenn had taken note of the frequent speeches on the idea during Ohira's election campaign, and the idea was one of the issues which arose during his meeting with Ohira in Tokyo in January 1979.

Glenn was also a participant in the Shimoda Conference, which discussed the idea earlier in 1977.

45 A series of sixteen Pacific Trade and Development Conferences has been held to date, and three more conferences are already planned to take place over the next three years. The first, in Tokyo in January 1968, examined the Pacific Free Trade Area proposal and alternative trading arrangements; the second, in Honolulu a year later, considered explicitly the interests and needs of the developing nations of the Pacific; the third was held in Sydney in August 1970 on issues of private direct investment in the Pacific region. A pattern had emerged which has resulted in the continuing series and in appropriate organisational arrangements. The fourth conference, on obstacles to trade in the Pacific area, was held in Ottawa in October 1971; the fifth, on structural adjustment in Asian–Pacific trade, was held in Tokyo in January 1973; the sixth, on technology transfer in Pacific economic development, was held in Mexico City in July 1974; the seventh, on relations among the larger and smaller nations of the Pacific, was held in Auckland in August 1975; the eighth, on trade and employment, was held in Thailand in July, 1976; the ninth, on the theme of the production, processing, financing and trade of natural resources in the Pacific Basin, was hosted by the United States Federal Reserve Bank in San Francisco in August 1977; the tenth was held at the Australian National University in Canberra in March 1979 on the emergence of ASEAN and its role in a changing Pacific and world economy; the eleventh examined the spectacular economic performance of the newly industrialising economies of Northeast Asia and their economic relations with other Pacific countries, and was held at the Korea Development Institute in Seoul in September 1980; the twelfth, in Vancouver in September 1981, examined the subject of the development of and trade in renewable resources; the thirteenth, on energy adjustment problems in the region, was organised jointly by the Philippine Institute of Development Studies and the Asian Development Bank and held in Manila in January 1983; the fourteenth, on Pacific financial interdependence, was organised by the Economic Society of Singapore in June 1984; the fifteenth, on Pacific industrial policies, was organised by the Japan Economic Research Center, Tokyo, in August 1985; and the sixteenth, on Pacific trade in services, was hosted

by the University of Wellington, New Zealand, in January 1987. Future conferences are scheduled for Indonesia (on technology issues), China (on the Pacific dimensions of China's industrialisation and modernisation), Malaysia, and the United States.

Conference papers and proceedings have been published, in sequence: Kiyoshi Kojima (ed.) *Pacific Trade and Development* Tokyo: Japan Economic Research Center, February 1968; Kiyoshi Kojima (ed.) *Pacific Trade and Development II* Tokyo: Japan Economic Research Center, April 1969; Peter Drysdale (ed.) *Direct Foreign Investment in Asia and the Pacific* Canberra: Australian National University Press, 1972; H.E. English and Keith Hay (eds) *Obstacles to Trade in the Pacific Area* Ottawa: Carleton University, 1972; Kiyoshi Kojima (ed.) *Structural Adjustments in Asian–Pacific Trade* Tokyo: Japan Economic Research Center, August 1973; Kiyoshi Kojima and Miguel S. Wionczek (eds) *Technology Transfer in Pacific Economic Development* Tokyo: Japan Economic Research Center, January 1975; L.V. Castle and Frank W. Holmes (eds) *Cooperation and Development in the Asia–Pacific Region: Relations Between Large and Small Countries* Tokyo: Japan Economic Research Center, 1976; Narongchai Akrasanee et al. (eds) *Trade and Employment in Asia and the Pacific* Honolulu: University of Hawaii Press, 1977; Lawrence B. Krause and Hugh T. Patrick (eds) *Mineral Resources in the Pacific Area* San Francisco: Federal Reserve Bank of San Francisco, 1978; Garnaut *ASEAN*; Hong and Krause *Trade and Growth*; H. Edward English and Anthony Scott (eds) *Renewable Resources in the Pacific* Ottawa: International Development Research Centre, 1982; Romeo Bautista and Seiji Naya (eds) *Energy and Structural Change in the Asia–Pacific Region* Manila: Asian Development Bank and Philippine Institute of Development Studies, 1984; Augustine Tan and Basant Kapur (eds) *Pacific Growth and Financial Interdependence* Sydney: Allen & Unwin, 1985; Hiromichi Mutoh, Sueo Sekiguchi, Kōtarō Suzumura, and Ippei Yamazawa (eds) *Industrial Policies for Pacific Economic Growth* Sydney: Allen & Unwin, 1986; and Leslie V. Castle and Christopher Findlay (eds) *Pacific Trade in Services* Sydney: Allen & Unwin, 1988.

A major joint research project, undertaken by a group of Australian economists centred on the Australian National University and a group of Japanese economists working from the Japanese Economic Research Center under the direction of Sir John Crawford and Dr Saburō Ōkita, has published, and continues to publish, a considerable volume of work on Australia, Japan and Western Pacific economic relations. See Crawford and Ōkita *Pacific Economic Relations* revised; also published as Crawford and Ōkita (eds) *Raw Materials*. In Australia this work is coordinated through the Australia–Japan Research Centre; in Japan the Japan Economic Research Center coordinates one major project on Western Pacific relations.

46   Drysdale 'Organisation' and Soesastro 'Institutional Aspects' provide a fairly comprehensive history of this thinking.
47   Drysdale 'Organisation' p.617.
48   Crawford and Ōkita *Pacific Economic Relations*.
49   Soesastro 'Institutional Aspects' pp.20–27; Drysdale and Patrick 'Regional Organisation' pp.18-19. See also Bernard Gordon 'Japan, the United States, and Southeast Asia' *Foreign Affairs* 56, 3, April 1978.
50   Peter Drysdale 'The Pacific Trade and Development Conference: A Brief History' *Pacific Economic Papers* No.112, Australia–Japan Research Centre, Australian National University, June 1984 provides a survey of this conference and reviews its impact.
51   ibid., p.1.
52   Drysdale and Patrick 'Regional organisation' appendix 4.

53 Drysdale and Patrick 'Regional organisation' p.16.
54 ibid., p.16; and Ross Garnaut and H.W. Arndt 'ASEAN and the Industrialisation of Southeast and East Asia' *Journal of Common Market Studies* XVII, 3, March 1979, pp.191–212.
55 Peter Drysdale 'The Proposal for an Organisation for Pacific Trade and Development Revisited' *Asian Survey* XXIII, 12, December 1983, pp.1293–304.
56 Soesastro 'Institutional Aspects' p.19.
57 Drysdale and Patrick 'Regional organisation'; Soesastro 'Institutional Aspects' pp.30–32.
58 Crawford and Ōkita *Pacific Economic Relations*.
59 Soesastro 'Institutional Aspects' p.19.
60 ibid., p.31.
61 ibid., pp.30–32.
62 Peter Drysdale 'Pacific Economic Integration: An Australian View' in Kojima *Pacific Trade and Development* pp.194–224; Drysdale 'Pacific Economic Integration'; Drysdale 'Japan, Australia'.
63 Kiyoshi Kojima 'Japan's Interest in Pacific Trade Expansion' in Kojima *Pacific Trade and Development* p.177.
64 Drysdale 'Pacific Economic Integration' in Kojima *Pacific Trade and Development* pp.208–09.
65 Drysdale and Patrick 'Regional Organisation' pp.6–7.
66 ibid., pp.35–36.
67 ibid., p.36.
68 ibid., pp.32–34.
69 The Pacific Basin Co-operation Study Group *Report on the Pacific Basin Co-operation Concept* Tokyo, 19 May 1980.
70 Crawford and Seow *Pacific Economic Cooperation* pp.1–6.
71 ibid., pp.27–32.
72 Soesastro 'Institutional Aspects' pp.36–37.
73 Narongchai Akrasanee et al. *ASEAN and the Pacific Community* Jakarta: Centre for Strategic and International Studies, 1981, pp.1–43.
74 *Issues for Pacific Economic Cooperation* a report of the Third Pacific Economic Co-operation Conference, Jakarta: Centre for Strategic and International Studies, March 1984.
75 ibid., pp.22–25.
76 ibid., pp.30–30.
77 Following the visit of Australian Prime Minister Hawke to the region in January 1984.
78 Meetings have so far taken place in Jakarta, Sydney and Seoul in this series of official consultations.
79 Such meetings and consultations are frequent among the countries of Europe and the Atlantic. Harris has stressed the point that such exchanges among Pacific countries are critical to building confident economic relations in the region; Stuart Harris 'Pacific Economic Cooperation: How Australia and Japan Fit In' address to the Australia–Japan Relations Symposium, Sydney, 19 March 1985.
80 ASEAN Dialogue Meetings, Jakarta, September 1984.
81 Importantly, of the countries which have been active in the Pacific Economic Cooperation conference process, Korea is excluded from the ASEAN–Pacific Dialogues.
82 Report of the International Standing Committee to the Fourth Pacific Economic Cooperation Conference, Seoul, April 1985.
83 ibid.
84 See Cooper *Economics of Interdependence* ch.3.

85   *Australia and Pacific Economic Cooperation: Report by the National Pacific Cooperation Committee to the Australian Government* Australian National University, October 1985; *Australia and Pacific Economic Cooperation: Second Report by the National Pacific Cooperation Committee to the Australian Government* Australian National University, July 1987.

86   ibid.

87   This point is stressed in a recent study, Lydia Dunn *In the Kingdom of the Blind: A Report on Protectionism and the Asian–Pacific Region* London: Trade Policy Centre, Special Report No.3, 1983. This report quite wrongly implies, though it does not say so directly, that proponents of Pacific economic cooperation arrangements such as the OPTAD proposal have had a different focus (see chapter 4).

88   Richard L. Schneider and Mark Borthwick 'Institutions for Pacific Regional Cooperation' *Asian Survey* XXIII, 12, December 1983, pp.1251–53.

9 The trade regime as an object of policy

The pursuit of national interest through a system of relatively free and voluntary economic exchange requires the collective act of establishing a framework for exchange — a system within which uncertainties and the threat of arbitrary action damaging to the interests of trading partners are reduced or eliminated. Such problems of collective choice in international economic policy coexist with the formation of recognisable international associations and communities. Moreover, the international agreements and understandings which are the product of such collective action are the important pillars upon which gainful and non-threatening economic exchange is built.[1]

Growing regional and global economic interdependence over the past several decades is in part the result of technological developments in industrial countries that have favoured both specialisation within larger and larger international markets and the lowering of transportation and communication costs. It also depends upon the various institutional and policy commitments that followed the Second World War and established a more secure framework for international exchange and settlement than had theretofore existed. These institutions are now under question. Strong industrial growth within a more open international economic system brought about significant change in the structure of world production and trade, as outlined earlier in this book. In turn, the economic and political adjustment to this change put its own pressure upon the institutions and governing principles which had helped to foster world trade and economic growth in this period. These pressures are now prominent. In this context, that arm of international economic policy which relates the pursuit of national economic interest to the choice of an appropriate regime for international trade and exchange assumes a very special significance.

The layers of integration within the international economy reflect, among other factors, the framework of tacit or explicit arrangements and understandings within which cooperative economic exchange has flourished in the postwar world. Trade and economic integration among industrial countries generally grew much more rapidly than trade among other countries in the earlier postwar period. Both the Atlantic and the European communities have taken economic integration further than most groups of countries, the latter within the framework of a discriminatory trade arrangement and measures encouraging broader economic and political union. In more recent years, economic growth in the Pacific, spurred on by the growth of Japan and, later, the newly industrialising countries of East Asia, has become a major force in the world economy, and closer integration among Pacific economies has resulted from their complementarity of economic structures, an intensive pattern of economic transactions fostered by proximity, and evolving political associations. The huge economic transformation taking place in the course of East Asian industrialisation, the growth of East Asian and Pacific economic interdependence, and the shift towards the Pacific and away from the Atlantic as the locus of world economic activity have profound implications for the international economic system, and for how to provide order in the principles, commitments and agreements whereby it is governed.

The framework of agreements and understandings for international economic exchange is neither permanent nor immutable. It is the product of economic and political circumstance and history and the artifact of social or political, as well as economic, interests and action. Changing circumstances reshape the coalition of interests in the international economy, and new conditions both encourage and require different forms and new focuses for policy coordination and economic association. The concern of international commercial diplomacy, in this context, is with the trade regime itself as an object of policy.

THE GATT LEGACY UNDER CHALLENGE

In the contemporary international economic policy environment, the most serious challenges to East Asian and Pacific development ambitions have emerged first in the area of trade policy.[2] The preceding argument has sought to demonstrate the interest of Pacific countries in preserving and extending a non-discriminatory trading regime in which access to international markets and established trade is kept open.[3] The argument stressed that characteristic of industrial transformation in East Asian countries whereby their trade growth has required the taking over of market shares from established exporters, first in labour-intensive manufactured goods, as Japan did from Britain in both the prewar and postwar periods and as other newly industrialising countries of East Asia have done from Japan, and in recent decades from one another.[4] An important conclusion is that arrangements which limit or discriminate against this type of trade growth and transformation would, by ossifying established trade shares, frustrate East Asia's development ambitions, adversely affect Pacific trade interests, and seriously limit the growth potential of the world economy. In the mid-1980s, two major forces are influencing the policy choices that Pacific countries face in promoting closer economic cooperation. The first derives from the changes that have taken place in the structure of world trade and are associated with the massive shifts in the balance of the world economy, centered on the decline of American economic power. The second is a result of the impact of the worst recession in the world economy since the Second World War on the conduct of commercial policy by the major industrial countries.

The thrust of the GATT trade regime and other international institutions established after the Second World War was towards the establishment of an open trade regime which embodied, importantly, the principles of 'non-discrimination', 'predictability', 'transparency' and 'openness'.[5] These principles steadily gained expression in successive GATT reviews and rounds of trade liberalisation, in the unconditional most-favoured-nation rule, in the adoption of tariffs as the principal and 'acceptable' form of trade protection, and in the 'binding' of tariff rates to negotiated levels.[6] In applying these principles and rules the architects of the GATT sought to avoid the experience of trade restrictions, bilateralism and uncertainty of the interwar years and develop a confident global framework within which the benefits of trade liberalisation would flow to all from the action of a relatively small number of major trading nations.[7]

A trading system incorporating these principles and rules was of particular importance to smaller countries seeking economic growth through trade expansion. One of the great achievements of United States and multilateral commercial diplomacy in the postwar period was undoubtedly the accommodation of Japan within the GATT most-favoured-nation trading framework, despite the initial application of Article XXXV permitting discrimination against Japan by many trading nations until the 1960s. Without appeal to GATT principles and the GATT framework, Japan would hardly have been able to achieve the economic growth and trade expansion that it did achieve in the first two decades or so immediately after the War.[8] One commercial diplomat has observed that:

> . . . a significant element (in the design of GATT) was the view of the body of international rules, customs and practices not only as governing the relationship of the strong countries towards each other but also as safeguards for the weaker partners in the international system. There was to be no repetition of what was seen as a particular evil of the 1930's — the operation of bilateral bargaining through which a strong country, by the sheer use of its commercial power and, even more objectionably, its political power, imposed its own desired patterns of trade upon a weaker trading partner . . .[9]

Certainly, while the economically and politically powerful nations may have held more sway in the conduct of commercial diplomacy than some of the founders of the GATT might have wished, the experience within the liberal trading environment it served to create after the War has been that dynamic new entrants into international markets have been able to expand their trade and market shares alongside the established economic powers.[10] An open international market where trade discrimination is constrained by general adherence to the most-favoured-nation rule allows the accommodation of new and competitive suppliers, for whom trade is a central factor to economic growth and industrialisation. And so, in the postwar period, the GATT regime has facilitated a major transformation in the geographic structure of world trade and economic power.

The rules of the GATT reflected agreement among diverse countries and did not seek to achieve the unattainable goal of free trade.[11] They allowed the right to maintain protection and to establish free trade area arrangements, at the same time as they aimed to create a confident framework for the pursuit of liberal trading policies.

The pressures of new and defensive protectionist coalitions against competition in the international economy and weak industrial growth in the 1980s threaten the legacy of the architects of the Atlantic Charter and the GATT.[12] The most-favoured-nation principle survives, but it is no longer accepted as a matter of course that commercial policies should be governed by that principle, and departures from it, especially in the application of non-tariff barriers to trade outside the purview of the GATT, are very widespread (as revealed in chapter 6) and threaten the basic principle of non-discrimination.[13] There has been some danger of the general abandonment of this principle[14] in the conduct of commercial diplomacy, which increasingly appeals to clout rather than to agreed rules in the settlement of trade issues. The most-favoured-nation principle is certainly on the defensive in significant areas of world trade, and there is a real fear that the dominance of the principle of equality in matters of trade protection could come to an end.[15]

The principle of non-discrimination in international trade has been eroded on several important fronts. The establishment of the European Economic Community and the extension of its discriminatory trading arrangements with other countries was the first major challenge to this principle to directly confront the countries of the Pacific.[16] The formation of the EEC itself *diverted* trade away from Pacific countries, such as Australia, New Zealand and Japan. Then, the EEC's agreements with associate members accorded preferential trading treatment inconsistent with the requirements of the GATT Article XXIV, which provided for the establishment of free trade areas and customs union arrangements.[17] The trend towards bilateralism was entrenched in the response of industrial countries to the trade and payments adjustments of the late 1960s and early 1970s, which saw the emergence of many discriminatory 'voluntary export restraints' (VERs), negotiated principally with Japan and other newly industrialising countries in the Pacific.[18] Later, in the 1980s, industrial country recession saw a mushrooming of these arrangements on a discriminatory basis, outside the aegis of the ineffective safeguard provisions of Article XIX of the GATT.[19] Whole industries, such as temperate-zone agriculture, were from the beginning exempted from the governance of the GATT; and others, such as textiles and clothing, have become subject to discriminatory agreements which limit open competition and protect established over new suppliers.[20] In the 1970s and 1980s discriminatory trade restraints extended to the steel trade, automobiles and electronics.[21] From the 1960s the extension of general preferences to developing countries posed a dilemma in the system and challenged the principle of non-discrimination in a fundamental way from another angle.[22] And, increasingly, the process of multilateral consultation and collective decisionmaking, judgment and agreement fell into disuse, while procedures for settling disputes, especially the complaints of the small against the strong economic powers, seemed ineffective.[23]

It may be true that many of these departures from GATT principles and rules aimed to accommodate protectionist pressures which might otherwise have threatened the achievements of trade liberalisation in the 1950s and 1960s, and that, through successful accommodation, the liberal trading framework has survived without systemic collapse — which it failed to do in the 1930s.[24] But in the mid-1980s the weight of derogations from GATT rules and principles threatens to reduce confidence in the open trading system which has been such an important vehicle for the trade expansion of the new industrialising countries. This is a central policy issue for the countries of East Asia and the Pacific.

These developments in the international trading system and the associated shift in the balance of economic power towards East Asia and the Pacific have created the need for a careful reassessment of the policy priorities and strategies of Pacific countries. Whereas 20 years ago the East Asian economies, including Japan, were a relatively insignificant component in world trade, this is no longer the case.[25] Western Pacific countries already account for between one-sixth and one-fifth of world trade, and in the next 10 years or so they are destined to rank alongside, and perhaps to surpass, the United States, accounting for over one-quarter of all world trade.[26]

Because it encompasses the whole range of industrial and non-industrial countries, the Pacific constituency of trade policy interests has the motive for addressing, as well as the potential to founder on, such issues as agricultural trade regulation, access for labour-intensive manufactures, safeguard arrangements, and 'orderly marketing'. The first question to ask is whether the principal Pacific players, the United States and Japan, have the *will* to address these issues in international trade diplomacy. The Atlantic constituency has sought to avoid dealing with these issues, or has tried to deal with them outside the established and generally agreed rules of trade.

THE PRINCIPAL PACIFIC PLAYERS

For Pacific countries, the game-play in international trade diplomacy revolves around the management of the economic relationship between the United States and Japan.[27] This is the most important relationship within the Pacific economy, and among the most important in the world. Japan and North America together account for 38 per cent of world production and 27 per cent of world trade, and their economic relationship is managed in the context of a broader alliance on economic and security matters. At the same time, all East Asian and Western Pacific countries depend very heavily on trade, capital and technology links with both countries, 60–70 per cent of their trade being with other Pacific countries, mainly the United States and Japan. In short, the United States and Japan are by far the world's as well as the

Pacific region's largest economies; they are the major trading partners for East Asian and Western Pacific economies; and their policy approaches are of systemic importance, as they are the maintainers or underminers of the GATT-based open international trading system because of the impact of the resolution of their trade policy problems upon the rules of the trading system and upon trade policy behaviour more broadly.[28]

The way in which trade and commercial policies had come to be practised in the Pacific by the mid-1980s focused sharply upon the serious imbalances between the United States and Japan and clouded the prospects for East Asian and Pacific trade and economic growth more generally.

Heightened tension in the management of the United States–Japan relationship in the first half of the 1980s resulted mainly from serious miscalculations in the macroeconomic policies of both countries and the lack of effective macroeconomic policy coordination. This was a recurrent problem from the late 1960s, but extreme imbalance, focused on rising United States current account deficits and Japanese surpluses, emerged very rapidly between 1981 and 1985. A United States current account surplus of US$6 billion in 1981 had been transformed into a deficit of US$141 billion by 1986, a deficit amounting to 3.3 per cent of American GNP. A Japanese current account surplus of US$4 billion in 1981 had grown to US$86 billion in 1986, running at 4.2 per cent of Japanese GNP.[29]

While the basic causes of each country's problem were separate and domestic, Japan's current account surplus became a symbol to many Americans of the *foreign* source of America's trade imbalance problem. Japan's surplus and the American deficit were not significantly a consequence of either Japan's 'closed economy' (as some American commentators insisted) or America's 'lack of competitiveness' (a popular view in Japan). They were mainly the products of extremely high savings and low government spending in Japan, and high government expenditure and a strong dollar in the United States in the first half of the 1980s.[30] Japanese capital market liberalisation provided the avenue for Japan to finance the growth of American debt.[31] Liberalisation of Japan's trade barriers is an important objective in itself, but it would have made little difference to Japan's bilateral surplus on current account with the United States at this time if all Japan's trade barriers had been removed immediately. During the period of rising current account surpluses, Japanese protection was falling. Elimination of Japan's trade barriers would, it has been estimated, have led to a US$5–8 billion expansion of United States exports at most.[32] The main adjustments for both Japan and the United States had therefore to be on the macroeconomic front, and those adjustments were set in train, rather belatedly, after the Plaza Agreement of September 1985 forced the pace through the large exchange-rate shift. Yet some dangers emerged in the way the United States–Japan relationship developed en route, and these dangers are important to the prospects for Pacific trade and economic diplomacy over the coming decades.

The main danger arose because both countries were diverted into attempts to resolve their global trade imbalances by action directed at each other (both negative and positive action: specific restrictions or surcharges, and bilateral market access arrangements). In the conduct of the United States–Japan relationship, specific trade issues came to dominate the policy approach.[33] Resolving these issues one by one had the cumulative effect of aggravating American perceptions of Japanese intransigence and unreasonableness and Japanese perceptions of American scapegoating.[34] The pattern involved Japanese procrastination on specific issues, American pressure, mobilisation of American pressure in Japan to shift positions, heightened American frustration, politicisation of the problem in America, and the lesson that Japan would respond if hit hard.[35]

A related and important danger, for Western Pacific and other countries, is that Japan-targeting by the United States and the American obsession in Japan leads both parties to negotiate bilateral deals which damage third parties as well as the whole trading system.

As Patrick[36] has pointed out, the most clear-cut spill-over effect of United States–Japan bilateral deals on East Asian economies comes from the 'voluntary export restrictions' (VERs) and 'orderly marketing agreements' (OMAs) restricting Japanese producers' access to the American market. In the short run smaller East Asian exporters might benefit to the degree to which they can develop competitor export capacity in restricted markets.[37] But in the longer run their very success generates United States reaction and an extension of specific bilateral import restrictions to them as well. The most prominent example of this process is, of course, the textiles trade: the Multi-Fibre Arrangement (MFA) now restrains textile exports from all East Asian economies, not only to American but also to European markets. The 'orderly marketing agreement' on colour television sets was soon extended from Japan to South Korea, Taiwan and Hong Kong. United States steel trade restrictions were more broadly based from the beginning, focusing as much on European dumping as Japanese cost efficiency. The 1980s United States–Japan bilateral restrictive arrangements on automobiles and semiconductors accelerated production in and exports from Korea, only to shift the threat of retaliation to that East Asian supplier. Because of the strength and pattern of East Asian industrialisation, the process of substitution from Japan to other East Asian economies is the normal pattern: so too has become the extension import quota and export restraint arrangements limiting access, and competition among suppliers, to the North American and European markets.[38]

The cry of 'specific reciprocity' as the guiding principle for trade and commercial policy has become stronger and stronger in the United States over this period. 'Specific reciprocity' (the careful equilibration of benefits in country-by-country and sector-by-sector settlements in which market-sharing arrangements are the goal and tit for tat is a legitimate strategy) is contrasted with the 'uncertain benefits' of 'diffuse reciprocity' (such as is embedded in the GATT system, under which multilateral negotiations and agreements foster a set of rules and norms in which reciprocity seeks an overall balancing of concessions).[39] 'Strategic trade policy'[40] and 'fair trade' are the intellectual and political slogans heralding this new American policy environment. In the 1980s the Reagan Administration clung to the rhetoric of 'diffuse reciprocity'; the political processes increasingly delivered the practice of 'specific reciprocity'.

The political processes and eventually the intellectual argument targeted on Japan in justifying the retreat from support for a global regime based upon multilateral agreements and 'diffuse reciprocity'. Krasner, for example, sees Japan as an economy which 'defies external penetration . . . Japanese institutions, both public and private, are linked in a dense network of reciprocal obligations', and he goes on to say that 'it is extremely difficult for new actors to pierce this network, whether they be Japanese or foreign; given the past system of formal closure, almost all foreign actors are bound to be new.'[41] Krasner concludes that:

> If domestic–political–economic structures vary, then similar universal rules, such as those codified in the GATT, can have very different behavioral outcomes. Tariff reductions in a market-oriented system like the United States will offer more opportunities to foreign producers than similar reductions in Japan, because buyers are more likely to consider only the costs and benefits of a specific transaction rather than to also incorporate assessments about past and future relationships with prospective suppliers. Diffuse reciprocity will not work even in the absence of conscious efforts at exploitation by the Japanese. The differences between the domestic structures of these two states guarantees [sic] that a universal open system based upon diffuse reciprocity will leave the United States with the 'sucker's payoff'.[42]

The recommendation is a policy of 'specific reciprocity' which, Krasner suggests, would yield economic benefit to the United States.[43]

It is not at all obvious that, if Japanese policy is, indeed, as non-market-oriented and 'outsider unfriendly'[44] as Krasner assumes relative to the United States, Europe or any other country, it is to anyone's economic disadvantage except primarily Japan's. Nor does such evidence of 'distance' between national markets recommend against the pursuit of multilateral specialisation in international commodity trade. Krasner certainly does not explain clearly why the alternative and new course in trade diplomacy should be chosen, except by innuendo. The evidence provided by careful studies of Japan's trade dependence and trade structure, such as those of Stern and Saxonhouse,[45] moreover, suggests that there is no significant difference between Japan's trade structure and those of other industrial countries, when account is taken of cross-national differences in factor endowments, including capital, labour and a variety of natural resources. The contention that Japanese institutions or reliance on a variety of informal barriers significantly influence the structure of trade cannot be supported on this evidence, nor can a convincing case be made that Japan's trade and domestic policies are the root causes of the existing bilateral trade imbalances.'[46]

These qualifications to Krasner's argument are not intended to suggest that Japanese trade liberalisation (of agriculture, in particular) is not an important interest for the United States and Japan's other trading partners, for Japan itself, and for the world trading system, nor that other commercial policy interests (such as those in the services trade area) are yet susceptible to treatment under commonly applied multilateral rules.[47] Furthermore, in the negotiations preparatory to the extension of an international systemic public good, such as are involved in changes to the trade regime through a new GATT round, interplay between the interests of 'specific reciprocity' (among the major groups of trading nations) and 'diffuse reciprocity' (the application of generalised rules and norms of behaviour) is a natural if not essential ingredient.[48] The first step in the process addresses the 'free rider' problem among the principal players, encouraging all of them to join in the exchange of concessions; the second delivers 'stable, beneficial agreements in complex multilateral situations'[49] involving domestic politics and international relations as well as economic interests. Certainly Japan's role in trade liberalisation and the negotiation of international settlements on other commercial policy, exchange rate and macroeconomic policy issues is a central element in Pacific economic policy, but it will only be supportive of broader Pacific policy objectives if it eschews 'specific reciprocity' in dealings with the United States and does not neglect third country interests and commitments to the multilateral trade and economic system.

In brief, the management of the United States–Japan economic relationship exposes an important challenge to East Asian and other Pacific countries. It confronts them with two alternative models for managing the trade system: the first is based on the GATT and a multilateral non-discriminatory system; the second involves managed trade in all the major sectors through the expansion of bilaterally based sector-specific import restrictions and trade controls. That is what the Uruguay Round of trade negotiations is fundamentally about.[50] If the Uruguay Round fails a broad retreat into sectoral and regional protectionism is likely to gather force, and that would be particularly damaging to the trade and development ambitions of countries in East Asia and the Pacific.

REGIONALISM WITHOUT DISCRIMINATION

The argument laid out in this book suggests that, even if a new round of multilateral negotiations within the GATT takes place as expeditiously as possible, there is likely to be much scope for additional Pacific trade policy action going beyond what can be achieved globally. In the regional context the potential benefits to exporters are highly visible because of the strong complementarity between the economies of the region and the high trade barriers that have limited opportunities for specialisation in the past (as observed in chapter 4). Those factors help to ensure that interests in export expansion can be effectively mobilised to counter protectionist interests in each country.

Regional negotiations, then, should not focus on discriminatory trade liberalisation, but should be based on most-favoured-nation principles. The concentration of Pacific countries' trade within the Pacific is such that most of the benefits from trade liberalisation on a most-favoured-nation basis are likely to accrue within the region. More fundamentally, any corrosion of the principle of non-discrimination would damage the capacity for transformation of international market shares that has been so essential to the success of East Asian industrialisation and trade growth.

The main 'external' influence on the possible extent and direction of trade liberalisation movements among East Asian and Western Pacific countries lies in the economic relationships of these countries with the United States. The United States is a major market for manufactured goods exports from the region. The Northeast Asian countries in particular are likely to see substantially more value in trade liberalisation movements if they include the United States. For its part, the United States has shown an increasing interest in the Western Pacific as the region has grown in importance, and the share of United States trade with the region has increased. Thus far, as is evident even in respect of Japan, the United States has tended to approach trade relations with particular East Asian countries in a case-by-case bilateral manner, the results of which have not always been consistent with most-favoured-nation principles.

The importance of the United States dictates that any proposals it advances for special trade relations between itself and Western Pacific countries be given serious attention. However, the nature of the United States interest is not automatically likely to coincide with that which Western Pacific countries otherwise may have. In particular, the much larger share of United States trade which is directed outside the Pacific means that the United States will tend to lean towards discriminatory trade arrangements with Western Pacific nations, rather than towards trade liberalisation on a most-favoured-nation basis.

In the lead-up to launching a new GATT Round, the United States shifted towards a trade diplomacy based on the conditional most-favoured-nation approach, seeking 'free trade area solutions' to its trade policy problems.[51] The agreement with Israel and the negotiation of a free trade arrangement with Canada were important targets in this policy approach (as well as the much-heralded Caribbean free trade arrangement). There were also suggestions at this time for some sort of 'free trade area' association between the United States and Western Pacific countries (ASEAN and other). It is not clear whether this United States suggestion was aimed at the ultimate establishment of a Pacific free trade area, or whether it was aimed at setting up a bilateral dealing mechanism between the United States and some Western Pacific countries on a different footing from, and separate from, United States bilateral dealings with Japan. Whichever was the case, Western Pacific countries have little interest in a 'free trade area' association of this kind, and should seek to direct discussions conducted on that basis with the United States into more constructive channels.

While it is almost certainly the case that a Pacific free trade area (if not subject to important exemptions) would provide net benefits to the participants, the idea is not consistent with the longer term interest of Western Pacific countries in more effective movement toward global trade liberalisation, and it may, because of the timing of discussions, result in the exclusion of some countries (such as China), with the effect of retarding their progress towards more open trade relations.

Discriminatory trade arrangements within the Pacific region, and discriminatory treatment of Japan by the United States and other Western Pacific countries or of other Western Pacific countries by Japan and the United States, are inconsistent with East Asian and Pacific trade policy interests and likely to damage the economic growth performance of countries in the region. If, on the other hand, the Pacific 'free trade area' suggestion is not intended to involve trade discrimination within the Pacific, it may provide a potentially valuable starting point for accelerating movement towards the negotiation of trade liberalisation on a most-favoured-nation basis, both in the region and more broadly. The important elements in such discussions should be to avoid any acceptance of the discrimination against non-Pacific countries implied by the term 'free trade area', and to work towards finding areas of reciprocal concession that can be offered on a most-favoured-nation basis.

The strategic problem in pursuing discussions under the 'free trade area' umbrella, then, is to maintain a focus on non-discrimination and to find areas of reciprocal concessions which are capable of sustaining United States interest in the discussions. From the viewpoint of Western Pacific countries, the most important concessions by the United States would relate to access to the United States markets for the manufactured products in which East Asian countries are most competitive.

For the United States to extend such concessions on a most-favoured-nation basis would not, with the exception of steel, have a strong impact on United States–Europe trade. The areas of greatest Japanese competitiveness do not now coincide closely with European competitiveness in the United States market. In fact, initial United States concessions to Japan could simply consist of the removal of trade arrangements such as 'voluntary export restraints' which discriminate against Japanese goods. However, concessions relevant to East Asian developing countries would affect United States trade with Latin America if offered on a most-favoured-nation basis. For this reason it would be sensible for the United States to engage Latin American countries in the process of reciprocation alongside Pacific discussions.

The main areas of concession which could be offered to the United States by Western Pacific countries are agricultural trade liberalisation and liberalisation of access to trade in services. The involvement of the United States in trade negotiations would make significant progress in agriculture more feasible, both because of United States interest in that area and because of the significance for Northeast Asian countries of the concessions which the United States would be able to offer in exchange.

Hitherto the United States has chosen to bargain about these issues on a country-by-country bilateral basis, seeking concessional access for United

States agricultural products rather than general agricultural trade liberalisation. Agricultural protection is commonly provided by administrative import quotas rather than by tariffs. These may be allocated so as to discriminate between suppliers. The disproportionately large share of a number of Asian food markets held by the United States today has its origins in shipments of PL480 food aid during the 1950s and 1960s. The United States considers that it 'bought' those high market shares through its aid program, and has negotiated vigorously with developing country governments to retain past market shares.[52]

More recently United States bilateral initiatives have been directed towards increasing American shares of East Asian commodity markets. In agriculture the important case in point concerns the Japanese beef trade. In the minerals trade coal markets have been affected in a similar way. In response to demands by the United States for greater access to the Japanese market, beef import restrictions have been altered so as to allow more United States imports, but this has been at the expense of third countries, particularly Australia. In the four years to 1983, the United States share in the volume of Japanese beef and offal imports rose from 31 per cent to 44 per cent, while the Australian share fell from 62 per cent to 49 per cent. The total import volume rose by less than 10 per cent during the period, however.[53] Also, the United States coal mining companies have been lobbying Japanese utilities to buy more United States coal. While these efforts have had only limited success, they threaten to encourage discrimination, through subsidy, against efficient third country suppliers. This form of bilateral commercial policy initiative is damaging to the interest in the non-discrimination principle, and must be constrained through regional agreement or multilateral settlement.

Bilateral commercial policy initiatives can also be brought into play where different exporters have divergent interests with respect to importer country protectionism.[54] One case in point that affects temperate-zone agricultural exporters relates to livestock products. As incomes and hence the demand for livestock products (meat, dairy products, eggs) rise in East Asia, farmers in these countries are looking to diversify production to satisfy this new domestic market. Since these countries are relatively densely populated and tend not to be low-cost producers of feedgrains, however, they have a comparative disadvantage in producing especially grass-fed and even grain-fed livestock. Domestic producers are therefore likely to be able to supply this growing demand only with the help of protection from imports of livestock products. Such protection, in turn, is likely to encourage a grain-intensive domestic livestock sector dependent on duty-free imports of feedgrains and soybean. Since the United States is the world's largest supplier of these feedstuffs and is a net importer of meat, it benefits from livestock protection in East Asia while Australasia, as a major source of red meat and milk products, loses.[55]

While the United States may have benefited from its country-by-country bilateral bargaining over access to East Asian commodity markets in the past, the benefits have been severely limited by the quantitative restrictions on overall agricultural trade. Movement towards more liberal agricultural trade would benefit Australasia, for example, relative to the United States by removing present discrimination, but would yield substantially greater gains to all agricultural exporters (including the United States) than have been achieved in existing bilateral dealings. Hence, Australia's initiative in forming the 'Cairns Group' of efficient agricultural exporters has sought to engage the United States and other agricultural exporters in the negotiation of a more general and phased liberalisation of the agricultural trading system.[56]

There are some prospects, then, that the 'free trade area' suggestion could be redirected in a manner consistent with the trade policy interests of Western Pacific countries. The advantage of pursuing discussions under that umbrella, so far as that is feasible, is that the United States is more likely to be prepared to exchange concessions through a process which it initiated, even though the outcome may differ markedly from its initial proposal.

At the global level, it is important to ensure that a clear Western Pacific voice is heard in multilateral trade negotiations. There is a need to maintain a process of consultation among Western Pacific nations which recognises the interdependence of the economies of the region and their mutual dependence on access to manufactured goods markets, particularly for Japanese exports.

PACIFIC PRIORITIES IN TRADE POLICY

The task now is to review the interests and policy priorities of Pacific countries as they emerge from the argument above and in the preceding chapters.

Established protection practices and their significant extension in the past decade or more are unlikely to be modified or checked through bilaterally focused efforts alone. Bilaterally focused negotiations, embodying the principle of 'specific reciprocity', are, indeed, likely to exacerbate the trend towards managed trade. Major liberalisation therefore requires the exchange of concessions and the reduction of trade and other commercial barriers under the aegis of multilateral negotiations, on as comprehensive a basis (in terms of country involvement, commodity and services coverage) as possible. East Asian and Pacific countries have a strong incentive to play a 'leadership' role in such multilateral trade negotiations within the GATT, and in other areas of economic diplomacy, in the years ahead. 'Leadership', in the trade context, could involve advancing the exchange of non-discriminatory trade concessions, through regional initiatives consistent with GATT most-favoured-nation principles. The trade prospects of the whole Pacific region (including the United States) are heavily dependent on East Asia's export prospects, and this coalition of interests provides a base for activist Pacific commercial diplomacy in the multilateral arena.

A major Pacific concern in the approach to multilateral negotiations within the GATT is the maintenance or improvement of access to markets for the manufactured exports of East Asian newly industrialising countries in North America, in Japan, in Australasia, and particularly in Europe. Historically, the economic growth of the region has depended on Japan's securing access to markets for its exports, and on those markets remaining open to 'next generation' East Asian suppliers as Japan's comparative advantage has shifted to more skill-intensive and technology-intensive products and services.

The Pacific contribution to multilateral trade negotiations needs to offer real hope of trade reforms in the area of improved access to markets for primary products, particularly agricultural products. Agricultural trade reform is a central interest for the United States, Australasia and some Southeast Asian exporters. The United States 'agricultural trade war' with Europe in the mid-1980s signalled the seriousness of that interest as a prelude to agreement on the agenda for the new GATT Round.[57] Agricultural exporters in the region therefore have reason to expect broad Pacific support for such reforms, yet immediate or significant progress within GATT negotiations will take some time. Meanwhile, there may be ways to pursue these interests effectively within the Pacific region, where much of the trade of Pacific agricultural exporters is concentrated.

The rapid emergence of Japan as a competitive producer of goods on the technological frontier, and therefore as a threat to established high-technology industries in Western Europe and North America, is engendering the same sort of protectionist responses in those countries as occurred in earlier decades when Japan threatened their established labour-intensive manufacturing industries. It is important for the Pacific economies in particular, and for the global economy generally, to ensure that these protectionist demands do not lead to a broadening of trade restrictions of the type encompassed in the Multi-Fibre Arrangement which resulted from those earlier competitive pressures.

The United States also pressed for discussions of barriers to trade in services to be placed on the agenda for the new GATT Round. As with merchandise trade, liberalisation of services trade on a global scale would yield substantial benefits, and United States interest in this area deserves the active support of all Pacific countries.[58] This support can be given on the basis that it would not divert attention from the commodity market access interests of the region but would complement the pursuit of those interests.

In the past the countries of the Western Pacific have not played a dominant role in the GATT or in other forums concerned with global trade and economic negotiations. With the shift of world economic power towards East Asia,[59] as argued in chapter 8, it is appropriate for this region, and Japan in particular, to play a more significant role both in promoting multilateral trade negotiations and in determining the agenda for negotiations. And it is very much in the interest of East Asia and other Western Pacific countries to encourage Japan to take up that responsibility, and to foster a stronger Pacific economic alliance to support Japan in that role. Japan's early call for the new round of multilateral trade negotiations through the GATT, and Australia's initiative in organising consultations on multilateral trade interests among officials of several Western Pacific countries, provided starting points for the commercial diplomacy needed to launch a round of trade negotiations of relevance to East Asian and Pacific countries.

HETEROGENEOUS VALUES AND COMMON PREFERENCES

How does this statement of interests and priorities square with the preferences for action revealed among the heterogeneous trade policy constituencies in Pacific countries?

In 1983 the Third Pacific Economic Cooperation Conference, held in Indonesia, commissioned the establishment of a Task Force on Trade Policy and Trade Negotiations to review the interests of East Asian and Pacific countries in global and regional trade policy initiatives.[60] As part of its work program, the Task Force undertook a survey of government, business and academic or research groups in East Asian and Pacific countries, the object of which was to identify priorities attached to the negotiation of trade policy issues throughout the region.[61] This survey was coordinated through the national institutions and Pacific cooperation committees involved in the work of the Pacific Economic Cooperation Conference in twelve countries.[62] Twenty-one trade policy issues or problems were nominated, and respondents were asked to rank their relative importance as issues for negotiation. The issues nominated included some of a general character, and others of a highly specific, new, and perhaps ephemeral nature.[63] The survey encouraged respondents to add other issues whose importance was felt to have been neglected, but few were suggested that had not, at least partly, been covered. While it is difficult to be entirely confident about how respondents interpreted the questionnaire, a clear ordering of policy priorities emerged from the survey. It may be that the responses were conditioned by perceptions of national interests, judgment of the prospects for negotiations on particular issues, individual assessments of the criticality of the issue for negotiation, or some other criterion: whatever the case, the uniformly high rankings that were given to the top ten issues reveal strong and common preference in the ordering of trade policy priorities and problems among the various and heterogeneous policymaking constituencies within the Pacific economy. Table 9.1 reports the rankings accorded to the top ten issues in terms of 'high, 'moderate' and 'low' priority.

The remaining issues nominated in the survey and by respondents from throughout the region received much lower rankings; none received more than thirteen 'high' priority rankings, and the bottom five received seven or fewer. Ranked in order of priority they are: GATT: dispute settlement; GATT: enforcement of codes; trade in services; trade in high-technology products; dumping; trade-related investment regulations; counter trade; steel; cartels for primary products; and counterfeiting.[64]

In its analysis of these findings the Task Force on Trade Negotiations drew attention to some interesting features of the structure of the responses to the survey.[65] For the most part the rankings were similar for government, business and research respondents. However, there were some exceptions. Government respondents placed the highest priority on safeguards, while others gave this issue no higher than seventh place. Surprisingly, business respondents ranked agriculture at the top and the Multi-Fibre Arrangement significantly lower than the other respondents, probably reflecting the particular nature of the business representation.

A comparison of national responses confirms the expectation that they would largely reflect the trading and investment interests of the individual countries. Where the rankings differ sharply, as they sometimes do between business and government respondents, this again appears to reflect the particular concerns of businessmen, from whom it is obviously more difficult to pick a single 'representative' than it is from the government and research sectors.

Table 9.1   The trade policy priorities of Pacific countries

Ranking	High	Moderate	Low
1 Access to low-penetrated developed country markets for manufactures	25	10	1
2 Voluntary export restraints, orderly marketing arrangements etc.	25	9	2
3 Agriculture (including processed products)	24	7	5
4 Subsidies and countervailing duties	22	13	1
5 Developing country participation in the GATT system	22	10	4
6 Safeguards	21	13	1
7 Generalised system of preferences	20	14	2
8 Tariff escalation and other trade restraints on natural resources (including processed resources)	20	11	5
9 Multi-Fibre Arrangement	20	9	4
10 Structural adjustment	17	18	1

Source: Pacific Economic Cooperation Conference *Report of the Task Force on Trade Policy and Trade Negotiations* Korea Development Institute, Seoul, April-May 1985, p.9

The issues given high priority encompass the special concerns of the industrialising countries of East Asia and their primary product suppliers in the Western Pacific, with whom there appears to be an exceptionally strong coincidence of policy interests. What is seen most clearly from this survey is that the issues to which East Asian and Pacific policymakers and those with policy influence attach priority for negotiation are indeed the issues emphasised in this book. Furthermore, they are issues at the very heart of the challenge that has emerged to the GATT trading regime itself. They constitute an agenda for reform of the international trading system which, if addressed effectively, would buttress the trade regime as it supports dynamic growth and change in world trade and constrain the coalition of interests that has formed against economic change and progress.

The salient issues to which a high order of importance is attached around the Pacific fall into three broad categories.[66]

The first group includes the first two issues identified as of high priority in Table 9.1 (developing country access to developed country markets for manufactures, and 'voluntary export restraints' and 'orderly marketing arrangements'), and also the Multi-Fibre Arrangement and the Generalised System of Preferences (GSP). The focus in these issues is very much upon access for newly industrialising countries to export markets for labour-intensive and other traditional manufactures. The powerful expression of the priorities of newly industrialising countries in the Pacific region is a reflection of the requirements of dynamic trade and transformation in the Pacific economy. The effective assertion of these priorities through international commercial diplomatic initiatives would redress the GATT's drift towards neglect of the principles of 'openness and non-discrimination', especially against the smaller or newly emerging economic powers.

The second group of issues relates to primary and processed resource products, including those of the agricultural, fisheries, forestry and mineral sectors. Agricultural protectionism has been virtually exempt from negotiation during all the postwar trade negotiations under the GATT. But agricultural exports are of major importance to four of the five most developed Pacific countries, and to a number of the Western Pacific developing countries as well. Tariff escalation (which is recorded as the eighth priority in Table 9.1) adds another dimension to this issue. It affects trade in mineral products (of importance to Australia, Canada and the United States, as well as Indonesia, Malaysia, Thailand, the Philippines and Papua New Guinea), tropical agricultural commodities (fruit, sugar, fish, hardwoods and rubber), and temperate-zone agricultural products (of importance to Australia, New Zealand, and North America). Pacific countries as a group are responsible for a substantial proportion of both world trade and production of many natural resource and agricultural products. The coalescence of a Pacific approach to negotiating primary product trade barriers through regulation within the GATT framework has the potential for remedying what has been a most intractable and fundamental problem for the international trade regime since the Second World War.[67]

The third group of issues relates to the management of adjustment to shifts in competitiveness in the international market place — in consequence of rapid change in the structure of industrial competitiveness, as has been witnessed in the East Asian economy, or because of the cyclic changes associated with international recession.[68] Specific measures such as subsidies, countervailing duties and safeguards represent means whereby countries seek to deal with the effects of increased import competition on domestic industries. Pacific countries clearly have a strong interest in the negotiation of codes which limit export subsidies so as to prevent protective reactions in defence of established industries in importing countries. The safeguards issue is one on which there has already been some negotiation in the GATT, but the results thus far are well short of guaranteeing non-discriminatory use of these measures.[69] 'As the world's most dynamic export-oriented economies', the Task Force concludes, 'Pacific countries have a particular interest in developing a safeguards system that places emphases upon adjustment rather than escape.'[70]

General guidance for the multilateral and regional liberalisation of trade may be found in the final three priorities listed in Table 9.1: more effective developing country participation in the GATT, more effective systems of preference for developing country exports, and emphasis on structural adjustment measures.

The first of these issues is central to the future role of East Asian industrialising and other developing countries within the GATT. The group of 77 UNCTAD countries in the past encouraged the de-coupling of the trade interests of developing countries from those of industrial countries, as it sought preferred treatment for developing country exports in international markets. In turn, industrial countries effectively de-coupled their own trading interests from those of developing countries as they extended the negative application of discriminatory trading arrangements to the exports of newly industrialising countries. But in the Pacific the interests of industrial and developing countries are not so readily separated in this way. There is no sharp distinction between developing and developed countries in the Pacific economy, and the progress of industrialisation in any one country inevitably involves it in a process of 'graduation' into full and equal obligation under the GATT and within the international trading system in the course of time.[71] Pacific countries (industrial and industrialising alike) now have every incentive to place the issue of 'graduation' on the agenda for international negotiation.

In whatever approaches are adopted to issues such as safeguards, 'voluntary export restraints' or 'orderly marketing arrangements', the thrust of Pacific interests is plainly towards effective structural adjustment as a logical approach to dynamism in international trade. The principal responsibility for adjustment policies rests with individual countries. But there is a strong Pacific interest in the collective encouragement of adjustment measures, through negotiation of the rules of trade and through the processes of consultation and exchange, at the government, industry and research levels, that are designed to make adjustment less costly.

There is a final group of issues which, although not included in the top ten on a ranking by equal vote, were rated highly important by respondents from the two largest Pacific economies — Japan and the United States — and these issues must be included in any complete and properly weighted ordering of Pacific trade policy priorities. These are the 'new issues' associated with trade in high-technology products, trade in services, and trade-related investment regulations.[72] A comprehensive trade policy strategy for Pacific countries, encompassing the concerns of the United States and Japan, requires these issues to be included in the agenda for action.

COALITION FOR COLLECTIVE ACTION

The potential for consensus among Pacific countries on trade policy matters appears considerable; and the collective leadership of Pacific countries could produce, through multilateral negotiations, a significant strengthening of the liberal elements in the international trade regime which have been so important to fostering trade growth and successful East Asian industrialisation.

Japan, of course, has a peculiarly crucial role to play in this. Yet Japan's position in welding together a coalition of Pacific countries to assume a collective leadership role in sustaining and buttressing the international trade regime has been ambivalent.

The reasons for this ambivalence are clear enough. Leadership responsibility, in this sense, is a privilege of the powerful, but it is also a real if necessary burden. Leadership carries with it the cost of doing what others cannot easily do, or will not do at all, in order to sustain and protect the international trading and economic system. For example, there is no way that the postwar trading and international economic system, with all its benefits to individual nation states, could have evolved as it did if the United States had not carried the prime burden, initially in terms of aid for reconstruction and development but more importantly in terms of the costs of trade adjustment and economic liberalisation, to deliver the international collective good of a relatively free trading system. A similar responsibility falls upon Japan today, not alone but in a very substantial measure. This represents a political as well as an economic burden for which there is only indirect recompense. The question is whether the Japanese community and its political leadership understand and will accept this leadership responsibility. It involves the effort of addressing tough political problems and of being a willing and active participant in building an international partnership and constituency in the Pacific that will make it manageable. Japan's domestic political problems are heavily focused on agriculture. But now that the Japanese economy is undergoing its own deep industrial adjustment because of the yen appreciation and domestic policies, Japan faces another important political test in resisting new claims for protection for declining industries (textiles, metals and electronics).[73] Leadership responsibility also has to be learned and understood. Japan's preoccupation with managing the United States relationship has led it to acquiesce in the settlement of problems with the United States in ways inconsistent with systemic responsibilities, as argued above. And finally, Japan's leadership responsibility has to be accepted by the countries that enter into its sway. Fears of Japanese dominance in East Asia and the Pacific inhibited the early development of policy dialogues, which was necessary to Japan's assumption of a leadership role in trade and economic policy matters, among the countries of the region and beyond.

Can Japan be persuaded to commit itself to a significant role in international commercial diplomacy based on Pacific trade interests in the years ahead? This will certainly be made easier if there is some sort of Pacific economic alliance and a purposeful effort towards the development of a strong and effective Pacific voice in these affairs.

Pacific countries can be engaged, on the basis of their common policy priorities, to advance a comprehensive program for trade negotiation and institutional reform under the auspices of the GATT. Such action would register the commitment of a significant group of developed and developing countries in the world economy — a group that will account for a larger and larger share of world production and trade towards the year 2000 — to the principles underlying the GATT regime, to the continued use of the multilateral framework, and to consideration of how to strengthen the institution itself. Initiatives within the Pacific region, compatible with GATT commitments, will set an example and add to the persuasiveness of diplomacy about the agenda for negotiation.[74] Countries outside the Pacific will be encouraged to respond in this process and to join in the reactivation of the trade liberalisation movement.

The importance of Pacific trade policy leadership rests on three foundations. First, the countries which have been active in developing a coalition of interests through the Pacific economic cooperation activities include all OECD developed countries outside Europe, as well as seven major East Asian newly industrialising countries. As a group they have a record of economic dynamism and economic performance, even in the recession of the 1970s and 1980s, which sets them ahead of other regions in the world economy. They are heavily committed to trade-oriented growth and outward-looking industrialisation and development policies.

Second, the growing importance of the Pacific economies makes it possible for them to make progress together and on their own, congruently with efforts through the GATT. They have powerful incentives for action within the region compatible with GATT principles and with a program for GATT negotiations. This action could include collective agreements which restrain the use of 'voluntary export restraints' and 'orderly marketing arrangements'; more generous import growth targets under the Multi-Fibre Arrangement; concurrent liberalisation of agricultural protection measures; de-escalation of tariffs affecting primary products of importance to Pacific countries on a most-favoured-nation basis; and collective agreement among Pacific countries on non-discriminatory subsidies, countervailing duties and safeguard practices.[75] This agenda for action is illustrative of a program for negotiation: its essential characteristic must be sufficient balance and comprehensiveness to accommodate the legitimate interests of all the countries, with their diverse resource endowments and complementary patterns of specialisation, within the Pacific economic community.

Third, the substantive issues for multilateral trade negotiation among Pacific countries are numerous and complex and the number of countries with significant interest are many. The preceding chapter outlined the evolving role of the Pacific Economic Cooperation Conference as an instrument for creating the climate for policy development and promoting the practice of policy cooperation in this and other areas.

The PECC links together the countries of the Pacific that are important to trade policy progress. Its unique format — encompassing governments, industry and academic participation within the one institution — and its coverage of developed and developing country interests make it an effective vehicle for advancing policy formulation through a process of persuasion and education. Its structure of national or member committees in most of the countries and regions which participate extends the work of forming an effective coalition on international trade and economic cooperation policies throughout the relevant national constituencies. The PECC's instigation of a Trade Policy Forum provides an institutional base from which the task of promoting the interests of Pacific countries in the trade regime can be given the attention it now needs as an important object of policy.

WHITHER THE RULES OF TRADE?

Thus far the concern has been to address the policy priorities and agenda for trade negotiations for Pacific countries in the last decade or so of the twentieth century. A new round of multilateral trade negotiations and settlements which confronted these issues would constitute a drastic reform of the trade regime, and would assuredly enhance the prospects for efficient trade specialisation and industrial growth in the Pacific and world economies. But there are longer term problems in the international trade system that are unlikely to be resolved in a round of multilateral or regional trade negotiations, and Pacific countries can usefully assist in setting the agenda for longer term reform.[76]

The first issue on the agenda for long-term reform relates to the role of developing countries in the GATT. No developing country, not even Japan before it achieved industrial maturity, was involved in the formation of the GATT regime. Indeed, developing country frustrations led to the emergence of UNCTAD in the early 1960s as a vehicle for the representation of their claims in the negotiation of trade and other international economic policy issues. Whatever its original promise, UNCTAD failed to deliver on these claims except in frugal measure.

The nature of the Pacific community, with its mixture of developed and developing countries, assigns for it a role in designing an international trading system which takes account of the reality that countries are at various stages of industrialisation and economic development, which encourages the use of trade policy to promote economic growth, and which serves the needs of all countries regardless of their stage of development. Such a system would have to incorporate principles such as matching rights with responsibilities and fully establishing non-discrimination as the dominant operating mode.

To assert non-discrimination as the dominant operating principle within the international trading system requires an assault on conditional most-favoured-nation approaches to the negotiation of international trade agreements or settlements. It also requires stronger tests in the application of Article XXIV of the GATT, permitting the formation of free trade areas. The 'free rider' problem can be addressed in the process of negotiation and through the linkage of trade benefits to other issues.

A second issue relates to the nature and purpose of the GATT itself. It was originally established as a stop-gap measure until a more permanent international trading organisation could be agreed upon. In the event, such an institution was never created, and the GATT survived and was given life. However, its incomplete and less than immaculate conception left the GATT without the capacities and instruments to perform adequately some functions which are essential to its purpose. Procedures for dispute settlement are less than adequate, for instance; the GATT secretariat is too small to provide the technical services required by the international trading system; and the regulation of agricultural trade falls largely outside its orbit. A GATT reform with the goals of ending discrimination and agricultural trade distortions is an important long-term objective to which Pacific countries might contribute with benefit both to themselves and to others.

A major conclusion of this book is that it is important for the countries of East Asia and the Pacific to ensure consistency between global goals and regional or bilateral collective action to foster closer economic cooperation in the pursuit of their economic development ambitions. A critical interest is the strength of an open and non-discriminatory world trading and economic system. Regional action can at times be by far the most effective route to furthering and fostering the pursuit of global objectives. At the same time, the collective leadership of Pacific countries presently provides the best hope for building a better international trade regime. Hence, the Pacific economy and the economic policy responses of East Asian and Pacific countries are increasingly central to the health of the world economy.

NOTES

Chapter 9

1   An insightful analysis of the interaction between the political agreements and
     understandings that constitute the regime for trade and the creation of
     opportunities for gainful international economic exchange is to be found in a paper
     by J.G. Crawford 'Australia as a Pacific Power' in W.G.K. Duncan (ed.)
     Australia's Foreign Policy Sydney: Angus & Robertson, 1938. Crawford's subject
     was East Asia's industrialisation before the Second World War and the political
     and economic turmoil that was associated with the response to it, the Great
     Depression, and the emergence of Japanese military expansionism in the Pacific.
     He distinguished a system of 'collective agreements', which provided
     acknowledgment of trading rights and freedoms within accepted rules, from a
     system of 'power politics', upon which empires were built through the exercise of
     might in varying degrees. Critical to his argument was the idea of a system of
     'collective agreements' which might govern the framework within which economic
     exchange took place. Crawford's work on this subject is reviewed by Peter
     Drysdale 'The Relationship with Japan: Despite the Vicissitudes' in L. Evans and
     J.D.B. Miller (eds) *Policy and Practice: Essays in Honour of Sir John Crawford*
     Canberra: Australian National University Press (Pergamon), 1987, pp. 66–81.
2   For a contemporary view of the challenges, see Soesastro 'Institutional Aspects'
     p.28; and 'Report of the Task Force on Trade Policy and Trade Negotiations' in
     Korea Development Institute (KDI) *Pacific Economic Cooperation: Issues and
     Opportunities* Seoul, 29 April–May 1985, ch.2, pp.61–73. These issues are
     reviewed in Peter Drysdale 'Pacific Growth and Economic Interdependence:
     Policy Priorities and Strategies' in Export–Import Bank of Japan *Second
     Symposium on Financial and Business Cooperation in Asia and the Pacific* Tokyo, 30
     October–1 November 1984, pp. 132–42.
3   See Colin J. Bradford 'ADCs' Manufactured Export Growth and OECD
     Adjustment' and 'Comments'; and David Yoffie and Robert Keohane
     'Responding to the "New Protectionism": Strategies for the ADCs' in Hong and
     Krause *Trade and Growth in the Pacific* pp. 476–514 and pp. 560–96.
4   Ross Garnaut and Kym Anderson 'ASEAN Export Specialisation and the
     Evolution of Comparative Advantage in the Western Pacific Region' in Garnaut
     ASEAN pp. 374–420 provide the first analysis of this question. For a recent
     exposition, see Kym Anderson et al. 'Pacific Economic Growth and the Prospects
     for Australian Trade' *Pacific Economic Papers* No. 122, Australia–Japan Research
     Centre, Australian National University, May 1985.
5   Dunn *Protectionism* p. 109; J.G. Crawford *Australian Trade Policy, 1942–1966*
     Canberra: Australian National University Press, 1968, pp. 127–76; Kenneth W.
     Dam *The GATT: Law and International Economic Organization* Chicago:
     University of Chicago Press, 1970; Gerard Curzon *Multilateral Commercial
     Diplomacy* London: Michael Joseph, 1965; GATT *Basic Instruments and Selected
     Documents, Third Supplement* 1955, and *Twenty-sixth Supplement* Geneva, 1980;
     Richard Snape 'Australia's Relations with GATT' *Economic Record* 60, 168,
     March 1984, p.17.
6   ibid., p.17, n.2. Snape notes that Harry Johnson says of non-discrimination, 'That
     principle has absolutely nothing to recommend it on grounds of either economic
     policy or the realities of international commercial diplomacy', but nevertheless

endorses it as the best principle available; see Harry Johnson *Trade Negotiations and the New International Monetary System* Graduate Institute of International Studies, Geneva, and Trade Policy Research Centre, London, 1976, pp.30-31. The argument in this book takes an opposite stance.

7   Dunn *Protectionism* ch.5.
8   ibid., p.110; see also Crawford *Australian Trade Policy* ch.10 on Japan, pp.351-88.
9   Sidney Galt *Developing Countries in the GATT System* Thames Essay No.13, London: Trade Policy Research Centre, 1978, p.10. Galt was a former Deputy Secretary of the Department of Trade and Industry in the British Government.
10   Harry G. Johnson 'World Trade Policy in the Post-Kennedy Round Era: a Survey of Alternatives, With Special Reference to the Position of the Pacific and Asian Regions' *Economic Record* 44, 106, June 1968, pp.152-67 and Peter Drysdale 'Trends in World Trade and World Trade Policy' in Ross Garnaut (ed.) 'Foreign Economic Relations of Papua New Guinea' *New Guinea Research Bulletin* No.56, Port Moresby and Canberra: Australian National University, 1974, pp.33-45 discuss the impact of the adjustment to these changes in the structure of the world economy on international economic policies in the late 1960s and early 1970s. For an early interpretation of bilateral elements in the United States-Japan relationship, see Gary Saxonhouse and Hugh Patrick 'Japan and the United States: Bilateral Tensions and Multilateral Issues in the Economic Relationship' in Donald Hellman (ed.) *China and Japan: A New Balance of Power* Lexington: D.C. Hamble, 1976, pp.96-157.
11   Dunn *Protectionism* ch.5.
12   KDI 'Task Force on Trade Policy' pp.65-9.
13   Note the parallel between these observations and those of Jacob Viner quoted in Snape 'Australia's Relations with GATT' pp.17-18. But although the most-favoured-nation principle still survives, it is no longer accepted as a matter of routine that the tariff relations between friendly countries should be governed by that principle, and departures from the principle are at the present moment more widespread and more important than at any time in the past century. It is quite apparent also that the idea of its general abandonment

> . . . is now receiving serious consideration in many quarters. The most-favoured-nation principle appears to be definitely on the defensive, and, while it has shown great survival power in the past, there is no ground for assurance that a concerted attack on it in which a number of countries participated simultaneously would not put an end to the dominance of the principle of equality of treatment in tariff matters.' Jacob Viner *International Economics* Glencore, Ill: Free Press, 1951, p.96.

14   The 'new reciprocity' bills before United States Congress are the most serious example in recent years. See also the proposals for introducing free trade area arrangements discussed later in this chapter.
15   KDI 'Task Force on Trade Policy' pp.65-9.
16   Johnson 'World Trade Policy'; Drysdale 'World Trade Trends'.
17   Drysdale 'World Trade Trends' p.36; Jean Royer 'Greater European Economic Integration' in Kiyoshi Kojima (ed.) *Structural Adjustment in Asian-Pacific Trade* Tokyo: Japan Economic Research Center, May 1973; Harold B. Malmgren 'Japan, the United States, and the Pacific Economy' *Pacific Community* April 1973, pp.307-25.
18   Dunn *Protectionism* ch. 5; KDI 'Task Force on Trade Policy'.
19   For earlier analyses, see KDI 'Task Force on Trade Policy' p.11; Dunn *Protectionism* p.112; David Robertson *Fail Safe Systems for Trade Liberalisation* Thames Essay No.12, London: Trade Policy Research Centre, 1977.

20   Gale Johnson *World Agriculture in Disarray* London: Macmillan, 1973; Donald
      B. Keesing and Martin Wolf *Textile Quotas Against Developing Countries* London:
      Trade Policy Research Centre, 1980.
21   Kent Jones *Steel Trade Policy in Crisis* London: Trade Policy Research Centre,
      1983; Hugh Patrick and Hideo Sato 'The Political Economy of the United States–
      Japan Trade in Steel' *Pacific Economic Papers* No. 88, Australia–Japan Research
      Centre, Australian National University, December 1981. For a review of these
      issues in the context of the United States–Japan trade relationship, see Japan–
      United States Economic Relations Group *Report of the Japan–United States
      Economic Relations Group*, prepared for the President of the United States and the
      Prime Minister of Japan, January 1981.
22   Harry G. Johnson *Economic Policies Towards Less Developed Countries* London:
      George Allen & Unwin, 1967, especially chs VI and VIII.
23   Dunn *Protectionism* p.124; see also Robert E. Hudee *Adjudication of International
      Trade Disputes* London: Trade Policy Research Centre, 1978.
24   Dunn *Protectionism* p.114.
25   Peter Drysdale, Ben Smith, Kym Anderson and Christopher Findlay 'Australia
      and the Pacific Economy' *Economic Record* 62, 176, March 1986, pp.60–6.
26   ibid.
27   Among the best reviews of recent developments in the United States–Japan
      economic relationship is Hugh Patrick, 'The Management of the United States–
      Japan Trade Relationship and its Implications for the Pacific Basin Economies',
      mimeo, background paper for the Project on the Impact of Japan–US Economic
      Relations on Other Pacific Basin Nations, US National Committee for Pacific
      Economic Cooperation. See also papers presented to the Conference on US–
      Canadian Trade and Investment Relations with Japan, Ann Arbor, Michigan,
      2–3 April 1987.
28   Peter Drysdale, 'Developments in Economic Relations between Japan, the United
      States and East Asia', mimeo, Australia–Japan Research Centre, Australian
      National University, 2 October 1987, p.2.
29   ibid., p.4.
30   Patrick 'US–Japan Relationship' pp. 5–11.
31   Colin McKenzie and Michael Stutchbury (eds) *Japan's Money Markets and the
      Future of the Yen* Canberra: Australia–Japan Research Centre, Australian National
      University (forthcoming).
32   C. Fred Bergsten and William R. Cline *The United States–Japan Economic Problem*
      Washington, DC: Institute for International Economics, January 1987, p.114.
33   For a review of these issues, see Yoko Sazanami 'Trade and Investment
      Patterns and Barriers for North America and Japan' conference on US–Canadian
      Trade and Investment Relations with Japan, University of Michigan, Ann Arbor,
      2–3 April 1987, Table 7.
34   Patrick 'US–Japan Relationship' pp.11–23.
35   idem.
36   idem.
37   David Yoffie 'The Newly Industrialising Countries and the Political Economy of
      Protectionism' *International Studies Quarterly* 25, 4, December 1981, pp.569–99.
38   Patrick 'US–Japan Relationship' pp.23–32.
39   Robert O. Keohane 'Reciprocity in International Relations' *International
      Organization* 40, 1, Winter 1986, pp.1–27 sets out the distinction between
      'specific' and 'diffuse' reciprocity most clearly. Stephen D. Krasner 'Trade
      Conflicts and the Common Defense: The United States and Japan' *Political
      Science Quarterly* 101, 5, 1986, pp.787–806 takes up the distinction to rationalise
      a strategy of 'specific reciprocity' in United States dealings with Japan.

40　Gene M. Grossman and J. David Richardson 'Strategic Trade Policy: A Survey of Issues and Early Analysis' *Special Papers in International Economics* No.15, Princeton University, April 1985, pp.1–34 provides a recent review of this literature. Among the more important contributions in the international relations literature which have encouraged this interest is Robert Axelrod *The Evolution of Cooperation* New York: Basic Books, 1983.

41　Krasner 'Trade Conflicts' p.789.

42　idem.

43　Krasner 'Trade Conflicts' pp.802–6.

44　A term coined by Patrick in 'US–Japan Relationship' p.15 to describe this perception. A preliminary analysis of the issues is contained in Richard Harris '"Market Access" in International Trade: A Theoretical Appraisal' conference on US–Canadian Trade and Investment Relations with Japan, Michigan, Ann Arbor, 2–3 April 1987.

45　Saxonhouse and Stern 'An Analytical Survey of Formal and Informal Barriers to International Trade and Investment in the United States, Canada, and Japan' pp.1–43. For a similar view, see Bergsten and Cline *United States–Japan Economic Problem*, and Gary Saxonhouse 'What's Wrong with Japanese Trade Structure?' *Pacific Economic Papers* No.137, Australia–Japan Research Centre, Australian National University, July 1986. For an alternative view, see Bela Balassa 'Japan's Trade Policies' *Weltwirtschaftliches Archiv* 122, 4, 1986, pp.745–90; William V. Rapp 'Japan's Invisible Barriers to Trade' in Thomas A. Dugel and Robert G. Hawkins (eds) 'Fragile Interdependence: Economic Issues' in *US–Japanese Trade and Investment* Lexington: Lexington Books, 1986.

46　Saxonhouse and Stern 'Formal and Informal Barriers' pp.32–33.

47　For a full review of problems in the codification of rules for trade in services, see Leslie V. Castle and Christopher Findlay (eds) *Pacific Trade in Services* Sydney: Allen & Unwin, 1988.

48　Keohane 'Reciprocity' pp.19–27.

49　ibid., p.19.

50　Patrick 'US–Japan Relationship' p.38.

51　For background to this policy approach, see Keith J. Hay and B. Andrei Sulzenko 'US Trade Policy and "Reciprocity"' *Journal of World Trade Law* 16, November–December 1982; William R. Cline '"Reciprocity": A New Approach to World Trade Policy?' Institute for International Economics *Policy Analyses in International Economics* No.2, Washington, DC, September 1982; A.J Wonnacott 'Aggressive US Reciprocity Evaluated with a New Analytical Approach to Trade Conflicts' Institute for Research on Public Policy *Essays in International Economics* Montreal, Canada, 1984. Officials defined 'reciprocity' as a strategy for opening foreign markets at this time. Free trade area strategies involve the reciprocation of 'preferred treatment in trade'.

52　Anderson and Hayami *Agricultural Protection*.

53　Aurelia George 'The Changing Pattern of Japan's Agricultural Import Trade: Implications for Australia' *Pacific Economic Papers* No.100, Australia–Japan Research Centre, Australian National University, January 1983; Aurelia George 'Japan's Beef Import Policies 1978–84: The Growth of Bilateralism' *Pacific Economic Papers* No. 113, Australia–Japan Research Centre, Australian National University, July 1984.

54　Patrick 'US–Japan Relationship' pp.34–35.

55　Anderson and Hayami *Agricultural Protection*.

56　*Australia and Pacific Cooperation* Second Report of the Australian National Pacific Cooperation Committee, Canberra, July 1987, p.9; Andy Stoeckel and Sandy Cuthbertson *Successful Strategies for Australian Trade* Canberra: Centre for

International Economics, 1987, ch.2.

57   ibid.

58   Leslie V. Castle and Christopher Findlay *Pacific Trade in Services* Sydney:
      Allen & Unwin, 1988.

59   There was symbolic but not substantial acknowledgment of this change in the
      Tokyo Round of Multilateral Trade Negotiations; see Dunn *Protectionism* ch.5.

60   Centre for Strategic and International Studies *Issues for Pacific Economic
      Cooperation* Jakarta: CSIS, March 1984, pp.22–24.

61   KDI 'Task Force on Trade Policy' pp.65–8.

62   ibid.

63   ibid.

64   ibid., p.65.

65   ibid., pp.65–8.

66   ibid., pp.66–7. The following section relies directly on the work of the Task Force
      on Trade Policy.

67   Crawford *Australian Trade Policy* chs 5 and 7; see also Curzon *Commercial
      Diplomacy* pp.166–248.

68   For an early analysis of this problem, see Crawford 'Australia as a Pacific Power'.

69   KDI 'Task Force on Trade Policy' pp.66–7.

70   ibid., p.67.

71   ibid.

72   C. Fred Bergsten and William R. Cline (eds) *Trade Policy in the 1980s* Cambridge:
      MIT Press for the Institute of International Economics, 1983.

73   Patrick 'US–Japan Relationship' p.35.

74   KDI 'Task Force on Trade Policy', and 'Comments' by T. Lloyd, Department of
      Trade and Industry, New Zealand, on this Report pp.176–8.

75   KDI 'Task Force on Trade Policy' p.69.

76   KDI 'Task Force on Trade Policy' pp.61–73.

10 Policy strategy

The countries of East Asia and the Pacific shape their approach to international economic policy in an environment in which their actions have an increasing influence on outcomes. Japan has been catapulted into a position of particular influence and responsibility. In matters of trade, finance, technology and development assistance, whatever Japan does or does not do interacts strongly with other countries, in the Pacific and globally. Under the umbrella of American economic and political power, and when they were a relatively small element in the world economy and trade, East Asian and Western Pacific countries enjoyed, paradoxically, a measure of foreign economic policy independence. When nations are able to take the actions of partner or rival nations as immutable, strategic behaviour plays no role. But policy interdependence now typifies the international and regional economies. And strategic interests in foreign economic policy are a paramount concern for Pacific countries.

A requirement for the development of policy strategies for the Pacific is the establishment of mechanisms for effective communication of dominant policy interests and policy priorities. This is a focal interest not only in the formation of policies and the development of a regime that aims to exploit the potential for trade and economic growth within East Asia and the Pacific, but also in the elaboration of policies that serve to project Pacific interests and define Pacific responsibilities in the global arena. The nature of the Pacific economy and its role in the historic shifts now unfolding in the world economy direct attention to these matters of policy coordination and vehicles for policy development.

The argument in this book has sought to explain how the economic cooperation interests among Pacific countries are targeted upon the development of mutually consistent approaches to such matters as trade policy in particular, foreign investment policy, aid policy, structural adjustment and other commercial policies. In the global arena, the Pacific countries share an immediate concern about the international coordination of macroeconomic policy and the management of the exchange rate and international financial system. In these matters, as well as in questions of international trade diplomacy, the interests of Pacific countries as a group are coming to converge on stronger support for the international economic system and, in this, there

256

is a close consistency between regional policy objectives and international economic policy goals.

The principal vehicle for economic policy consultation within the Pacific is the Pacific Economic Cooperation Conference (PECC) process. Apart from political-level consultations on a sub-regional basis (such as within ASEAN), the PECC affords the most comprehensive opportunities for discussion of interests in policy coordination among Pacific countries, and its work has been important in defining the goals of Pacific economic cooperation since the beginning of the 1980s.

Compared with the elaborate mechanisms for consultation on economic policy matters that have evolved within Europe, or the consultative processes that are enshrined in the work of the OECD, those in the Pacific are as yet quite rudimentary. Nonetheless, they incorporate some essential features and additional functions quite uniquely suited to the problems of encouraging policy coordination among Pacific economies.

The essential features are: support for the enhancement of information about policy practices and economic data to assess policy interests; the opportunity for interchange on policy matters among officials of Pacific countries; and encouragement to seek policy convergence through the exploration of common interests and problems. The PECC's unique structure and operating modalities, including the 'non-official' but informed character of its deliberations, are essential to its functioning (around the constraints of Pacific diplomacy) and constitute a special strength in its role of policy development within the Pacific. In a policy environment that is subject to rapid change, the anticipation of new policy issues, the need to change old policy approaches and adopt new ones, and the need for increased transparency of policy interests, recommends against the representation of policy positions, and their entrenchment, in the formal bureaucratic structure of government-to-government arrangements.

The success of economic policy consultation among Pacific countries was reviewed in chapter 8. The measure of success is obviously not linked to the impact of consultations on action by *all* countries in the region or *all* members involved. That is an unrealistic and improper test of success. The importance of such deliberations derives from their impact upon policy initiatives encouraged and facilitated among participating countries where and as they are required. This test is the same as that which might be applied to other consultative bodies, such as the OECD.

Indeed, all the Pacific Five are also members of the OECD, and the question arises of how their role in the PECC relates, if at all, to their role in that organisation. Of course, the perspectives which dominate policy discussion and consultation within the OECD do not reflect the principal interests of East Asia and the Pacific, despite Japan's membership for over 20 years. Nor is additional membership, of Korea for example, likely to change the direction of policy thinking within the OECD. The limits to change within the Paris-based organisation stem from its origins, the concentration of its membership, its established bureaucracies, its history, and the purpose of the organisation, focused as it still is upon the concerns of the European industrial democracies, not those of newly industrialising countries. Nor does it make sense to compromise that purpose. But interests surrounding economic development in East Asia and the Pacific require a different association, with a different structure, a wider range of membership and clearly different economic policy interests. Pacific interests already challenge some of the most important assumptions of economic policy in Europe — on agriculture, trade policy and structural adjustment. The dialogue with Japan within the OECD has addressed this challenge in only the most limited way. In time, the opportunity and the need may arise to strengthen the policy dialogue between the OECD and East Asian and Pacific countries, within the framework of the PECC's own contribution to the definition of a Pacific international economic policy agenda.

Throughout the argument of this book, the interest of East Asian and Pacific countries in a non-discriminatory trade regime, supportive of their own industrialisation and trade growth ambitions as well as the global GATT-based trade system, is a dominant theme. The important conclusion is that collective leadership is necessary to sustain the regional and global trade and development regime in the years ahead; and that the Pacific is emerging as an effective domain for the exercise of international economic policy leadership.

Before turning to the issue of policy leadership, there is one remaining question that needs to be addressed: about the compass of the Pacific economy and the role of countries on the periphery of, but nonetheless involved in, Pacific economic or political affairs, such as the Latin American countries, the Soviet Union and the communist states of East Asia. Until relatively recently China might have been included among countries on the periphery of developments in the Pacific but that is no longer so. There can be no question that the course of economic reform and modernisation is firmly established in China. Already China has sought, and been admitted to, full membership of the PECC. The forces that underlie China's specialisation in the world economy will, in the longer term, probably not be so dissimilar to those that have shaped trade and industrial growth in the rest of East Asia. Of course, China still differs enormously in the degree to which intervention and non-market factors affect resource allocation in the economy. But this is undergoing epochal change. Pacific countries are vitally interested in cooperation with China in the process of further involvement in the open multilateral system of trade. There are many dimensions of such cooperation: through participation in the GATT, in the approach of China's bilateral economic partners, and in regional consultations in the Pacific, within the PECC. The successful accommodation of China is a major challenge for effective multilateral cooperation in the Pacific and world economies, and the continuing drive of East Asian industrialisation.

The Latin American countries and the Soviet Union are now more actively involved, or interested in becoming more actively involved, in Pacific economic cooperation. Successful reform in the Soviet economy may, in future, make more extensive economic cooperation with Pacific countries feasible. Meanwhile, within the framework of PECC task force activities, the Soviet Union has begun a modest dialogue in areas of particular interest — in minerals and energy, fisheries and agriculture — as too have the Latin American countries. The structured and non-exclusive character of dialogues at this level in the Pacific give Pacific economic cooperation activities a policy and diplomatic stamp appropriate to the pluralist constituency, the representation of whose interests they seek to serve.

Finally, there is the issue of international economic leadership, as the economic power of the United States has begun to wane, and that of Japan and the Pacific has grown. Much of the commentary on the transfer of the responsibilities of international economic leadership around the decline of America's hegemonic power has been cast in terms of their transfer from one hegemony to another. Nowhere is this perspective more entrenched in thinking than it is in discussion of the changing status of the United States and Japan.[1] This is not the place to inquire into the political, intellectual or, indeed, the psychological wellsprings of this view of the transfer of hegemonic power, but rather to note simply that the evidence and argument of this book suggests that other outcomes are more likely.

The structure and shape of the world economy has changed vastly over the past 25 years, with the emergence first of Europe and now East Asia and the Pacific, beyond North America, as new centres of economic power. While it is reasonable to share the anxiety of those who hanker for a regime made strong by the economic and political patronage of a dominant leader,[2] there is no single nation that can now, or in the foreseeable future, fill that role. The economic and political challenge for the future is therefore to strengthen the processes of collective leadership in global economic management.

Much of the effort of international macroeconomic management appears to devolve upon the United States, Europe (West Germany), and Japan. But this conception of international economic leadership responsibilities is too circumscribed. The force of East Asian industrialisation has already transformed the contours of world economic power and influence. Japan is no mere appendage of the Atlantic economy.[3] It is embedded as well in the East Asian and Pacific economy and polity. So, for that matter, is Australia. Japan also sits alongside China, a huge country undergoing the greatest economic and social revolution in modern times. Japan cannot be dealt with easily and separately any longer, in a comfortable condominium with North America and Europe.[4]

The message is that an increasing (not dominant) leadership role for Japan must be found within a pluralist structure of world economic power, encompassing the effective representation of broader Pacific and global interests, as well as those of the United States and Europe.

Yet despite Japan's prominent position in the Pacific and world economy, it cannot presume to project Pacific interests without an infrastructure of regional consultation and cooperation to make the development of Pacific positions practicable. Such mechanisms are evolving because of the region's growing industrial might and economic interdependence; because reduction of policy uncertainties offers large potential gains through a stronger framework for regional economic relations; and because they assist the communication of the diverse policy objectives of very different countries and of the smaller and weaker economic partners in the Pacific region. Growing knowledge among Pacific countries of each others' institutions and policy practices strengthens the level of mutual confidence in national economic policies and reduces psychological and political barriers to the movement of commodities and capital and the relocation of production, all of which help to improve international welfare.

A key conclusion is that the Pacific belongs to no single nation — not Japan, despite its new-found economic power, nor China, despite the scale of its industrial promise, nor, any longer, America. The responsibilities of Pacific economic policy leadership are bound to be developed as shared responsibilities. The huge and rewarding task of establishing a degree of intimacy among the heterogeneous nations of the Pacific upon which confident policy strategies can be promulgated and executed in support of international systemic objectives is a challenge to which Pacific countries are now — fortunately — at last beginning to turn.

NOTES

Chapter 10

1   Among the first American works that signalled this perspective was Ezra Vogel *Japan as No.1* Tokyo: Charles Tuttle & Co., 1979.
2   Charles P. Kindleberger 'International Public Goods without International Government' *American Economic Review* 71, 1, March 1986, pp.1–13.
3   C. Fred Bergsten 'Economic Initiatives and World Politics' *Foreign Affairs* 65, 4, Spring 1987, pp.770–94.
4   Stephen D. Krasner 'Trade Conflicts and the Common Defense: The United States and Japan' *Political Science Quarterly* 101, 5, 1986, p.806.

BIBLIOGRAPHY

ADB (Asian Development Bank) *Southeast Asia's Economy in the 1970s* New York: Longman, 1971
_____ *Southeast Asia's Economy: Development Policies in the 1970s* Harmondsworth: Penguin, 1972
Akrasanee, Narongchai et al. (eds) *Trade and Employment in Asia and the Pacific* Honolulu: University of Hawaii Press, 1977
_____ *ASEAN and the Pacific Community* Centre for Strategic and International Studies, Jakarta, 1981
Aliber, Robert (ed.) *The Political Economy of Monetary Reform* London: Macmillan, 1977
Allen, Thomas 'Direct Investment of United States Enterprises in Southeast Asia' *ECOCEN Study* No.2, Economic Cooperation Centre for the Asian and Pacific Region, Bangkok, March 1973
Anderson, Kym 'On the Gains and Losses from Beef Import Quotas in Japan and Korea' *Pacific Economic Papers* No.90, Australia–Japan Research Centre, Australian National University, February 1982
_____ 'Intensity of Trade Between Pacific Basin Countries' *Pacific Economic Papers* No.102, Australia–Japan Research Centre, Australian National University, July 1983
_____ (ed.) 'East Asian and West European Agricultural Policies: Implications for Australia' *Pacific Economic Papers* No.143, Australia–Japan Research Centre, Australian National University, January 1987
Anderson, Kym and Baldwin, Robert E. 'The Political Market for Protection in Industrial Countries' in A.M. El-Agraa *Protection, Cooperation, Development and Integration*
Anderson, K., Drysdale, P., Findlay, C., Phillips, P., Smith, B. and Tyers, R. 'Pacific Economic Growth and the Prospects for Australian Trade' *Pacific Economic Papers* No. 122, Australia–Japan Research Centre, Australian National University, May 1985
Anderson, Kym and Garnaut, Ross 'Australia's Trade Growth with Developing Countries' *Pacific Economic Papers* No.102, Australia–Japan Research Centre, Australian National University, July 1982
Anderson, Kym and Garnaut, Ross *Australian Protectionism: Extent, Causes and Effects* Sydney: Allen & Unwin, 1987
Anderson, Kym and George, Aurelia (eds) *Australian Agriculture and Newly Industrialising Asia: Issues for Research* Australia–Japan Research Centre, Australian National University, 1980
Anderson, Kym and Hayami, Yūjirō (eds) *The Political Economy of Agricultural Protection* Sydney: Allen & Unwin, 1986
Anderson, Kym and Park, Young-il 'China and the International Relocation of World Textile and Clothing Activity' paper prepared for a pre-AAES Conference Workshop on Development in China's Food and Fibre Markets: Their International Significance, held at the University of Adelaide, 9 February 1987 (also published as *Pacific Economic*

Papers No. 158, Australia–Japan Research Centre, Australian National University, April 1988)

Anderson, Kym and Smith, Ben 'Changing Economic Relations Between the Asian ADCs and Resource-Exporting Advanced Countries of the Pacific Basin' in Hong and Krause (eds) *Trade Growth of the Advanced Developing Countries in the Pacific Basin*, Korea Development Institute Press, Seoul: Korea, 1981

Anderson, Kym and Tyers, Rod 'Agricultural Policies of Western Europe and East Asia and their Effects on Traditional Food Exporters' in Anderson (ed.) *Pacific Economic Papers* No. 143, Australia-Japan Research Centre, Australian National University, January, 1987

Anderson, Kym et al. 'Australia's Agricultural Trade with Northeast Asia' *Australia-Japan Economic Relations Research Project Research Paper* No.63, Australian National University, December 1979

Arndt, H.W. 'PAFTA: An Australian Assessment' *Intereconomics* 10, 1967

—— 'Professor Kojima on the Macro-economics of Foreign Direct Investment' *Hitotsubashi Journal of Economics* 15, 11, 1974.

—— 'Financial Development in Asia' *Asian Development Review* 1, 1, 1983

—— 'Financial Development in Asia' *Asian Development Bank Journal* 1, 1, March 1983

Arndt, Heinz and Garnaut, Ross 'ASEAN and the Industrialisation of East Asia' *Journal of Common Market Studies* 17, 3, March 1979

Arrow, Kenneth *Social Choice and Individual Values* New York: Witary, 1951

Asian Survey XXIII, 12, December 1983 (special issue on 'Perspectives on the Pacific Community Concept')

Association for the Promotion of International Cooperation *Japan's Official Development Assistance, 1986 Annual Report* Tokyo, March 1987

Aubrey, Henry *Atlantic Economic Cooperation: The Case of the OECD* New York: Praeger, for the Council on Foreign Relations, 1967

Australia and Pacific Cooperation: see NPCC, July 1987.

Au Yeong, Josephine, Financing of Japanese Direct Foreign Investment, PhD dissertation, Australian National University, Canberra, 1987

Axelrod, Robert *The Evolution of Cooperation* New York: Basic Books, 1983

Balassa, Bela 'Japan's Trade Policies' *Weltwirtschaftliches Archiv* 122, 4, 1986

—— 'Trade Liberalisation and "Revealed" Comparative Advantage' *Manchester School of Economic and Social Studies* 33, 2, May 1965

—— 'Export Incentives and Export Performance in Developing Countries: A Comparative Analysis' *Weltwirtschaftliches Archiv* I, 1978

—— 'The Changing Pattern of Comparative Advantage in Manufactured Goods' *Review of Economics and Statistics* 61, 2, 1979

—— *Developing Strategies in Semi-industrial Economies* Baltimore: Johns Hopkins University Press, 1982

Baldwin, Robert *Economic Development and Export Growth: A Study of Northern Rhodesia 1920-1960* Berkeley: University of California Press, 1966

—— 'Beyond the Tokyo Round Negotiations' *Thames Essay* No.22, Trade Policy Research Centre, London, 1979

—— 'US Political Pressures against Adjustment to Greater Imports' in Hong and Krause *Trade and Growth in the Pacific*

Banno, Junji 'Foreign Policy and Attitudes to the Outside World, 1868–1945' in Drysdale and Kitaōji *Japan and Australia*

Bartlett, Randall *Economic Foundations of Political Power* New York: The Free Press, 1973

Basic Treaty of Friendship and Co-operation between Australia and Japan Canberra: Commonwealth of Australia, June 1976

Bautista, Romeo and Naya, Seiji (eds) *Energy and Structural Change in the Asia–Pacific Region* Manila: Asian Development Bank and Philippine Institute for Development Studies, 1983

Bell, Coral, Collins, Hugh and Garnaut, Ross 'Conclusion: The Nexus between Economics, Politics and Strategy' in Dibb (ed.) *Australia's External Relations*

Bergsten, C. Fred 'The Threat from the Third World' *Foreign Policy* II, Summer 1973
—— 'The Response to the Third World' *Foreign Policy* 17, Winter 1974–75
—— *Toward a New World Trade Policy: The Maidenhead Papers* Lexington: Lexington Books, 1975
—— 'Economic Imbalances and World Politics' *Foreign Affairs* 65, 4, Spring 1987

Bergsten, C. Fred and Cline, William R. *The United States–Japan Economic Problem* Institute for International Economics, Washington, DC, January 1987

Bergsten, C. Fred and Cline, William R. (eds) *Trade Policy in the 1980s* Cambridge, Mass.: MIT Press, for the Institute of International Economics, 1983

Bergsten, C. Fred and Krause, Lawrence (eds) *World Politics and International Economics* Washington, DC: The Brookings Institution, 1975

Bhagwati, Jagdish *Trade, Tariffs and Growth* Cambridge, Mass.: MIT Press, 1969
—— *Foreign Trade Regimes and Economic Development: Anatomy and Consequences of Exchange Control Regimes* Cambridge, Mass.: Ballinger, 1978

Bhagwati, Jagdish and Krueger, Anne (eds) *Trade Strategies for Economic Development: The Asian Experience* Manila: Asian Development Bank, 1975

Bickerdike, C. 'The Theory of Incipient Taxes' *Economic Journal* 17, March 1907

Bigman, David and Reutlinger, Shlomo 'National and International Policies toward Food Security and Price Stabilization' *American Economic Review, Papers and Proceedings* 69, May 1979

Booth, Anne and McCawley, Peter (eds) *The Indonesian Economy during the Suharto Era* Kuala Lumpur: Oxford University Press, 1981

Bradford, Colin J. 'ADCs' Manufactured Export Growth and OECD Adjustment' and 'Comments' in Hong and Krause *Trade and Growth of the ADCs*

Branson, William 'Trends in United States International Trade and Comparative Advantage: Analysis and Prospects' in *International Economic Policy Research* Washington, DC: National Science Foundation, 1980, pp.22–48

Breton, Albert 'The Economics of Nationalism' *Journal of Political Economy* 72, 4, August 1964

Brown, A.J. *Applied Economics: Aspects of the World Economy in War and Peace* London: Allen & Unwin, 1941

Brown, Lester *World Without Borders: The Interdependence of Nations* New York: Vintage, for the Foreign Policy Association, 1973

Buchanan, James 'An Economic Theory of Clubs' *Economica* 32, 25, February 1965
—— *The Limits of Liberty: Between Anarchy and Leviathan* Chicago: University of Chicago Press, 1975
—— 'Markets, States and the Extent of Morals' *American Economic Review* 68, 2, May 1978

Buchanan, J.M. Tollison, R.D. and Tullock, G. (eds) *Towards a Theory of the Rent-Seeking Society* College Station: Texas A & M University Press, 1980

Buchanan, James and Tullock, Gordon *The Calculus of Consent* Ann Arbor: University of Michigan, 1962

Bull, Hedley *The Anarchical Society: A Study of Order in World Politics* London: Macmillan, 1977

Burnett, Robin and Burnett, Alan *Australia–New Zealand Economic Relations: Issues for the 1980s* Canberra: Australian National University Press, 1981

Bush, W. and Mayer, L. 'Some Implications of Anarchy for the Distribution of Property' *Journal of Economic Theory* 8, 4, August 1974

Castle, Leslie V. and Findlay, Christopher (eds) *Pacific Trade in Services* Sydney: Allen & Unwin, 1988

Castle, Leslie V. and Holmes, Frank W. (eds) *Cooperation and Development in the Asia-*

Pacific Region: Relations between Large and Small Countries Tokyo: Japan Economic Research Center, 1976

Caves, Richard E. 'Economic Models of Political Choice: Canada's Tariff Structure' *Canadian Journal of Economics* 9, 1976

Caves, Richard and Jones, Ronald *World Trade and Payments: An Introduction* Boston: Little, Brown & Co., 1973

Centre for Strategic and International Studies *Issues for Pacific Economic Cooperation* Jakarta: CCIS, March 1984

Chamberlin, John 'Provision of Collective Goods as a Function of Group Size' *American Political Science Review* 68, 2, June 1974

Chenery, Hollis 'Restructuring the World Economy' *Foreign Affairs* 53, 2, January 1975

Chūshōkigyō-chō (Small and Medium Enterprises Agency) *Chūshō kigyō hakusho Shōwa-57 nenban* [White Paper on small and medium-sized enterprises, 1982] Tsūshōsangyō-chō (Ministry of International Trade and Industry), 1982

Cleveland, Harold *The Atlantic Idea and its European Rivals* New York: McGraw–Hill, for the Council on Foreign Relations, 1966

Cline, William R. '"Reciprocity": A New Approval to World Trade Policy?' *Policy Analyses in International Economics* No.2, Institute for International Economics, Washington DC, September 1982

Cole, David C. and Patrick, Hugh 'Financial Development in the Pacific Basin Market Economies' in Tan and Kapur *Pacific Growth*

Cole, Robert, Totten, George and Uyehara, Cecil *Specialist Parties in Postwar Japan* New Haven: Yale University, 1966

Commission of the European Community, Report on the Operation during 1975 of the system set up by the Lome Convention for Stabilising Export Earnings (Brussels)

Connelly, Phillip and Pelman, Robert *The Politics of Scarcity: Resource Conflicts in International Relations* London: Oxford University Press, 1975

Conybeare, John A.C. 'Public Goods, Prisoners' Dilemmas and the International Political Economy' *International Studies Quarterly* 28, 1984

Cooper, C. and Massell, B. 'A New Look at Customs Union Theory' *Economic Journal* 75, December 1965

Cooper, Richard *The Economics of Interdependence: Economic Policy in the Atlantic Community* New York: McGraw–Hill, 1968

―――― 'Financial Aspects of Economic Cooperation around the Pacific' in Kojima *Pacific Trade and Development*

―――― 'Worldwide versus Regional Integration: Is There an Optimal Size of the Integrated Area? *Yale Economic Growth Center Discussion Paper* No.220, November 1974

―――― 'Natural Resources and National Security' *Resources Policy* 1, 4, June 1975

―――― 'Prolegomena to the Choice of an International Monetary System' in Bergsten and Krause *World Politics*

―――― 'A New International Economic Order for Mutual Gain' *Foreign Policy* 26, Spring 1977

―――― (ed.) *A Re-Ordered World: Emerging International Economic Problems* Washington, DC: Potomac Association, 1973

Corbet, Hugh and Jackson, Robert (eds) *In Search of a New World Economic Order* London: Croom Helm/Trade Policy Research Centre, 1974

Corden, W.M. *Trade Policy and Economic Welfare* Oxford: Oxford University Press, 1971

Cox, Robert and Jacobsen, Harold (eds) *The Anatomy of Influence: Decision Making in International Organizations* New Haven: Yale University, 1973

Crawford, J.G. 'Australia as a Pacific Power' in Duncan *Australia's Foreign Policy*

―――― *Australian Trade Policy, 1942-1966 — A Documentary History* Canberra: Australian National University Press, 1968

―――― 'The Pacific Basin Cooperative Concept' Speech to the 13th Annual Meeting of the Pacific Basin Economic Council, Sydney, 6 May 1980

Crawford, J.G., Ōkita, Saburō et al. *Australia, Japan and Western Pacific Economic Relations* report presented to the Australian and Japanese Governments, Canberra: Australian Government Publishing Service, 1976 (also referred to as the *Crawford–Ōkita Report*)

_____ *Raw Materials and Pacific Economic Integration* London: Croom Helm, 1978 (revised version of Crawford and Ōkita 1976)

Crawford–Ōkita Report: see Crawford and Ōkita, 1976

Crawford, Sir John and Seow, Greg (eds) *Pacific Economic Cooperation: Suggestions for Action* Petaling Jaba, Selangor, Malaysia: Heinemann Asia, for the Pacific Community Seminar, 1981

Crawford, J.G. et al. 'Australian Agriculture and Trade with Japan' *Australia–Japan Economic Relations Research Project Research Paper* No.27, Australian National University, July 1975

Cummings, Bruce 'The Origins and Development of the Northeast Asian Political Economy: Industrialization, Product Cycles, and Political Consequences' *International Organization* 38, Winter 1984

Curzon, Gerard *Multilateral Commercial Diplomacy: GATT and its Impact on National Commercial Policies and Technique* London: Michael Joseph, 1965

Curzon, Gerard and Curzon, Victoria 'GATT: Traders' Club' in Cox and Jacobsen (eds) *The Anatomy of Influence*

Dahl, Robert and Tufte, Edward *Size and Democracy* Stanford: Stanford University Press, 1973

Dam, Kenneth *The GATT: Law and International Economic Organization* Chicago: University of Chicago Press, 1970

Dasgupta, P. and Heal, G. *Economic Theory and Exhaustible Resources* Welwyn: Cambridge University Press, 1979

Deese, D.A. and Nye, Joseph S. (eds) *Energy and Security* Cambridge, Mass.: Ballinger (with Harper & Row), 1981

Denison, Edward E. and Chung, William K. *How Japan's Economy Grew So Fast: The Source of Postwar Expansion* Washington, DC: The Brookings Institution, 1976

Department of Trade and Resources (Australia) *Multilateral Trade Negotiations: Australia–European Economic Community Bilateral Settlement* Canberra, November 1979

_____ *Multilateral Trade Negotiations: Australia–Japan Bilateral Settlement* Canberra, November 1979

Destler, I., Satō, H., Clapp, P. and Fukui, H. *Managing an Alliance: The Politics of US–Japanese Relations* Washington, DC: The Brookings Institution, 1976

Deutsch, Karl et al. *Political Community and the North Atlantic Area* Princeton: Princeton University Press, 1957

Diaz–Alejandro, Carlos 'North–South Relations: The Economic Component' in Bergsten and Krause (eds) *World Politics*

Dibb, Paul (ed.) *Australia's External Relations in the 1980s: The Interaction of Economic, Political and Strategic Factors* Canberra: Croom Helm, 1983

Dornbush, Rudiger and Frenkel, Jacob (eds) *International Economic Policy: The Theory and Evidence* Baltimore: Johns Hopkins University Press, 1979

Drysdale, Peter 'Japanese–Australian Trade' in Sissons *Papers on Modern Japan*

_____ 'Australia, Japan and New Zealand: The Prospects for Western Pacific Economic Integration' *Economic Record* September 1967

_____ 'Japan, Australia and Pacific Economic Integration' *Australia's Neighbours* November–December 1967

_____ Japanese–Australian Trade: An Approach to the Study of Bilateral Trade Flows, PhD dissertation, Australian National University, Canberra, 1967

_____ 'Pacific Economic Integration: An Australian View' in Kojima *Pacific Trade and Development*

_____ 'Pacific Economic Integration: The Evolution of a New Approach to Regional Trade and Development Policies' *Australia's Neighbours* October–December 1968

_____ 'Japan, Australia and New Zealand: The Prospects for Western Pacific Economic Integration' *Economic Record* 45, 111, September 1969

_____ 'Minerals and Metals in Japanese–Australian Trade' *The Developing Economies* 18, 2, June 1970

_____ 'Japan in the World Economy: The Decade Ahead' in Stockwin *Japan and Australia in the Seventies* Sydney: Angus & Robertson, 1972 (first prepared in 1970 for the Australian Institute of International Affairs)

_____ 'Trends in World Trade and World Trade Policy' in Garnaut 'Foreign Economic Relations' *New Guinea Research Bulletin* 56 Australian National University, 1974

_____ 'An Organisation for Pacific Trade, Aid and Development: Regional Arrangements and the Resource Trade' in Krause and Patrick *Mineral Resources*

_____ 'Australia's Economic Relations with Asia and the Pacific — Past Perspectives and Future Prospects' in Hanson and Roehl *The United States and the Pacific Economy* (also published in *Current Affairs Bulletin* 55, 11, April 1979)

_____ 'Australia and Japan in the Pacific and World Economy' in Drysdale and Kitaōji *Japan and Australia*

_____ 'The Proposal for an Organisation for Pacific Trade and Development Revisited' *Asian Survey* XXIII, 12, December 1983

_____ 'Pacific Growth and Economic Interdependence' in Export–Import Bank of Japan *Second Symposium*

_____ 'The Pacific Trade and Development Conference: A Brief History' *Pacific Economic Papers* No.112 Australia–Japan Research Centre, Australian National University, June 1984

_____ 'Building the Foundations of a Pacific Community' in Shishido and Satō' *Economic Policy and Development*

_____ 'The Pacific Basin and Its Economic Vitality' in James W. Morley (ed.) *US Annals of Political Science* Academy of Political Sciences, New York, 36, 1, 1986

_____ 'Developments in Economic Relations between Japan, the United States and East Asia' Conference on 'Business Opportunities in Northeast Asia' held in Melbourne, 2 October 1987

_____ 'The Relationship with Japan: Despite the Vicissitudes' in Evans and Miller *Policy and Practice*

_____ (ed.) *Direct Foreign Investment in Asia and the Pacific* Canberra: Australian National University Press, 1972

Drysdale, Peter and Garnaut, Ross 'Trade Intensities and the Analysis of Bilateral Trade Flows in a Many-Country World' *Hitotsubashi Journal of Economics* 22, 2, February 1982

Drysdale, Peter and Kitaōji, Hironobu (eds) *Japan and Australia: Two Societies and Their Interaction* Canberra: Australian National University Press, 1981

Drysdale, Peter and Kojima, Kiyoshi (eds) *Australia–Japan Economic Relations in International Context: Recent Experience and the Prospects Ahead* Australia–Japan Economic Relations Research Project, Australian National University, 1978

Drysdale, Peter and Patrick, Hugh 'Evaluation of a Proposed Pacific Regional Economic Organisation' *Australia–Japan Economic Relations Research Project Research Paper* No.61, Australian National University, July 1979 (also published by the US Congressional Research Service as *An Asian–Pacific Regional Economic Organization: An Exploratory Concept Paper* Washington, DC: US Government Printing Office, July 1979)

Drysdale, Peter and Rix, Alan 'Australia's Trading Patterns' *Current Affairs Bulletin* 55, 11, April 1979

Drysdale, Peter and Shibata, Hirofumi (eds) *Federalism and Resource Development: The Australian Case* Sydney: Allen & Unwin, 1986

Drysdale, Peter, Smith, Ben, Anderson, Kym and Findlay, Christopher 'Australia and the Pacific Economy' *Economic Record* 62, 176, March 1986

Duncan, W.G.K. (ed.) *Australia's Foreign Policy* Sydney: Angus & Robertson, 1938

Dunn, Lydia *In the Kingdom of The Blind: A Report on Protectionism and the Asian-Pacific Region* Special Report No.3, Trade Policy Centre, London, 1983

Economic Planning Agency (Japan) *2000 Nen no Nihon (kakuron) — tajuteki na keizaishakai no anzen o motomete* [Japan in the year 2000 (detailed discussion) — in search of security for a diverse economic society] Economic Planning Agency, Tokyo, 1982

Edgeworth, F. 'The Theory of International Values' *Economic Journal* 4, March 1894

El-Agraa, A.M. (ed.) *Protection, Cooperation, Development and Integration: Essays in Honour of Hiroshi Kitamura* London: Macmillan, 1987

English, H.E. 'Canada and Pacific Trade Policy' in Kojima (ed.) *Pacific Trade and Development*

English, H.E. and Hay, Keith (eds) *Obstacles to Trade in the Pacific Area* Ottawa: Carleton University, 1972

English, H.E. and Scott, Anthony (eds) *Renewable Resources in the Pacific* Ottawa: International Development Research Centre, 1982

EPAC (Economic Planning Advisory Council) 'International Trade Policy' Council Paper No. 18, Canberra: Australian Government Publishing Service, 1986

Erb, Guy 'Controlling Export Controls' *Foreign Policy* Winter 1974

ESCAP (Economic and Social Commission for Asia and the Pacific) Secretariat 'ASEAN Foreign Investment from Pacific Sources' in United Nations ESCAP 'ASEAN and Pacific Economic Cooperation' *Development Papers* No.2, 1983

Evans, L. and Miller, J.D.B. (eds) *Policy and Practice: Essays in Honour of Sir John Crawford* Canberra: Australian National University Press (Pergamon), 1987

Evans, John W. *The Kennedy Round in American Trade Policy: The Twilight of the GATT?* Cambridge, Mass.: Harvard University Press, 1971

Export–Import Bank of Japan *Business Cooperation between Asia-Pacific and Japan in the Eighties* Report of Symposium, Tokyo, 26–27 May 1980

—— *Second Symposium on Financial and Business Cooperation in Asia and the Pacific* Tokyo, 30 October–1 November 1984

Farrands, Chris, 'Textiles Diplomacy: The Making and Implementation of European Textile Policy 1974–1978' *Journal of Common Market Studies* September 1979

Feld, Werner 'Atlantic Interdependence and Competition for Raw Materials in the Third World' *The Atlantic Community Quarterly* 14, 3, Fall 1976

Felder, Gershon et al. 'Storage with Price Uncertainty in International Trade' *International Economic Review* 18, 3, October 1977

Findlay, Christopher, Anderson, Kym and Drysdale, Peter 'China's Trade and Pacific Economic Growth' *Pacific Economic Papers* (forthcoming) Australia–Japan Research Centre, Australian National University

Findlay, Christopher, Phillips, Prue and Tyers, Rodney 'China's Merchandise Trade: Composition and Export Growth in the 1980s' *ASEAN–Australian Economic Papers* No.19, ASEAN–Australian Project, Australian National University, 1985

Findlay, Ronald 'Comments on Export-Led Industrialisation' in Hong and Krause *Pacific ADCs*

Findlay, R. and Wellisz, S. 'Some Aspects of the Political Economy of Trade Restrictions' *Kyklos* 36, 1983

Finger, J.M. and Yeats, A.J. 'Effective Protection by Transportation Costs and Tariffs: A Comparison of Magnitudes' *Quarterly Journal of Economics* 90, February 1976

Finlayson, Jack A. and Zacher, Mark W. 'The GATT and the Regulation of Trade Barriers: Regime Dynamics and Functions' *International Organization* 35, 4, Autumn 1981

Fishlow, A., Diaz-Alejandro C., Fagen, R. and Hansen, R. *Rich and Poor Nations in the World Economy* New York: McGraw-Hill, for the Council on Foreign Relations, 1978

Fleming, J. M. 'Domestic Financial Policies under Fixed and Floating Exchange Rates' *IMF Staff Papers* November 1962

Forum on Minerals and Energy *Report of the Fifth Pacific Economic Cooperation Conference, Vancouver, November 16-19,* 1986 Canadian Chamber of Commerce, Ottawa, 1987

Fox, J.J. et al. (eds) *Indonesia: Australian Perspectives* Research School of Pacific Studies, Australian National University, 1980

Frank, Charles R., Kim, Kwang Suk and Westphal, Larry E. *Foreign Trade Regimes and Economic Development: South Korea* New York: Columbia University Press, for the National Bureau of Economic Research, 1975

Frey, Bruno S. 'The Public Choice View of International Political Economy' *International Organization* 38, 1, 1984

Fukui, Haruo (ed.) *Public Policies and Policymaking in Post-Oil Crisis Japan* Berkeley: University of California Press (forthcoming)

GATT (General Agreement on Tariffs and Trade) *Basic Instruments and Selected Documents, Third Supplement* Geneva, 1955

—— *Trends in International Trade: A Report by a Panel of Experts* (the Haberler Report) Geneva, 1958

—— *Basic Instruments and Selected Documents, Twenty-sixth Supplement* Geneva, 1980

Galt, Sidney 'Developing Countries in the GATT System' *Thames Essay* No. 13, Trade Policy Research Centre, London, 1978

—— Gardner, Richard N. *Sterling–Dollar Diplomacy: The Origins and the Prospects of our International Economic Order* New York: McGraw-Hill, 1969

—— 'The Hard Road to World Order' *Foreign Affairs* 52, 3, April 1974, pp.556-76

Garnaut, Ross, Australian Trade with Southeast Asia: A Study of Resistances to Bilateral Trade Flows, PhD dissertation, Australian National University, Canberra, 1972

—— 'The Importance of Industrialisation in Southeast and East Asia to an Open Australian Economy' in Drysdale and Kojima (eds) *Australia–Japan Economic Relations*

—— 'Survey of Recent Developments' *Bulletin of Indonesian Economic Studies* 15, 3, November 1979

—— 'General Repercussions of the Resources Boom in the Segmented Indonesian Economy' in Fox et al. *Indonesia*

—— (ed.) 'Foreign Economic Relations of Papua New Guinea' *New Guinea Research Bulletin* No.56, Australian National University, Port Moresby and Canberra, 1974

—— (ed.) *ASEAN in a Changing Pacific and World Economy* Canberra: Australian National University Press, 1980

Garnaut, Ross and Anderson, Kym 'ASEAN Export Specialisation and the Evolution of Comparative Advantage in the Western Pacific Region' in Garnaut *ASEAN*

Garnaut, Ross and Arndt, H.W. 'ASEAN and the Industrialisation of Southeast and East Asia' *Journal of Common Market Studies* XVII, 3, March 1979

Garnaut, Ross and Baxter, Paul, in consultation with Anne O. Krueger *Exchange Rate and Macro-Economic Policy in Independent Papua New Guinea* Report to the Papua New Guinea Government, Canberra: Development Studies Centre, Australian National University, February 1983

Garnaut, Ross and Clunies-Ross, Anthony *The Taxation of Mineral Rents* Oxford: Oxford University Press, 1983

George, Aurelia, The Strategies of Influence: Japan's Agricultural Cooperative (Nōkyō) as a Pressure Group, PhD dissertation, Australian National University, Canberra, 1980

—— 'The Comparative Study of Interest Groups in Japan: An International Framework' *Pacific Economic Papers* No.95, Australia–Japan Research Centre, Australian National University, December 1982

—— 'The Changing Patterns of Japan's Agricultural Import Trade: Implications for Australia' *Pacific Economic Papers* No. 100, Australia–Japan Research Centre, Australian National University, January 1983

_____ 'Japan's Beef Import Policies, 1978–84: The Growth of Bilateralism' *Pacific Economic Papers* No.113, Australia–Japan Research Centre, Australian National University, July 1984

_____ 'Agricultural Politics and Policymaking' in Fukui *Public Policies* (forthcoming)

George, Geoff 'Japan's Oil Import Policies in the Age of "Multipolar Diplomacy"' *Australia–Japan Economic Relations Research Project Research Paper* No.8, Australian National University, April 1974

Gift, Richard 'Trading in a Threat System: the US–Soviet Case' *Journal of Conflict Resolution* 13, 4, December 1969

_____ Girgis, Maurice 'Development and Trade Patterns in the Arab World' *Weltwirtschaftliches Archiv* 109, 1973

Gordon, Bernard 'Japan, the United States, and Southeast Asia' *Foreign Affairs* April 1978

Gordon, Bernard and Rothwell, Kenneth (eds) *The New Political Economy of the Pacific* Cambridge, Mass.: Ballinger, 1975

Grossman, Gene M. and Richardson, J. David *Strategic Trade Policy: A Survey of Issues and Early Analysis* Special Papers in International Economics No.15, Princeton, April 1985

Gunasekera, Don, Intra-industry Trade in East Asia, PhD dissertation, Australian National University, Canberra, 1987

Haas, Ernst 'International Integration: The European and the Universal Process' *International Organization* 15, 3, Summer 1961

_____ 'Turbulent Fields and the Theory of Regional Integration' *International Organization* 30, 2, Spring 1976

Haas, Michael *International Systems: A Behavioral Approach* New York: Chandler, 1974

Haberler Report: *see* GATT, 1958

Hamada, T. 'The Steel Industry and Japan — Its Role in the Japanese Economy' address to the American Chamber of Commerce in Japan, Tokyo, 13 March 1969

Hamada, Kōichi 'Japanese Investment Abroad' in Drysdale *Direct Foreign Investment*

_____ 'On the Political Economy of Monetary Integration: A Public Economics Approach' in Aliber *The Political Economy of Monetary Reform*

_____ 'Macroeconomic Strategy and Coordination under Alternative Exchange Rates' in Rudiger Dornbusch and Jacob Frenkel (eds) *International Economic Policy: The Theory and Evidence* Baltimore: Johns Hopkins University Press, 1979

Han Sung-joo (ed.) *Community-Building in the Pacific Region: Issues and Opportunities* Seoul: Asiatic Research Center, Korea University, 1981

Hancock, W.K. *Survey of British Commonwealth Affairs* Vol. II, London: Oxford University Press, 1940

Hanson, Kermit and Roehl, Thomas (eds) *The United States and the Pacific Economy in the 1980s* Seattle: University of Washington, 1980

Harris, Richard '"Market Access" in International Trade: A Theoretical Appraisal' paper presented at a conference on US–Canadian Trade and Investment Relations with Japan, Ann Arbor, University of Michigan, 2–3 April 1987

Harris, Stuart 'The Commodities Problem and the International Economic Order: What Rules of What Game?' in Oppenheimer *Basic Issues*

_____ Australian Security and Resources Diplomacy: An Economic Viewpoint' Paper presented to ANZAAS Conference, Canberra, January 1975

_____ 'Agricultural Trade and its International Trade Policy Context' *CRES Working Paper* R/WP 37, Centre for Resource and Environmental Studies, Australian National University, 1979

_____ 'Australian Agriculture and World Commodity Trading Arrangements' paper presented to the Annual Conference of the Australian Agricultural Economics Society, University of Adelaide, February 1980

—— 'International Practice and Mores in Resources Policy' *Australian Outlook* 35, 3, December 1981

—— *Energy in the Asia–Pacific Region* London: Gower, for the Royal Institute of International Affairs, 1983

—— 'Pacific Economic Cooperation: How Australia and Japan Fit In' address to the Australia–Japan Relations Symposium, Sydney, 19 March 1985

Harris, Stuart and Ikuta, Toyoaki *Australia, Japan and the Energy Coal Trade* Canberra and Tokyo: Australia–Japan Research Centre, 1982

Harris, Stuart and Oshima, Keichi (eds) *Australia and Japan: Nuclear Energy Issues in the Pacific* Canberra and Tokyo: Australia–Japan Research Centre, 1980

Harris, Stuart, Salmon, Mark and Smith, Ben 'Analysis of Commodity Markets for Policy Purposes' *Thames Essay* No. 17, Trade Policy Research Centre, London, 1978

Harsanyi, John *Essays on Ethics, Social Behaviour, and Scientific Explanation* Dordrecht: Reidel (originally published in *Australian Journal of Politics and History* 11, 1965)

—— *Rational Behaviour and Bargaining Equilibrium in Games and Social Situations* Cambridge: Cambridge University Press, 1977

Hasenpflug, Hugo 'The Stabilization of Export Earnings in the Lome Convention: A Model Case?' in Suvant and Hasenpflug *The New International Economic Order*

Hastings, Peter and Farran, Andrew (eds) *Australia's Resources Future: Threats, Myths and Realities in the 1980s* Melbourne: Nelson, 1978

Hawtrey, R. *Economic Aspects of Sovereignty* London: Longmans, Green & Co., 1930

Hay, Keith J. and Sulzenko, B. Andrei 'US Trade Policy and "Reciprocity"' *Journal of World Trade Law* 16, November–December 1982

Hayden, Eric W. 'Internationalisation of Japan's Financial System' Occasional Paper of the Northeast Asia–United States Forum on International Policy, December 1980

Haynes, Stephen E., Hutchinson, Michael M. and Mikesell, Raymond F. 'Japanese Financial Policies and the US Trade Deficit' *Essays in International Finance* No.162, Princeton, April 1986

Helleiner, G.K. 'The Political Economy of Canada's Tariff Structure: An Alternative Model' *Canadian Journal of Economics* 10, 1977

Hellman, Donald (ed.) *China and Japan: A New Balance of Power* Critical Choices for Americans, Vol. XII, Lexington: D.C. Heath, 1976

—— (ed.) *Southern Asia: The Politics of Poverty and Peace* Critical Choices for Americans, Vol.XIII Lexington: D.C. Heath, 1976

Hemmi, Kenzō 'Japanese Agricultural Policy and Australian Trade Prospects' in Hemmi and Allen 'Structural Adjustment'

Hemmi, Kenzō and Allen, G.C. 'Structural Adjustment of Japanese Agriculture' *Australia–Japan Economic Relations Research Project Research Paper* No.11, Australian National University, May 1974

Hewson, John R. 'Offshore Banking in Singapore: A Case Study in Offshore Banking in Australia' *Commissioned Studies and Selected Papers* Part II, Canberra: Australian Financial System Enquiry, Australian Government Publishing Service, 1982

—— 'The Internationalisation of Banking' in Tan and Kapur *Pacific Growth*

'Hickman, B.G., Kuroda, Y. and Lau, L.J. 'The Pacific Basin in World Trade — An Analysis of Changing Trade Patterns 1955–75' *Empirical Economics* 4, 1, 1979

Hill, Hal and Johns, Brian 'The Role of Direct Foreign Investment in Developing East Asian Countries' *Weltwirtschaftliches Archiv* 121, 1985

Hillman, J.S., Johnson, D.G. and Gray, R. 'Food Reserve Policies for World Food Security: A Consultant Study on Alternative Approaches' United Nations, FAO, ESC/72/2, January 1975

Hirschman, Albert *National Power and the Structure of Foreign Trade* Berkeley and Los Angeles: University of California Press, 1945

Holmes, Sir Frank et al. *Closer Economic Relations with Australia: Agenda for Progress*

Wellington, NZ: Institute of Policy Studies, 1986

Holsti, Ole R., Siverson, Randolph M. and George, Alexander L. (eds) *Changes in the International System* Boulder, Col.: Westview, 1980

Kong, Wontack 'Capital Accumulation, Factor Substitution, and the Changing Factor Intensity of Trade: The Case of Korea (1966–72)' in Hong and Krueger *Trade and Development in Korea*

Hong, Wontack and Krause, Lawrence B. (eds) *Trade and Growth of the Advanced Developing Countries in the Pacific Basin* Seoul: Korea Development Institute, 1981

Hong, Wontack and Krueger, Anne O. (eds) *Trade and Development in Korea* Seoul: Korea Development Institute, 1975

Hooper, Paul F. (ed.) *Building a Pacific Community* Honolulu: University of Hawaii Press, 1982

Hormats, Robert 'The World Economy under Stress' *Foreign Affairs* 64, 3, 1986

Horne, James 'National, International and Sectional Interests in Policymaking: The Evolution of the Yen Bond Market, 1970–82' *Pacific Economic Papers* No.98, Australia–Japan Research Centre, Australian National University, December 1982

———— *Japan's Financial Markets: Conflict and Consensus in Policymaking* Sydney: Allen & Unwin, 1985

Horsefield, Keith *The International Monetary Fund, 1945–1965* Washington, DC: IMF, 1967

Hsing, M.H. 'Taiwan: Industrialisation and Trade Policies' in Hsing, Power and Sicat *Taiwan and the Philippines*

Hsing, M.H., Power, J.H. and Sicat, G.P. *Taiwan and the Philippines: Industrialisation and Trade Policies* London: Oxford University Press, for the OECD, 1971

Hudee, Robert E. *Adjudication of International Trade Disputes* London: Trade Policy Research Centre, 1978

Hughes, Barry 'Transactional Analysis: The Impact of Operationalization' *International Organization* 25, 1, Winter 1971

———— 'Transaction Data and Analysis: In Search of Concepts' *International Organization* 25, 3, Summer 1972

Hunsberger, Warren *Japan and the United States in World Trade* New York: Harper & Row, for the Council on Foreign Relations, 1964

Ichimura, Shinichi 'Japan: The Rising Sun or Sinking Ship: The Energy Problem and the Food Shortage' *Center for South-East Asian Studies Discussion Paper* No.74, Kyoto, July 1974

———— 'Debt Problems of Developing Countries' *Pacific Economic Papers* Special Paper, Australia–Japan Research Centre, Australian National University, November 1984

Inoguchi, Takashi 'Trade, Technology and Security: Implications for East Asia and the West' *Pacific Economic Papers* No.147 Australia–Japan Research Centre, Australian National University, May 1987

Issues for Pacific Economic Co-operation report of the Third Pacific Economic Co-operation Conference, Jakarta: Centre for Strategic and International Studies, March 1984

Itagaki, Yoichi 'Economic Nationalism and the Problem of Resources' *The Developing Economies* 11, 3, September 1973

Jacoby, Neil, Nehemkis, Peter and Eells, Richard *Bribery and Extortion in World Business: A Study of Corporate Political Payments Abroad* New York: Macmillan, 1977

Japan Economic Research Center *Measures for Trade Expansion of Developing Countries* Tokyo: Japan Economic Research Center, October 1966

Japan Member Committee: *see* PBEC, 1968

Japan Pacific Cooperation Study Group *Report on Pacific Basin Cooperation Concept* (Ōhira Study Group Report) Prime Minister's Office, Tokyo, 1982

Japan–United States Economic Relations Group *Report of the Japan–United States Economic Relations Group* prepared for the President of the United States and the Prime Minister of Japan, January 1981

JETRO (Japan External Trade Organisation) *Sekai to Nihon no kaigai no chokusetsu tōshi* [World and Japanese direct foreign investment] Tokyo: JETRO, 1987

Johansson, J. and Moinpour, R. 'Objective and Perceived Similarity among Pacific Rim Countries' *Columbia Journal of World Business* 12, 4, Winter 1977

Johansson, J.K. and Spick, Robert S. 'Trade Interdependence in the Pacific Rim and the EC. A Comparative Analysis' *Journal of Common Market Studies* XX, 1, September 1981

Johnson, Gale *World Agriculture in Disarray* London: Macmillan, 1973

───── 'Impact of Farm Support Policies on International Trade' in Corbet and Jackson *A New World Economic Order*

Johnson, Harry 'Optimum Tariffs and Retaliation' *Review of Economic Studies* 21, 2, 1953–54

───── *Money, Trade and Economic Growth: Survey Lectures in Economic Theory* London: George Allen & Unwin, 1962

───── 'The Economic Theory of Customs Unions' in *Money, Trade and Economic Growth* London: George Allen & Unwin, 1962

───── 'An Economic Theory of Protectionism, Tariff Bargaining, and the Formation of Customs Unions' *Journal of Political Economy* 73, June 1965

───── *Economic Policies Towards Less Developed Countries* London: George Allen & Unwin, 1967

───── *Comparative Cost and Commercial Policy Theory for a Developing World Economy* Stockholm: Almqvist & Wicksell, 1968

───── (ed.) *Economic Nationalism in Old and New States* London: George Allen & Unwin, 1968

───── 'World Trade Policy in the Post-Kennedy Round Era: A Survey of Alternatives, with Special Reference to the Position of the Pacific and Asian Regions' *Economic Record* June 1968

───── *Trade Negotiations and the New International Monetary System* Graduate Institute of International Studies, Geneva, and Trade Policy Research Centre, London, 1976

Joint Coal Board (Australia) *Annual Report* 1976–77 Sydney: New South Wales Printing Office, 1978

───── *Annual Report 1977–78*

Jones, Kent *Steel Trade Policy in Crisis* London: Trade Policy Research Centre, 1983

Josling, T.E. 'Agriculture in the Tokyo-Round Negotiations' Trade Policy Research Centre, London, 1977

Kaneko, Ikuyo and Imai, Kenichi, 'Japan's Firms and Markets in Comparative Perspective' paper prepared for the Workshop on Corporate Organisation and Trade in Technology and Services, Australia-Japan Research Centre, Australian National University, Canberra, 27 February 1987

───── 'A Network View of the Firm' paper prepared for the First Hitotsubashi–Stanford Conference, Stanford, 29 March–April 1987

Kapoor, A. *Foreign Investments in Asia* Princeton: Darwin, 1972

Kasper, Wolfgang and Parry, Thomas (eds) *Growth, Trade and Structural Change in an Open Australian Economy* Sydney: Centre for Applied Economic Research, University of New South Wales, 1978

KDI (Korea Development Institute) *Pacific Economic Cooperation: Issues and Opportunities* Seoul, 29 April–1 May 1985.

Keesing, D.B. 'Outward-looking Policies and Economic Development' *Economic Journal*, 77, June 1967

Keesing, D.B. and Wolf, M. 'Textile Quotas against Developing Countries' *Thames Essay* No.23, Trade Policy Research Centre, London, 1980

Kemp, Geoffrey 'Scarcity and Strategy' *Foreign Affairs* 56, 2, January 1978

Keohane, Robert O. 'The Theory of Hegemonic Stability and Changes in International

Economic Regimes: 1967–1977' in Holsti et al. *Changes in the International System*
_____ 'The Demand for International Regimes' *International Organization* 36, 2, 1982
_____ 'Reciprocity in International Relations' *International Organization* 40, 1, Winter 1986
Keohane, Robert and Nye, Joseph *Power and Interdependence: World Politics in Transition* Boston: Little, Brown & Co., 1977
Kindleberger, Charles *Foreign Trade and the National Economy* New Haven: Yale University, 1962
_____ *Power and Money: The Economics of International Politics and the Politics of International Economics* London: Macmillan, 1970
_____ *The World in Depression, 1929–39* Berkeley: University of California Press, 1974
_____ *Government and International Trade* Essays in International Finance No.129, Princeton, July 1978
_____ 'Dominance and Leadership in the International Economy' *International Studies Quarterly* 25, 1981
_____ 'International Public Goods without International Government' *American Economic Review* 71, 1, March 1986
Kissinger, Henry, Address to the Fourth Ministerial Meeting of the United Nations Conference on Trade and Development (UNCTAD), Nairobi, 6 May 1976, published in *The Atlantic Community Quarterly* 14, 2, Summer 1976
Kleiman, Ephraim 'Trade and the Decline of Colonialism' *Economic Journal* 86, 343, September 1976
_____ 'Cultural Ties and Trade: Spain's Role in Latin America' *Kyklos* 31, 2, 1978
Knorr, Klaus *Power and Wealth: The Political Economy of International Power* London: Macmillan, 1973
Kojima, Kiyoshi *Sekai keizai to Nihon bōeki* [The world economy and Japan's foreign trade] Tokyo: Keisō Shobō, 1962
_____ 'The Pattern of International Trade Among Advanced Countries' *Hitotsubashi Journal of Economics* 5, 1, June 1964
'A Pacific Economic Community and Asian Developing Countries' *Hitotsubashi Journal of Economics* 7, 1, June 1966
_____ 'Japan's Interest in Pacific Trade Expansion' in Kojima *Pacific Trade and Development*
_____ *Japan and a Pacific Free Trade Area* London: Macmillan, 1971
_____ 'An Organisation for Pacific Trade, Aid and Development: A Proposal' *Australia–Japan Economic Relations Research Project Research Paper* No.40, Australian National University, September 1976
_____ *Japan and a New World Economic Order* Tokyo: Charles Tuttle & Co., 1977
_____ *Direct Foreign Investment: A Japanese Model of Multinational Business Operations* London: Croom Helm, 1978
_____ 'Japan's Resource Security and Foreign Investment in the Pacific: A Case Study of Bilateral Devices between Advanced Countries' in Krause and Patrick *Mineral Resources*
_____ 'Economic Cooperation in a Pacific Community' *Asia Pacific Community* Spring 1981
Kojima, Kiyoshi (ed.) *Pacific Trade and Development* Tokyo: Japan Economic Research Center, 1968
_____ (ed.) *Pacific Trade and Development II* Tokyo: Japan Economic Research Center, 1969
_____ (ed.) *Structural Adjustments in Asian–Pacific Trade* Tokyo: Japan Economic Research Center, 1973
Kojima, Kiyoshi and Wionczek, Miguel S. (eds) *Technology Transfer in Pacific Economic Development* Tokyo: Japan Economic Research Center, January 1975

Kolhagen, Stephen 'The Characteristics, Motivations, and Effects of Japanese and United States Direct Investments in the Pacific Basin' *Explorations in Economic Research* 3, 2, Spring 1976

Komiya, Ryūtarō 'Commentary on Economic Assumptions of the Case for Liberal Trade' in Bergsten *Toward a New World Trade Policy*

Komiya, Ryūtarō and Itoh, Motoshige 'International Trade and Trade Policy of Japan' *Tokyo University Discussion Paper* 85–F-16, January 1986 (based on a paper prepared for the Japan Political Economy Research Conference, East–West Center, Hawaii, August 1984)

Krasner, Stephen D. 'The Tokyo Round: Particularistic Interests and Prospects for Stability in the Global Trading System' *International Studies Quarterly* 23, 4, December 1979
_____ 'Structural Causes and Regime Consequences: Regimes as Intervening Variables' *International Organization* 36, 2, 1982
_____ 'Trade Conflicts and the Common Defense: The United States and Japan' *Political Science Quarterly* 101, 5, 1986

Krause, Lawrence B. 'The Pacific Economy in an Interdependent World' in Hanson and Roehl (eds) *The United States and the Pacific Economy in the 1980s*
_____ *US Economic Policy toward the Association of Southeast Asian Nations: Meeting the Japanese Challenge* Washington, DC: The Brookings Institution, 1982

Krause, Lawrence and Nye, Joseph 'Reflections on the Economics and Politics of International Economic Organisations' in Bergsten and Krause *World Politics*

Krause, Lawrence B. and Patrick, Hugh T. (eds) *Mineral Resources in the Pacific Area* San Fransisco: Federal Reserve Bank of San Francisco, 1978

Krause, Lawrence B. and Sekiguchi, Sueo (eds) *Economic Interaction in the Pacific Basin* Washington, DC: The Brookings Institution

Kraus, M.B. 'Recent Developments in Customs Union Theory: An Interpretative Survey' *Journal of Economic Literature* 10, June 1972.

Kravis, Irving '"Availability" and Other Influences on the Commodity Composition of Trade' *Journal of Political Economy* 64, 2, April 1956

Krueger, Anne O. 'The Political Economy of the Rent-Seeking Society' *American Economic Review* 64, 3, June 1974
_____ *Growth, Distortions and Patterns of Trade among Many Countries* Princeton, NJ: International Finance Section, Princeton University, 1977
_____ *Foreign Trade Regimes and Economic Development: Liberalization Attempts and Consequences* Cambridge, Mass.: Ballinger, 1978

Krueger, Anne O., Lary, Hal B., Monson, Terry and Akrasanee, Narongchai (eds) *Trade and Employment in Developing Countries I: Individual Studies* Chicago: University of Chicago Press, 1981

Lee Sheng Yi 'Developing Asian Financial Centres' in Tan and Kapur *Pacific Growth*

Le Vine, Victor, The Bribe Goes Global: Preliminary Reflections on the New Transnational Aspects of Political Corruption, mimeo, Edinburgh Congress of the International Studies Association, August 1976

Leibenstein, Harvey *General X-Efficiency Theory and Economic Development* New York: Oxford University Press, 1978

Lillich, Richard B. 'Economic Coercion and the International Legal Order' *International Affairs* 51, 3, July 1975

Lindberg, Leon *The Political Dynamics of European Economic Integration* Stanford: Stanford University Press, 1963

Lindblom, Charles *Politics and Markets: The World's Political–Economic Systems* New York: Basic Books, 1977

Linder, Staffan Burenstam *The Pacific Century: Economic and Political Consequences of Asian–Pacific Dynamism* Stanford: Stanford University Press, 1986

Lipsey, R. 'The Theory of Customs Unions: Trade Diversion and Welfare' *Economica* 24, February 1957

_____ 'The Theory of Customs Unions: A General Survey' *Economic Journal* 70, September 1960

Lipsey, R. and Lancaster, K. 'The General Theory of Second Best' *Review of Economic Studies* 24, 1956–57

Little, Ian, Scitovsky, Tibor and Scott, Maurice *Industry and Trade in Some Developing Countries* London: Oxford University Press, 1970

Lloyd, Peter 'Japan and Australia in the Multilateral Trade Negotiations; *Australia–Japan Economic Relations Research Project Research Paper* No.20, Australian National University, March 1975

_____ *Economic Relations between Australia and New Zealand* Department of Economics, Research School of Pacific Studies, Australian National University, 1976

Lloyd, T. 'Comments' in KDI Task Force, Department of Trade and Industry, New Zealand

Lockwood, William W. *The Economic Development of Japan: Growth and Structural Change 1868–1938* Princeton, NJ: Princeton University Press, 1954

Luce, Duncan and Raiffa, Howard *Games and Decisions: Introduction and Critical Survey* New York: John Wiley & Sons, 1957

Luo Yuan Zheng 'The Management of China's Modernisation and Its Impact on the Rest of the World' *Australian Journal of Management* 7, 1, June 1982

McCawley, Peter and Manning, Christopher 'Survey of Recent Developments' *Bulletin of Indonesian Economic Studies* XII, 3, November 1976

McDougall, I.A. 'Prospects for the Economic Integration of Japan, Australia and New Zealand' in Kojima *Pacific Trade and Development II*

McKenzie, Colin and Stutchbury, Michael (eds) *Japan's Money Markets and the Future of the Yen* Australia–Japan Research Centre, Australian National University, Canberra, (forthcoming)

McKern, R.B. *Multinational Enterprise and Natural Resources* Sydney: McGraw-Hill, 1976

McKinnon, Ronald I. 'Foreign Trade Regimes and Economic Development: A Review Article' *Journal of International Economics*, 9, 1979

_____ 'Issues and Perspectives: An Overview of Banking Regulation and Monetary Control' in Tan and Kapur *Pacific Growth* (also published as *Pacific Economic Papers* No.117, Australia–Japan Research Centre, Australian National University, December 1984)

Malmgren, Harald B. 'Japan, the United States, and the Pacific Economy' *Pacific Community* April 1973

_____ 'International Order for Public Subsidies' *Thames Essay* No.11, Trade Policy Research Centre, London, 1977

Manning, Christopher 'Labour Surplus to Labour Scarcity? — The Impact of Rapid Economic Growth and the Green Revolution on Labour Markets in Rural Java' paper presented to the 31st Annual Conference of the Australian Agricultural Society, Adelaide, 9–12 February 1987

March, Robert M. 'The Australia–Japan Sugar Negotiations *Australia–Japan Economic Relations Research Project Research Paper* No. 56, Australian National University, March 1979

Mayer, Wolfgang 'Theoretical Considerations on Negotiated Tariff Settlements' *Oxford Economic Papers* No. 33, February 1981

Meadows, D.H. et al. *The Limits of Growth* London: Earth Island, 1972

MEF (Pacific Minerals and Energy Forum) *PECC Forum on Minerals and Energy* Jakarta, 6–8 July 1986, Papers and Report, Australian National University, October 1987

Menadue, John 'Roles and Problems in Pacific Economic Cooperation' paper presented at the 3rd Symposium on Pacific Cooperation, sponsored by the Pacific Basin Economic Council of Japan, Tokyo, 24 March 1987

Merciai, Patrizio 'Safeguard Measures in GATT' *Journal of World Trade Law* 15, 1, January/February 1981

Michaely, Michael *Concentration in International Trade* Amsterdam: North–Holland, 1962
_____ *Theory of Commercial Policy* Oxford: Philip Allan, 1977
Mikesell, Raymond F. (ed.) *Foreign Investment in the Petroleum and Mineral Industries* Baltimore: Johns Hopkins University Press, 1971
Mill, John Stuart *Principles of Political Economy with some of their Applications to Social Philosophy* any edition: first published 1848
Ministry of International Trade and Industry (Japan) 'Resources Development and Imports of Japan' in *Modern Government and National Development* MITI, Tokyo, July 1970
_____ *Outlook on Resources Problems* MITI, Tokyo, 4 October 1971
Moran, Theodore *Multinational Corporations and the Politics of Dependence: Copper in Chile* Princeton: Princeton University Press, 1974
Morris-Suzuki, Tessa 'Japan and the Pacific Basin Community' *The World Today* December 1981
Morse, R.A. (ed.) *The Politics of Japan's Energy Strategy* Berkeley: Institute of East Asian Studies, University of California, 1981
Mueller, Dennis 'Public Choice: A Survey' *Journal of Economic Literature* 14, 2, June 1976
Mundell, Robert A. *International Economics* New York: Macmillan, 1968
_____ *Man and Economics: The Science of Choice* New York: McGraw–Hill, 1968
Murota, Yasuhiro 'Options for a Resource-Poor Developed Country — Japan' in Krause and Patrick *Mineral Resources*
Murray, Tracy, Schmidt, Wilson and Walter, Ingo 'Alternative Forms of Protection against Market Disruption' *Kyklos* 31, 4, 1978
Mutoh, Hiromichi, Sekiguchi, Sueo, Suzumura, Kōtarō and Yamazawa, Ippei (eds) *Industrial Policies for Pacific Economic Growth* Sydney: Allen & Unwin, 1986
Nakakita, Thu 'The World Economy in the 1990s' *Look Japan* January 1987
National Science Foundation *International Economic Policy Research Paper*, and Proceedings of a Colloquium held in Washington, DC, 3–4 October 1980
Naya, Seiji and James, William 'External Shocks, Policy Responses and External Debt of Asian Developing Countries' in Tan and Kapur *Pacific Growth*
Nelson, Charles G. 'European Integration: Trade Data and Measurement Problems' *International Organization* 28, 3, 1974
von Neumann, John and Morgenstern, Oskar *Theory of Games and Economic Behavior* Princeton, NJ: Princeton University Press, 1947
Nozick, Robert *Anarchy, State, and Utopia* Oxford: Basil Blackwell, 1974
NPCC (National Pacific Cooperation Committee, Australia) *Australia and Pacific Economic Cooperation: Report by the National Pacific Cooperation Committee to the Australian Government* Australian National University, October 1985
_____ *Australia and Pacific Economic Cooperation: Second Report by the National Pacific Cooperation Committee to the Australian Government* Australian National University, July 1987
Odaka, Konosuke *Motor Vehicle Industry in Asia: A Study of Ancillary Firm Development* Singapore: Singapore University Press, 1983
OECD *The Impact of the Newly Industrialising Countries on Production and Trade in Manufactures* Paris, OECD, June 1979
Ōhira Study Group Report: *see* Japan Pacific Cooperation Study Group
Ohlin, Bertil 'Some Insufficiencies in the Theories of International Economic Relations' *Essays in International Finance* No.34, Princeton University, September 1979
Ōkita, Saburō 'Natural Resources Dependency and Japanese Foreign Policy' *Foreign Affairs* 52, 4, July 1974
_____ 'Japan's High Dependence on Imports of Raw Materials' in Crawford and Ōkita *Raw Materials*
Oksenberg, Michael 'China's Confident New Nationalism' *Foreign Affairs* 65, 3, February 1987

Olson, Mancur *The Logic of Collective Action: Public Goods and the Theory of Groups* Cambridge, Mass.: Harvard University Press, 1965

_____ 'The Principle of "Fiscal Equivalence": The Division of Responsibilities Among Different Levels of Government' *American Economic Review* 59, 2, May 1969

_____ 'Increasing Incentives for International Cooperation' *International Organization* 25, 4, Autumn 1971

Olson, Mancur and Zeckhauser, Richard 'An Economic Theory of Alliances' *Review of Economics and Statistics* 8, 3, August 1976

Oppenheimer, Peter (ed.) *Issues in International Economics* London: Oriel Press, 1978

Ozawa, Terutomo *Multinationalism Japanese Style: The Political Economy of Outward Dependency* Princeton, NJ: Princeton University Press, 1979

Pacific Economic Cooperation Conference *Report of the Task Force on Minerals and Energy* Australia–Japan Research Centre, Australian National University, July 1983

_____ *Report on the Task Force on Capital Flows* Fourth Pacific Economic Cooperation Conference, Seoul, April–May 1985

Pacific Basin Co-operation Study Group *Report on the Pacific Basin Co-operation Concept* Tokyo, 19 May 1980

Pangestu, Mari 'Japanese and Other Foreign Investment in the ASEAN Countries' *Australia–Japan Economic Relations Research Project Research Papers* No.73, Australian National University, 1980

Park, Young-il 'The Changing Pattern of Textile Trade in Northeast Asia' paper presented to the Australia–Japan Research Centre Workshop on Northeast Asia Trade, Australian National University, 25 March 1987

Patrick, Hugh 'United States Foreign Economic Policy Towards Japan and the Pacific' *Australia–Japan Economic Relations Research Project Research Paper* No.32, Australian National University, November 1975

_____ 'American Foreign Economic Policy Towards the Western Pacific' in Crawford and Ōkita *Raw Materials*

_____ 'Options for a Resource-Poor Developed Country — Japan: A Comment' in Krause and Patrick *Mineral Resources*

_____ 'United States–Japan Political Economy: Is the Partnership in Jeopardy?' in Hanson and Roehl *The United States and the Pacific Economy* (also published as *Australia–Japan Economic Relations Research Project Research Paper* No. 59, Australian National University, May 1979)

_____ The Management of the United States–Japan Trade Relationship and its Implications for the Pacific Basin Economies, Background Paper for Project on the Impact of Japan–US Economic Relations on other Pacific Basin Nations, United States National Committee for Pacific Economic Cooperation (mimeo), Columbia University, May 1987

Patrick, Hugh and Satō, Hideo 'The Political Economy of the United States–Japan Trade in Steel' *Pacific Economic Papers* No.88, Australia–Japan Research Centre, Australian National University, December 1981

PBEC (Pacific Basin Economic Council) Japan Member Committee *Pacific Economic Community Statistics* Tokyo: PBEC Japan Member Committee, 1986

PECC (Pacific Economic Cooperation Conference), Report of the International Standing Committee to the Fourth PECC, Seoul, April 1985

Penrose, Edith 'Profit Sharing between Producing Countries and Oil Companies in the Middle East' *Economic Journal* June 1959

Phelps, E. (ed.) *Economic Justice* Harmondsworth: Penguin, 1973

Pincus, J.J. *Pressure Groups and Politics in Antebellum Tariffs* New York: Columbia University Press, 1977

Plano, Jack and Olton, Roy *International Relations Dictionary* New York: Holt, Rinehart & Winston, 1969

Pomery, John 'Uncertainty and International Trade' in Dornbusch and Frenkel *International Economic Policy*

Puchala, Donald J. and Hopkins, Raymond F. 'International Regimes: Lessons from International Analysis' *International Organization* 36, 2, 1982

Pugel, Thomas A. and Hawkins, Robert G. (eds) *Fragile Interdependence: Economic Issues in US-Japanese Trade and Investment* Lexington: Lexington Books, 1986

Purcell, W.A. 'The Nature and Extent of Japanese Commercial and Economic Interests in Australia 1932–1941' *Australia–Japan Economic Relations Research Project Research Paper* No.53, Australian National University, 1978

Ranis, Gustav 'Challenges and Opportunities Posed by Asia's Super Exporters: Implications for Manufactured Exports from Latin America' *Quarterly Review of Economics and Business* 21, 2, Summer 1981

Rapp, William V. 'Japan's Invisible Barriers to Trade' in Dugel and Hawkins *Fragile Interdependence*

'Raw Materials and Political Risk' submission by European mining companies to the Commission of the European Communities, 1976

Rawls, John *A Theory of Justice* Cambridge, Mass.: Harvard University Press, 1972

Riger, H.C. 'ASEAN Cooperation and Intra-ASEAN Trade' *Research Notes and Discussions Paper* No.57, Institute of Southeast Asian Studies, Singapore, 1985

Rix, Alan *Japan's Economic Aid* London: Croom Helm, 1980

Robertson, David 'Fail Safe Systems for Trade Liberalisation' *Thames Essay* No.12, Trade Policy Research Centre, London, 1977

Robson, Peter *The Economics of International Integration* London: George Allen & Unwin, 1980

Roemer, John 'The Effect of Sphere of Influence and Economic Distance on the Commodity Composition of Trade in Manufactures' *Review of Economics and Statistics* 59, 3, August 1977

Royer, Jean 'Greater European Economic Integration' in Kojima *Structural Adjustment*

Russett, Bruce *International Regions and the International System* Chicago: Rand McNally & Co., 1967

—— (ed.) *Economic Theories of International Politics* Chicago: Markham, 1968

Russett, Bruce and Sullivan, John 'Collective Goods and International Organization' *International Organization* 25, 4, Autumn 1977

Saeki, Kiichi (ed.) *The Search for Japan's Comprehensive Guideline in the Changing World — National Priorities for the 21st Century* [Kokusai kankyō no henka to Nihon no taiō: Nijūichi seiki e no teigen] Kamakura: Nomura Research Institute, 1978

Sakakibara, Eisuke 'The Internationalisation of Tokyo's Financial Markets' in Tan and Kapur *Pacific Growth*

Sakurai, Makoto 'Japanese Direct Investment: Studies on its Growth in the 1970s' *Discussion Paper* No.397, Economic Growth Center, Yale University, 1982

Sampson, Gary and Yeats, Alexander 'Tariff and Transport Barriers Facing Australian Exports' *Journal of Transport Economics and Policy* 11, 2, May 1977

Satō H. and Destler, I, *Coping with US-Japanese Economic Conflicts* Lexington: Lexington Books, 1982

Saxon, Eric and Anderson, Kym 'Japanese Agricultural Protection in Historical Perspective' *Pacific Economic Papers* No.92, Australia–Japan Research Centre, Australian National University, July 1982

Saxonhouse, Gary R. 'What's Wrong with Japanese Trade Structure?' *Pacific Economic Papers* No.137, Australia–Japan Research Centre, Australian National University, July 1986

Saxonhouse, Gary and Patrick, Hugh 'Japan and the United States; Bilateral Tensions and Multilateral Issues in the Economic Relationship' in Hellman *China and Japan*

Saxonhouse, Gary R. and Stern, Robert M. 'An Analytical Survey of Formal and Informal

Barriers to International Trade and Investment in the United States, Canada and Japan' paper presented at a conference on US–Canadian Trade and Investment Relations with Japan, Ann Arbor, University of Michigan, 2–3 April 1987

Sazanami, Yōko 'Trade and Investment Patterns and Barriers for North America and Japan' paper presented at a conference on US–Canadian Trade and Investment Relations with Japan, Ann Arbor, University of Michigan, 2–3 April 1987

Scalapino, Robert *The Japanese Communist Movement, 1920–1966* Berkeley: University of California Press, 1967

Scalapino, Robert A. and Wanandi, Jusuf (eds) *Economic, Political and Security Issues in Southeast Asia in the 1980s* Berkeley: Institute of East Asian Studies, University of California, 1982

Schneider, Richard L. and Borthwick, Mark 'Institutions for Pacific Regional Co-operation' *Asian Survey* XXIII, 12, December 1983

Sekiguchi, Sueo *Japanese Direct Foreign Investment* Montclair: Allenheld & Osmen & Co., 1979

———— *Japanese Direct Foreign Investment in ASEAN* Singapore: Institute of Southeast Asian Studies, 1982

———— 'Nihon no chokusetsu tōshi to Nihon–ASEAN kankei' [Japanese direct investment and the Japan–ASEAN relationship] Keizai Kenkyū,' 33, 4, October 1982

———— (ed.) *Kantaiheiyōken to Nihon no chokusetsu tōshi* [The Pacific Basin and Japan's direct foreign investment] Tokyo: Nihon Keizai Kenkyū Sentā, 1982

Sekiguchi, Sueo and Krause, Lawrence B. 'Direct Foreign Investment in ASEAN by Japan and the United States' in Garnaut (ed.) *ASEAN*

Sen, Amartya *Collective Choice and Social Welfare* San Francisco: Holden–Day, 1970

———— *On Economic Equality* Oxford: Clarendon, 1973

———— 'Personal Utilities and Public Judgements: Or What's Wrong with Welfare Economies?' *Economic Journal*, 89, 355, September 1979

Shibata, Hirofumi 'A Note on the Equivalence of Tariffs and Quotas' *American Economic Review* 58, 1968

Shishido, Toshio and Ryūzō Satō (eds) *Economic Policy and Development: New Perspectives* Dover: Auburn, 1985

Silk, Leonard 'The US and the World Economy' *Foreign Affairs* 65, 3, 1986

Simkin, C.F.G. 'Closer Economic Ties with New Zealand' Discussion Paper No.8, Centre for Economic Policy Research, Australian National University, 1980

Sissons, D.C.S. (ed.) *Papers on Modern Japan* Canberra: Australian National University Press, 1965

Smith, Adam *An Inquiry into the Nature and Causes of the Wealth of Nations* any edition: first published 1776

Smith, Ben 'Australian Minerals Development, Future Prospects for the Mining Industry and Effects on the Australian Economy' in Kasper and Parry *Growth, Trade and Structural Change*

———— 'Long-Term Contracts for the Supply of Raw Materials' in Crawford and Ōkita *Raw Materials*

———— 'The Japanese Connection' in Hastings and Farran (eds) *Australia's Resources Future*

———— 'Security and Stability in Minerals Markets: The Role of Long-term Contracts' *The World Economy* 2, 1, January 1979

———— 'Bilateral Commercial Arrangements in Energy Coal Trade' in Harris and Ikuta *Australia, Japan and the Energy Coal Trade*

———— 'The Role of Resource Development in Australian Economic Growth' Discussion Paper No. 167, Centre for Economic Policy Research, Australian National University, Canberra, May 1987

Smith, Ben and Drysdale, Peter 'Stabilisation and the Reduction of Uncertainty in Bilateral Minerals Trade Arrangements' *Australia–Japan Economic Relations Research Project*

Research Paper No.65, Australian National University, December 1979

Smith, Ben and Ulph, Alistair 'The Impact of Developed Country Environmental Policy on the Trade of Developing Countries in the ESCAP Region' paper prepared for the UNEP/ESCAP Project on Environment and Development; released as *CRES Report R/R5*, Centre for Resource and Environmental Studies, Australian National University, 1979

Soesastro, Hadi 'Institutional Aspects of ASEAN Pacific Economic Cooperation' ESCAP Report on ASEAN and Pacific Economic Cooperation, Bangkok, June 1982; see also Soesatro and Sung-joo Han *Pacific Economic Cooperation*

Soesastro, Hadi 'Institutional Aspects of Pacific Economic Cooperation' in Soesastro and Sung-boo Han *Pacific Economic Cooperation; see also* Soesastro 'Institutional Aspects' June 1982

Soesastro, Hadi and Sung-joo Han (eds) *Pacific Economic Cooperation: The Next Phase* Jakarta: Centre for Strategic and International Studies, 1983

Snape, Richard 'Australia's Relations with GATT' *Economic Record* March 1984

Statistical Yearbook of the Republic of China, 1985

Stern, Robert M. 'Changes in US Comparative Advantage: Issues for Research and Policy' in National Science Foundation *International Economic Policy Research*

Stevens, Dana and Foster, James The Possibility of Democratic Pluralism' *Economica* 45, 180, November 1978

Stockwin, J.A.A. (ed.) *Japan and Australia in the Seventies* Sydney: Angus & Robertson, 1972

Stoeckel, Andy and Cuthbertson, Sandy *Successful Strategies for Australian Trade* Canberra: Centre for International Economics, 1987

Stone, Julius *The Atlantic Charter* Sydney: Angus & Robertson, 1943

Strange, Susan 'International Economic Relations I: The Need for an Interdisciplinary Approach' in Roger Morgan (ed.) *The Study of International Affairs: Essays in Honour of Keith Younger* London: Oxford University Press, 1972

Stuckey, John 'Joint Ventures in the Aluminium Industry' *Australia-Japan Economic Relations Research Projects Research Paper* No.67, Australian National University, December 1979
_____ *Vertical Integration in the Aluminium Trade* Cambridge, Mass.: Harvard University Press, 1983

Suhartono, R.B. 'Industrial Cooperation in ASEAN' in Mutoh et al. (eds) *Industrial Policies for Pacific Economic Growth*

Suttmeier, Richard 'Japanese Reactions to United States Nuclear Policy: Domestic Origins of an International Negotiating Position' *Orbis* 22, 3, 1978

Suvant, K.P. and Hasenpflug, H. (eds) *The New International Economic Order — Confrontation or Cooperation between North and South* Frankfurt: Campus Verlag, 1977

Swearingen, Rodger *Communist Strategy in Japan 1945-1960* Santa Monica: Rand Corporation, 1965

Takayema, Yasuo 'Don't Take Japan for Granted' in Cooper *A Re-Ordered World*

Tan, Augustine H.H and Kapur, Basant (eds) *Pacific Growth and Financial Interdependence* Sydney: Allen & Unwin, 1986

Task Force on Capital Flows: see Pacific Economic Cooperation Conference, 1985

Teese, C.F. 'A View from the Dress Circle in the Theatre of Trade Disputes' *The World Economy* 5, 1, March 1982

Trends in International Trade: A Report by a Panel of Experts: see GATT, 1958

Tsao Yuan 'Capital Flows Among Pacific Basin Economies' in Tan and Kapur (eds) *Pacific Growth and Financial Interdependence*

Tsuchiya, Keizō 'Japanese Agriculture and Problems in Importing Farm Products' in Anderson et al. 'Agricultural Trade'

Tsukehira, Toshio *The Postwar Evolution of Communist Strategy in Japan* Cambridge, Mass.: MIT 1954

Tsurumi, Yoshihiro *The Japanese are Coming: A Multinational Interaction of Firms and Politics* Cambridge, Mass.: Ballinger, 1976

Tullock, G. 'The Welfare Cost of Tariffs, Monopolies and Theft' *Western Economic Journal* 5, 1967

Tyers, Rodney 'Effects on ASEAN of Food Trade Liberalisation in Industrial Countries' Paper presented to the Second Western Pacific Food Trade Workshop, Jakarta, 22–23 August 1982

―――― 'Distortions in World Food Markets: A Quantitative Assessment' background paper prepared for the World Bank's *World Development Report 1986* National Centre for Development Studies, Australian National University, Canberra, 1986

―――― (ed.) *Food Security in Asia and the Pacific: Issues for Research* Report of the 1st Meeting of the Food Security Working Group, 18–30 June 1979, East–West Resource Systems Institute, Hawaii, 1979

Tyers, Rodney, Phillips, Prue and Drysdale, Peter 'Projecting Matrices of International Trade Flows: The Case of Australian and Pacific Basin Trade' Australia–Japan Research Centre, Australian National University (forthcoming in *Journal of Economics and International Relations*)

Tyers, Rodney and Sekboonsarng, Sutad, Some Aggregate Trends in the Structure and Stability of Staple Food Markets in the Asia–Pacific Region, mimeo, paper presented at the 3rd biennial meeting of the Agricultural Economics Society of Southeast Asia, Kuala Lumpur, 27–29 November 1979

United Nations *A Guide to the United Nations Charter* United Nations Department of Public Information, 1947

US Senate Committee on Finance *MTN Studies: 1* 'Results for US Agriculture' Washington, DC, June 1979

―――― *MTN Studies: 2* 'Tokyo–Geneva Round: Its Relation to US Agriculture' Washington, DC, June 1979

Vernon, Raymond *Two Hungry Giants: The United States and Japan in the Quest for Oil and Ores* Cambridge, Mass.: Harvard University Press, 1983

Viner, Jacob *International Economics* Glencore, Ill.: Free Press, 1951

Viviani, Nancy 'Australia and Japan: Approaches to Development Assistance Policy' *Australia–Japan Economic Relations Research Project Research Paper* No.37, Australian National University, March 1976

Vogel, Ezra *Japan as Number One* Tokyo: Charles Tuttle & Co., 1979

de Vylder, Stefan *Allende's Chile* Cambridge: Cambridge University Press, 1974

Wallensteen, Peter 'Scarce Goods as Political Weapons: The Case of Food' *Journal of Peace Research* XIII, 4, 1976

Walter, Ingo 'Nontariff Barriers and the Export Performance of Developing Economies' *American Economic Review* 61, Papers and Proceedings, 1971

Welfield, John 'Australia–Japan in Asian–Pacific International Politics: Some Problems and Projects' in *Australia–Japan Relations Symposium, 1977, Summary of Papers and Discussion*, Canberra: Embassy of Japan, 1977

―――― 'Australia and Japan in the Cold War' in Drysdale and Kitaōji (eds) *Australia and Japan*

―――― *An Empire in Eclipse: Japan in the Postwar American Alliance System* London: The Athlone Press, 1988

WIDER (World Institute for Development Economics Research) 'Mobilising International Surpluses for World Development: A WIDER Plan' WIDER, Helsinki and Tokyo, May 1987

Wilkinson, Bruce W. 'A Re-estimation of the Effects of the Formation of a Pacific Free Trade Area' in Kojima *Pacific Trade II*

Williams, Charlotte 'The Pacific Community: A Modest Proposal' *Australia–Japan Economic Relations Research Project Research Paper* No. 55, Australian National University, March 1979

Willrich, Mason *Energy and World Politics* New York: Free Press, 1975

Wolf, Charles and Weinschrott, David 'International Transactions and Regionalism: Distinguishing "Insiders" from "Outsiders"' *American Economic Review* 63, 2, May 1973

Wonnacott, A.J. 'Aggressive US Recioprocity Evaluated with a New Analytical Approach to Trade Conflicts' *Essays in International Economics* Institute for Research and Public Policy, Montreal, 1984

Wonnacott, Paul and Wonnacott, Ronald 'Is Unilateral Tariff Reduction Preferable to a Customs Union ? The Curious Case of the Missing Foreign Tariffs' *American Economic Review*, 71, 4, September 1981

World Bank *World Development Report 1983* New York: Oxford University Press, 1983
―――― *World Development Report 1986* Washington, DC: World Bank, 1986

Yamazawa, Ippei 'Intensity Analysis of World Trade Flows' *Hitotsubashi Journal of Economics*, 11, 2, February 1971
―――― 'Renewal of the Textile Industry in Developed Countries and World Textile Trade' *Hitotsubashi Journal of Economics* 24, 1, June 1983

Yates, P. Lamartine *Forty Years of Foreign Trade* London: George Allen & Unwin, 1959

Yoffie, David B. 'Orderly Marketing Agreements as an Industrial Policy' *Public Policy* 29, Winter 1981
―――― 'The Newly Industrialising Countries and the Political Economy of Protectionism' *International Studies Quarterly*, 25, 4, December 1981

Yoffie, David and Keohane, Robert 'Responding to the "New Protectionism": Strategies for the ADCs' and 'Comments' in Hong and Krause *Trade and Growth of the ADCs*

Yoshihara, Kunio *Japanese Investment in Southeast Asia* Kyoto: Kyoto University, 1978
―――― *Sōgo Shōsha: Vanguard of the Japanese Economy* Kuala Lumpur: Oxford University Press, 1983

Yoshino, Michael *Japan's Multinational Enterprises* Cambridge, Mass.: Harvard University Press, 1976

Yoshitomi, Masaru 'Recent US–Japan Financial Interactions under Flexible Exchange Rates' in Tan and Kapur *Pacific Growth*

Yoshitomi, Masaru and the Japanese Economic Planning Agency World Model Group 'The Insulation and Transmission Mechanisms of Floating Exchange Rates Analysed by the EPA World Economic Model' Economic Planning Agency, Tokyo, 1984

Young, Oran R. 'Regime Dynamics: The Rise and Fall of International Regimes' *International Organization* 36, 2, 1982

Yuan-li, Wei *Japan's Search for Oil: A Case Study of Economic Nationalism and International Security* Stanford: Hoover Institution Press, 1977

INDEX

Italicised page numbers are for tables/figures. References to footnotes are to the page in the text in which they occur. A reference such as 203 & n1 means that the footnote continues the discussion of the text.